The Colossal
Cookie Cookbook

The Colossal Cookie Cookbook

Over 425 quick and easy recipes, plus expert tips

on mixing, baking, and storing

EDITED BY
Deborah Gray

CONTRIBUTING AUTHORS:
Catherine Atkinson; Kathryn Hawkins; Dawn Stock; Janet Mannings; Katy Holder;
Fiona Hunter; Emma Patmore; Alison Austin

CHARTWELL
BOOKS, INC.

A QUINTET BOOK

Published by Chartwell Books
A Division of Book Sales, Inc.
114 Northfield Avenue
Edison, New Jersey 08837

This edition produced for sale in the U.S.A., its
territories and dependencies only.

ISBN 0 7858 1052 8

Reprinted 2000

This book was designed and produced by
Quintet Publishing Limited
6 Blundell Street
London N7 9BH

Creative Director: Richard Dewing
Art Director: Paula Marchant
Designers: Siân Keogh and
Sandra Marques at Axis Design
Managing Editor: Diana Steedman
Senior Project Editor: Toria Leitch
Editor: Jane Donovan
Photographer: Ferguson Hill
Food Stylist: Labeena Ishaque

Material in this book also previously appeared in
Breakfast Bakes; The Complete Biscuit and Cookie
Book; New Jewish Cooking, Elizabeth Wolf Cohen; The
Complete Book of Gingerbread, Valerie Barrett; High
Fiber Cooking, Rosemary Moon; Kids' kitchen Sugar
and Spice, Nicola Fowler

Typeset in Great Britain by
Central Southern Typesetters, Eastbourne
Manufactured in Hong Kong
Printed in China

Contents

INTRODUCTION 6

ALL-DAY
COOKIES
22

AROUND
THE WORLD
66

SPECIAL
COOKIES FOR
GIFTS
106

CHOCOLATE
COOKIES
152

CHILDREN'S
COOKIES
198

NUT COOKIES
336

COOKIES FOR
SPECIAL DIETS
240

BAR COOKIES
376

COOKIES
FOR FESTIVE
OCCASIONS
256

SAVORY
COOKIES
418

FRUIT
COOKIES
296

INDEX 460

Introduction

Seeping out from the corners of every shopping mall, every sidewalk café, and every bakery comes wafting the irresistible scent of baking butter, sugar, chocolate, and vanilla. Cookies, it seems, are everywhere, and now, with the purchase of this book, the aromas from your kitchen can pervade your neighborhood. The fruits of your labors can fill jars on the worktop, be displayed at table sales, be donated to parties, wing their way to distant relatives in the mail, all to the delight of cookie fiends everywhere. For is there anyone who can resist a cookie? Cookies seem to appeal to the child in us. They appear sweeter and more intensely flavored than most cakes, they are crunchy and soft, they are nutty and chocolately, they are easy to handle—they are the perfect comfort food.

Take comfort in the knowledge that this book is the only cookie book that you will ever need to own. It contains a unique collection of favorites from all over the world. The word "cookie" comes from the Dutch "koekje" meaning little cake, and this book contains recipes from Holland as well as France, Italy, Britain, Scandinavia, Eastern Europe, and Australia. Every culture, it seems, has its cookies characterized by the availability of local ingredients and the temperament of its inhabitants. So rustic oaty cookies come from northern Europe, almond-studded biscotti from Italy, spicy Lebkuchen from Eastern Europe and delicate Madelaines from the elegance of Marcel Proust's Paris. Then, of course, there are the American cookies themselves. Many of these are jumbo cookies stuffed with goodies or smaller, simpler cookies baked straight from the refrigerator. Here you will find recipes for family favorites and elegant classics alongside new ideas for the new millennium.

A comprehensive introduction provides all the background information in the art of cookie baking to turn you into a master of the art. Take time out to read this section before you begin, then return to your kitchen and enjoy yourself. If you have kids at hand rope them in too, they will enjoy the process of baking cookies and it's a good way to have fun with them on wet afternoons. Get them involved in the decorating, especially at holiday times, and your cookies will take on a certain home-made charm. No kids? Then why not bake with a friend? That way you'll have twice the choice without extra effort and have lots of laughs in the process. After all, you can be really serious about cookies, but who can deny that part of their charm lies in their frivolity.

The only problem with this book is the amazing choice it offers, and the wonderful photographs make all the cookies look so tempting. Maybe go for the Toll House Cookie, or the original recipe for the ever-popular Chocolate Chip Cookie or perhaps the White Chocolate and Apricot—eat one with a glass of cold milk to make the perfect snack while browsing through the other recipes to select your next cookie.

Be assured that whichever recipe you choose, the instructions are clearly written and easy to follow and the ingredients are listed in order of use. With this fabulous cookbook to guide you, you can't go wrong.

The Ins and Outs of Cookie Mastery

By simply following the recipe instructions on the following pages you will be able to bake a huge variety of sensational cookies, but it does help to know a little about the equipment and techniques you will be using. You might want your cookies just that little bit larger, chewier, or crisper than the recipe suggests and by understanding the principles of cookie production you will be able to fine tune your baking to suit your taste.

Tools of the Trade

These are listed roughly in the order of use.

● A set of dry measuring cups, a set of measuring spoons, and a liquid measure are all essential. Cooking is chemistry, and in order to get the optimum results careful attention should be paid to measuring the ingredients accurately. Pour or scoop ingredients into the measures and level with the straight edge of a knife. For butter or other fat, pack down firmly in the measure, then level with a knife.

● A set of mixing bowls, preferably microwave-safe for melting butter and chocolate in the microwave as well as on top of a double boiler.

● A food mixer and/or food processor. A food mixer is great for combining butter and sugar and beating in eggs. It is still best to fold in dry ingredients by hand as it is easy to over mix in a machine and risk making the dough tough. A food processor will blend the butter and sugar easily but doesn't result in quite such a light, fluffy mixture as doing it in a food mixer. However, it is probably preferable to doing it by hand with a wooden spoon, which can be quite hard on the arms. The food processor is brilliant for chopping and grinding nuts, chopping fruits, and for making shortbread and pastry dough.

● A sifter or sieve.

● A wire whisk, or two—one large and one small.

● A grater for grating the rind from citrus fruits and for grating fresh ginger and nutmeg.

● Spoons. A wooden one, plus several teaspoons and tablespoons for mixing and measuring.

● Knives. A sharp pointed knife and a straight knife for leveling are both useful.

placed on a large baking sheet, they tend to burn. To avoid this use a small baking sheet or try turning a 8 x 8 inch baking pan over and baking on the back. Avoid using pans with edges such as jelly roll pans, since they prevent good air circulation around the baking cookies.

For baking bar cookies a nonstick 13 x 9 in and 8 x 8 in pans are required. Some recipes also call for a jelly roll pan. If you have to use an ovenproof glass baking dish for bar cookies, then be aware that glass retains more heat while cooking than metal. Avoid overcooking and scorched edges by reducing the oven temperature by 25°F.

● A metal spatula for removing cookies from the baking sheet. Use thin, heatproof plastic if your non-stick surface will be damaged by metal.

● A timer.

● At least two wire cooling racks.

● A pastry brush.

● Two or three baking sheets. There are a lot out there to choose from. Heavy gauge aluminum sheets are excellent as they conduct heat evenly and swiftly. Nonstick sheets are good too, but avoid those that are very dark in color as they absorb too much heat which means that cookies may burn more easily. If yours are dark, compensate by cooking your cookies on a sheet of aluminum foil. Insulated baking sheets are not as good as they are cracked up to be—they consist of two layers of aluminum separated by a locked in air space. Crisp cookies do not crisp well on them, and soft cookies spread out too much on them. If you are using insulated sheets, allow a minute or two extra cooking time and mound cookies generously before cooking.

To maintain optimal air circulation in the oven, baking sheets should be four inches shorter and narrower than the oven. For some obscure reason to do with heat circulation, if there are too few cookies

COOKIE TYPES

The ingredients for most cookies are pretty much the same—sugar, butter and a little egg, bound with flour and flavored with vanilla, spices, chocolate, fruits or nuts. However, the proportions and treatment of these basic ingredients differ, resulting in a range of cookies with various textures and flavors.

Drop Cookies

These are probably the simplest and most versatile type of cookie. They are called drop cookies as the dough is soft enough to drop off the spoon and onto the baking sheet. Use the size of spoon recommended in the recipe and encourage the mixture to drop off the spoon by pushing with a second teaspoon. The basic batter usually consists of butter (or margarine or shortening) and sugar beaten together until light and fluffy. Eggs are then beaten in, followed by flour combined with

leavening ingredients and flavorings, either subtle or robust. In addition, textual ingredients are added, the most common of these being oats, coconut, nuts, or chocolate chips.

Space the cookies according to the instructions which will take account of the cooking spread, and bake in a moderate oven. For soft or cakey cookies the mixture should be left well mounded on the cookie sheet. For a cookie with a deliciously soft, chewy center and a crisp edge, remove the cookies from the oven as soon as the edges turn golden and while the middles are still soft and paler in color. The more even the color and the firmer the cookie to touch, the crisper the cookies will be. If you want to make crisper cookies, spread the mixture out a little using the back of the spoon before baking. Some very crisp drop cookies such as Florentines require that the butter and sugar are first melted together to begin the caramelization prior to baking, others replace some or all of the sugar with syrup. Such cookies generally contain very little flour which helps them to spread out on the baking sheet. Make sure you space these cookies far apart on the baking sheet.

Refrigerator Cookies

The advantage of refrigerator cookies is that the ingredients used to make up the dough can be made in advance and kept in the refrigerator for up to two weeks before being cooked. This encourages cooking on demand so that wonderful fresh cookies can be cooked as and when required without the need to prepare fresh dough each time you want to bake a batch. These are the perfect cookies for those who only have time to prepare food and bake on the weekend, or for anyone who doesn't have the self control necessary to leave half a batch of cookies in the storage tins!

Rolled Cookies

Rolled cookies are the delight of holiday cooks. These tempting cookies can be rolled out and cut into shapes using cookie cutters, or simply cut into discs using the top of a drinking glass. Rolled cookie dough is similar to that made for refrigerator cookies and often requires refrigerating before rolling and pressing. After chilling, roll the dough on a lightly floured board to a thickness of ⅛ to ¼ inch. Some cooks prefer to roll the dough between two sheets of thicker quality plastic wrap so that the dough can be returned to the refrigerator before cutting. Dip the cookie cutter into flour before pressing through the dough, then press down firmly to ensure that the dough is cut right through. Gently pull away any scraps, which can be combined and re-rolled. These cookies are cooked in a moderate to moderately hot oven until very slightly golden around the edges and firm to the touch. They tend to be very fragile and need to be removed from the baking sheets after they have cooled for one or two minutes. Use a thin metal spatula or fish slice to transfer the hot cookies to cooling racks. Rolled cookies freeze well for up to 1 month so they can be made before the holidays and decorated when required.

The dough for refrigerator cookies is quite stiff, so that they are easiest to prepare in the food mixture or food processor. The dough is then molded into a log or into a thin, oblong brick and wrapped in plastic wrap. Due to their high fat content, the dough must then be chilled for at least 3 hours to firm up so that the cookies hold their shape and become crisp when cooked. Slice the cookies according to the instructions given in the recipe using a thin, sharp blade. Space an inch or so apart on the baking sheet in a moderate oven. If you decide to increase the thickness of the cookies, decrease the temperature of the oven slightly to ensure that the cookies are crisp throughout. The best way to check that these cookies are done is to sacrifice one and break it in half. Check to see that there is no dark, doughy strip in the center of the cookie and that the texture is even throughout.

Pressed Cookies

A plate of delicate pressed cookies always looks fancy but they are simple to make using a commercial cookie press. They are the perfect cookie for those who would love to make festive cookies, but lack the skill or time to do the fancy decorations.

The dough for pressed cookies needs to be soft enough to be squeezed through a cookie press but firm enough to hold its shape. Extra care must be taken to ensure that the butter and sugar are beaten until really light and fluffy and the flour should be gently folded in

cakes producing a denser and moister bar. For this reason the bars with a crumb or shortbread base often require that the oven temperature be reduced after an initial part-cooking of the base. Always cook bar cookies in the pan size recommended. Using a smaller pan will produce thicker cookies which will need a longer cooking time and would alter the proportions of crust to cake.

As a general rule these cookies are done when a toothpick inserted into the center of the pan comes out clean. However, some bar cookies, such as brownies, are best slightly softer and fudgier than most others. Remove from the oven as soon as the center is set and the brownies are just beginning to pull away from the edges of the pan. Most soft, chewy brownies can be cut with a sharp, serrated knife when cooled. Crisp bar cookies, however, must be cut after five to ten minutes before they become firm. Do not cut bar cookies too big. Three inch squares are ample, after all they are supposed to be cookies. Generally bar cookies keep well if left in the baking pan covered with an airtight lid or a piece of foil.

by hand. If the mixture is too stiff to press, then add a few drops of milk; if it is too soft, then place in the refrigerator until firm enough to hold its shape. For spritz-type cookies, the dough is generally pressed out onto ungreased, cold baking sheets and dredged with colored sugar or decorated with nuts prior to cooking. To prevent the cookies from spreading and loosing their shape, the baking sheets are placed in the refrigerator to allow the cookies to firm up before baking in a moderate oven. Remove from the oven and transfer to the cooling racks as for rolled cookies.

Bar Cookies

These cookies fall half way between a cake and a cookie. They can be thick and chewy, thin and crispy, or light and cakey. Some combine two textures having a crispy outer shell (usually shortbread or crumb based) and a rich, soft center. Most of these cookies are baked in a moderate to moderately low oven; the cooler oven slows the process of aeration called for in lighter

To Market

It goes without saying that good quality ingredients make the best cookies, however, most of the ingredients required for the cookies in this book can be bought at the average grocery store and are not expensive. The most important thing is to make sure that the ingredients are fresh—nuts left over from last Christmas and rock hard apricots should be replaced, as should spices kept in a warm kitchen in full sunlight.

Flour

Most recipes call for all-purpose flour which you can buy bleached and unbleached (the latter is probably preferable;) sifted or unsifted. It is just as well to sift even presifted flour as it settles when left standing on the shelf. Always sift flour when told to do so by the recipe. Do not substitute cake flour unless stated in the recipe as an option—cake flour contains less gluten and is more powdery than all-purpose flour and will produce a lighter textured cookie. If cake flour is all you have, then for each cup of flour called for in the recipe, remove two tablespoons of flour, then sift well. Likewise, do not use self-rising flour unless it is specifically mentioned, as this already contains leavening agents and could create dramatic eruptions in the oven if used in conjunction with other leavening agents. Substitute 1 cup of all-purpose flour plus 1½ tablespoons baking powder and a pinch of salt for 1 cup self-rising flour.

Butter

This one is a soul searcher. Butter has an incomparable flavor in baked goods but we all know that butter is high in saturated fat and cholesterol both of which should be avoided. The problem is that the only substitute is regular, non-diet margarine and this is not much healthier. The process which turns liquid polyunsaturated oils into the solid fats found in margarine causes the fats to saturate making them no better than those found naturally in butter. The softer margarines and spreads are healthier but have a greatly increased liquid content than should be used in baking. In some recipes with plenty of other flavors, hard margarine may be substituted for butter although the resulting cookie will be a little softer due to the higher water content of even hard margarine. However, where the butter is absolutely essential for a recipe, such as in shortbread, there is really no substitute. Maybe the solution is to make smaller buttery cookies and eat less of them.

Unsalted butter is best for baking as it allows the cook to fine tune the salt content of the cookies themselves. Always use unsalted butter when recommended in the recipe. If you only have salted butter to hand, then cut the amount of salt in the recipe by at least half.

Salt was originally added to butter as a preservative, so surplus unsalted butter is best kept in the freezer in order to retain its freshness. Use butter at room temperature when making cookies that need initial beating of butter and sugar, particulary if you are beating by hand as this will cut out some of the hard work. If you need to do this quickly, place the butter on a dish and put it in the microwave on MEDIUM and heat for 10 to 15 seconds (exact timings vary with machines.) In other recipes where the butter is cut into the flour, very cold butter is essential as the small particles of butter in the mixture melt while cooking creating tiny air pockets resulting in the characteristic light, crunchy texture.

A few recipes call for lard, which comes from pork, or for vegetable shortening, both of which create short, flaky pastries and cookies. Use as directed on the packet. If you wish to substitute vegetable shortening for butter, then reduce the amount used by 20%.

Sugar

Sugars add flavor and texture as well as sweetness to the cookies. Use the type of sugar indicated in the recipe. Brown sugar is white sugar with syrup added to it, molasses in the case of brown sugar and generally a lighter syrup in conjunction with a little molasses in light brown sugar. Consequently, brown sugar tends to make moister cookies than white sugar. The darker the sugar the moister and more intense the flavor. Store brown sugar in airtight containers to prevent it drying out. To soften already hard brown sugar, add a slice of apple and seal with the sugar in a plastic container for a few days; alternatively, heat gently in the microwave, checking frequently until softened but not melted.

Many recipes call for granulated sugar or for a finer white sugar, superfine. The sugar crystals in superfine sugar are very small and will melt quicker than those in granulated sugar, so do not substitute.

Vanilla sugar may be asked for especially as a decoration. To make vanilla sugar simply place a vanilla bean or two in a sealed container with about 1½ cups of sugar. Leave for a week to allow the flavor to infuse; add additional sugar as required and replace the vanilla beans about once every six months.

Eggs

The eggs used in this book are large unless otherwise specified. It is important to use the correct sized egg or the mixture will be too dry or too wet. Eggs are easier to separate when they are cold but are best used in baking when at room temperature. Very cold eggs tend to curdle the mixture. If you forget to bring eggs up to room temperature, place in a bowl of warm water for a few minutes. Egg whites should always be used at room temperature to ensure that they whisk to their maximum volume. Always whisk egg whites in a clean bowl that is completely dry and free of grease. If there is even a speck of egg yolk remaining with the white it will not whisk satisfactorily. Start again with a new egg.

Chocolate

The brand of chocolate you select is a matter of taste (and budget); some swear by readily available brands, others purchase special chocolates by mail order. What is not interchangeable is the type of chocolate you choose. If the recipe calls for semisweet or bittersweet chocolate, that is what you should use. Be particularly careful when buying white chocolate chips that you are indeed buying chocolate and not vanilla flavored chips. Different chocolates have different quantities of cocoa butter and sugar so altering the chocolate alters the chemistry of the cookie. Always melt chocolate very slowly over a double boiler or on a MEDIUM heat in

the microwave (initially for 1 minute then in 20 second bursts); either way, remove the chocolate from the heat when it is about half melted and stir well until the remainder dissolves.

Cocoa powder is the pure thing not cocoa or chocolate drink mixes. Dutch Process is probably the best type to use as it has been processed with a small amount of alkali making it less bitter to taste and darker than its untreated counterpart.

Nuts

It is important that nuts are as fresh as possible since they do go rancid over time. Buy whole nuts which keep their flavor longer, and chop in the food processor or by hand as required. Store in airtight containers, in

the refrigerator if you have space. If nuts soften, place in a 300°F oven for a few minutes to recrisp. Some recipes call for nuts to be toasted to give a richer flavor. This is best done in an ungreased skillet on the stove-top where they can be stirred and watched continuously. Otherwise, place on a baking sheet in a 350°F oven and cook for about 15 minutes, stirring occasionally and watching carefully, especially toward the end of cooking as nuts burn quickly and seemingly without warning. Coconut and oats can be treated in the same way.

Dried Fruit

As with nuts, the fresher the better. As a preference, buy dried fruit at a whole food store with a good selection and a regular turnover, as this is likely to be fresher than the packaged fruit (and nuts) found in the grocery store (this is also true for nuts and special grains as well.) You are also much more likely to find fruits that have not been treated with sulfur in the whole food shop. Try to avoid fruit drying out by storing it in the appropriate containers and always sealing the packet when you put it away. To rehydrate fruit, seep hot water on to it for 10 to 15 minutes.

Candied Fruit

This is best bought in specialist cook stores as it is much better than the bulk variety bought in the markets at holiday times.

Oats and Granola

Do not confuse quick oats with rolled oats. Quick oats are rolled oats chopped finer and they absorb more liquid during cooking. Use the type specified in the recipe. Usually the recipes call for plain granola without fruit unless otherwise stated.

Flavorings

Spices loose the intensity of their flavor quite quickly so need replacing frequently. To prolong their life keep in a cool, dark place and certainly out of direct sunlight. Use pure vanilla extracts not artificial flavoring as this does not come close to the real thing. Similarly freshly squeezed lemon and orange juice and freshly grated rind are an absolute must. Bottled juice is a poor flavor substitute.

PREPARE THAT PAN

There are several schools of thought with regard to pan preparation. Some prefer to very lightly brush their baking sheets with a little oil using a pastry brush or mister spray, and find that sufficient to stop their cookies from sticking. Others grease with shortening using a paper towel. However, avoid butter as it burns at a relatively low temperature and salted butter tends to make cookies stick to the sheet. Or you can line the sheets with aluminum foil, which needs oiling or with

nonstick silicone or parchment paper which does not. Both paper types can be wiped clean after use with a paper towel and reused several times. Using liners allows you to prepare all the cookies at once then simply slide onto the baking sheets as soon as they become available. Never slide a sheet of prepared cookies onto a warm baking sheet. The sheet must be absolutely cold before it is reused or the fat in the cookies will melt and the cookies spread before they reach the hot air of the oven.

A more recent invention is the very lightweight, flexible silicone mat that can replace parchment lining paper and be reused almost endlessly. These are particularly good for very thin, delicate cookies such as gingerbread men and cut shapes. Liners of the same material are also available for baking pans.

INTO THE OVEN

Cookies must be put into a preheated oven. Most ovens take around 10 minutes to heat up to temperature so switch your oven on when you begin preparation. Every oven is different, so the times given in this book may be a little different from those in your oven. Trust your eyes and your commonsense. If you persistently find the timings at variance, test the temperature of your oven using a cooking thermometer then calibrate with the thermostat reading; alternatively call for an engineer to check your oven. For optimum heat circulation, cook one cookie sheet at a time in the center of the oven. If you cook two sheets simultaneously, then reverse the sheets half way through cooking time working quickly to prevent the oven temperature falling too dramatically. When cooking two sheets at once, the cookies will need a little extra cooking time.

For evenly cooked cookies, space as directed in the recipe for consistent air circulation.

INGREDIENT	ALTITUDE		
	3,000 ft	5,000ft	7,000ft
Reduce baking powder For each teaspoon reduce by	⅛ teaspoon	⅛ to ¼ teaspoon	¼ teaspoon
Reduce sugar For each cup reduce by	0–1 tablespoon	0 to 2 tablespoons	1 to 4 tablespoons
Increase liquid For each cup add	1 to 2 tablespoons	2 to 4 tablespoons	3 to 4 tablespoons
Increase temperature by	0–10°F	10–25°F	25–35F

ARE THEY DONE YET?

Check the cookies a couple of minutes before the suggested cooking time is up to make sure that the cookies are not already cooked. Observe the color and touch the cookies gently to see if they spring back or feel soggy. Different types of cookies have different tell tale signs for doneness and these will be given in the recipe. Also follow the cooling instructions closely as some need to stay on the baking sheet to continue cooking for a few minutes while others need to get onto a wire rack fairly quickly to prevent sticking. Cut bar cookies according to the directions using a serrated edged knife and a gentle sawing motion. This method is less likely to rip the dough than cutting directly through the cake with a sharp knife.

HIGH ALTITUDE COOKING

Many sea-level cookie recipes work well without adjustments. However, above 3000 feet the atmospheric becomes pressure lower, liquid boils quicker and evaporation is therefore greater, which concentrates the flavor more, particularly sugars; in practical terms this means that chocolate chip and other drop cookies are slightly flatter and sweeter than at sea level. To compensate, adjust the recipes if necessary using the chart above as a guide. Reducing the quantity of fat and/or increasing the quantity of flour may help too. For sour cream-based doughs do not reduce the leavening beyond ½ teaspoon per 1 cup sour cream. Avoid using self-rising flour as this already contains leavening agents (1 cup of self rising flour contains 1½ tablespoons of baking powder and a pinch of salt). Getting the recipe just right may require some element of trial and error—begin with small incremental changes until the cookies are baked to perfection.

KEEPING COOKIES FRESH

With a few exceptions, cookies are best eaten on the day that they are cooked.

WHAT WENT WRONG

The following are the most common causes for disappointment.

PROBLEM	REASON	REMEDY
Cookies stick to baking sheet Cookies too cool	Baking sheet not greased or unevenly greased Greasing with salted butter	Cookies should be removed from baking sheet 1 to 2 minutes after cooking. Return to the oven for a couple of minutes and remove from sheet immediately. Follow instructions below for overgreased sheets. Salted butter can make cookies stick to baking sheets.
Cookies break or crumble when removed from baking sheet	Delicate butter-rich cookies can be very fragile	Leave on baking sheet for 2 minutes before removing to cooling rack. Lift carefully with thin metal spatula.
Cookies too Dry Cookies are Overbaked	Oven too hot	Check oven thermostat. Check cookies a few minutes before suggested cooking time is up. Trust your judgement when testing for doneness. Place half an apple in the storage box with the cookies to moisten.
Cookies too moist	Cookies are underdone	Check oven thermostat. Do not remove from oven unless the cookies test done even if the cooking time is up. Return to the oven for a few minutes.

PROBLEM	REASON	REMEDY
Dough too soft Won't roll or hold its shape Dough too wet Dough too warm	Maybe too much liquid or fat or insufficient flour	Measure the ingredients carefully. Add extra flour. Place in the refrigerator for 30 minutes.
Dough won't hold together and is crumbly Dough too dry	Too much flour, or insufficient fat or liquid	Check that correct sized eggs have been used. Measure ingredients carefully. Add a little soft butter or a little milk.
Cookies spread across baking sheet and touch each other	Cookies placed too close together Baking sheet overgreased Cookies placed on warm baking sheet	Follow recipe instructions for spacing. Use a pastry brush dipped in vegetable oil and wipe the sheet thinly and evenly with oil. Allow baking sheets to cool between batches.
Cookies are not evenly cooked	Cookies of uneven sizes on one sheet Oven cooks unevenly	Always cook cookies of a similar size on one sheet. Turn cookie sheets round during cooking and reverse sheets if cooking two at a time.
Cookies burnt on bottom but not top	Poor baking sheets Overgreasing Greasing with butter Cooking too low in oven	Avoid very thin or very dark baking sheets or line such sheets with foil. This causes cookies to spread too much. Butter burns at a lower temperature—use oil or shortening. Cookies are best cooked on the middle shelf. If cooking two sheets, reverse half way through cooking time.

Cookie dough, for all but cakey cookies that contain leavening ingredients (baking powder, baking soda, self-rising flour, or cream of tartar,) will keep in the refrigerator at least overnight, some types for as much as two or three days.

Cool cookies completely before wrapping and storing to prevent them from going soft.

Dough can be safely frozen for up to four months. The flavors do become less intense after the first month after which the dough may also pick up that characteristic freezer taste. Be sure to wrap the dough well, then place in an airtight plastic container. When freezing frosted cookies, place a sheet of waxed paper in between the layers.

Store cookies in airtight containers to prevent soft cookies becoming hard and crisp cookies becoming soft. If possible store in the refrigerator to retain the fresh cooked flavor. For crisp cookies do not shut the container completely, a slight air flow helps them stay crisp in all but the most humid climates. For this reason, crisp cookies are the best type to keep in ceramic cookie jars. A little crumpled, clean tissue paper placed at the bottom of the jar to absorb moisture also helps keep them crisp. If you must keep soft cookies in jars, place them first in self-sealing plastic bags.

Never mix crisp and soft cookies when storing.

To recrisp cookies, place in a 300°F oven for a few minutes, remove and cool. To revitalize soft cookies that have hardened, place a piece of apple, or a slice of bread in the container. Replace every day or two. This trick can be used to prolong storage particularly in very dry climates.

Cookies keep best in the refrigerator in plastic boxes. Defrost cookies in their wrappings for between 15 to 30 minutes. To accelerate the defrosting process, defrost in the microwave on MEDIUM for about 40-60 seconds.

DECORATIONS GALORE

This is the point where the great cookie cook and the artist shoot off in different directions. For some, decoration means a dollop of frosting or a sprinkling of sugar; others take pride in their decorating skills and pipe fancy lines and designs of great beauty.

A BASIC DECORATOR'S FROSTING

   2 cups powdered sugar

   ½ tsp vanilla

   2 Tbsp half and half or milk

Beat together the ingredients until of spreading consistency and color.

This quantity is sufficient to decorate 3 to 5 dozen cookies. Thin this mixture down a little and it becomes a useful cookie paint.

Another option is to use an egg wash. Mix together 1 egg yolk and ½ tsp water. Divide the resulting mixture if desired and tint with food colors. This mixture can then be painted onto cookies prior to cooking. For a blue tint use egg white in place of yolk. Tinted evaporated milk can also be used as a subtle glaze in place of egg wash.

The recipes in this book give you the information needed to decorate the cookies, but when out shopping look for unusual decorations, such as colored sugars, sprinkles, shaped chocolate pieces, and candied flowers that might come in handy. Small seasonal templates can be used as a stencil and dusted with powdered sugar colored with decorator's coloring dust for effective, simple decorations.

COOKIES BY MAIL

Cookies make the perfect gift, whatever the occasion. Wrapped in gift boxes or bags, or in seasonal storage tins they are always greeted with delight. There is also a tradition of sending cookies in the mail. For cookies by mail, line a sturdy box or tin with foil or cellophane and place some crumbled tissue paper or cellophane on the base. Select cookies that will stand the journey such as drop or bar cookies, or those containing fruits. Thin, delicate crisp cookies decorated with the finest piping make the worse travelers—if you must send these, place a few cookies on a piece of card, then wrap securely with plastic wrap. Place plenty of crumbled tissue in between the cardboard layers in the box and around the edges. Pack other more robust cookies in layers separating each with a layer of paper or cellophane. Then pack crumbled paper in the top of the box and in any gaps around the edges. Place the box in a plastic bag and seal well (incase the package encounters inclement weather) then, pack in a larger, sturdy box surrounded by a layer or packaging foam pieces or crumbled paper. Make sure that the box of cookies does not move around at all. Send by overnight mail if possible, although most cookies can cope with a few days in the regular post.

All-day Cookies

Who says you can't eat cookies at any time of the day? In this chapter there are cookies for breakfast, brunch, morning coffee, lunch boxes, afternoon snacks, after dinner, and night-time nibbles. Many are quick to make, so there is no excuse—get baking and enjoy them fresh from the oven.

Breakfast

Try not to miss this most important meal of the day and there is no excuse now with this selection of tempting, nutritious cookies.

Granola Bars	24
Maple Syrup Cookies	24
Banana Cookies	27
Pine Nut Oat Cookies	27
Apricot Slices	28
Pumpkin Seed and Bran Cookies	29
Lime Cookies	30
Honey and Oat Cookies	32
Sesame Seed Sensations	33

Brunch

Substantial cookies for a late brunch at weekends.

Orange Shortbread	34
Currant and Almond Cookies	34
Cornflake and Golden Raisin Drop Cookies	35
Double Banana Cookies	35
Cream Cheese Puff Swirls	36
Nut Chewies	37
Maple Syrup Tartlets	38
Orange Spritz Cookies	39
Jam Thumbprints	40
Crunchy Cereal Bites	41

Morning Coffee

Delight your friends with the smell of fresh baked cookies when they call in for coffee. These cookies make a perfect snack.

Ginger Bites	42
Popcorn Balls	43
Butter, Currant, and Coconut Cookies	43
Pear Cookies	44
Chocolate Swirls	45
Peanut Shortbread Bars	46
Ginger and Coffee Creams	47

Lunch Box

The cookies in this section are hearty enough for brunches or lunches, or whenever you need an energy-giving snack. They are portable too and ideal for when you have a busy schedule but still need a quick bite to eat.

Apricot and Cheese Cookies	49
Apple and Cinnamon Cookies	49
Chocolate and Cream Cheese Marble Fudge Bars	50
Spiced Molasses Drops	52
Milk Cookies	53
Peanut and Lemon Crunch Bars	53

Afternoon Snacks

The cookies featured in this part of the book are generally smaller and more delicate than the cookies for brunch or lunch. These cookies have also been chosen as their flavors offer a wide range of tastes from which to choose your snack.

Cranberry Crunch	54
Maple Walnut Drops	55
Blueberry Streusel Bakes	56
Coconut Cookies	57
Cinnamon Palmiers	57

After-dinner Delicacies

These cookies are small, delicate, and bite size; ideal to serve up after a meal of several courses with coffee when entertaining. They may be small, but they are very tempting so make a good selection for your guests to choose from.

Mini Florentines	58
No-bake Chocolate Delights	59
Minute Meringues	60
Maple Pecan Wafers	60

Night-time Nibbles

Cardomom Cookies	61
Chocolate Pretzels	62
Nut Rocks	62
Tropical Fruit Cookies	64
Honey and Date Comforts	65

Granola Bars

Preparation time: 15 minutes ● Cooking time: 25 minutes ● Makes: 12 bars

Ideal for those who need to eat breakfast on the move, grab a bar and a piece of fruit and this will set you up for the day.

INGREDIENTS

⅓ *cup clear/runny honey*
1 stick margarine
¼ *cup packed dark brown sugar*
¼ *cup packed light brown sugar*
2½ *cups rolled oats*
3 Tbsp slivered almonds
3 Tbsp chopped walnuts
⅓ *cup raisins*
⅓ *cup chopped dried dates*
⅓ *cup chopped dried apricots*

Preheat oven to 350°F. Grease a shallow 11 x 7-inch baking pan or line with a sheet of nonstick baking parchment.

● Gently melt the honey, margarine, and sugars in a saucepan until well combined, taking care not to boil the mixture. Stir in the oats, nuts, and dried fruits, mixing well.

● Press the mixture into the baking pan and bake in the center of the oven for about 25 minutes, until golden. Leave to cool in the pan for 5 minutes. Cut into bars.

● Leave to cool completely before removing granola bars from the pan. Store in an airtight container.

Maple Syrup Cookies

Preparation time: 15 minutes ● Cooking time: 12 to 15 minutes ● Makes: About 12 to 14

These simple cookies are delicately flavored with maple syrup.

INGREDIENTS

1 stick lightly salted butter
½ *cup packed light brown sugar*
1 egg, beaten
1½ *cups all-purpose flour*
2 Tbsp maple syrup

Preheat oven to 350°F. Grease two large baking sheets or line with nonstick baking parchment.

● Beat the butter and sugar together in a mixing bowl. Beat in the egg, then add the flour and maple syrup.

● Place 12 to 14 equal-sized spoonfuls of the mixture onto the baking sheets, allowing 3 inches for spreading. Flatten the mounds of mixture a little with the back of the spoon. Bake in the oven for about 12 to 15 minutes, until pale golden. Remove from the oven and allow to cool for one minute to allow the cookies to firm, before removing with a thin metal spatula to a wire rack to cool completely. Store in an airtight container.

Banana Cookies

Preparation time: 15 minutes ●
Cooking time: 10 to 12 minutes ● *Makes: 12*

Great served with a quickly whizzed smoothie or shake.

INGREDIENTS

1 stick lightly salted butter
½ cup packed light brown sugar
1 egg, beaten
1½ cups all-purpose flour
1⅔ cups dried banana chips, chopped

Preheat oven to 350°F. Grease two large baking sheets or line with nonstick baking parchment.

● Beat the butter and sugar together in a mixing bowl until pale and fluffy. Beat in the egg and flour. Stir in three-quarters of the chopped banana chips and place twelve equal-sized spoonfuls of the mixture onto the baking sheets, allowing 3 inches for spreading. Flatten the mounds of cookie mixture a little using the back of the spoon.

● Sprinkle the remaining banana chips equally over the twelve cookies and press in very lightly. Bake for about 10 to 12 minutes, until pale golden. Remove from the oven and allow to cool for one minute to allow the cookies to firm, before removing with a thin metal spatula to a wire rack to cool completely. Store in an airtight container.

Pine Nut Oat Cookies

Preparation time: 10 minutes ●
Cooking time :10 to 12 minutes ● *Makes: 12*

A high fiber start to the day.

INGREDIENTS

⅓ cup packed dark brown sugar
2¼ cups rolled oats
¼ cup oatmeal
⅔ cup pine kernels
½ cup peanut or canola oil
1 egg, beaten

Preheat oven to 375°F. Grease two large baking sheets or line with nonstick baking parchment.

● Place the sugar, oats, oatmeal, and pine kernels in a mixing bowl and mix together. Add the oil and egg and mix all the ingredients together thoroughly to form a crumble mixture.

● Place small tablespoonfuls of the mixture 4 inches apart on the baking sheets and flatten with a fork to make 3 inch circles. If necessary, bring the crumble mixture together and place any loose pine kernels back on top of the cookies. Bake in the oven for 10 to 12 minutes or until golden-brown. Leave for 1 minute to firm before removing with a thin metal spatula to cool on a wire rack. Store in an airtight container.

Apricot Slices

Preparation time: 45 minutes ● Cooking time: 25 to 30 minutes ● Makes: About 12 bars

The fresh tang of apricots combined with the comforting oats makes this a great breakfast cookie.

INGREDIENTS

⅓ cup dried apricots
2 Tbsp granulated sugar
⅔ cup unsweetened clear apple juice
1 cup all-purpose flour
1 tsp baking soda
1¼ cups rolled oats
¼ cup packed light brown sugar
1 stick lightly salted butter

Preheat oven to 375°F. Grease a shallow 11 x 7-inch baking pan or line with nonstick baking parchment.

● Chop the apricots into quarters and place in a saucepan with the granulated sugar and apple juice.

Bring to a boil, cover and simmer for 15 minutes or until the apricots have softened and nearly absorbed all of the apple juice. Leave to cool completely, then place in a blender and process until smooth.

● Mix together the flour, baking soda, oats, and brown sugar in a mixing bowl. Blend in the butter using fingertips, until the mixture resembles bread crumbs.

● Press half of the crumbly oat mixture over the base of the baking pan. Spread the apricot purée evenly over the oat mixture, using a thin metal spatula wetted with a little cold water to help ease of spreading. Cover with the remaining oat mixture, pressing the mixture down lightly. Bake in the oven for 25 to 30 minutes, until pale golden. Leave to cool in the pan before cutting into 12 equal-sized bars. Store in an airtight container.

Pumpkin Seed and Bran Cookies

Preparation time: 10 minutes • Cooking time: 10 to 12 minutes • Makes: 12

Packed with goodness, try these deliciously crunchy cookies any time of day.

INGREDIENTS

1 stick lightly salted butter
½ cup packed light brown sugar
½ cup packed dark brown sugar
1 egg, beaten
1¼ cups all-purpose flour
⅔ cup bran
⅓ cup pumpkin seeds

Preheat oven to 350°F. Grease two large baking sheets or line with nonstick baking parchment.

● Beat the butter and sugars together in a mixing bowl until the mixture turns paler and fluffy. Beat in the egg, flour, and bran. Stir in three-quarters of the pumpkin seeds.

● Place 12 equal-sized spoonfuls of the mixture onto the baking sheets, allowing 3 inches for spreading. Flatten the mounds of mixture a little with the back of the spoon and sprinkle the remaining pumpkin seeds evenly over the cookies. Bake for about 10 to 12 minutes, until golden and just firm. Remove from the oven and allow to cool for one minute to allow the cookies to firm, then remove with a thin metal spatula to a wire rack to cool completely. Store in an airtight container.

Lime Cookies

Preparation time: 15 minutes ● *Cooking time: 12 to 14 minutes* ● *Makes: 12*

Lime adds a zestful tang to wake up your tastebuds.

INGREDIENTS

1 stick lightly salted butter

½ cup granulated sugar

1 egg, beaten

1½ cups all-purpose flour

Finely grated rind of 1 lime

2 Tbsp fresh lime juice

FILLING

¾ stick unsalted butter, softened

1½ cups confectioners' sugar, sifted

1 Tbsp grated lime rind

2 tsp fresh lime juice

Preheat oven to 350°F. Grease two large baking sheets or line with nonstick baking parchment.

● Beat the butter and sugar together in a mixing bowl until pale and fluffy. Beat in the egg, flour, lime rind, and lime juice.

● Place 12 equal-sized spoonfuls of the mixture onto the baking sheets, allowing 3 inches all round for spreading. Flatten the mounds of mixture a little using the back of the spoon. Bake the cookies in the oven for about 12 to 14 minutes, until pale golden.

● Remove from the oven and allow to cool on the sheets for one minute to allow the cookies to firm, before removing with a thin metal spatula to a wire rack to cool completely.

● To make the filling, in a small bowl beat together the butter and confectioners' sugar until soft and stir in the lime rind and juice for a soft frosting. Sandwich the cookies together with the filling. Store them in an airtight container.

Honey and Oat Cookies

Preparation time: 15 minutes ● Cooking time: 10 to 12 minutes ● Makes: 14

Sweet and delicious honey and oats in a cookie jar breakfast.

INGREDIENTS

1 stick lightly salted butter

½ cup packed light brown sugar

2 Tbsp clear/runny honey

1 egg yolk

1½ cups self-rising flour

Pinch ground pumpkin pie spice

⅔ cup rolled oats

Preheat the oven to 350°F. Meanwhile, grease two large baking sheets.

● Beat together the butter and sugar in a mixing bowl until pale and fluffy. Beat in the honey and egg yolk, then stir in the flour, mixed spice, and oats until well combined.

● Divide the mixture into 14 equal-sized pieces and roll into balls using your fingertips. Place the cookies onto the baking sheets 3 inches apart, to allow for spreading. Bake for 10 to 12 minutes until golden and just firm. Leave to cool for one minute to allow the cookies to firm, before removing them with a thin metal spatula to a wire rack to cool. Store in an airtight container.

Sesame Seed Sensations

Preparation time: 10 minutes ● *Cooking time: 12 to 15 minutes* ● *Makes: About 12*

Sesame seeds have a strong flavor which bursts through the oaty base in this cookie.

INGREDIENTS

⅓ cup packed light brown sugar

2¼ cups rolled oats

¼ cup oatmeal

⅓ cup sesame seeds

½ cup peanut or canola oil

1 egg, beaten

Preheat the oven to 375°F. Grease two large baking sheets or line with nonstick baking parchment.

● Place the sugar, oats, oatmeal, and sesame seeds in a mixing bowl and mix. Add the peanut or canola oil and beaten egg and mix all the ingredients thoroughly to form a crumble mixture.

● Place small tablespoons of the mixture 3 to 4 inches apart on greased baking sheets and flatten with a fork to make 3-inch circles. If necessary, bring the crumbly mixture together. Bake in the oven for 12 to 15 minutes or until golden-brown. Leave on the baking sheets for 1 minute to firm before carefully removing with a thin metal spatula to cool the cookies on a wire rack. Store in an airtight container.

Orange Shortbread

Preparation time: 10 minutes ● Cooking time: 1 hour ● Makes: About 16

Home-baked shortbread is crisp and light and this version is delicately flavored with orange rind.

INGREDIENTS

1 stick lightly salted butter

1 cup all-purpose flour

½ cup confectioners' sugar

⅓ cup plus 1 Tbsp cornstarch

Grated rind of 1 orange

Preheat oven to 325°F. Grease a shallow baking pan measuring 7 x 7-inches or line with nonstick baking parchment.

● With fingertips gently work the butter, flour, confectioners' sugar, cornstarch, and orange rind together in a mixing bowl. Bring the mixture together to make a soft dough.

● Press the mixture evenly into the pan and smooth the surface. Lightly prick the surface evenly all over with a fork. Bake for 40 minutes then reduce the temperature to 275°F and bake for a further 15 to 20 minutes, or until lightly browned. Leave to cool completely in the pan and cut into 16 equal-sized bars with a sharp knife. These cookies are best eaten on the day they are made.

Currant and Almond Cookies

Preparation time: 15 minutes + chilling ● Cooking time: 8 to 10 minutes ● Makes: 16

The combination of currants and nuts in these cookies makes them both crunchy and chewy—delicious.

INGREDIENTS

2 sticks lightly salted butter

½ cup packed light brown sugar

1½ cups self-rising flour

½ cup slivered almonds

½ cup currants

Preheat oven to 400°F. Grease two large baking sheets with nonstick baking parchment.

● Beat together the butter and sugar in a mixing bowl until pale and fluffy. Beat in the flour and almonds then stir in the currants. If the dough is too soft to handle, cover and chill in the refrigerator for 30 minutes.

● Form the cookie dough into a roll about 2½ inches in diameter. Cut into ½-inch slices and place well apart on the baking sheets to allow for spreading.

● Bake the cookies in batches in the oven for 8 to 10 minutes, until light brown. Leave to cool for five minutes on the sheets before removing with a thin metal spatula to a wire rack to cool completely.

Cornflake and Golden Raisin Cookies

Preparation time: 25 minutes ● Cooking time: 10 to 15 minutes ● Makes: 18

Soft chewy cookies that are very easy to make.

INGREDIENTS

1 stick soft margarine
½ cup packed light brown sugar
1 egg, beaten
1¼ cups self-rising flour
2 cups cornflakes
½ cup golden raisins

Preheat oven to 350°F. Grease several baking sheets or line with nonstick baking parchment.

● Beat together the margarine and sugar in a mixing bowl until pale and fluffy. Beat in the egg. Stir in the flour with the cornflakes and golden raisins and mix everything together until well combined.

● Place mounds of the mixture onto the baking sheets, leaving big spaces in between to allow for spreading.

● Bake the cookies in the oven for 12 to 15 minutes, until golden brown. Lift onto wire racks to cool completely. Store in an airtight container.

Double Banana Cookies

Preparation time: 25 minutes ● Cooking time: 12 to 15 minutes ● Makes: 16

These wholesome cookies contain oats, banana chips, and fresh chunks of banana.

INGREDIENTS

1 stick soft margarine
½ cup packed light brown sugar
1 egg, beaten
1½ cups self-rising flour
⅔ cup porridge oats
½ cup chopped candied pineapple
¼ cup crumbled banana chips
1 banana, chopped

Preheat oven to 350°F. Grease several baking sheets or line with nonstick baking parchment.

● In a mixing bowl beat together the margarine and sugar until pale and fluffy. Beat in the egg. Stir in the flour with the oats, candied pineapple, banana chips, and fresh banana and mix everything together until well combined.

● Place mounds of the mixture onto the baking sheets, leaving big spaces in between to allow for spreading.

● Bake the cookies in the oven for 12 to 15 minutes, until golden brown. Lift onto wire racks to cool completely. Store in an airtight container.

Cream Cheese Puff Swirls

Preparation time: 10 minutes ● Cooking time: 12 to15 minutes ● Makes: About 18

You can use any dried fruit to flavor these creamy pastry treats.

INGREDIENTS

8 oz ready rolled puff pastry, thawed, if frozen

4 oz fine chopped dried apricots

½ cup cream cheese

Preheat oven to 425°F. Grease two large baking sheets or line with nonstick baking parchment.

● Place the puff pastry on a lightly floured surface and if necessary roll to make a rectangle measuring 11 x 9-inches.

● In a bowl mix the apricots and cream cheese together thoroughly. Spread the mixture evenly all over the surface of the pastry. Holding one of the short sides, roll the pastry up to make a log. Cut across the pastry roll with a sharp knife to make ¼-inch thick slices.

● Place the pastry swirls onto the prepared baking sheets allowing 1 inch in between them for spreading. If necessary, reshape into neat circles and pat down slightly. Bake for 12 to 15 minutes, or until the pastry is golden-brown and crisp. Best if eaten warm when freshly made, but can be cooled and kept in the refrigerator for 24 hours.

Nut Chewies

Preparation time: 25 minutes + cooling ● *Cooking time: 12 to 15 minutes* ● *Makes: About 36*

This cookie is almost all nuts and fruit. They are soft and chewy and don't last long—especially at a picnic.

INGREDIENTS

1 cup unblanched whole almonds

½ cup pecan or walnut halves

½ cup blanched hazelnuts

1 cup all-purpose flour

1 tsp baking soda

¼ tsp salt

1 stick unsalted butter

½ cup granulated sugar

3 Tbsp dark brown sugar

1 egg

1 tsp vanilla essence

½ cup raisins

½ cup golden raisins

Preheat oven to 375°F. Place nuts on a large baking sheet and toast until golden and fragrant, 5 to 7 minutes, stirring occasionally. Pour onto a plate and cool completely, then roughly chop. Grease two large baking sheets or line with nonstick baking parchment.

● Into a small bowl, sift together the flour, baking soda, and salt. In a large bowl, beat the butter until soft, beat in the sugar until the mixture becomes light and fluffy. Beat in the egg and vanilla until combined. Stir in the flour mixture followed by the raisins, golden raisins, and nuts until evenly distributed.

● Drop heaped tablespoons of the mixture, at least 2 inches apart onto baking sheets. Bake in the oven until set and golden, 12 to 15 minutes, rotating the baking sheets during cooking. Cool the cookies slightly, then transfer to wire racks to cool completely. Store in an airtight container.

Maple Syrup Tartlets

Preparation time: 30 minutes + chilling ● *Cooking time: 15 to 20 minutes* ● *Makes: About 17*

These little tartlets are delicious served warm with more maple syrup poured over the top.

INGREDIENTS

FOR THE PASTRY BASE

1 stick margarine

1 Tbsp milk

1½ cups all-purpose flour

FILLING

8 Tbsp maple syrup

TOPPING

½ stick margarine

¼ cup packed light brown sugar

6 Tbsp self-rising flour

½ tsp baking powder

¼ tsp vanilla extract

1 egg, beaten

1 Tbsp milk

Preheat the oven to 375°F. Grease two shallow muffin pans or eight 3½-inch individual tartlet pans.

● To make the pastry base, place the margarine, milk, and flour together in a bowl and mix together to make a dough. If the pastry is too soft to handle, cover and refrigerate for at least 30 minutes to become firm.

● On a lightly floured surface, roll out the pastry thinly and cut into 3-inch circles using a fluted pastry cutter. Re-roll and cut the pastry to make as many pastry circles as possible. Line the tartlet pans with the pastry circles. Place one teaspoonful of maple syrup in each small pastry shell.

● To make the topping, beat together the margarine and sugar until pale and fluffy. Add the flour, baking powder, vanilla, egg, and milk, mix thoroughly. Divide the mixture evenly over the maple syrup covered tartlet bases. Bake in the oven for 15 to 20 minutes, until golden. Eat warm, served with more maple syrup or cool and store in an airtight container.

Orange Spritz Cookies

Preparation time: 40 minutes ● *Cooking time: 25 minutes* ● *Makes: About 96*

A very tangy cookie that never loses its appeal. These are great for brunch or for social parties at school, church, or tennis club, for example.

INGREDIENTS

3 cups all-purpose flour	Grated rind of 1 orange
½ tsp pumpkin pie spice	¼ cup fresh squeezed orange juice
¼ tsp salt	½ tsp almond extract
3 sticks unsalted butter	½ cup orange marmalade
⅔ cup superfine sugar	Slivered almonds, to decorate

Preheat oven to 375°F. ● In a medium bowl, sift together flour, spice, and salt. In a large bowl beat butter until creamy. Add the sugar and continue beating until light and fluffy. Beat in egg, orange rind, and orange juice until well blended. Stir in flour until well combined.

● Divide the dough into quarters. Working with one-quarter at a time, fill a cookie press fitted with a ribbon or bar plate. Press 12-inch strips overlapping lengthwise, onto one side of an ungreased baking sheet, making a base about 3 inches wide. Pat down strips to flatten. Refill the press with dough, if necessary, and press a border along each side of strips, leaving a shallow trough in the center. Press out a little dough and use to make 2 ends (this will prevent the marmalade from oozing out onto the baking sheet.)

● Bake strips for 15 minutes. Remove baking sheets from oven, and using the back of a spoon, press down a center trench in each strip. Fill with marmalade to just below the edges.

● Return the baking sheet to the oven and bake until the edges are golden and the marmalade bubbling, 10 to 12 minutes. Remove baking sheets to wire rack and cool until set, about 3 minutes. Using another baking sheet or long metal spatula, slide each long strip onto wire rack to cool for about 5 minutes. Slip each strip onto a work surface and while still warm, trim the edges and cut into 1 inch cookies.

Jam Thumbprints

Preparation time: 20 minutes + chilling ● *Cooking time: 15 to 17 minutes* ● *Makes: 14*

A cookie classic. Using a selection of jams or preserves makes a plate of these look really pretty.

INGREDIENTS

1¼ sticks lightly salted butter

⅓ cup light brown sugar

1 egg yolk

2 cups all-purpose flour

14 tsp seedless fruit jam or preserves

Grease two large baking sheets or line with nonstick baking parchment.

● Beat together the butter and sugar until light and fluffy. Beat in the egg yolk and stir in the flour. Cover and refrigerate for about an hour, or until firm enough to handle. Preheat oven to 350°F, then divide the mixture into 14 equal-sized pieces and roll into balls using your hands. Place at least 1 inch apart on the baking sheets. Press your thumb into the center of each cookie ball to make a hollow indentation.

● Bake in the oven for about 10 to 12 minutes until pale brown and just firm. If the centers of the cookies have risen slightly, gently pat back down with the back of a teaspoon. Fill each hollow with a teaspoon of jam or preserves and bake for a further 5 minutes. Remove the cookies to a wire rack to cool using a thin metal spatula. Store in an airtight container.

Crunchy Cereal Bites

Preparation time: 10 minutes ● Cooking time: 20 minutes ● Makes: 10

A great favorite with children and adults alike.

INGREDIENTS

½ stick margarine

¼ cup superfine sugar

½ cup all-purpose flour

2 cups crisp rice cereal

1 egg, beaten

Preheat oven to 350°F. Grease a large baking sheet or line with nonstick baking parchment.

● Beat together the margarine and sugar until the mixture is light and fluffy.

● Beat in the egg, until well combined. Then stir in the flour and the cereal, taking care not to crush the cereal. Shape into 10 equal-sized balls and place on the baking sheet. Bake for about 20 minutes, until lightly browned. Eat warm, or cool on a wire rack. These cookies are best eaten on the day they are made.

Ginger Bites

Preparation time: 10 minutes ● *Cooking time: 15 minutes* ● *Makes: About 12*

Ginger cookies work well with foaming milky latte.

INGREDIENTS

4 Tbsp light brown sugar
½ stick lightly salted butter
2½ Tbsps molasses
1½ cups self-rising flour
1 tsp ground ginger
½ tsp baking powder

Preheat oven to 350°F. Grease two large baking sheets or line with nonstick baking parchment.

● Beat together the sugar, butter, and molasses until it becomes lighter in color and fluffy. Mix in the flour, ginger, and baking powder until well combined. Roll the mixture into walnut sized balls using your hands and place 2 to 3 inches apart on the baking sheets to allow for spreading. Flatten the cookies slightly using your fingers or the back of a fork. Bake in the oven for about 15 minutes, until flattened and slightly firm to the touch. Leave to cool on the baking sheets then remove and store in an airtight container.

Popcorn Balls

Preparation time: 10 minutes ● Cooking time: 20 minutes ● Makes: 8

The popcorn adds an airy crunch to these cookies.

INGREDIENTS

½ stick margarine

2 Tbsp superfine sugar

6 Tbsp all-purpose flour

2 eggs, beaten

4 cups ready-made plain or sweetened popcorn

Preheat oven to 350°F. Grease a large baking sheet or line with nonstick baking parchment.

● Beat together the margarine and sugar in a large mixing bowl until light and fluffy. Stir in the egg. Add the flour and the popcorn and mix thoroughly, so that the popcorn is evenly coated. The mixture will combine sufficiently so that it will form balls.

● Make 8 equal-sized ball-shaped cookies with the mixture and place on the baking sheet. Bake for about 20 minutes, until lightly browned. Serve immediately, while warm.

Butter, Currant & Coconut Cookies

Preparation time: 15 minutes + chilling ● Cooking time: 8 to 10 minutes ● Makes: 16

These cookies are crisp on the day they are made, but if stored in an airtight container they soften and become quite chewy—both are delicious.

INGREDIENTS

2 sticks lightly salted butter

¾ cup packed light brown sugar

1½ cups self-rising flour

1 cup packed flaked, sweetened coconut

¾ cup currants

Preheat oven to 400°F. Grease two large baking sheets or line with nonstick baking parchment.

● Beat together the butter and sugar in a mixing bowl until pale and fluffy. Beat in the flour and coconut. Stir in the currants. If the dough is too soft to handle, cover and chill in the refrigerator for about 1 hour to firm.

● Form the cookie dough into a roll about 2½ inches in diameter. Cut into ½ inch slices and place well apart to allow for spreading as the cookies double in size. Reshape into neat rounds, if necessary.

● Bake the cookies in batches in the oven for about 8 to 10 minutes, until light brown. Allow to cool for 5 minutes to firm on the baking sheet, before removing with a thin metal spatula to a wire rack to cool completely.

Pear Cookies

*Preparation time: 15 minutes ● Cooking time:
12 to 14 minutes ● Makes: About 12 to 14*

**You will want to add dried pears to many more recipes
after enjoying these cookies. Other dried fruits such as
apricots, can also be substituted.**

INGREDIENTS

1 stick lightly salted butter

½ cup packed light brown sugar

1 egg, beaten

1½ cups all-purpose flour

5 oz chopped ready to eat dried pears

Preheat oven to 350°F. Grease two large baking
sheets or line with nonstick baking parchment.
● Beat the butter and sugar together in a mixing bowl
until pale and fluffy. Beat in the egg and flour. Stir in the
chopped pear.

● Place 12 to 14 equal-sized spoonfuls of the cookie
mixture onto the baking sheets, allowing 2 to 3 inches
for spreading. Flatten the mounds of mixture a little
using the back of the spoon. Bake the cookies in the
oven for about 12 to 14 minutes, until pale golden.
Remove from the oven and leave to firm on the baking
sheets for one minute, before removing with a thin
metal spatula to a wire rack to cool completely. Store in
an airtight container.

Chocolate Swirls

44

Chocolate Swirls

Preparation time: 5 minutes ● *Cooking time: 10 to 12 minutes* ● *Makes: About 18 to 20*

Using ready made puff pastry makes these cookies very quick and easy to make.

INGREDIENTS

8 oz ready made and rolled puff pastry, thawed if frozen

3-4 Tbsp chocolate spread

Preheat oven to 425°F. Grease two large baking sheets or line with nonstick baking parchment.

● Place the puff pastry on a lightly floured surface and if necessary roll to make a rectangle measuring 11 x 9-inches. Spread the chocolate spread evenly all over the surface of the pastry. Holding one of the short sides, roll the pastry up to make a long roll. Cut across the pastry roll with a sharp knife to make ¼-inch thick slices.

● Transfer the pastry swirls onto the baking sheets allowing a little space for spreading. If necessary, reshape into neat circles and pat down slightly. Bake for 8 minutes in the center of the oven until golden-brown, then carefully turn the pastries over and bake for a further 2 to 4 minutes until golden. Using a thin metal spatula, remove the chocolate swirls to a wire rack to cool completely.

Peanut Shortbread Bars

Preparation time: 15 minutes ● *Cooking time: 50 minutes* ● *Makes: 10 bars*

These filling bars are extra tasty when spread with peanut butter.

INGREDIENTS

2 sticks lightly salted butter

2 cups all-purpose flour

¼ cup confectioners' sugar

1 cup roasted, salted peanuts

Preheat oven to 350°F. Grease a shallow 11 x 7-inch baking pan or line with nonstick baking parchment.
● Beat together the butter, flour, and sugar in a mixing bowl until well combined. Add three-quarters of the peanuts and using your hand, lightly bring the mixture together to form a soft dough.
● Press the mixture into the prepared pan with a lightly floured hand and smooth the surface. Evenly sprinkle over the remaining peanuts and lightly press into the top of the shortbread mixture. Bake for about 50 minutes, until a pale, golden-brown and firm to touch.
● Leave to cool completely in the pan before cutting into 10 even-sized bars. Store in an airtight container. Best eaten on the day made but can be kept in the refrigerator for 2 to 3 days.

Ginger and Coffee Creams

Preparation time: 30 minutes ● Cooking time: 15 to 20 minutes ● Makes: About 25

Crisp ginger nut cookies sandwiched together with a coffee cream; perfect with a large mug of steaming coffee.

INGREDIENTS

1½ cups all-purpose flour

2 tsp baking powder

1 tsp baking soda

2 tsp ground ginger

1 tsp pumpkin pie spice

1 Tbsp superfine sugar

1 stick lightly salted butter or margarine

½ cup dark corn syrup

FROSTING

½ stick unsalted butter, softened

3 Tbsp superfine sugar

1 tsp coffee extract

7 Tbsp confectioners' sugar

Preheat oven to 375°F. Grease or line two baking sheets with nonstick baking parchment.

● Sift together the flour, baking powder, baking soda, ginger, and spice. Stir in the sugar and make a well in the center. Melt the butter, then stir in the syrup and pour the mixture into the well. Mix to give a soft but not sticky dough.

● Take half teaspoons of the mixture and roll into balls. Place on the baking sheets leave space between the cookies as they will spread while cooking. Flatten them slightly. Bake for 15 to 20 minutes until set. Leave to cool for a few minutes, then transfer onto wire racks to cool completely.

● To prepare the frosting, beat the butter and superfine sugar together with the coffee extract until well blended. Gradually beat in the confectioners' sugar and mix to a stiff paste. Sandwich the cookies together with the frosting. Best eaten on the day filled, but may be stored in an airtight container for 2 to 3 days although the filling will cause the cookies to soften.

Apricot and Cheese Cookies

Preparation time: 15 minutes ● Cooking time: 15 to 18 minutes ● Makes: About 14

Tangy sweet apricots complement these cheese cookies.

INGREDIENTS

5 oz fine chopped no-soak, dried apricots
¼ stick lightly salted butter
2 cups all-purpose flour
6 Tbsp grated Cheddar cheese
1 egg, beaten
3–4 Tbsp milk

Preheat oven to 375°F. Grease two large baking sheets or line with nonstick baking parchment.

● Cut the dried apricots into small pieces. In a mixing bowl, blend the butter into the flour to resemble bread crumbs. Stir in two-thirds of the grated cheese, three-quarters of the chopped dried apricots, and the egg. Add sufficient milk to form a dough.

● On a lightly floured surface, roll the cookie dough out to ¼ inch thick and cut the dough into 2 x 3-inch rectangular cookies. Re-roll and repeat. Place the cookies onto the baking sheets, brush with any remaining milk and sprinkle over the reserved grated cheese and apricots. Bake for about 15 to 18 minutes, until golden-brown. Remove from the baking sheet with a thin metal spatula and cool on a wire rack. Store in an airtight container in the refrigerator for up to 2 days.

Apple and Cinnamon Cookies

Preparation time: 15 minutes + chilling ● Cooking time: 25 minutes ● Makes: 12

These cookies are best eaten the same day, but can be stored in an airtight container for 2 days.

INGREDIENTS

2 sticks lightly salted butter
1 cup confectioners' sugar
4 drops vanilla extract
1 tsp ground cinnamon
2 cups all-purpose flour
1⅓ cups cornstarch
3 Tbsp apple sauce
1 eating apple, peeled, cored, and chopped

Preheat oven to 350°F. Grease two large baking sheets or line with nonstick baking parchment.

● Beat the butter, confectioners' sugar, vanilla, and cinnamon until well combined. Stir in the flour, cornstarch, apple sauce, and diced apple until it forms a well mixed but crumbly dough. If the mixture is soft and sticky, refrigerate for at least 30 minutes to firm.

● Divide the mixture into 12 equal-sized pieces and using your hands shape into balls. Place the cookie balls onto the baking sheets, 3 inches apart and flatten slightly with a fork. Bake in the oven for about 25 minutes, until golden. Leave to cool on the baking sheet for 5 minutes to firm before removing with a thin metal spatula to a wire rack to cool completely.

Chocolate and Cream Cheese Marble Fudge Bars

Preparation time: 20 minutes • Cooking time: 40 to 45 minutes • Makes: 12 bars

These are very rich and sticky fudge bars which can be wrapped in waxed paper and make wonderful lunch box fillers.

INGREDIENTS

FOR THE CHOCOLATE BASE

1½ sticks lightly salted butter

3 oz semi-sweet chocolate

1 cup packed light brown sugar

1 cup packed dark brown sugar

2 eggs, beaten

1 cup all-purpose flour

6 drops vanilla extract

TOPPING

1¼ cups cream cheese

½ cup packed light brown sugar

1 egg, beaten

4 drops vanilla extract

Preheat oven to 350°F. Grease a shallow 7 x 11-inch baking pan and line with waxed paper and then grease again.

● To make the chocolate base; melt the butter and chocolate in a small saucepan over a gentle heat, taking care not to boil the mixture.

● In a mixing bowl, whisk together the light and dark brown sugars with the eggs until well combined, then whisk in the melted butter and chocolate mixture. Stir in the flour and vanilla. Pour the mixture into the prepared pan.

● Make the topping. Beat together the cream cheese, sugar, egg, and vanilla until the mixture thickens to a spooning consistency. Randomly place spoonfuls of the mixture over the chocolate mixture in the baking pan and, using the tip of a sharp knife, make swirling patterns drawing the knife through the two mixtures to combine lightly. Bake in the oven for about 40 to 45 minutes, or until the mixture is firm to touch and the tip of a sharp knife comes out clean when inserted into the center of the cookie mixture. Cool in the pan and cut into 12 equal-sized bars. Store in an airtight container in the refrigerator for up to 2 days.

Spiced Molasses Drops

Preparation time: 15 minutes ● *Cooking time: 14 to 20 minutes* ● *Makes: About 40*

These cookies are bite-size, and packed with a rich spicy flavor

INGREDIENTS

1 cup all-purpose flour

1 tsp ground cinnamon

$^{1}/_{2}$ tsp ground ginger

$^{1}/_{2}$ tsp ground nutmeg

$^{1}/_{4}$ tsp ground cloves

$^{1}/_{2}$ tsp baking soda

$^{1}/_{2}$ tsp salt

$^{1}/_{2}$ stick butter or margarine, softened

$^{1}/_{2}$ cup shortening

$^{1}/_{4}$ cup molasses

$^{1}/_{2}$ cup packed dark brown sugar

1 egg

GLAZE

1 $^{1}/_{2}$ cups confectioners' sugar

3 tsp water

$^{1}/_{2}$ tsp vanilla essence

Preheat oven to 375°F. Grease two large baking sheets or line with nonstick baking parchment.

● In a medium bowl, sift together flour, cinnamon, ginger, nutmeg, cloves, baking soda, and salt. In a large bowl beat the butter or margarine, shortening, molasses, brown sugar and egg until well blended. Stir in flour-spice mixture until combined.

● Drop teaspoons of mixture 1 inch apart onto 2 large ungreased baking sheets. Bake until crisp and golden, 7 to 10 minutes. Cool slightly on wire racks, then remove cookies onto wire racks to cool completely. Repeat with remaining mixture.

● For the glaze, mix the confectioners' sugar, water, and vanilla until smooth. Arrange cookies on a rack over a baking sheet (to catch drips) and drizzle with glaze. Allow glaze to dry completely. Store in an airtight container.

Milk Cookies

Preparation time: 15 minutes ●
Cooking time: 15 to 20 minutes ● *Makes: About 14*

Serve milk cookies spread with savory toppings such as hummus, cream cheeses, and pâtés.

INGREDIENTS

¼ stick margarine
⅔ cup milk
2 cups all-purpose flour
1 tsp baking powder
Pinch of salt

Preheat oven to 350°F. Grease two large baking sheets or line with nonstick baking parchment.

● Place the margarine and milk in a small saucepan and heat gently to melt the margarine, taking care not to boil the milk. Leave to become tepid. Place the flour, baking powder and salt in a mixing bowl and add sufficient of the cooled milk and melted margarine mixture to form a dough. Knead the mixture until smooth.

● On a lightly floured surface, roll out the dough to ⅛-inch thick. Using a plain 3-inch round cutter, cut out the cookies and place on the baking sheet. Re-roll and cut out the dough to make as many cookies as possible.

● Lightly prick the surface of each cookie with the prongs of a fork several times. Bake in the oven for 15 to 20 minutes, until lightly golden all over. Remove the cookies with a thin metal spatula to a wire rack to cool completely. Store in an airtight container.

Peanut and Lemon Crunch Bars

Preparation time: 10 minutes + chilling
● *Makes: About 6 bars*

Peanut butter is a certain favorite and makes these cookies a nutritious treat.

INGREDIENTS

½ stick lightly salted butter
¼ cup light brown sugar
3 Tbsp honey
3 Tbsp crunchy peanut butter
Grated rind of 1 lemon
2 cups crisp rice breakfast cereal
2 cups cornflake breakfast cereal

Grease a 8-inch square, shallow baking pan or line with nonstick baking parchment.

● Place the butter, sugar, honey, and peanut butter into a large saucepan and heat gently to melt the butter and dissolve the sugar. Do not boil the mixture. When the ingredients are melted and well combined, remove from the heat.

● Stir the lemon rind, crisp rice, and cornflake breakfast cereals into the melted mixture carefully so as not to crush the cereals. Mix well. Spoon the mixture into the pan and level the surface. Leave to set for at least 30 minutes in a cool place, then cut into 6 equal-sized bars. Store in an airtight container.

Cranberry Crunch

Preparation time: 15 minutes ● *Cooking time: 10 to 12 minutes* ● *Makes: 14*

Dried cranberries are full of flavor and would go well with a cup of lemony herb tea.

INGREDIENTS

1 stick lightly salted butter

½ cup packed light brown sugar

2 Tbsp honey

1 egg yolk

1½ cups self-rising flour

⅔ cup rolled oats

½ cup dried cranberries

Preheat oven to 350°F. Grease two large baking sheets or line with nonstick baking parchment.
● Beat together the butter and sugar in a mixing bowl until pale and fluffy. Beat in the honey, egg yolk, flour, and oats until well combined. Stir in the cranberries.
● Divide the mixture into 14 equal-sized pieces and roll into balls using the fingertips. Place the cookies 2 to 3 inches apart to allow for spreading onto the prepared baking sheets. Bake in the oven for about 10 to 12 minutes until golden and just firm. Leave to cool for one minute to allow the cookies to firm, before removing them with a thin metal spatula to a wire rack to cool. Store in an airtight container.

Maple Walnut Drops

Preparation time: 30 minutes + chilling ● *Cooking time: 13 to 15 minutes* ● *Makes: About 48*

These cookies are bursting with flavor and make a great cookie to come back to after an afternoon out.

INGREDIENTS

¾ cup raisins

2½ cups all-purpose flour

1 tsp salt

¼ tsp baking powder

¼ tsp baking soda

1 tsp ground cinnamon

½ tsp ground nutmeg

1½ sticks unsalted butter

½ cup packed dark brown sugar

2 eggs

2 Tbsp maple syrup

⅓ cup cold, strong black coffee

1½ cups coarse chopped walnuts

In a small bowl, cover the raisins with hot water, stand for 15 minutes to plump. Drain the raisins and pat dry; set aside. Into a medium bowl sift together the flour, salt, baking powder, baking soda, cinnamon, and nutmeg.

● In a large bowl, beat the butter until soft, then beat in the sugar until light and fluffy. Beat in the eggs one at a time, beating well after each addition, then beat in the maple syrup.

● In three batches add the flour mixture and the black coffee ending with the flour. If the mixture seems to stiff, add a little extra coffee or water, but the mixture should be thick enough to drop. Stir in the walnuts and raisins and refrigerate until chilled, at least 30 minutes.

● Preheat oven to 350°F. Grease or line two baking sheets with nonstick baking parchment.

● Drop dough by heaped teaspoon on the baking sheets 2 inches apart (keeping the remaining dough refrigerated.) Bake until golden and firm to the touch, 13 to 15 minutes. Rotate baking sheets halfway through cooking. Remove the baking sheets to wire racks to allow to cool slightly, then, using a metal spatula, remove the cookies onto wire racks to cool completely. Store in an airtight container.

Blueberry Streusel Bakes

Preparation time: 20 minutes ● Cooking time: 55 to 60 minutes ● Makes: 12 bars

This recipe uses blueberry jam, but plum, apricot, or even pineapple preserves would be equally delicious.

INGREDIENTS

BASE

1 stick lightly salted butter

½ cup packed light brown sugar

1 cup all-purpose flour

FILLING

7 Tbsp blueberry jam or preserves

TOPPING

1¼ cups all-purpose flour

½ tsp baking powder

⅓ cup packed light brown sugar

1 stick lightly salted butter

½ cup chopped almonds

Grated rind 1 lemon

Preheat oven to 350°F. Grease a 7 x 11-inch baking sheet or line with nonstick baking parchment.

● To make the base, beat together the butter and sugar in a mixing bowl until pale and fluffy. Stir in the flour to form a soft dough. Press the mixture down, evenly over the base of the baking pan using the back of a spoon or lightly floured hand. Lightly prick the dough with a fork several times. Bake the dough in the oven for 15 minutes, until just firm. Remove from the oven and spread the blueberry jam or preserves all over the dough base.

● To make the topping, place the flour, baking powder, and sugar in a mixing bowl and blend in the butter, until the mixture resembles even-sized crumbs. Stir in the almonds and grated lemon rind. Sprinkle the topping over the jam or preserves. Bake in the oven for about 40 to 45 minutes until golden. Cool before cutting into bars. Store in an airtight container.

Coconut Cookies

Preparation time: 15 minutes ● *Cooking time:
10 to 12 minutes* ● *Makes: About 24*

An old-fashioned tea-time favorite.

INGREDIENTS

½ cup packed light brown sugar

2 sticks lightly salted butter

3 cups all-purpose flour

¼ cup flaked sweetened coconut

Preheat oven to 375°F. Grease two large baking sheets or line with nonstick baking parchment.
● Place the sugar, butter, and flour in a mixing bowl and with fingertips, blend the mixture together until it resembles bread crumbs. Add the coconut and work the mixture together to form a dough. Do not be tempted to add any liquid as the crumb mixture will upon kneading come together to make a smooth dough.
● On a lightly floured surface, halve the mixture and make two long rolls about 1½-1¾-inches in diameter. Cut into ½-inch slices. Place the cookies on the baking sheets, 1 inch apart to allow for spreading during baking. Bake in the oven for 10 to 12 minutes, until a pale light brown. Allow to cool for 1 minute before removing to a wire rack to cool completely. Store in an airtight container.

Cinnamon Palmiers

Preparation time: 10 minutes ● *Cooking time:
10 to 12 minutes* ● *Makes: 18 to 20*

A variation on the French classic.

INGREDIENTS

8 oz ready made and rolled puff pastry, thawed, if frozen

3 Tbsp packed dark brown sugar

1 tsp ground cinnamon

Preheat oven to 425°F. Grease two large baking sheets or line with nonstick baking parchment.
● Place the pastry on a lightly floured surface and if necessary roll out to a 11 x 9-inch rectangle.
● In a small bowl mix together the sugar and cinnamon. Sprinkle two-thirds of the cinnamon mixture evenly over the surface of the pastry. Fold each of the shortest pastry sides into the center, press down and sprinkle over the remaining cinnamon mixture. Fold each pastry side in half again so they meet in the center. Brush the pastry with cold water and fold over to make a long roll. Cut across the roll to make ¼-inch slices and place on the baking sheets 1-inch apart to allow for spreading.
● Bake in the oven for 8 minutes until golden, then carefully using a thin metal spatula, turn the palmiers over and cook for a further 3 to 5 minutes to brown and crisp the other side. Remove from the baking sheet with a thin metal spatula and cool on a wire rack. Best eaten when made, but can be kept in an airtight container for a few days, although they will lose their crispness.

Mini Florentines

Preparation time: 25 minutes ● Cooking time: 10 minutes ● Makes: About 16

Don't reserve these fantastic cookies for the festive season.

INGREDIENTS

¼ stick lightly salted butter

2 Tbsp light brown sugar

2 tsp molasses

½ cup fine chopped candied cherries

2 Tbsp fine chopped walnuts

2 Tbsp raisins

2 Tbsp candied citrus peel

¼ cup all-purpose flour

2 oz semi-sweet chocolate

Preheat oven to 325°F. Grease and line a large baking sheet with nonstick baking parchment. In a small saucepan, melt the butter, sugar, and molasses over a low heat, taking care not to boil the mixture. When the ingredients are melted and well combined, stir in the cherries, walnuts, raisins, candied mixed peel, and flour. Mix thoroughly.

● Place small heaped teaspoonfuls of the mixture onto the baking sheet at least 1 inch apart to allow for spreading. Bake in the oven for about 10 minutes, until the mixture has spread slightly and is bubbling. Remove the cookies from the oven and allow to cool slightly to firm, before lifting off with a thin metal spatula and placing on a wire rack to cool completely.

● Break the chocolate in small pieces and place in a small bowl over a pan of hot water. Melt the chocolate very slowly, taking care not to boil or get water in the chocolate. When the chocolate has melted, stir and remove from the heat. Using a pastry brush, cover the base of each Florentine with a little of the melted chocolate and leave chocolate side up on the wire rack until set. If desired, when the chocolate is very nearly set, make a wavy line pattern with the back of a fork on each chocolate Florentine. When the chocolate has set, store the Florentines in an airtight container.

No-bake Chocolate Delights

Preparation time: 15 minutes + setting ● *Makes: About 18 to 20*

A cross between a cookie and a truffle—and so easy to make.

INGREDIENTS

1⅔ cups pound cake crumbs

⅓ cup candied cherries, quartered

⅓ cup raisins

2 oz semi-sweet chocolate

¼ stick lightly salted butter

2 Tbsp milk

Place the cake crumbs, quartered cherries, and raisins into a mixing bowl. Break the chocolate into small pieces and place in a small heatproof bowl with the butter and milk over a saucepan of hot, but not boiling, water. Carefully melt all of the ingredients and stir into the sponge and fruit mixture. Mix together thoroughly to combine all of the ingredients and then leave to cool for a short while until the mixture is cool enough to handle.

● Using a teaspoon, place heaped spoonfuls of mixture on waxed paper in a single layer on a baking sheet. Chill the chocolate cookies in the refrigerator for at least 1 hour, to firm. Remove from the waxed paper and store in an airtight container.

Minute Meringues

Preparation time: 10 minutes ● *Cooking time: 45 minutes* ● *Makes: 26*

Tiny bubbles of airy sugar—irresistible!

INGREDIENTS

1 egg white
¼ cup packed light brown sugar
1 tsp cornstarch

Preheat oven to 275°F. Line two baking sheets with edible rice paper or nonstick baking parchment.
● Place the egg white in a grease free mixing bowl and whisk until soft peaks form. Whisk in half of the sugar and all of the cornstarch, until well combined. Add the remaining sugar and whisk until shiny and fairly stiff.
● Spoon the meringue mixture carefully into a decorating bag fitted with a small star tube and then pipe small wavy lines about 2 inches long and small rosettes directly onto the lined baking sheets, leaving 1 inch between them to allow for a little spreading during the cooking process. Bake in the oven for about 45 minutes, until pale brown and crisp. Remove from the oven and cool completely, before removing from the baking parchment. If using rice paper, remove as much as possible, but any left on the base of the meringues is edible. Store in an airtight container.

Maple Pecan Wafers

Preparation time: 25 minutes ● *Cooking time: 48 minutes* ● *Makes: About 24*

These elegant wafers are ideal served with ice cream. Be sure to use real maple syrup, not the artificial flavoring—it makes a big difference.

INGREDIENTS

2 cups pecan halves
½ stick unsalted butter
1 cup unpacked dark brown sugar
⅓ cup all-purpose flour
1 tsp maple syrup
¼ tsp salt
1 egg, lightly beaten

Preheat oven to 375°F. Line a large baking sheet with aluminum foil. Set aside 24 perfect pecan halves, then chop the remaining nuts.
● In a medium saucepan over a low heat, melt the butter. Remove from the heat and stir in the sugar, flour, maple syrup, salt, and egg until well blended. Drop tablespoonfuls, at least 3 inches apart on the baking sheet, place a reserved pecan halve into the center of each.
● Bake the wafers for 12 minutes, remove the baking sheet to a wire rack to cool slightly, then transfer the cookies onto a wire rack to cool completely. Cook the baking sheet and reline, then repeat with another batch of cookies. When the wafers are cool, peel off foil and store in an airtight container with waxed paper between the layers.

Cardamom Cookies

Preparation time: 10 minutes ● Cooking time: 15 minutes ● Makes: 14

Fresh cardamom seeds have a distinctive but subtle flavor characteristic of the Eastern Mediterranean.

INGREDIENTS

1 stick lightly salted butter

½ cup confectioners' sugar

1 cup all-purpose flour

3 drops almond extract

6 cardamom pods, split and seeds lightly crushed

⅓ cup chopped walnuts

Preheat oven to 350°F. Grease two large baking sheets or line with nonstick baking parchment.
● Place the butter, confectioners' sugar, and flour in a large mixing bowl and beat together thoroughly. Stir in the almond extract, crushed cardamom seeds, and chopped walnuts until well combined and the dough has a firm texture.
● Using your hands, shape the dough into 14 equal-sized balls and place 2-inches apart on the baking sheets. Bake in the oven for about 15 minutes, or until lightly browned. Remove with a thin metal spatula to a wire rack to cool completely. Store in an airtight container.

Chocolate Prezels

Preparation time: 40 minutes + chilling ●
Cooking time: 10 to 15 minutes ● Makes: 30

These delicious prezels are surprisingly easy to form.

INGREDIENTS

1½ cups all-purpose flour

¼ tsp salt

3 Tbsp unsweetened cocoa powder

1 stick unsalted butter

½ cup superfine sugar

1 egg, beaten

1 tsp vanilla extract

GLAZE

1 egg white, lightly beaten

Sugar crystals, for sprinkling

Sift together the flour, salt, and cocoa powder. In a separate bowl, beat the butter until creamy, add the sugar and continue beating until light and fluffy. Beat in the egg and vanilla until well blended. Gradually add the flour mixture until combined. Turn dough onto a piece of plastic wrap and seal. Refrigerate until firm.

● Preheat oven to 375°F. Grease two large baking sheets or line with nonstick baking parchment.

● With lightly floured hands, roll dough into about 30 1½-inch balls. Roll into a "rope" about 9 inches long. Bring each end of the "rope" together to meet in the center. Twist the ends together, and press to the middle of the "rope" to form the prezel shape. Transfer to the baking sheets.

● Brush each prezel with egg white to glaze, then sprinkle with sugar crystals. Bake until firm, 10 to 12 minutes. Cool and tranfer to wire racks to cool completely. Store in an airtight container.

Nut Rocks

Preparation time: 20 minutes + chilling ●
Cooking time: 15 minutes ● Makes: 12

Crunchy cookies with the hint of oranges and almonds.

INGREDIENTS

1 stick lightly salted butter

¼ cup packed light brown sugar

Grated rind 1 orange

1 egg, separated

1 cup all-purpose flour

¼ cup ground almonds

Beat the butter and sugar together in a mixing bowl until pale and fluffy. Beat in the orange rind, egg yolk, and flour. Refrigerate for at least 30 minutes.

● Preheat oven to 350°F. Grease two large baking sheets or line with nonstick baking parchment. Using your hands, divide the cookie dough into 12 equal-sized balls and roll each in the lightly beaten egg white then in the ground almonds to coat evenly. Place the almond covered balls on the baking sheets at least 1 inch apart. Bake for about 15 minutes, until just firm and light brown. Remove the cookies immediately from the baking sheet with a thin metal spatula, to prevent them from sticking, and cool on a wire rack. Store in an airtight container.

Tropical Fruit Cookies

Preparation time: 15 minutes ● *Cooking time: 12 to 15 minutes* ● *Makes: 12*

Almost every fruit under the sun is now available dried—try a new flavor or use your favorites, the choice is yours.

INGREDIENTS

1 stick lightly salted butter

½ cup granulated sugar

1 egg, beaten

1½ cups all-purpose flour

⅔ cup chopped ready-to-eat dried exotic fruit (papaya, mango, pineapple, or melon)

Preheat oven to 350°F. Grease two large baking sheets or line with nonstick baking parchment.

● Beat the butter and sugar together in a mixing bowl until pale and fluffy. Beat in the egg and flour. Stir in the chopped exotic fruit mix.

● Place 12 equal-sized spoonfuls of the mixture onto the baking sheets, allowing 2 to 3 inches in between them for spreading. Flatten the mounds of mixture a little with the back of the spoon. Bake in the oven for about 12 to 15 minutes, until pale golden on top. Remove from the oven and leave to firm for one minute. Transfer to a wire rack using a thin metal spatula and cool completely. Store the cookies in an airtight container.

Honey and Date Comforts

Preparation time: 10 minutes ● *Cooking time: 12 to 15 minutes* ● *Makes: About 12 to 14*

Comfort food at bedtime.

INGREDIENTS

1 stick lightly salted butter
½ cup packed light brown sugar
1 egg, beaten
1½ cups all-purpose flour
2 Tbsp honey
⅔ cup chopped dried dates

Preheat oven to 350°F. Grease two large baking sheets or line with nonstick baking parchment.

● Beat the butter and sugar together in a mixing bowl until pale and fluffy. Beat in the egg, flour, and honey. Stir in the chopped dates.

● Place 12 to 14 equal-sized spoonfuls of the mixture onto the baking sheets, allowing 2 to 3 inches in between for spreading. Flatten the mounds of mixture a little with the back of the spoon. Bake in the oven for about 12 to 15 minutes, until pale golden. Remove from the oven and leave the cookies to firm for one minute on the baking sheets before removing with a thin metal spatula to a wire rack to cool completely. Store in an airtight container.

Around the World

The cookie is not a new phenomenon, most countries have little treasures that are loved by their people. Looking at the following selection, it is clear to see national influences such as almonds from Italy, spices from the Middle East, thick cream from Britain, and pecans and maple syrup from North America. There are stunning similarities too, in the use of butter, sugar, and spices which are used universally to create a treat that's always a pleasure to eat.

These cookies make excellent desserts. Espresso Biscotti would make a delightful finale to an Italian meal, serve the Spanish Churros after paella, and the Coconut Fortune Cookies after a stir-fry.

North America

The American nation has taken the idea of the cookie and run with it. Cookies are everywhere, and they are bigger, more action-packed, and more adventurous than their traditional ancestors.

Pennsylvanian Shoofly Slices	68
New Orleans Oat Cookies	69
Peanut Butter and Jelly Cookies	71
Rocky Road	72
Raisin Rockies	73
Refrigerator Cookies	74
Pecan Tassies	75

Britain

Known as "biscuits" in the British Isles, cookies are eaten accompanied by a cup of tea or with steaming hot cocoa at bedtime.

Grantham Gingerbreads	76
Whole-wheat Rounds	77
Scottish Shortbread	78
Cornish Fairings	78

Western Europe

Steeped in history and culture, Western Europe has a long culinary tradition as clearly exemplified in its magnificent cookies as in any of its fancy sauces.

Amaretti	81
Fior di Mandorle	81
Espresso Biscotti	82
Panforte di Siena	83
Almond Macaroons	84
Vanilla Crescents	85
Ischl Cookies	87
Spanish Churros	88
Parisian Palmiers	89
Cigarettes Russes	90
Fours Poches	90
Sablés Nantais	91
Rascals	92
Eponges	93
Chrabeli Bread	94
Zitron	95
Dutch Butter Cookies	96

Further Afield

Eastern Europe, Scandinavia, Australia, New Zealand, India, and China all have their own traditional cookie recipes. Typical ingredients include nuts, sour cream, fresh fruit juice, and all kinds of spices.

Polish Macaroons	97
Lepeshki	98
Finnish Fingers	98
Danish Piped Cookies	99
Scandinavian Slices	99
Grated Peach Shortcake	101
Chunky Macadamia Cookies	102
Anzacs	102
Baklava	104
Jalebi	105
Coconut Fortune Cookies	105

Pennsylvanian Shoofly Slices

Preparation time: 40 minutes ● Cooking time: 35 minutes ● Makes: 14 slices

This cookie owes its origin to the shoofly pies popular in the Southern States.

INGREDIENTS

1½ cups all-purpose flour

pinch of salt

2 Tbsp confectioners' sugar

1 stick lightly salted butter

FILLING

¼ cup corn syrup

¼ cup molasses

⅔ cup boiling water

1 tsp baking soda

2½ cups all-purpose flour

1 tsp ground ginger

1 tsp ground cinnamon

1 stick lightly salted butter

¾ cup packed light brown sugar

Preheat oven to 350°F. Lightly grease a 11 x 7-inch pan. Sift the flour, salt, and confectioners' sugar into a mixing bowl. Blend in the butter until the mixture resembles fine bread crumbs. Add enough cold water to make a firm dough. Roll out on a lightly floured surface and use to line the base and sides of the pan. Chill in the refrigerator while making the filling.

● Put the corn syrup and molasses in a heatproof pitcher and pour over the boiling water. Stir until well-mixed, then add the baking soda and mix again. Leave to stand for 5 minutes.

● Sift the flour, ginger, and cinnamon into a bowl. Blend in the butter until the mixture resembles bread crumbs. Stir in the packed light brown sugar. Spoon half the crumb mixture evenly over the base of the pan. Slowly pour over the syrup and molasses mixture, then spoon over the remaining crumb mixture.

● Bake immediately for 35 minutes, or until lightly set. The mixture will rise a little as it cooks, but will sink again as it cools. Leave to cool in the pan. Divide the baked mixture into 14 slices.

New Orleans Oat Cookies

Preparation time: 20 minutes ● Cooking time: 10 minutes ● Makes: 20

The food of New Orleans has been influenced by African, Spanish, and French cuisines as seen in these delicious cookies.

INGREDIENTS

1 stick lightly salted butter

½ cup packed light brown sugar

1 egg, beaten

1½ cups self-rising flour

⅓ cup fine oatmeal

1⅓ cups rolled oats

3 Tbsp pumpkin seeds

Pumpkin seeds, to decorate

Preheat oven to 375°F. Lightly grease two baking sheets or line with nonstick baking parchment.

● Beat the butter and sugar until light and fluffy. Add the beaten egg, a little at a time, beating between each addition. Sift the flour over the butter mixture and work into the butter mixture with the oatmeal, oats, and pumpkin seeds.

● Roll out on a lightly floured surface to about ¼-inch thick. Stamp out rounds with a 2½-inch plain cutter. Place on the baking sheets, spacing slightly apart. Press a few pumpkin seeds on the top of each to decorate. Bake for 10 minutes, until golden brown. Leave on the baking sheets for 5 minutes, then remove and cool on a wire rack. Store in an airtight container.

Peanut Butter and Jelly Cookies

Preparation time: 25 minutes ǀ chilling ● Cooking time: 15 minutes ● Makes: 24

The great combination of peanut butter and jelly not only appears as a sandwich filling, but in these giant crunchy cookies as well.

INGREDIENTS

¾ cup unsalted peanuts

1 stick unsalted butter

½ cup superfine sugar

⅓ cup packed light brown sugar

1 Tbsp seedless raspberry jam or preserves

½ cup smooth or crunchy peanut butter

1 tsp vanilla extract

1 egg, beaten

1½ cups all-purpose flour

2 tsp baking powder

Preheat oven to 350°F. Lightly grease 2 baking sheets or line with nonstick baking paper. Spread the peanuts on a baking sheet and roast in the oven for 5 minutes, until beginning to turn brown. Allow to cool, then rough chop.

● Beat the butter and sugars until light and fluffy. Add the jam or preserves, peanut butter, and vanilla, then beat until thoroughly mixed. Gradually add the egg, a little at a time, beating well after each addition. Sift the flour and baking powder into the bowl. Stir into the mixture with the chopped nuts to make a soft dough. Wrap the dough in plastic wrap and chill in the refrigerator for 1 hour.

● Preheat oven to 350°F. Divide the dough into 24 pieces. Roll each piece into a ball the size of a walnut. Put the cookies onto the prepared baking sheets, spacing well apart. Flatten slightly with a fork. Bake for 15 minutes or until golden brown. Leave on the baking sheets for 3 to 4 minutes, then remove with a thin metal spatula and cool on a wire rack.

VARIATION

Hazelnut Cookies

● Add ½ cup hazelnut butter and ¾ cup chopped roasted hazelnuts instead of the peanut butter and unsalted peanuts.

Rocky Road

Preparation time: 25 minutes ● *Cooking time: 10 minutes* ● *Makes: 18*

Both children and adults love this sumptuously wicked treat.

INGREDIENTS

	TOPPING
¾ cup all-purpose flour	14 oz semi-sweet chocolate
2 Tbsp unsweetened cocoa powder	½ stick unsalted butter
Scant ¼ cup confectioners' sugar	¼ cup candied cherries
½ stick lightly salted butter	1 cup mini marshmallows
1 egg yolk	⅓ cup unsalted peanuts
1 Tbsp milk	

Preheat oven to 350°F. Grease and line the base of a 7 x 11-inch pan with nonstick baking parchment.

● Sift the flour, cocoa powder, and confectioners' sugar into a bowl. Cut the butter into small pieces and blend in until the mixture resembles bread crumbs. Add the egg yolk and milk to the dry ingredients and mix to a firm dough. Knead on a lightly floured surface until smooth, then press into the base of the pan. Prick all over with a fork, then bake for 10 minutes. Leave to cool while making the topping.

● Break the chocolate into pieces and put in a bowl with the butter over a saucepan of near-boiling water. Heat gently until melted, stirring occasionally. Remove from the heat and allow to cool for 3 minutes. While the chocolate is melting, snip the cherries into quarters with oiled scissors. Stir into the chocolate with the mini marshmallows and peanuts.

● Quickly pour the topping over the base, gently shaking the pan to spread the mixture. Leave to set at room temperature. Cut into small squares and store in the refrigerator until ready to serve.

Raisin Rockies

Preparation time: 20 minutes ● *Cooking time: 15 minutes* ● *Makes: 16*

The raisins in these tasty cookies are soaked in orange juice to make them plump and juicy.

INGREDIENTS

½ cup raisins

2 Tbsp orange juice

1 stick lightly salted butter

¼ cup superfine sugar

¼ cup packed light brown sugar

Grated rind ½ orange

1 egg, beaten

1½ cups all-purpose flour

½ tsp baking soda

Put the raisins in a small bowl. Sprinkle over the orange juice, stir, cover with plastic wrap and leave to soak for at least 2 hours, or overnight in the refrigerator.

● Preheat oven to 350°F. Lightly grease two baking sheets. Beat the butter, sugars, and orange rind together until light and fluffy. Gradually add the egg, beating well between each addition. Sift the flour and baking soda together and work into the butter mixture with the soaked raisins to make a soft dropping mixture.

● Drop heaped teaspoonfuls onto the prepared baking sheets, spacing well apart. Bake for 15 minutes until lightly browned. Leave on the baking sheets for 5 minutes, then remove and cool on a wire rack. Store in an airtight container.

VARIATION

Apricot and Almond Rockies

● Substitute ½ cup chopped dried apricots for the raisins and mix in ¼ cup chopped blanched almonds.

Refrigerator Cookies

Preparation time: 20 minutes ● Cooking time: 10 to 12 minutes ● Makes: 40

**Also known as icebox cookies, this cookie dough will keep for up to a week in the refrigerator.
It freezes well too so you can make it ahead and bake as necessary.**

INGREDIENTS

2 cups all-purpose flour

1 tsp baking powder

1 stick lightly salted butter

½ cup superfine sugar

1 egg

½ tsp vanilla extract

Sift the flour and baking powder into a mixing bowl. Cut the butter into small pieces and blend in until the mixture resembles bread crumbs. Stir in the sugar. Beat the egg with the vanilla, add to the dry ingredients and mix to a firm dough. Shape into a roll about 2-inches in diameter and wrap in plastic wrap or foil. Chill in the refrigerator for at least 2 hours, or until needed.

● When ready to bake the cookies, preheat oven to 375°F. Lightly grease three baking sheets or line with nonstick baking parchment.

● Unwrap the dough and cut into ¼-inch slices. Arrange on the baking sheets, spacing slightly apart. Bake for 10 to 12 minutes or until golden-brown. Leave on the baking sheets for 5 minutes, then transfer to a wire rack to cool.

VARIATIONS

Fruit and Nut

● Stir ½ cup chopped raisins and ½ cup chopped walnuts into the dry ingredients. Replace the vanilla extract with almond extract.

Cherry and Almond

● Stir ¼ cup chopped candied cherries and ½ cup chopped blanched almonds into the dry ingredients. Replace the vanilla extract with almond extract.

Double Chocolate Chip

● Replace ¼ cup flour with ¼ cup unsweetened cocoa powder and stir 2 oz semi-sweet or white chocolate chips into the dry ingredients.

Pecan Tassies

Preparation time: 30 minutes ● Cooking time: 20 minutes ● Makes: 24

These American tassies from the Southern Pecan-growing regions taste as delicious as they sound. Considered a "cookie" it is really a mini tartlet. Tender cream cheese pastry filled with a caramelized pecan center.

INGREDIENTS

CREAM CHEESE PASTRY

1 cup all-purpose flour
1 Tbsp sugar
¼ tsp salt
¼ tsp ground nutmeg
1 stick unsalted butter, softened
¼ cup cream cheese, softened

PECAN FILLING

1 egg
⅓ cup packed dark brown sugar
1 tsp vanilla extract
1½ Tbsp unsalted butter, melted
½ cup chopped toasted pecans
24 pecan halves, for decoration

First, lightly butter two x 12-cup or one x 24-cup muffin pan.

● Into a medium bowl, sift the flour, add the sugar, salt, and nutmeg. Add the butter and cream cheese, and using fingertips or food processor, blend together until a soft dough forms. Cover the bowl and refrigerate until just firm enough to roll out, about 10 minutes.

● On a lightly floured surface, roll the pastry to ⅜-inch thick. Using a 2½-inch cutter cut out 24 circles. Carefully line the muffin cups with a pastry circle, gently pressing pastry onto the bottom and sides of cups. Refrigerate for 20 to 30 minutes. (If using a 12-cup muffin pan, refrigerate remaining dough and cut out once the first batch is cooked.)

● In a medium bowl, beat the eggs until foamy. Gradually beat in the brown sugar, vanilla, and melted butter. Sprinkle an equal amount of chopped pecans into each cup. Carefully pour a little filling into each muffin cup, and top with a pecan half.

● Bake the tassies until the tops are puffed and the filling set with golden pastry edges, about 20 minutes. Remove to a wire rack to cool, 20 to 30 minutes. Using the top of a sharp knife, gently loosen the edge of the pastry from each muffin cup and unmold each tassie. Either serve warm or cool completely, then store in an airtight container.

TIP

Filling can be made with toasted chopped walnuts, hazelnuts, macadamias, or even pine nuts, but pecans are traditional.

Grantham Gingerbreads

Preparation time: 15 minutes ● *Cooking time: 35 minutes* ● *Makes: 25*

**These crisp pale spiced cookies are also known as White Buttons in the Norfolk fenlands
of Eastern England where they are rolled in sugar after cooking.**

INGREDIENTS

1 stick lightly salted butter

1¼ cups superfine sugar

1 egg, beaten

2¼ cups self-rising flour

1 tsp ground ginger

¼ tsp ground cinnamon

Preheat oven to 300°F. Lightly grease two baking sheets or line with nonstick baking parchment.
● Beat the butter and sugar together until pale and fluffy. Gradually add the egg, beating well after each addition. Sift the flour and spices into the mixture and work in to make a firm dough.
● Roll into small walnut-sized balls and place on the prepared baking sheets, spacing slightly apart. Bake for 35 minutes, or until well-risen, crisp and light golden. Leave on the baking sheets for 2 to 3 minutes, then remove and cool on a wire rack.

VARIATION

● For spicier cookies, sprinkle with 2 tablespoons superfine sugar mixed with ¼ teaspoon each of ground ginger and cinnamon before baking.

Whole-wheat Rounds

Preparation time: 20 minutes ● Cooking time: 20 minutes ● Makes: 20

**These very English savory cookies are sometimes spread with butter and served with cheese.
The amount of sugar may be varied, depending how sweet you like them.**

INGREDIENTS

2 cups plain whole-wheat flour
½ cup fine oatmeal
½ tsp salt
½ stick lightly salted butter
¼ cup shortening
4 Tbsp soft light brown sugar
½ beaten egg
2 Tbsp milk
2 Tbsp fine oatmeal, for sprinkling

Preheat oven to 350°F. Lightly grease two baking sheets or line with nonstick baking parchment.

● Put the flour, oatmeal, and salt in a bowl and stir together. Blend in the butter and shortening until the mixture resembles fine bread crumbs. Stir in the sugar. Add the beaten egg and mix to a firm dough. Lightly knead for a few seconds until smooth.

● Roll out the dough on a floured surface to a thickness of ⅛-inch. Cut into rounds using a 2½-inch plain cutter and lift onto the prepared baking sheets.

● Brush the rounds very lightly with milk and sprinkle with the oatmeal. Prick all over with a fork and bake for 20 minutes, until slightly darkened. Leave on the baking sheets for 2 minutes, then remove and cool on a wire rack.

Scottish Shortbread

Preparation time: 15 minutes+ chilling time ●
Cooking time: 30 to 40 minutes ●
Makes: One 7-inch shortbread round

Generations of Scots have baked this simple delicious cookie. As with all "traditional" recipes there are many variations, but it is always made with butter.

INGREDIENTS

1 stick lightly salted butter

2 Tbsp superfine sugar

1¼ cups all-purpose flour

3 Tbsp ground rice

1 Tbsp superfine sugar, for dusting

Lightly grease a baking sheet or line with nonstick baking parchment.

● Put the butter in a mixing bowl and beat until soft and creamy. Stir in the sugar. Sift in the flour and mix in with the semolina or ground rice. Lightly knead on a floured surface for a few seconds until smooth.

● Roll out the dough to a 6-inch circle, then press into an 7-inch shortbread mold. Unmold onto the prepared baking sheet. If you haven't got a shortbread mold, press the mixture into a 7-inch false-bottomed pie pan. Prick all over and mark into 8 wedges. Chill in the refrigerator for 1 hour.

● Preheat oven to 325°F.

● Bake for 35 to 40 minutes, or until a pale golden-brown. Remove from the oven and dust with superfine sugar. Leave on the baking sheet or remove from the pan, leaving the shortbread on the base for 15 minutes, then cool on a wire rack. Store in an airtight container.

Cornish Fairings

Preparation time: 15 minutes ●
Cooking time: 12 to 15 minutes ● *Makes: 16*

These sweet ginger cookies were sold in the market town of Launceston at the annual fair where maids were hired.

INGREDIENTS

1½ cups self-rising flour

1½ tsp ground ginger

Pinch of freshly grated nutmeg

5 Tbsp lightly salted butter

5 Tbsp light brown sugar

3 Tbsp corn syrup

3 Tbsp molasses

1½ tsp baking soda

Preheat oven to 350°F. Lightly grease two baking sheets or line with nonstick baking parchment.

● Sift the flour, ginger, and nutmeg into a large mixing bowl. Blend in the butter until the mixture resembles find bread crumbs. Stir in the sugar.

● Gently warm the corn syrup and molasses in a small pan. Stir in the baking soda, then immediately add to the dry and mix together to a soft dough.

● Roll the dough into walnut-sized balls and place on the prepared baking sheets. Flatten with a thin metal spatula to about ½-inch thick. Bake for 12 to 15 minutes until the cookies have darkened slightly and have a cracked appearance. Leave on the baking sheets for 10 minutes, or until firm, then cool on wire racks.

Amaretti

Preparation time: 15 minutes ●
Cooking time: 12 minutes ● *Makes: 30*

**Wrap these after-dinner almond cookies in pairs with
pretty pastel tissue paper for an authentic appearance.**

INGREDIENTS

1 egg white
2 tsp amaretto liqueur
¼ tsp almond extract
1½ cups ground almonds
1 cup confectioners' sugar
2 Tbsp confectioners' sugar, for dusting

Preheat oven to 350°F. Line two baking sheets with nonstick baking parchment.

● Lightly whisk the egg white with a fork until slightly frothy. Add the amaretto liqueur and almond extract and whisk again.

● Put the ground almonds in a bowl and sift in the confectioners' sugar. Make a well in the middle, add the egg white mixture and stir to a stiff dough. Divide the dough into 30 pieces, then roll each into a ball. Place on the prepared baking sheets, spacing slightly apart.

● Bake for 12 minutes, or until the cookies are golden-brown. Dust with confectioners' sugar. Leave on the baking sheets for 2 minutes, then transfer to a wire rack to cool. When completely cold wrap in pairs in colored tissue paper.

TIP

Amaretto is a sweet almond liqueur. An orange or coffee liqueur may be used instead.

Fior di Mandorle

Preparation time: 20 minutes + chilling ●
Cooking time: 15 minutes ● *Makes: 20*

**These sweet almond cookies, flavored with cinnamon are
Arabic in origin, but are made throughout Sicily.**

INGREDIENTS

1¼ sticks lightly salted butter, softened
½ cup superfine sugar
1 Tbsp honey
1 cup all-purpose flour
½ tsp ground cinnamon
¾ cup ground almonds
Superfine sugar and cinnamon, to dust

Preheat oven to 350°F. Lightly grease two baking sheets or line with nonstick baking parchment.

● Beat the butter, sugar, and honey together until light and fluffy. Sift the flour and cinnamon into the bowl and work into the butter mixture with the ground almonds. Lightly knead on a floured surface until smooth. Wrap in plastic wrap and chill in the refrigerator for 30 minutes.

● Roll out the dough on a floured surface to a thickness of ¼-inch and cut into 3-inch squares. Carefully transfer to the prepared baking sheets, spacing slightly apart. Chill for a further 30 minutes.

● Bake for 15 minutes, or until light golden-brown. As soon as the cookies come out of the oven, dust with a little superfine sugar and ground cinnamon. Leave on the baking sheets for 5 minutes, then remove with a thin metal spatula and cool on a wire rack. Store in an airtight container.

Espresso Biscotti

Preparation time: 20 minutes ● Cooking time: 30 minutes ● Makes: 20 slices

The name of these crisp Italian cookies means twice baked. They're wonderful served with steaming black coffee or cappuccino, although traditionally they are dipped into chilled sweet wine.

INGREDIENTS

⅔ cup unblanched almonds

2¼ cups all-purpose flour

1½ tsp baking powder

Pinch of salt

¾ stick unsalted butter

½ cup superfine sugar

2 eggs, beaten

2 Tbsp cooled strong espresso coffee

Preheat oven to 350°F. Lightly grease a baking sheet or line with nonstick baking parchment.

● Place the almonds on a baking sheet and roast in the oven for 5 minutes. Allow to cool, then grind in a nut grinder or food processor until fine.

● Sift the flour, baking powder, and salt into a mixing bowl. Cut the butter into small pieces and blend into the flour until the mixture resembles bread crumbs. Stir in the sugar and ground almonds. Make a well in the middle. Mix the egg and coffee together and add to the dry ingredients. Mix to a firm dough.

● Lightly knead on a floured surface for a few seconds until smooth, then shape into 2 rolls about 2½-inches in diameter. Transfer to the prepared baking sheet and bake for 20 minutes until lightly browned. Leave to cool for 5 minutes, then cut with a serrated knife into ½-inch slices. Arrange on the baking sheet, cut-side-down and bake for a further 10 minutes, until golden brown and dry to the touch. Store the biscotti in an airtight pan for at least 24 hours, before serving.

Panforte di Siena

Preparation time: 35 minutes ● Cooking time: 40 minutes ● Makes: 12 slices

A specialty of Siena in Italy, thin slices of this rich fruit and nut cookie are traditionally served at Christmas.

INGREDIENTS

½ cup candied citrus peel

½ cup candied pineapple

¼ cup candied cherries

½ cup candied papaya or mango

⅔ cup whole unblanched almonds

½ cup walnut pieces

⅓ cup all-purpose flour

1 tsp ground cinnamon

¼ tsp ground coriander

¼ tsp ground cloves

¼ tsp ground nutmeg

1 cup granulated sugar

3 Tbsp cold water

Rice paper

2 Tbsp confectioners' sugar, to dust

Preheat oven to 325°F. Cut the rice paper to fit the base of a 8-inch false-bottomed pan. Lightly grease the pan, then line with the rice paper.

● Chop the fruit and nuts and put in a mixing bowl with the flour and spices. Put the sugar in a small heavy-bottomed saucepan with the water and heat very gently until the sugar dissolves. Turn up the heat and boil the syrup for 3 to 4 minutes, or until it reaches 220°F on a sugar thermometer. Pour the syrup over the dry ingredients and mix well.

● Spoon the mixture into the prepared pan and level the top. Bake for 40 minutes. Remove from the oven; it will still be soft, but will firm up as it cools. Leave in the pan for 5 minutes, then loosen the edges with a thin metal spatula and remove from the pan. Allow to cool on the base. When completely cold, remove the base and dust with confectioners' sugar. Cut into very thin slices to serve. Store in an airtight container.

TIP

If you haven't got a sugar thermometer, boil the syrup to "short-thread stage"; remove a little of the syrup in a teaspoon, cool for a minute then press between your finger and thumb and pull out slightly; it should form a short thread.

Almond Macaroons

Preparation time: 25 minutes + cooling ● *Cooking time: 12 to 15 minutes* ● *Makes: About 24*

In Italy, macaroons are often sandwiched together with a little apricot jam—delicious.

INGREDIENTS

3 Tbsp currants
3 Tbsp Marsala wine, or orange juice
1 cup slivered almonds, lightly toasted
1 cup superfine sugar
1 Tbsp all-purpose flour
1 egg white
¼ tsp almond extract
1 cup slivered almonds

Preheat oven to 350°F. Grease or line two baking sheets with nonstick baking parchment.

● In a small bowl combine the currants and Marsala or orange juice and microwave on HIGH for 30 to 60 seconds. Allow to sit until the moisture is absorbed, 3 to 5 minutes. Cool completely.

● In a food processor fitted with a metal blade, process the almonds, sugar, and flour until finely ground. Add egg white and almond extract, and process until the mixture forms a dough. Stir in the plumped currants by hand.

● Place the untoasted almonds on a plate. Wet your hands, and using a teaspoon of the dough, shape into ¾-inch balls. Roll balls in pine nuts, pressing lightly to cover completely. Place balls 1½-inches apart on the baking sheets, flatten slightly to a disk shape.

● Bake until almonds are golden, 12 to 15 minutes, rotating the baking sheets halfway through cooking time. Allow to cool slightly, then transfer to wire racks. Store in an airtight container.

Vanilla Crescents

Preparation time: 25 minutes + chilling ● *Cooking time: 15 minutes* ● *Makes: 25*

Forming a horseshoe or crescent shape these "Kipferln" symbolize good luck.

INGREDIENTS

⅓ cup unblanched almonds

1 cup all-purpose flour

1 stick unsalted butter, chilled

2 Tbsp superfine sugar

1 egg yolk

1 tsp vanilla extract

1 cup confectioners' sugar

Lightly grease a baking sheet or line with nonstick baking parchment. Chop the almonds very finely. Sift the flour into a bowl. Cut the butter into pieces and blend it into the flour until the mixture resembles fine bread crumbs.

● Stir in the chopped almonds and sugar. Mix the egg yolk and vanilla together, add to the dry ingredients and mix to a soft dough. Lightly knead on a floured surface until smooth. Wrap in plastic wrap and chill in the refrigerator for 20 minutes.

● Preheat oven to 350°F. Roll teaspoonfuls of the cookie dough into small crescents and place on the prepared baking sheets. Bake for 15 minutes until pale golden. As soon as you remove the cookies from the oven, thickly dredge with confectioners' sugar. Leave on the baking sheet for 5 minutes, then remove and cool on a wire rack. Store in an airtight container.

VARIATION

● Coat the cookies with vanilla sugar. Store a vanilla pod in a sealed jar of superfine sugar for at least a week. Leave the pod and top up with sugar as it is used.

Ischl Cookies

Preparation time: 30 minutes + chilling ● *Cooking time: 15 minutes* ● *Makes: 12*

These jam-filled cookies are named after the famous resort in the Austrian Alps.

INGREDIENTS

1 stick lightly salted butter

¼ cup superfine sugar

1 egg, beaten

1 Tbsp ground almonds

1¾ cups all-purpose flour

4 Tbsp cornstarch

¼ tsp ground cinnamon

3 Tbsp raspberry jam or preserves

3 Tbsp apricot jam or preserves

3 Tbsp lemon curd

1 Tbsp confectioners' sugar

Lightly grease two baking sheets or line with nonstick baking parchment.

● Beat the butter and sugar until creamy. Gradually add the egg, beating well after each addition, then beat in the ground almonds. Sift over the flour, cornstarch, and cinnamon and stir in to make a soft dough. Wrap in plastic wrap and chill in the refrigerator for 30 minutes.

● Preheat oven to 350°F. Roll out on a lightly floured surface to ⅛-inch thick. Cut the dough into 3-inch rounds with a plain cutter. Cut a leaf or flower design from the middle of half the squares with a 1-inch cutter. Transfer to the baking sheets. Bake for 15 minutes, until golden. Leave on the baking sheets for 5 minutes, then transfer to a wire rack to cool.

● Warm and sieve the jam or preserves. Spread a third of the uncut cookies with each of the jams and the third with lemon curd. Place the cookies with cut-out middles on top, so that the jam or curd shows through. Lightly dust with sieved confectioners' sugar before serving. The cookies should be eaten on the same day that they are filled.

Spanish Churros

Preparation time: 15 minutes ● *Cooking time: 10 minutes* ● *Makes: 25*

These are freshly made and sold as a snack on street stalls throughout Spain to be eaten while you stroll along.

INGREDIENTS

¾ stick slightly salted butter

1 cup water

1 cup all-purpose flour

3 Tbsp superfine sugar

3 eggs

Oil for deep frying

Put the butter and water in a saucepan and heat gently until melted. Meanwhile, sift the flour and ½ teaspoon of the sugar onto a piece of waxed paper.

● Bring the butter and water to a fast boil, then add the sifted flour and sugar all at once. Remove the pan from the heat and beat vigorously. Leave to cool for 5 minutes.

● Lightly beat the eggs and gradually add to the mixture, beating until very smooth and glossy. Spoon the mixture into a decorating bag fitted with a ½-inch star tube.

● Half fill a pan with oil and heat to 375°F. Pipe five 4-inch lengths of the mixture at a time into the hot oil. Fry for about 2 minutes, or until golden and crisp. Remove from the oil with slotted spoon and drain on kitchen paper. Repeat until all the mixture is used up. Serve warm or cold, dredged with remaining sugar.

TIP

If preferred dust the churros with confectioners' sugar mixed with a little ground cinnamon instead of the superfine sugar.

Parisian Palmiers

Preparation time: 20 minutes ● Cooking time: 10 minutes ● Makes: 20

These light-as-air French puff pastry cookies have a sugary glaze which caramelizes as they cook.

INGREDIENTS

½ cup superfine sugar

8 oz puff pastry, thawed if frozen

Preheat oven to 450°F. Lightly grease two baking sheets or line with nonstick baking parchment.
● Sprinkle half the sugar evenly over the work surface or on a pastry board, then roll out the pastry into a rectangle about 10 x 12-inches. Trim the edges to neaten, then sprinkle with the remaining sugar.
● Roll the two longer sides to the center to make a double roll. Cut into ½-inch slices and transfer to the prepared baking sheets, spacing slightly apart. Bake for 10 minutes, or until well-risen, golden-brown and crisp. Remove from the baking sheets and cool on a wire rack.

VARIATIONS

Cinnamon Palmiers

● Mix the sugar with 1 teaspoon ground cinnamon before sprinkling.

Jam Palmiers

● Sandwich together in pairs with ⅔ cup heavy cream, lightly whipped and 3 tablespoons warmed and sieved apricot jam or preserves.

Cheese Palmiers

● Fine grate ½ cup Gruyere or Swiss cheese and ¼ cup Parmesan cheese. Mix with 1 teaspoon paprika and use instead of the sugar. Sandwich together in pairs with ¾ stick unsalted butter flavored with 2 teaspoons tomato paste.

Cigarettes Russes

Preparation time: 20 minutes ●
Cooking time: 4 to 5 minutes per sheet ● Makes: 25

These crisp cigar-shaped cookies make a delicious accompaniment to ice creams and mousses.

INGREDIENTS

½ stick unsalted butter
2 egg whites
½ cup superfine sugar
½ cup all-purpose flour
½ tsp vanilla extract

Preheat oven to 375°F. Line a baking sheet with nonstick baking parchment.

Melt the butter over a low heat, then leave to cool.

● Whisk the egg whites until stiff peaks form. Gradually add the sugar a tablespoon at a time, whisking between each addition. Sift half the flour over the whisked mixture and trickle the melted butter around the edge. Carefully fold in. Sift the remaining flour over the mixture and fold in with the vanilla extract.

● Drop teaspoonfuls of the mixture onto the prepared baking sheets, spacing well apart. Spread the mixture thinly and evenly to form a circle 4-inch in diameter. Bake for 5 to 6 minutes, or until golden-brown around the edges. It is best to bake only 3 Cigarettes at a time as they need to be rolled quickly while warm, before the mixture hardens.

● Using a metal spatula, carefully remove the cookies, one at a time from the baking sheet while still hot. Roll immediately around the oiled handle of a wooden spoon. Remove and leave on a wire rack to cool. Repeat with the remaining cookie mixture until used up.

Fours Poches

Preparation time: 30 minutes ● Cooking time: 15
minutes ● Makes: 30

These tiny almond treats are perfect for serving with after-dinner coffee and can be made several days ahead. In France the word "poche" refers to a decorating bag, hence the name of these cookies.

INGREDIENTS

2 egg whites
½ cup superfine sugar
1¼ cups ground almonds
¼ tsp almond extract
Rice paper
Whole hazelnuts, walnut pieces and quartered candied cherries, to decorate

Preheat oven to 350°F. Line two baking sheets with rice paper.

● Whisk the egg whites until stiff, then fold in the superfine sugar, ground almonds, and almond extract.

● Spoon the mixture into a decorating bag fitted with a ½-inch star tube and pipe small rosettes onto the rice paper. Decorate each with a hazelnut, walnut, or candied cherry. Bake for 15 minutes, until light golden-brown. Leave on the baking sheets for 2 to 3 minutes, then cool on a wire rack. Remove surplus rice paper when cold. Store in an airtight container.

Sablés Nantais

Preparation time: 25 minutes + chilling ● *Cooking time: 15 minutes* ● *Makes: 25*

These cookies come from the French region of Nantes. "Sable" is the French word for sand, and reflects their golden crumbly texture.

INGREDIENTS

1 stick unsalted butter

1 cup confectioners' sugar

1 tsp vanilla extract

1 egg, separated

1 egg yolk

1½ cups all-purpose flour

¼ tsp baking powder

Put the butter in a mixing bowl and beat until soft. Sift over the confectioners' sugar and beat the mixture until light and fluffy. Beat in the egg yolks, one at a time, then beat in the vanilla. Sift the flour and baking powder over the butter mixture and mix to a soft dough. Lightly knead on a floured surface for a few seconds until smooth. Wrap in plastic wrap and chill in the refrigerator for 1 hour.

● Preheat oven to 375°F. Lightly grease two baking sheets or line with nonstick baking parchment.

● Roll out the cookie dough on a floured surface to a ¼-inch thickness and stamp out rounds using a fluted 2-inch cutter. Transfer to the prepared baking sheets.

● Lightly beat the egg white. Mark crisscross patterns on top of the cookies with the back of a knife or with a fork. Brush with the egg white, then bake for 15 minutes, until golden-brown. Leave on the baking sheets for 3 minutes, then transfer to a wire rack to cool.

Rascals

Preparation time: 30 minutes + chilling ● *Cooking time: 20 minutes* ● *Makes: 20*

Known as "Spitzbuben", these Viennese vanilla and lemon cookies are sandwiched together with plum jam.

INGREDIENTS

2 sticks lightly salted butter
½ cup vanilla sugar
Grated rind 1 lemon
2½ cups all-purpose flour
1 egg, separated
1 egg yolk
3 Tbsp superfine sugar, for sprinkling
½ cup plum jam or preserves
2 tsp lemon juice

Lightly grease two baking sheets or line with nonstick baking parchment.

● Beat the butter, vanilla sugar, and lemon rind together until mixed. Sift in the flour and stir into the mixture with the egg yolks to make soft dough. Wrap in plastic wrap and chill for 30 minutes.

● Preheat oven to 325°F. Roll out the dough on a lightly floured surface to a thickness of ¼-inch. Use a 2½-inch round or star cutter to cut out about 40 cookies. Transfer to the prepared baking sheets, spacing slightly apart. Lightly whisk the egg white and brush over the tops of half the cookies, then sprinkle generously with superfine sugar.

● Bake for 20 minutes, until lightly browned. Leave on the baking sheets for 2 to 3 minutes, then transfer to a wire rack to cool.

● Gently heat the plum jam or preserves in a pan, then sieve. Use to sandwich the cookies together in pairs with a plain cookie on the bottom and a sugar dusted one on top.

Eponges

Preparation time: 25 minutes ● *Cooking time: 9 to 10 minutes* ● *Makes: 20*

"Eponges" is the French word for sponge and is thought to be the name given to these cookies because they look like sea sponges.

INGREDIENTS

2 egg whites

2 Tbsp superfine sugar

½ cup confectioners' sugar

½ cup ground almonds

Scant 1 cup blanched almonds, finely chopped

3 oz seedless raspberry jam or preserves

1 Tbsp confectioners' sugar, to dust

Preheat oven to 375°F. Line two baking sheets with nonstick baking parchment.

● Whisk the egg whites until soft peaks form, then gradually add the superfine sugar, whisking after each addition until the mixture is stiff and glossy.

● Sift the confectioners' sugar and ground almonds together and fold in. Spoon the mixture into a decorating bag fitted with a ½-inch plain tube and pipe small rounds onto the baking sheets, spacing them slightly apart.

● Sprinkle with the chopped almonds and bake for 9 to 10 minutes, until golden. The "eponges" will rise slightly during cooking, and shrink again as they cool. Remove from the baking sheets and cool on a wire rack. When cool, sandwich together in pairs with the jam or preserves. Dust with confectioners' sugar before serving. Esponges are best eaten on the day they are made.

Chrabeli Bread

Preparation time: 20 minutes + standing ● *Cooking time: 10 minutes* ● *Makes: 25*

These crisp and light Mediterranean cookies are usually served with black coffee or eaten as a simple snack. Before baking they're left on the baking sheet to dry overnight.

INGREDIENTS

3 egg whites

½ cup confectioners' sugar

1¼ cups all-purpose flour

4 Tbsp cornstarch

Put the egg whites in a large mixing bowl. Sift the confectioners' sugar over the egg whites, then whisk until the mixture will hold stiff peaks.

● Sift over the flour and gently fold in until combined, taking care not to over mix. Cover the bowl with a damp cloth and leave for 1 hour.

● Line two baking sheets with nonstick baking parchment, then lightly dust with the cornstarch. Knead the dough on a lightly floured surface for a minute or so until smooth.

● Take walnut sized pieces of the mixture and shape into ovals. Using scissors, snip three cuts down one side, then place on the prepared sheets, bending the cookies slightly to open up the cuts. Keep dipping your hands in flour when shaping the cookies, to prevent them sticking. Leave uncovered overnight to allow the cookies to dry out.

● The following day, preheat oven to 400°F. Bake the cookies for 10 minutes, until very pale brown. Remove from the baking sheets and cool on a wire rack.

Zitron

Preparation time: 30 minutes ● Cooking time: 10 minutes ● Makes: 20

These tangy Swiss cookies have a double helping of lemon, in both the filling and frosting.

INGREDIENTS

1 cup all-purpose flour

¼ cup self-rising flour

¾ cup ground almonds

1 stick lightly salted butter

2 Tbsp confectioners' sugar

1 egg yolk

FILLING

1 stick unsalted butter

1½ cups confectioners' sugar

Grated rind 1 lemon

FROSTING

1½ cups confectioners' sugar

About 4 tsp lemon juice

Yellow food coloring

● For the frosting, sift the confectioners' sugar into a bowl and stir in enough lemon juice to make a thick frosting. Add a drop of yellow food coloring to make a pale yellow. Use to frost the tops of the cookies. Leave to set before serving.

Preheat oven to 350°F. Lightly grease two baking sheets or line with nonstick baking parchment.

● Sift the flours into a bowl. Stir in the ground almonds, then blend in the butter until the mixture resembles fine bread crumbs. Sift the confectioners' sugar and stir in. Add the egg yolk and mix to a dough.

● Lightly knead the dough for a few seconds, then roll out on a floured surface to a ⅛-inch thickness. Cut into rounds using a 3-inch plain cutter and transfer to the baking sheets. Bake for 10 minutes, until lightly browned. Leave on the baking sheets for 2 minutes, then transfer to a wire rack to cool.

● For the filling, beat the butter, sifted confectioners' sugar, and lemon rind until light and fluffy. Use to sandwich the cookies together in pairs.

Dutch Butter Cookies

Preparation time: 25 minutes + chilling ● *Cooking time: 15 to 20 minutes* ● *Makes: 30*

**These lemon-scented cookies are known as "Botermopen" and should always
be made with unsalted butter for the best flavor.**

INGREDIENTS

1½ sticks unsalted butter

Grated rind ½ lemon

¼ cup superfine sugar

¼ cup packed light brown sugar

½ tsp almond or vanilla extract

2 cups all-purpose flour

½ cup raw sugar

Beat the butter until creamy, then add the lemon rind, sugars, and almond or vanilla extract and beat until light and fluffy. Sift over the flour and stir into the mixture to make a firm dough. Lightly knead on a floured surface for a few seconds until smooth. Divide the dough in half, wrap each piece in plastic wrap and chill in the refrigerator for 30 minutes.

● Shape each piece into a roll about 6-inches long. Sprinkle the raw sugar over a piece of waxed paper and roll them to coat with sugar. Wrap the rolls in plastic wrap or foil and chill in the refrigerator for at least 2 hours or overnight.

● Preheat oven to 325°F. Cut each roll into 15 slices and space slightly apart on the baking sheets. Bake for 15 to 20 minutes or until light golden and firm. Leave on the baking sheets for 3 minutes, then transfer the cookies to a wire rack to cool.

Polish Macaroons

Preparation time: 25 minutes ● *Cooking time: 15 to 20 minutes* ● *Makes: 16*

**These "Makaroniki" are sprinkled with poppy seeds before baking.
Halved blanched almonds may also be used to decorate these cookies.**

INGREDIENTS

¾ cup blanched almonds

1 cup superfine sugar

2 Tbsp cornstarch

2 egg whites

¼ tsp almond extract, optional

1 Tbsp poppy seeds

Rice paper

Preheat oven to 375°F. Line two baking sheets with rice paper.

● Spread the blanched almonds on a tray and roast for 5 minutes, or until just beginning to brown. Allow to cool, then grind them finely in a nut grinder or food processor.

● Mix together the ground almonds, sugar, and cornstarch. Lightly whisk the egg whites and add to the dry ingredients, with the almond extract if using, to make a thick paste.

● Spoon the mixture into a decorating bag fitted with a plain ½-inch tube. Pipe 16 rounds of the mixture on the prepared baking sheets, spacing well apart. Sprinkle each with a few poppy seeds. Bake for 15 to 20 minutes, or until lightly browned. Leave on the baking sheets for 5 minutes, then remove and cool on a wire rack. Tear away any excess rice paper when cold.

Lepeshki

Preparation time: 20 minutes ●
Cooking time: 10 minutes ● *Makes: 20*

These creamy Russian cookies are shortened with sour cream rather than butter and sprinkled with slivered almonds before baking.

INGREDIENTS

2 cups self-rising flour

Pinch of salt

½ cup superfine sugar

1 Tbsp ground almonds

1 egg, separated

⅔ cup sour cream

½ tsp vanilla extract

½ cup slivered almonds

Preheat oven to 400°F. Lightly grease two baking sheets or line with nonstick baking parchment.
● Sift the flour and salt into a mixing bowl. Stir in the superfine sugar and ground almonds. Reserve 1 tablespoon egg white. Mix the rest with the egg yolk, sour cream, and vanilla extract. Add to the dry ingredients and mix to a firm dough. Lightly knead on a floured surface until smooth.
● Roll out to ⅓-inch thick and stamp into rounds using a 3-inch cutter. Place on the prepared baking sheets, spacing slightly apart. Brush the tops with the reserved egg white and sprinkle with slivered almonds. Bake for 10 minutes until lightly browned. Leave on the baking sheets for 5 minutes, then transfer the cookies to a wire rack to cool.

Finnish Fingers

Preparation time: 25 minutes ●
Cooking time: 12 minutes ● *Makes: 12*

These golden log-shaped cookies have a crumbly airy texture and a topping of chopped almonds.

INGREDIENTS

1½ sticks unsalted butter

½ cup confectioners' sugar

1 tsp vanilla extract

1½ cups all-purpose flour

⅓ cup cornstarch

¼ cup blanched almonds or pistachios, chopped

FILLING

½ stick unsalted butter

¾ cup confectioners' sugar

Preheat oven to 350°F. Lightly grease a baking sheet or line with nonstick baking parchment.
● Put the butter in a mixing bowl and beat until creamy.
● Sift over the confectioners' sugar, add the vanilla and beat until light and fluffy. Sift the flour and cornstarch over the butter mixture and fold in.
● Spoon the mixture into a decorating bag fitted with a ¾-inch plain tube and pipe 2½-inch lengths onto the prepared baking sheets, spacing well apart. Sprinkle with the chopped nuts. Bake for 12 minutes, until pale golden-brown. Leave on the baking sheets for 3 to 4 minutes, then remove and cool on a wire rack.
● For the filling, beat the butter until softened. Sift over the confectioners' sugar and beat until light and fluffy. Use to sandwich pairs of the cookies together.

Danish Piped Cookies

Preparation time: 30 minutes ●
Cooking time: 12 minutes ● Makes: 30

These classic buttery cookies from Denmark melt in the mouth and are perfect with morning coffee.

INGREDIENTS

2 cups unsalted butter
½ cup superfine sugar
1 egg yolk
1½ cups all-purpose flour
½ cup self-rising flour
¾ cup ground almonds

GLAZE

2 Tbsp superfine sugar
2 Tbsp milk

Preheat oven to 375°F. Lightly grease two baking sheets or line with nonstick baking parchment.

● Beat the butter in a bowl until creamy. Add the superfine sugar and mix until blended, then beat in the egg yolk. Sift the plain and self-rising flours over the butter mixture and stir in with the ground almonds.

● Spoon into a decorating bag fitted with a ½-inch star tube and pipe scrolls, fingers or whirls as liked onto the prepared baking sheets. Bake for 10 to 12 minutes until pale golden.

● Meanwhile, prepare the glaze. Mix the superfine sugar and milk together in a small saucepan and heat gently to dissolve. As soon as you remove the cookies from the oven, brush with the milk glaze. Leave on the baking sheets for 5 minutes, then transfer to a wire rack to cool.

Scandinavian Slices

Preparation time: 25 minutes + chilling ●
Cooking time: 10 minutes ● Makes: 20

This dark, spicy cookie mixture is chilled overnight to let the flavors develop.

INGREDIENTS

1 stick lightly salted butter
½ cup superfine sugar
2½ Tbsp corn syrup
2 tsp honey
½ cup slivered almonds
2 tsp ground cinnamon
1 tsp ground ginger
½ tsp ground cardamom
½ tsp baking soda
1 tsp water
1¾ cups all-purpose flour

Put the butter, sugar, syrup, and honey in a small pan and heat gently until the butter has melted. Stir in almonds and spices and bring to a boil. Remove from the heat. Mix the baking soda and water together and stir into the mixture.

● Sift the flour into a bowl and make a well in the middle. Pour in the melted mixture and mix. Cool, then turn out and knead on a floured surface until smooth. Shape into a block 2-inches in diameter. Wrap in plastic wrap and chill in the refrigerator overnight.

● Preheat oven to 350°F. Lightly grease two baking sheets or line with nonstick baking parchment.

● Cut the block into ⅛-inch slices and place on the baking sheets, slightly apart. Bake for 10 minutes, until slightly darkened and crisp. Cool on the baking sheets.

Grated Peach Shortcake

Preparation time: 20 minutes + chilling ● Cooking time: 45 minutes ● Makes: 8 wedges

**It's not the peaches that are grated in this chunky Australian cookie,
but the buttery shortcake that sandwiches it together.**

INGREDIENTS

2 sticks lightly salted butter

⅓ cup packed light brown sugar

1 egg

1 Tbsp sunflower oil

1 tsp vanilla extract

3½ cups all-purpose flour

¼ cup cornstarch

2 tsp baking powder

½ cup dried peaches

3 Tbsp peach or orange juice

½ cup peach or apricot jam or preserves

Lightly grease and line the base of a round 8-inch false-bottomed pan.

● Beat the butter until creamy, then add the light brown sugar and mix until light and fluffy. Beat the egg, oil, and vanilla together. Gradually add to the butter mixture, beating well between each addition. Sift the flour, cornstarch, and baking powder together. Stir into the butter mixture to make a stiff dough. Knead on a lightly floured surface until smooth. Wrap and chill the dough in the refrigerator for 15 minutes.

● Meanwhile, fine chop the peaches and put in a small saucepan with the fruit juice. Heat gently for 3 to 4 minutes, until the fruit juice is absorbed. Remove from the heat and stir in the jam or preserves.

● Preheat oven to 300°F. Cut the dough in two and coarsely grate one half into the prepared pan, so that it covers the base evenly. Spoon over the warm peach jam or preserves mixture. Grate the rest of the cookie dough evenly over the jam or preserves.

● Bake for 45 minutes or until lightly browned. Leave to cool in the pan Cut the shortcake into wedges to serve.

VARIATION

Grated Pineapple Shortcake

● Substitute candied pineapple for the dried peaches, simmer in pineapple juice, and use pineapple instead of peach jam or preserves.

Chunky Macadamia Cookies

Preparation time: 20 minutes • Cooking time: 15 minutes • Makes: About 25

Macadamia trees are native to the woodlands of Australia and produce small white buttery nuts.

INGREDIENTS

½ stick unsalted butter
¼ cup shortening
½ cup packed light brown sugar
1 egg, beaten
2 cups all-purpose flour
½ tsp baking powder
¾ cup macadamia nuts
4 Tbsp milk

Preheat oven to 350°F. Lightly grease two baking sheets or line with nonstick baking parchment.

● Put the butter and shortening in a mixing bowl and beat until soft. Add the packed light brown sugar and cream together until light and fluffy. Gradually add the egg, beating well between each addition.

● Sift the flour and baking powder into the bowl and fold into the butter mixture with the nuts and milk to make a fairly firm dough. Place small teaspoonfuls of the mixture onto the prepared baking sheets, spacing well apart. Bake for 12 to 15 minutes, until light golden-brown. Leave to cool on the baking sheets for 5 minutes, then transfer to a wire rack to cool.

VARIATION

Chocolate Macadamia Cookies

● Substitute ¼ cup unsweetened cocoa powder for ¼ cup of the flour.

Anzacs

Preparation time: 15 minutes • Cooking time: 20 minutes • Makes: 40

These well-known Australian cookies were named after the Australian New Zealand Army Corps (ANZAC).

INGREDIENTS

1½ cups all-purpose flour
1 cup rolled oats
1 cup sweetened flaked coconut
1 cup dark brown sugar
1 stick lightly salted butter
2 Tbsp honey
½ tsp baking soda
2 tsp milk

Preheat oven to 350°F. Lightly grease three baking sheets or line with nonstick baking parchment.

● Sift the flour into a mixing bowl. Add the oats, coconut, and sugar and mix well. Make a well in the middle. Put the butter and honey in a small pan and gently heat until melted, stirring occasionally. Remove from the heat. Blend the baking soda with the milk and stir into the melted mixture. Pour into the dry ingredients and mix well.

● Drop heaped teaspoonfuls of the mixture onto the baking sheets, spacing well apart. Bake for 20 minutes, until browned. Leave on the baking sheets for 5 minutes, then transfer to a wire rack to cool.

Baklava

Preparation time: 25 minutes ● Cooking time: 30 minutes ● Makes: 16

These layers of phyllo pastry filled with nuts and soaked in syrup are eaten in the Middle East, Greece, and Turkey.

INGREDIENTS

1 cup chopped mixed nuts such as hazelnuts and almonds

½ cup golden superfine sugar

1 tsp ground cinnamon

¼ stick unsalted butter

4 oz phyllo pastry, thawed if frozen

SYRUP

¾ cup granulated sugar

2 Tbsp lemon juice

2 tsp orange-flower or rose-flower water

Preheat oven to 350°F. Lightly brush the sides of a 11 x 7-inch shallow pan with oil.

● Put the nuts, sugar, and cinnamon in a bowl and mix together. Melt the butter and allow to cool.

● Cut the pastry to fit the pan. Brush the base of the pan with melted butter, then lay a sheet of pastry over the base of the pan. Brush its top with more melted butter and repeat with three more sheets of pastry. Sprinkle over half of the nut mixture. Top with three more sheets of pastry, brushing butter between the layers, then sprinkle over the remaining nut mixture. Continue layering and buttering the phyllo pastry until it is used up.

● Press down the edges to seal, then mark the top layer into 16 squares or diamonds. Bake for 30 minutes, until a rich golden-brown and crisp.

● While the pastry is in the oven, put the granulated sugar and lemon juice in a small pan. Heat over a very low heat until the sugar has dissolved. Bring to a boil and simmer for 2 minutes. Stir in the orange-flower or rose-flower water. Pour the hot syrup over the pastry as soon as it comes out of the oven. Leave to cool in the pan, then cut into squares or diamonds and remove from the pan.

TIP

When using phyllo pastry, cover it with a damp dish towel, to prevent it drying out.

Jalebi

Preparation time: 20 minutes •
Cooking time: 20 minutes • *Makes: 16-20*

These Indian batter coils are deep-fried, then soaked in a saffron and cardamom syrup.

INGREDIENTS

2 cups all-purpose flour
¼ oz easy-blend dried yeast
¼ cup plain yogurt
1¼ cups warm water
Sunflower oil for deep-frying

SYRUP

1 cup granulated sugar
Large pinch saffron strands
6 cardamom pods, lightly crushed
1¼ cups water

Sift the flour into a bowl and stir in the easy-blend dried yeast. Make a well in the middle. Add the yogurt and water and gradually blend in the flour to make a thick batter. Cover the bowl with a dish towel and leave the batter for 2 hours.

• Meanwhile, make the syrup. Put the sugar, saffron, and cardamom pods in a pan with the water. Heat gently, stirring occasionally until the sugar dissolves. Bring to a boil and simmer for 1 minute. Strain the syrup into a bowl.

• Half-fill a deep saucepan with oil and heat to 375°F. Stir the batter, then pour through a basting spoon in a steady stream into the oil to form coils, making 4 or 5 at a time. Deep fry for about 30 seconds, then turn over and continue cooking until deep golden. Remove from the pan and drain on kitchen paper, then immerse in the sugar syrup for 2 to 3 minutes. Repeat with remaining batter and syrup until used up. Serve straight away.

Coconut Fortune Cookies

Preparation time: 30 minutes •
Cooking time: 5 minutes • *Makes: 36*

Everyone knows these Chinese cookies, this one has a pretty texture provided by a little grated coconut.

INGREDIENTS

2 egg whites
½ cup confectioners' sugar, sifted
1 tsp coconut or almond extract
2 Tbsp unsalted butter, melted
5 Tbsp all-purpose flour, sifted
¼ cup fine shredded coconut, toasted and chopped

Grease and flour two baking sheets. Using a glass 3-inches in diameter, mark two circles in diagonal corners of the baking sheet, to allow cookies to spread.

• In a medium bowl, beat the egg whites until foamy. Gradually beat in confectioners' sugar, coconut or almond extract, and melted butter. Fold in the flour until well blended.

• Drop á teaspoonful of batter in the center of each marked circle and, using the back of a spoon, spread evenly to cover the circle. Sprinkle each cookie with a little toasted coconut.

• Bake one sheet at a time until the edges are lightly browned, about 5 minutes. Remove the baking sheet to a wire rack, and working quickly, use a thin-bladed metal spatula to loosen the edges of the cookie. Set on a board and fold in half, then curve each cookie over the rim of a glass creating the classic shape. Hold for 30 seconds, then place on a wire rack to cool completely. Repeat with the remaining cookies, if the cookies become too firm, return to the oven for 30 seconds.

Special Cookies for Gifts

Cookies make the perfect gift, especially for those who have everything. These simple food gifts add a personal touch and are the perfect way to show that you care. Here are a variety of gift suggestions ranging from ideas for birthday presents to the perfect hostess gift. There are cookies to congratulate the parents of a new baby, "congratulations" on an engagement and "get well" to cheer up someone who is sick. Often it is hard to know what to take to a party as a little thank you to present to your host or hostess— make cookies and you are onto a sure winner. Why not gift-wrap extra-luxurious cookies and make a contribution to the meal?

Birthdays

Present Cookies	108
Birthday Cake Cookies	109
Coconut Meringues	110
Cassis Pink Cookies	111
Candied Cherry Slices	112
Vanilla Cream Cheese Cutouts	112
Coffee and Walnut Numbers	113

Family Celebrations

Star Cookies	114
Pink and White Meringues	115
Chocolate Cookies	117
Marmalade Moons	117
Maple Syrup Tuiles	118
Short Cake with a Hint of Rose	118
Poppy Seed Cookies	119
Orange Flower Cookies	121
Chocolate Macaroons	122
Coconut Curls	122
Classic Butter Sables	124

Romantic Anniversaries

Valentine's Cookies	125
Valentine Passion Fruit Swirls	126
Chocolate Initials	127
Lover's Scrolls	128
Pine Nut Horseshoes	129
Wedding Bells	130
Golden Ginger Cookies	131
Cranberry Cookies	132
Lemon Rings	133
Pine Nut Biscotti	133
Confetti Cookies	134

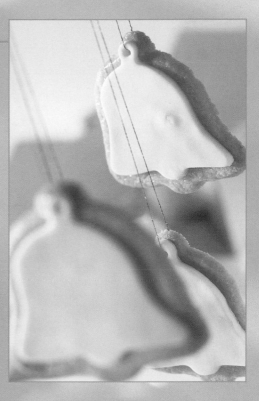

Special Occasions

Butter Viennese Fingers	135
Two-toned Cookies	136
Chocolate-dipped Palmiers	136
Lime and Coconut Hearts	137
Rosemary and Lime Cookies	139
Smiling Faces	139
Pecan Pinwheel Cookies	140
Fantailed Shortbread	142
Sesame Cracker Cookies	142
Coffee Meringue Snails	143
Almond Tiles	144
Hazelnut and Nutmeg Cookies	145
Cardamom Crisps	146
Double Chocolate Mint Sandwiches	148
Strawberry Jam Sandwiches	149
Real Vanilla Cookies	150
Bitter Chocolate Discs	151

Present Cookies

Preparation time: 35 minutes ● Cooking time: 15 minutes ● Makes: 11

If you can't find number cutters, trace some numbers, cut them out, and use them as a template.

INGREDIENTS

1¼ cups all-purpose flour, sifted

½ cup ground almonds

1 stick lightly salted butter, cut into small pieces

1 egg, yolk

¾ cup chopped candied pineapple

DECORATION

7 oz ready-to-roll fondant frosting

Food colorings

1 Tbsp apricot jam or preserves, warmed

Preheat oven to 350°F. Grease several baking sheets or line with nonstick baking parchment.

● Place the flour and ground almonds in a mixing bowl and blend in the butter using your fingers until the mixture resembles fine bread crumbs. Stir in the egg yolk and chopped candied pineapple and using your hands bring all the ingredients together to form a soft dough.

● On a lightly floured surface, roll out the dough to about ¼-inch thick and stamp out squares using a 3-inch cutter. Lift on to the baking sheets and re-roll the trimmings as necessary. Prick the squares with a fork. Bake the cookies for 15 minutes or until lightly golden at the edges. Transfer to a wire rack to cool.

● To decorate the cookies, place the frosting in a bowl and add a few drops of coloring, knead the frosting until soft and smooth. On a surface lightly sprinkled with confectioners' sugar, roll out the frosting and stamp out the numbers "2" and "1" to make ten "21s."

● Brush the apricot jam over the surface of each cookie and lay the numbers "21" on each cookie. Cut the trimmings from the frosting into thin strips and place over the squares and numbers, to represent lengths of ribbon around a present. Store these cookies in an airtight container.

Birthday Cake Cookies

Preparation time: 25 minutes ● Cooking time: 15 minutes ● Makes: 18

These cookies are made from all the ingredients you expect to find in a fruit cake, making them a clever birthday gift.

INGREDIENTS

1 stick lightly salted butter, softened

½ cup packed light brown sugar

1 egg, beaten

1 Tbsp brandy or dark rum

1¼ cup all-purpose flour, sifted

¼ tsp baking powder

½ cup chopped blanched almonds

⅓ cup chopped candied cherries

½ cup candied citrus peel

½ cup golden raisins

1 Tbsp chopped angelica, optional

Confectioners' sugar, for dusting

Preheat oven to 350°F. Grease several baking sheets or line with nonstick baking parchment.

● In a mixing bowl beat together the butter and sugar until light and fluffy. Beat in the egg and brandy. Stir in the flour, baking powder and all the remaining ingredients and mix everything together, until evenly combined.

● Place mounds of the mixture onto the baking sheets and bake for 15 minutes or until golden-brown. Lift onto wire racks to cool. Dust the cookies lightly with confectioners' sugar and store them in an airtight container until needed.

TIP

The angelica gives good color to these cookies, but is not essential to the flavor.

Coconut Meringues

Preparation time: 30 minutes ● *Cooking time: 1 hour and 30 minutes* ● *Makes: 20*

These elegant meringues, dipped in chocolate, would be perfect for a little girl's birthday.

INGREDIENTS

4 egg whites

Pinch of salt

1 cup superfine sugar

⅔ cup sweetened flaked coconut

4 oz semi-sweet chocolate

Preheat oven 250°F. Line several baking sheets with nonstick baking parchment.

● In a large mixing bowl whisk the egg whites and salt using a hand held electric mixer until they form stiff peaks. Whisk in the sugar, a little at a time until the mixture is glossy but still very stiff. Fold in the coconut.

● Using a decorating bag fitted with a medium star tube, pipe the meringue mixture into loops to make long shapes on the baking sheets. Bake the meringues for 1 hour and 30 minutes or until they can lift off the paper easily. Store in an airtight container until needed.

● To decorate, melt the chocolate in the microwave or in a bowl over simmering water; cool. Dip one end of each meringue in melted chocolate and leave to set on waxed paper.

TIP

Sandwich the meringues together in pairs with 1¼ cups of whipped cream for a real treat!

Cassis Pink Cookies

Preparation time: 40 minutes ● *Cooking time: 10 to 15 minutes* ● *Makes: 15*

These very elegant cookies are only for the grown ups! They are flavored with crème de cassis liqueur for a distinct taste.

INGREDIENTS

2 cups all-purpose flour, sifted

¾ cup confectioners' sugar

1¼ sticks butter, cut into small pieces

¾ cup fine chopped blanched almonds

2 Tbsp crème de cassis or kirsch liqueur

DECORATION

½ stick unsalted butter, softened

1 cup confectioners' sugar, sifted

1 Tbsp crème de cassis or kirsch liqueur

8 oz marzipan

Pink food coloring

1 Tbsp raspberry jam or preserve, warmed

Preheat the oven to 350°F. Grease several baking sheets or line with nonstick baking parchment.

● Place the flour and confectioners' sugar in a mixing bowl and blend in the butter using your fingers until the mixture resembles fine bread crumbs. Stir in the chopped almonds and crème de cassis and mix all the ingredient together to a firm dough.

● On a lightly floured surface, roll out the dough to about ¼-inch thick. Stamp out 30 circles using a 2½-inch fluted cutter. Re-roll the trimmings as necessary and lift on to the prepared baking sheets.

● Bake the cookies for 10 to 15 minutes or until just beginning to turn golden at the edges. Transfer to a wire rack to cool.

● To decorate the cookies, first make the frosting by beating together the butter and confectioners' sugar in a bowl to give a fluffy consistency. Gradually beat in the crème de cassis. Set aside. Add a few drops of pink coloring to the marzipan in a small bowl and knead until soft and smooth. On a clean surface lightly sprinkled with confectioners' sugar, roll out the marzipan quite thinly and stamp out 15 circles using a 2½ inch fluted cutter.

● Brush 15 of the cookies with the warmed raspberry jam and place a circle of marzipan on top, this will become the top of the cookies. Using the butter frosting as the filling, sandwich the cookies together using the marzipan cookie for the top and the plain cookies for the base.

Candied Cherry Slices

Preparation time: 30 minutes + chilling ●
Cooking time: 15 to 20 minutes ● *Makes: 18 slices*

Make these chunky slices of cookie with lots of sticky candied cherries and ground almonds for a birthday surprise.

INGREDIENTS

1 stick butter, softened

⅓ cup superfine sugar

1 egg yolk

1¼ cups all-purpose flour, sifted

½ cup ground almonds

¼ cup chopped blanched almonds

¾ cup candied cherries, quartered

In a mixing bowl, beat together the butter and sugar until light and fluffy. Beat in the egg yolk.

● Add the flour, ground almonds, blanched almonds, and candied cherries and using your hands bring the mixture together to form a firm dough. Shape into a 6 x 2-inch bar shape. Wrap and chill for 30 minutes. Meanwhile, line several baking sheets with nonstick baking parchment.

● Preheat oven to 350°F. Slice the bar into 18 equal slices and lift onto the baking sheets. Bake the cookies for 15 to 20 minutes or until evenly golden. Transfer to a wire rack to cool.

TIP

Melt 5 oz of chocolate into a small bowl, dip in one end of the cookie and place on a sheet of waxed paper and leave to set.

Vanilla Cream Cheese Cutouts

Preparation time: 20 minutes + chilling ●
Cooking time: 10 to 12 minutes ● *Makes: 36*

These tender cookies are prefect with just a simple sugar and nut topping.

INGREDIENTS

1 stick butter, softened

3 oz package cream cheese

1 cup all-purpose flour

1¼ cups confectioners' sugar

1 tsp vanilla extract

TOPPING

1 Tbsp sugar

1 tsp ground cinnamon

2 Tbsp fine chopped almonds

1 egg

Beat together the butter and sugar in a bowl until creamy. Add the flour, sugar, and vanilla extract and mix to form a soft dough. Wrap the dough in plastic wrap and refrigerate until firm, about 1 hour.

● Line 2 baking sheets with nonstick baking parchment. On a lightly floured surface roll half the dough to ⅛-inch thick (keep remaining dough refrigerated). Using a floured 2-inch cutter, cut out as many rounds as possible. Arrange 1 inch apart on the baking sheets. Repeat with remaining dough and trimmings. Chill.

● Preheat oven to 350°F. For the topping stir together the sugar, cinnamon, and almonds. In a separate bowl, lightly beat the egg with 1 tablespoon cold water. Brush the tops of the cookies with the egg and sprinkle with a little of the sugar-nut mixture. Bake for 12 to 15 minutes until golden. Transfer to a wire rack to cool.

Coffee and Walnut Numbers

Preparation time: 35 minutes ● *Cooking time: 15 minutes* ● *Makes: 14*

This coffee flavored cookie is made even more delicious by being dipped in semi-sweet and white chocolate.

INGREDIENTS

1 Tbsp instant coffee

1 Tbsp boiling water

1½ cups self-rising flour

1 stick butter, cut into small pieces

¾ cup superfine sugar

¾ cup fine chopped walnuts

1 egg yolk

DECORATION

2 oz white chocolate, broken into pieces

2 oz semi-sweet chocolate, broken into pieces

Preheat the oven to 350°F. Grease several baking sheets or line with nonstick baking parchment.

● Dissolve the instant coffee with the boiling water and allow to cool.

● Place the flour in a mixing bowl and blend in the butter using your fingertips until the mixture resembles fine bread crumbs. Stir in the sugar, walnuts, egg yolk, and cooled coffee and mix together well to form a firm dough.

● On a lightly floured work surface, roll out the dough to about ½-inch thick and stamp out the numbers "1" and "8" using cutters. Re-roll the trimmings to make 14 pairs of numbers and transfer to the baking sheets. Prick each cookie with a fork.

● Bake the cookies for 15 minutes, or until lightly golden-brown and transfer to a wire rack to cool.

● To decorate the cookies, melt the chocolate by placing each one in a separate bowl. Place each of these bowls over a saucepan of simmering water, stir fequently until the chocolate has melted. Dip the number "8" in the white chocolate and the number "1" in the semi-sweet chocolate and place on a piece of baking paper to set. Store these cookies in an airtight container.

Star Cookies

Preparation time: 45 minutes ● Cooking time: 10 to 15 minutes ● Makes: 16

Say "congratulations" with a crisp vanilla cookie base shaped into a star-shape and then decorated with ready rolled white fondant frosting.

INGREDIENTS

1 stick lightly salted butter, softened

½ cup superfine sugar

1 egg, beaten

1 tsp vanilla extract

2 cups all-purpose flour, sifted

DECORATION

14 oz ready-to-roll fondant frosting

2 Tbsp apricot jam or preserve

Preheat oven to 350°F. Grease several baking sheets or line with nonstick baking parchment.

● In a mixing bowl beat together the butter and sugar until pale and fluffy. Beat in the egg and vanilla. Add the flour and bring the mixture together to form a soft dough.

● On a lightly floured work surface, roll out the dough to a ¼-inch thick, stamp out 16 stars using a 4-inch star shaped cutter. Re-roll trimmings and place the cookies onto a baking sheet. Bake the cookies for 10 to 15 minutes or until golden-brown. Transfer to a wire rack and leave to cool.

● Knead the frosting until soft and smooth. Brush each cookie with warmed apricot jam or preserve. Roll out the frosting on a work surface lightly sprinkled with confectioners' sugar. Stamp out 16 stars using the same size cookie cutter and press a white star onto each cookie, re-rolling if necessary. Leave to set and store in an airtight container.

Pink and White Meringues

Preparation time: 30 minutes ● Cooking time: 1 hour and 30 minutes ● Makes: 20

These pastel meringues, which are as light as air and melt in the mouth, are ideal for a Christening celebration.

INGREDIENTS

4 egg whites

Pinch of salt

1 cup superfine sugar

Red food coloring

1¼ cups heavy cream, whipped lightly

Preheat oven to 250°F. Line several baking sheets with nonstick baking paper.

● In a large clean bowl, using a balloon whisk or hand held electric mixer, whisk together the egg whites and salt until they form stiff peaks. Whisk in the sugar a little at a time, the meringue should start to look glossy. Continue whisking in the sugar until all the sugar has been incorporated and the meringue is thick, shiny and stands in stiff peaks. Transfer half the meringue to another bowl, add a few drops of food coloring to create a pastel pink color.

● Fill a decorating bag with the white meringue, using a ¾-inch star tube, pipe about 20 small whirls on to the baking sheets. Repeat with the pink meringue.

● Bake the meringues for 1 hour and 30 minutes until they are dry and crisp and the swirls can be easily lifted off the paper. Leave to cool completely.

● Just before serving, sandwich the meringues together in pairs with the whipped cream. Store unfilled meringues in an airtight container. Once filled, meringues should be eaten within a few hours.

Chocolate Oat Cookies

Preparation time: 20 minutes ● Cooking time: 20 minutes ● Makes: 16

These chunky oat cookies with their chocolate topping will be a great edible birthday gift.

INGREDIENTS

½ cup all-purpose flour, sifted

2 cups rolled oats

1 tsp sesame seeds

1 tsp baking powder

1 stick lightly salted butter, cut into small pieces

½ cup superfine sugar

1 egg, beaten

6 oz milk or white chocolate, melted

Preheat oven to 350°F. Grease several baking sheets or line with nonstick baking parchment.

● In a mixing bowl place the flour, oats, sesame seeds, and baking powder. Blend in the butter, superfine sugar, and beaten egg to make a firm dough. Alternatively, place all these ingredients in a food processor and pulse until the mixture comes away from the sides of the bowl.

● On a lightly floured surface, roll out the dough to ¼-inch thick. Using a 3-inch cutter, stamp out 16 rounds. Lift onto the baking sheets. Bake for 20 minutes until golden-brown. Transfer to a wire rack to cool.

● Spread each cookie with melted chocolate and allow to set.

Marmalade Moons

Preparation time: 25 minutes + chilling ● Cooking time: 10 to 12 minutes ● Makes: 20

Reward your child after their first day at school with these delicious moon-shaped cookies.

INGREDIENTS

1½ cups all-purpose flour, sifted

¼ cup ground almonds

½ cup packed light brown sugar

¾ stick butter, cut into small pieces

1 egg yolk

3 Tbsp orange marmalade

Confectioners' sugar for dusting

Place the flour, ground almonds, and sugar in a mixing bowl and using your fingers blend in the butter until the mixture resembles fine bread crumbs. Add the egg yolk and marmalade and bring the mixture together to form a soft ball. Wrap and chill for 30 minutes.

● Preheat the oven to 350°F. Grease several baking sheets or line with nonstick baking parchment.

● On a lightly floured work surface roll out the dough to about ¼-inch thick. Using a 4½-inch round cutter, stamp out rounds, then cut away a quarter of each round making a crescent shape. Re-roll the trimmings as necessary and lift onto the baking sheets. Prick the cookies well with a fork.

● Bake the cookies for 10 to 12 minutes or until lightly golden. Transfer to a wire rack to cool. Just before serving, dust with confectioners' sugar. Store in an airtight container.

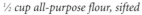
Maple Syrup Tuiles

Preparation time: 25 minutes ● *Cooking time: 8 to 10 minutes* ● *Makes: 21*

Store these very delicate Mother's Day cookies in an airtight container.

INGREDIENTS

½ stick lightly salted butter

½ cup superfine sugar

2 Tbsp chopped almonds

3 Tbsp maple syrup

½ cup all-purpose flour, sifted

Preheat oven to 350°F. Line 2 to 3 baking sheets with nonstick baking parchment.

● In a saucepan, gently heat the butter, superfine sugar, almonds, and maple syrup until the butter has melted. Remove from the heat. Add the flour and mix together until thoroughly blended.

● Spoon four teaspoonfuls of the mixture well apart on the baking sheets, bake for 8 to 10 minutes until bubbly and the cookies have spread to a lacy texture. Remove from the oven, leave to cool for one minute, then lift off with a thin, metal spatula and curl around a rolling pin to mold into tuile shapes.

● Shape the remaining cookies in the same way leave to go cold and crisp. Handle the tuiles very carefully once baked.

TIP

If the tuiles have hardened before you have shaped them, pop them back in the oven for a few seconds to soften them.

Shortcake with a Hint of Rose

Preparation time: 25 minutes ● Cooking time: 25 to 30 minutes ● Makes: 10

These thick rounds of delicate shortbread have been flavored with an extract of rose water.

INGREDIENTS

1½ cups all-purpose flour, sifted

¾ stick butter, cut into small pieces

⅓ cup superfine sugar

1 egg yolk

2 Tbsp rose water

Raw sugar for sprinkling, optional

Preheat oven to 300°F. Grease several baking sheets or line with nonstick baking parchment.

● Place the flour in a mixing bowl and blend in the butter using your fingertips until the mixture resembles fine bread crumbs. Stir in the sugar, egg yolk, and rose water, then bring everything together with your hands to form a soft dough. On a lightly floured surface roll out the dough to about ¼-inch and using a 3-inch cutter, stamp out rounds and lift onto the baking sheets and prick with a fork. Repeat as necessary.

● Sprinkle with raw sugar and bake the cookies for 25 to 30 minutes or until lightly golden. Transfer to a wire rack to cool.

Poppy Seed Cookies

Preparation time: 25 minutes + chilling ● Cooking time: 10 to 12 minutes ● Makes: 36

These crisp sweet cookies with a hint of orange are ideal for serving with dessert.

INGREDIENTS

1 cup minus 2 Tbsp all-purpose flour, sifted

1 cup confectioners' sugar

1 stick butter, softened

1 egg, beaten

1 Tbsp poppy seeds

Grated rind from half an orange

1 Tbsp honey

Place the flour and confectioners' sugar into a mixing bowl and blend in the butter using your fingers until the mixture resembles fine bread crumbs.

● Add the egg, poppy seeds, orange rind, and honey and combine all the ingredients into a firm dough. On a lightly floured work surface, roll out the dough to a 9-inch log, wrap and chill for 30 minutes or up to 2 hours until firm.

● Preheat oven to 350°F. Grease several baking sheets or line with nonstick baking parchment.

● Slice the log into about 36 even slices and place them slightly apart on the baking sheets. Bake the cookies for 10 to 12 minutes or until lightly golden. Transfer to a wire rack to cool. These cookies can be frozen for up to a month.

Orange Flower Cookies

Preparation time: 35 minutes + chilling ● *Cooking time: 15 minutes* ● *Makes: 13*

These pretty cookies, sandwiched together with an orange butter cream are perfect for a Mother's Day tea.

INGREDIENTS

1½ sticks lightly salted butter, softened

¾ cup confectioners' sugar, sifted

Grated rind from 1 orange

1¾ cups all-purpose flour, sifted

½ cup English pudding custard mix or cornstarch

plus ½ tsp vanilla extract

FILLING

¾ stick unsalted butter softened

1½ cups confectioners' sugar, sifted

1 tsp grated orange rind

2 tsp fresh orange juice

Confectioners' sugar for dusting

In a mixing bowl beat together the butter and confectioners' sugar until light and fluffy. Stir in the orange rind, flour, and custard mix or cornstarch and combine all the ingredients well. Using your hands bring the mixture together to form a soft ball. Wrap and chill for 30 minutes.

● Preheat the oven to 350°F. Grease several baking sheets or line with nonstick baking parchment.

● On a lightly floured work surface, roll out the dough to about ¼-inch thick. Using a 2-inch flower-shaped cutter, stamp out 26 flower shapes or rounds and transfer to the baking sheets. Bake the cookies for 15 minutes, or until lightly golden-brown and transfer to a wire rack to cool.

● To decorate the cookies, in a small bowl beat together the butter and confectioners' sugar until soft and stir in the orange rind and juice for a soft frosting. Sandwich the cookies together with some butter cream and dust with confectioners' sugar before serving. Store these cookies in an airtight container for up to 1 week.

Chocolate Macaroons

Preparation time: 25 minutes ● Cooking time: 25 minutes ● Makes: 20

Show how much you care, by presenting these classic cookies enhanced by the addition of chocolate to your Father.

INGREDIENTS

3 oz semi-sweet chocolate
2 egg whites
Pinch of salt
¾ cup plus 2 Tbsp superfine sugar
1 cup ground almonds
5 candied cherries, halved
1 Tbsp almond pieces

Preheat oven to 300°F. Line several baking sheets with nonstick baking parchment. Melt the chocolate in the microwave or in a bowl over simmering water. Allow to cool.

● In a large bowl, whisk the egg whites with the salt until they form stiff peaks. Gradually whisk in the sugar a little at a time. Fold in the ground almonds and cooled melted chocolate and mix well together.

● Place tablespoonfuls, spaced well apart on the baking sheets and spread into circles about 2 inches across and decorate half the cookies with cherries and the remainder with almonds. Bake the cookies for 25 minutes or until firm, transfer to a wire rack and leave to cool. Store in an airtight container and eat within one week.

Coconut Curls

Preparation time: 25 minutes ● Cooking time: 6 to 8 minutes ● Makes: 18

These stunning cookies are ideal to serve with coffee or as an accompaniment to a creamy dessert.

INGREDIENTS

¼ cup butter
⅓ cup superfine sugar
3 Tbsp corn syrup
¾ cup all-purpose flour, sifted
2 Tbsp sweetened flaked coconut

Preheat oven to 375°F. Line 2 to 3 baking sheets with nonstick baking parchment.

● In a saucepan gently heat the butter, sugar, and corn syrup until the butter has melted. Remove from the heat. Add the flour and coconut and mix together until well blended.

● Spoon 3 tablespoons of the mixture, well apart, on the baking sheets and spread out to a 2 inch circle, bake for 6 to 8 minutes until bubbly and the cookies have spread to a lacy texture.

● Remove from the oven, leave to cool for one minute, then lift off with a thin, metal spatula and curl around a rolling pin to mold into a curl. Shape the remaining cookies in the same way. Leave to go cold and crisp.

TIP

Handle these cookies very carefully once baked.

Classic Butter Sables

Preparation time: 25 minutes + chilling • Cooking time: 15 minutes • Makes: 20

**These buttery cookies will be so popular, you will be baking a double batch for the next time.
They would make an ideal gift for Grandparents' Day.**

INGREDIENTS

2 cups all-purpose flour, sifted

Pinch of salt

¾ cup confectioners' sugar

1¼ sticks lightly salted butter, cut into small pieces

2 egg yolks

2 tsp vanilla extract

1 egg beaten, to glaze

In a mixing bowl place the flour, salt, and confectioners' sugar. Blend in the butter, until the mixture resembles fine bread crumbs, add the egg yolks with the vanilla and combine all the ingredients together to form a soft dough. Alternatively, place all the ingredients in a food processor and pulse until the mixture comes away from the sides of the bowl in a soft dough.

● Preheat the oven to 350°F. Grease or line 2 baking sheets with nonstick baking parchment.

● On a lightly floured work surface, roll out the dough to about ¼-inch thick. Cut out rounds using a 2-inch cutter and lift onto the baking sheets. Brush the cookies very carefully with the beaten egg and chill for 30 minutes.

● Brush again with beaten egg, then mark with the back of a fork, across the cookie to make a pattern. Bake the cookies for 15 minutes or until evenly golden. Transfer to a wire rack to cool.

● To assemble the sables, stack them together in neat bundles and tie with colored ribbon. Add labels marked with the names of your grandparents (or other family members) to the cookies. Store in an airtight container and eat within one week.

Valentine's Cookies

Preparation time: 30 minutes + chilling ● *Cooking time: 15 minutes* ● *Makes: 22*

This two toned dough creates a stunning effect, guaranteed to impress your Valentine!

INGREDIENTS

1½ sticks butter, softened

¾ cup confectioners' sugar, sifted

2¼ cups all-purpose flour, sifted

few drops of pink food coloring

Granulated sugar, for sprinkling

In a mixing bowl beat together the butter and confectioners' sugar until light and fluffy. Fold in the flour and bring all the ingredients together using your hands to form a soft dough. Take half the dough and add a few drops of coloring to turn the dough pink. Wrap the two doughs separately and chill for 30 minutes.

● Preheat oven to 350°F. Grease several baking sheets or line with nonstick baking parchment.

● On a lightly floured work surface, roll out each dough to about ¼-inch thick. Using a 2-inch and 1-inch heart-shaped cutter, stamp out hearts from the dough and lift onto the baking sheets. Re-position the centers to alternate the colors. Sprinkle with the granulated sugar. Bake the cookies for 15 minutes or until lightly golden. Allow to cool on the baking sheets, before transferring to a wire rack to cool completely. Store these cookies in an airtight container to keep fresh.

Valentine Passion Fruit Swirls

Preparation time: 30 minutes ● *Cooking time: 15 minutes* ● *Makes: 26*

These delicately flavored cookies are crisp to the touch but have a melt-in-the-mouth buttery taste.

INGREDIENTS

4 passion fruit

1½ sticks butter, softened

1 cup confectioners' sugar

1 cup plus 2 Tbsp all-purpose flour, sifted

Confectioners' sugar for dusting

Scoop out the flesh and seeds from the passion fruit and push through a fine sieve. Using a teaspoon, push the seeds against the side of the sieve to extract as much juice as possible. (You should be able to extract about 4 tablespoons of passion fruit juice, discard the black seeds.)

● Preheat the oven to 350°F. Grease several baking sheets or line with nonstick baking parchment.

● In a mixing bowl beat together the butter and confectioners' sugar until very soft (this will take about 5 minutes.) Then beat in the passion fruit juice and the flour to give a soft consistency. Using a decorating bag fitted with a medium star tube, pipe small "s" shapes on the baking sheets, spacing them well apart. Bake the cookies for 15 minutes. Allow to cool slightly on the sheets then transfer to a wire rack to cool completely. Dust with confectioners' sugar before serving. Store in an airtight container.

Chocolate Initials

Preparation time: 20 minutes + chilling ● *Cooking time: 20 minutes* ● *Makes: 18*

These incredibly crisp chocolate cookies are the perfect choice for decorating with the initials of the happy couple!

INGREDIENTS

1 egg, separated

½ cup superfine sugar

4 oz semi-sweet chocolate, finely grated

1½ cups all-purpose flour, sifted

2 Tbsp orange juice

DECORATION

2 oz semi-sweet chocolate, melted

In a mixing bowl whisk the egg white until soft, but not dry and fold in the superfine sugar. Stir in the chocolate, flour, egg yolk, and orange juice and bring the mixture together with your hands to make a soft dough. Wrap and chill for 30 minutes.

● Preheat the oven to 350°F. Grease several baking sheets or line with nonstick baking parchment.

● On a lightly floured work surface, roll out the dough to about ¼-inch thick. Using a 2-inch round cutter, stamp out the cookies, re-rolling the dough as necessary and transfer onto the baking sheets. Bake the cookies for 15 to 20 minutes, or until crisp. Transfer to a wire rack and leave to cool.

● Decorate the cookies by piping initials with melted chocolate using a paper decorating bag. Leave to set then store in an airtight container.

Lover's Scroll

Preparation time: 25 minutes + chilling ● *Cooking time: 15 minutes* ● *Makes: 24*

These sticky buttery cookies are delicious fresh from the oven.

INGREDIENTS

1½ cups all-purpose flour, sifted

1 stick butter, cut into small pieces

¼ cup superfine sugar

Grated rind from ½ lemon

2 Tbsp milk

FILLING

½ stick butter, softened

¼ cup packed light brown sugar

Grated rind from ½ lemon

1 egg beaten, for glaze

¾ cup mixed dried fruit

⅓ cup chopped candied cherries

Place the flour in a mixing bowl and blend in the butter using your fingers until the mixture resembles fine bread crumbs. Stir in the sugar, lemon rind, and milk and using your hands bring all the ingredients together to form a dough. Wrap and chill for 30 minutes.

● Meanwhile beat the butter and sugar together in a mixing bowl until light and fluffy, then stir in the lemon rind.

● On a lightly floured surface roll out the dough to a 6 x 11-inch rectangle. Brush with beaten egg and spread over the butter and sugar mixture, keeping within ½-inch of the edges. Sprinkle over the mixed dried fruit and candied cherries and very lightly press down.

● Roll up the pastry from one long side to the center, then roll up the other side so the two rolls meet, using a little egg brush along the point where the rolls meet. Wrap and chill for a further 1 hour.

● Preheat the oven to 350°F. Grease and line several baking sheets with nonstick baking paper.

● Using a sharp knife, slice the roll into about 24 even pieces and lift on to the baking sheets. Bake the cookies for 15 minutes or until lightly golden. Allow to cool on the sheets for a minute before transferring to a wire rack to cool completely.

Pine Nut Horseshoes

Preparation time: 30 minutes ● Cooking time: 15 minutes ● Makes: 10

Coated with sweet and crunchy pine nuts, these cookies say "Good Luck" in an edible way.

INGREDIENTS

3 oz white chocolate, broken into pieces

2 cups all-purpose flour, sifted

1 stick lightly salted butter, cut into small pieces

¼ cup superfine sugar

⅔ cup chopped dried apricots

1 egg, beaten, for glazing

1 cup pine nuts

Confectioners' sugar for dusting

Preheat oven to 350°F. Grease several baking sheets or line with nonstick baking parchment.

● First melt the chocolate by placing the pieces of chocolate in a small bowl and put this in double boiler over simmering water, stir frequently until the chocolate has melted. Allow to cool.

● Place the flour in a mixing bowl and blend in the butter using your fingers until the mixture resembles fine bread crumbs. Stir in the sugar, apricots, and cooled chocolate and bring all the ingredients together to a firm dough. On a lightly floured surface divide the dough into 10 equal-sized balls.

● Roll out each ball to about 9-inch thick sausage shapes and then curve it in the middle to resemble a horseshoe shape. Lay the pine nuts on a large plate in a single layer.

● Brush each cookie with beaten egg and lift onto the plate and flatten slightly to coat each horseshoe with the pine nuts. Lift onto the prepared baking sheets and bake the cookies for 15 minutes or until lightly golden. Transfer to a wire rack to cool. Just before serving dust with confectioners' sugar.

Cranberry Cookies

Preparation time: 45 minutes + chilling ● *Cooking time: 30 minutes* ● *Makes: 16*

These stunning ruby-colored cookies are great for special wedding anniversaries.

INGREDIENTS

¾ cup cranberries

⅓ cup superfine sugar

1 Tbsp water

2 cups all-purpose flour, sifted

¾ cup confectioners' sugar, sifted

1¼ sticks lightly salted butter, cut into small pieces

Granulated sugar, for dusting

Place the cranberries, sugar, and water in a small saucepan and set over a medium heat until the sugar dissolves. Reduce the heat and simmer uncovered for 8 to 10 minutes until the mixture is very thick, almost like jelly; cool.

● Place the flour and confectioners' sugar into a mixing bowl and blend in the butter using your fingertips until the mixture resembles fine bread crumbs, add the cooled cranberry sauce mixture and bring all the ingredients together to form a soft ball. Wrap and chill for 30 minutes.

● Preheat oven to 350°F. Grease several baking sheets or line with nonstick baking parchment.

● On a lightly floured work surface, roll out the dough to about ¼-inch thick and stamp out 3-inch fluted ovals or rounds, re-rolling the dough as necessary; there should be about 16. Transfer to the baking sheets.

● Bake the cookies for 15 minutes or until they are lightly golden at the edges. Transfer to a wire rack to cool. Just before serving sprinkle with granulated sugar.

Lemon Rings

Preparation time: 35 minutes ● Cooking time:
10 to 15 minutes ● Makes: 16

**These cookies are sandwiched together with a lemon
butter frosting to symbolize wedding rings.**

INGREDIENTS

¼ stick butter, softened

½ cup superfine sugar

1 egg, beaten

2 cups self-rising flour

Grated rind from 1 lemon

2 Tbsp lemon juice

FROSTING

½ stick unsalted butter, softened

1 cup confectioners' sugar

2 tsp lemon juice

1 tsp grated lemon rind

Confectioners' sugar, for dusting

Preheat oven to 350°F. Grease several baking sheets or line with nonstick baking parchment.

● In a mixing bowl beat together the butter and sugar until light and fluffy. Beat in the egg. Fold in the flour, lemon rind, and lemon juice and mix all the ingredients together to a firm dough. On a lightly floured surface roll out the dough to about ¼-inch thick. Using a 2½-inch and 1-inch cutter, cut out rings from the dough, carefully removing the central circle and lift on to the baking sheets. Re-roll the trimmings as necessary. Bake the cookies for 10 to 15 minutes. Transfer to a wire rack to cool.

● To decorate the cookies, in a mixing bowl beat together the butter and confectioners' sugar to give a fluffy consistency. Gradually beat in the lemon juice and rind. Sandwich the rings together with the filling and dust with confectioners' sugar before serving.

Pine Nut Biscotti

Preparation time: 30 miniutes ● Cooking time:
35 to 40 minutes ● Makes: 13

**Pine nuts and ground cinnamon are used to flavor these
crisp cookies. Serve them with black coffee after a meal.**

INGREDIENTS

1 egg

7 Tbsp superfine sugar

1 cup all-purpose flour, sifted

½ tsp baking powder

1 tsp ground cinnamon

⅔ cup pine nuts

Confectioners' sugar for dusting

Preheat oven to 350°F. Grease a large baking tray or line with nonstick baking parchment.

● In a mixing bowl whisk together the egg and sugar with an electric hand-held mixer until pale and thick (ribbons of mixture should leave a trail from the whisk as you lift it).

● Fold in the flour, baking powder, cinnamon, and pine nuts and mix everything together to form a soft dough. Turn out onto a lightly floured work surface and roll into a 9-inch long log. Transfer onto the prepared baking sheet and flatten the dough until it is about ¾-inch thick.

● Bake the dough for about 30 minutes or until golden and firm. Leave to cool for about 5 minutes. Transfer to a cutting board and using a serrated bread knife cut the log on the diagonal into ½-inch thick slices. Lift onto the baking sheet and cook for a further 10 to 15 minutes or until crisp.

● Transfer to a wire rack to cool. Dust with confectioners' sugar and store these cookies in an airtight container for up to one week.

Confetti Cookies

Preparation time: 50 minutes ● *Cooking time: 10 to 12 minutes* ● *Makes: 35 small cookies*

These tiny crisp cookies with a delicate hint of lime are decorated with clear frosting to resemble confetti.

INGREDIENTS

1 cup all-purpose flour, sifted

1 tsp grated lime rind

3 Tbsp confectioners' sugar

5 Tbsp butter, cut into small pieces

DECORATION

1 cup confectioners' sugar, sifted

1 Tbsp water

Blue, yellow, and pink food colorings

Preheat oven to 350°F. Grease several baking sheets or line with nonstick baking parchment.

● In a large mixing bowl place the flour, grated lime, and confectioners' sugar. Blend in the butter, using your fingertips, until the mixture begins to form together in a soft ball. On a lightly floured surface roll out the dough to ¼-inch thick and using 1½-inch selection of small cutters, stamp out different shapes. Re-roll the trimmings to make about 35 cookies in all and lift on to the baking sheets. Bake for 10 to 12 minutes or until lightly golden. Transfer the cookies to a wire rack and leave to cool completely.

● To decorate the cookies, mix the confectioners' sugar with sufficient water to form a thin frosting and divide into four bowls. Color the frosting blue, yellow, and pink, leaving one quarter white. Spread a little frosting on each cookie and allow to set. Gift-wrap in colored cellophane bags to look just like confetti!

Butter Viennese Fingers

Preparation time: 25 minutes ● *Cooking time: 10 to 15 minutes* ● *Makes: 20*

These cookies look very impressive, they are crisp on the outside but have a melt-in-the-mouth texture.

INGREDIENTS

1½ sticks butter, softened

3 Tbsp confectioners' sugar, sifted

1½ cups all-purpose flour, sifted

DECORATION

2 oz semi-sweet chocolate, broken into pieces

Preheat oven to 350°F. Grease several baking sheets or line with nonstick baking parchment.

● In a large mixing bowl beat together the butter and confectioners' sugar until very soft (this will take about 5 minutes), beat in the flour until thoroughly mixed and a soft consistency.

● Using a decorating bag fitted with a medium star tube, pipe 3-inch long finger shapes on the baking sheets, or spread the mixture evenly and mark fingers. Bake for 10 to 15 minutes or until pale golden. Cut into fingers, if necessary, and transfer to a wire rack to cool.

● To decorate the cookies, place the chocolate in a small bowl and put this in a double boiler set over a saucepan of simmering water and stir frequently until the chocolate has melted. Dip the ends of each cookie in the chocolate and allow to set on a piece of waxed paper or baking parchment.

Two-toned Cookies

Preparation time: 30 minutes + chilling ●
Cooking time: 10 to 12 minutes ● *Makes: 32*

Once you have mastered the basic technique, have fun creating different cookie patterns.

INGREDIENTS

1½ sticks butter, softened

¾ cup confectioners' sugar

1 cup plus 2 Tbsp all-purpose flour, sifted

½ tsp grated lemon rind

2 Tbsp unsweetened cocoa powder, sifted

1 egg white, to glaze

In a mixing bowl, beat together the butter and sugar until light and fluffy. Stir in the flour and lemon rind, then combine the ingredients to form a soft ball. Transfer half the mixture to another bowl and stir in the cocoa powder. Wrap separately and chill for 30 minutes.
● Preheat oven to 350°F. Grease several baking sheets or line with nonstick baking parchment.
● On a lightly floured work surface divide each dough in half and roll into four sausage shapes about 12-inches long and ½-inch wide. Using the egg white, brush the sausage shapes and stack together alternating the colors. Cut the log shape into 32 slices and lift onto the baking sheets. Bake the cookies for 10 to 12 minutes. Transfer to a wire rack to cool completely. Store the cookies in an airtight container.

Chocolate-dipped Palmiers

Preparation time: 20minutes ●
Cooking time: 10 minutes ● *Makes: 40*

These cookies are so simple to make, but look so delicate that they never fail to impress.

INGREDIENTS

½ cup fine chopped hazelnuts

2 Tbsp granulated sugar

½ tsp ground cinnamon

sugar for rolling

8 oz fresh or frozen puff pastry, thawed if frozen

1 egg, lightly beaten

8 oz semi-sweet chocolate

Preheat oven to 450°F. Lightly grease 2 baking sheets or line with nonstick baking parchment.
● In a bowl, combine hazelnuts, sugar and cinnamon.
● Cut the pastry into quarters and sprinkle a little sugar. Roll out the pastry into a rectangle. Lightly brush with beaten egg, then sprinkle with half the nut mixture.
● Roll the two sides to the centre to make a double roll. Brush with more beaten egg and sprinkle with more nut mixture. Fold the outside edges inward to meet edge to edge in the center.
● Cut into 1-inch slices and transfer to the prepared baking sheets, spacing slightly apart; open out to form "V" shapes. Refrigerate for 15 minutes. Bake for 10 minutes, or until puffed up and lightly golden-brown. Transfer to a wire rack to cool.
● Melt the chocolate in a small bowl set over a saucepan of simmering water until smooth. Line baking sheets with waxed paper. Dip each palmier halfway into the chocolate and place on lined baking sheets. Allow to set.

Lime and Coconut Hearts

Preparation time: 35 minutes ● Cooking time: 15 minutes ● Makes: 16

Ideal for any journey, the exotic flavors of coconut and lime are reminiscent of the Caribbean.

INGREDIENTS

2 cups all-purpose flour, sifted

¼ cup rice flour

1½ sticks butter, cut into small pieces

½ cup superfine sugar

1 cup unsweetened flaked coconut

Grated rind from 1 lime

2 Tbsp milk

DECORATION

7 Tbsp confectioners' sugar, sifted

3 tsp cold water

Grated rind from 1 lime

Preheat oven to 350°F. Grease several baking sheets or line with nonstick baking parchment.

● Place the flour and rice flour in a mixing bowl and add the butter. Blend in the butter using your fingers until the mixture resembles fine bread crumbs, add the sugar, coconut, lime rind, and milk and mix all the ingredients together to form a soft dough.

● On a lightly floured work surface, roll out the dough to about ¼-inch thick, stamp out hearts using a 3-inch heart-shaped cutter and lift onto the baking sheets. Bake the cookies for 15 minutes or until they are lightly golden. Transfer to a wire rack to cool.

● To decorate the cookies, mix the confectioners' sugar with the cold water and mix to a thin frosting. Fill a paper decorating bag with frosting and drizzle it over the cookies, sprinkle with lime rind and allow the frosting to set. Store in an airtight container.

Rosemary and Lime Cookies

Preparation time: 25 minutes ● Cooking time: 15 to 20 minutes ● Makes: 30

The combination of fresh rosemary with lime results in a crisp scented cookie.

INGREDIENTS

½ stick lightly salted butter, softened

¼ cup light brown sugar

1 egg, separated

Grated rind from 1 lime

1¾ cups all-purpose flour, sifted

2 Tbsp lime juice

2 tsp finely chopped fresh rosemary

Granulated sugar for sprinkling

Preheat oven to 350°F. Grease several baking sheets or line with nonstick baking parchment.

● In a mixing bowl beat together the butter and sugar until light and fluffy. Beat in the egg yolk and lime rind. Add the flour and begin to work the mixture into a soft dough. Add the lime juice and rosemary and using your hands bring the dough together in a soft ball.

● On a lightly floured surface, roll out the dough to ¼-inch thick, stamp out diamond shapes using a 3-inch cutter. Re-roll the trimmings and stamp out more shapes and place on the baking sheets.

● Lightly whisk the egg white in a small bowl, gently brush over the surface of each cookie, then sprinkle with a little granulated sugar. Bake the cookies for 15 to 20 minutes or until lightly golden. Transfer to a wire rack to cool. Store the cookies in an airtight container for up to one week.

Smiling Faces

Preparation time: 35 minutes ● Cooking time: 15 minutes ● Makes: 16

These coffee flavored cookies will cheer up a special friend!

INGREDIENTS

1 Tbsp instant coffee

1 Tbsp of hot water

2 cups all-purpose four, sifted

¾ cup confectioners' sugar, sifted

1¼ sticks butter, cut into small pieces

DECORATION

6 Tbsp confectioners' sugar

3 tsp water

Preheat oven to 350°F. Grease several baking sheets or line with nonstick baking parchment.

● Dissolve the coffee with the hot water and allow to cool.

● Place the flour and confectioners' sugar in a mixing bowl and blend in the butter using your fingertips until the mixture resembles fine bread crumbs. Pour in the cooled coffee and bring all the ingredients together to form a soft dough.

● On a lightly floured surface, roll out the dough to about ¼-inch thick. Using a 3-inch cutter, stamp out rounds and lift on to the prepared baking sheets, re-rolling the dough as necessary. Prick the cookies with a fork. Bake for about 15 minutes or until crisp. Transfer to a wire rack to cool.

● To decorate, mix the confectioners' sugar with sufficient cold water to make a thin frosting. Using a paper decorating bag, pipe smiling faces onto the cookies. Allow to set. Store in an airtight container.

Pecan Pinwheel Cookies

Preparation time: 25 minutes + chilling ● Cooking time: 20 minutes ● Makes: 24

A cinnamon cookie base is sprinkled with pecan nuts and orange rind then rolled up and cut into pinwheels.

INGREDIENTS

1½ cups all-purpose flour, sifted

1 tsp ground cinnamon

½ cup sugar

1 stick lightly salted butter, cut into small pieces

1 Tbsp maple syrup

FILLING

⅓ cup smooth peanut butter

2 Tbsp maple syrup

Grated rind from 1 orange

½ cup chopped pecan nuts

2 Tbsp maple syrup, optional

Place the flour, cinnamon, and sugar in a mixing bowl and using your fingers blend in the butter until the mixture resembles fine bread crumbs. Add the maple syrup and mix everything together with your hands to form a soft dough. Wrap and chill for 30 minutes.

● On a lightly floured work surface roll out the dough to a 12 x 7-inch rectangle. In a small bowl combine the peanut butter and maple syrup, beat using a wooden spoon until soft enough to spread. Spread this mixture over the rectangle leaving a 1-inch border around the edge of the dough. Sprinkle over the orange rind and pecan nuts. Starting from the long end, roll up the dough tightly into a "sausage" shape. Wrap and chill for 30 minutes.

● Preheat the oven to 350°F. Grease several baking sheets or line with nonstick baking parchment.

● Using a sharp knife cut the log into 24 equal slices (discarding the first and last slice, which have little filling) and lift onto the baking sheets. Bake the cookies for 20 minutes or until lightly golden. Drizzle with maple syrup to glaze, if liked. Transfer to a wire rack to cool. Store in an airtight container until required.

Fantailed Shortbread

Preparation time: 25 minutes ● Cooking time: 35 to 40 minutes ● Makes: 8

This classic buttery shortbread is very rewarding to make—and a great gift.

INGREDIENTS

1 stick butter, softened
¼ cup superfine sugar
1 cup minus 2 Tbsp all-purpose flour, sifted
2 Tbsp rice flour
Pinch of salt
2 Tbsp fine chopped mixed nuts, to sprinkle

Preheat oven to 300°F. Grease a baking sheet or line with nonstick baking parchment.

● In a mixing bowl beat together the butter and sugar until light and fluffy. Add the flour, rice flour, and salt and mix everything together to form a soft dough. On a lightly floured surface, roll out the dough to form a neat circle about 8-inch across and ¼-inch thick.

● Transfer to the prepared baking sheet, then crimp the edges with your fingertips and mark into 8 even wedges with a sharp knife. Prick with a fork, sprinkle with the chopped nuts, and bake for about 35 to 40 minutes until lightly golden.

● Allow to cool slightly on the tray before transferring to a wire rack to cool completely. Cut along the scored lines to divide into 8 wedges.

Sesame Cracker Cookies

Preparation time: 20 minutes ● Cooking time: 15 minutes ● Makes: 15

Serve these savory cookies with chunks of Cheddar cheese.

INGREDIENTS

1½ cups whole-wheat flour
¾ cup oat bran
½ tsp salt
1 tsp baking powder
½ oz superfine sugar
2 Tbsp sesame seeds
1 stick butter, cut into small pieces
1 Tbsp water

Preheat oven to 375°F. Grease several baking sheets or line with nonstick baking parchment.

● In a mixing bowl place the whole-wheat flour, oat bran, salt, baking powder, sugar, and sesame seeds and give a good mix. Blend in the butter, using your fingers, until the mixture resembles fine bread crumbs. Add sufficient cold water (about 1 tablespoon) and work all the ingredients together into a firm dough.

● On a lightly floured work surface, roll out the dough to about ¼-inch thick and using a 3-inch round cutter, stamp out 15 circles and lift onto the baking sheets, re-rolling the dough as necessary. Prick the cookies with a fork. Bake for 15 minutes. Transfer to a wire rack to cool, then store these cookies in an airtight container.

Coffee Meringue Snails

Preparation time: 25 minutes ● *Cooking time: 1 hour and 30 minutes* ● *Makes: 15*

The addition of coffee to the meringue makes it quite soft when piping but the taste is delicious. Any gardener should see the funny side of making a snail cookie!

INGREDIENTS

1 Tbsp instant coffee

1 Tbsp of boiling water

4 egg whites

Pinch of salt

2 cups superfine sugar

DECORATION

3 Tbsp confectioners' sugar

1 tsp of water

Black food coloring

Mix the coffee with the boiling water in a small jug and allow to go cold. Preheat the oven to 250°F. Line several baking sheets with nonstick baking parchment.
● In a large clean bowl, using a balloon whisk or hand-held electric mixer, whisk together the egg whites and salt until they form stiff peaks. Whisk in the sugar a little at a time, the meringue should start to look glossy.
● Continue whisking in the sugar until it has been incorporated and the meringue is thick and shiny and stands in stiff peaks. Fold in the coffee and mix through.
● Fill a decorating bag with the meringue, using a ¾-inch plain tube, pipe about 15 "snail" shapes. Bake the meringues for 1 hour and 30 minutes until they are dry and crisp and can be easily lifted off the paper.
● To decorate the snails, mix the confectioners' sugar with the water and mix to form a thin frosting. Add a few drops of coloring. Fill a paper decorating bag with the black frosting and decorate each snail with eyes and mouths. Store the meringues in an airtight container.

Almond Tiles

Preparation time: 45 minutes ● *Cooking time: 4 to 5 minutes per batch* ● *Makes: 30*

These are one of the most popular French cookies, "tuiles aux amandes", so called because they resemble the curved roof tiles seen all over France.

INGREDIENTS

½ cups whole blanched almonds, lightly toasted

scant cup superfine sugar

3 Tbsp unsalted butter

2 egg whites

½ tsp almond extract

¼ cup all-purpose flour, sifted

¾ cup slivered almonds

In a food processor fitted with a metal blade, process the toasted almonds with 2 tablespoons of the sugar until fine crumbs form.

● Preheat oven to 400°F. Generously butter 2 baking sheets or line with nonstick baking parchment.

● In a medium bowl beat the butter until creamy, add the sugar and beat until light and fluffy. Gradually beat in the egg whites and almond extract until well blended. Sift over the flour and fold into the butter mixture, then fold in the almond-sugar mixture.

● Begin by working in batches of 4 cookies on each sheet. Drop tablespoonfuls of batter about 6-inches apart on the baking sheet. With the back of a moistened spoon, spread each mound of batter into very thin 3-inch rounds. Each round should be transparant. If you make a few holes, the batter will spread and fill them in. Sprinkle tops with slivered almonds.

● Bake, one sheet at a time, until the edges are browned and the centers are just golden, 4 to 5 minutes. Remove baking sheet to a wire rack, working quickly, use a thin-bladed metal spatula to loosen the edge of a hot cookie and transfer to a rolling pin or glass tumbler. Gently press, side down, to shape each cookie. If the cookie becomes too firm to transfer, return to the oven for 30 seconds to soften, the proceed as above. When cool, transfer immediately to airtight containers in single layers. These cookies are very fragile.

Hazelnut and Nutmeg Cookies

Preparation time: 30 minutes + chilling ● *Cooking time: 15 to 18 minutes* ● *Makes: 24*

The crunchy hazelnuts and spicy nutmeg make these a great treat for morning coffee.

INGREDIENTS

2 sticks lightly salted butter, softened

⅔ cup superfine sugar

2 egg yolks

1 tsp vanilla extract

2½ cups self-rising flour, sifted

½ tsp ground nutmeg

¾ cup chopped hazelnuts

Confectioners' sugar for dusting, optional

In a mixing bowl cream together the butter and sugar until light and fluffy. Beat in the egg yolks and vanilla extract, add the flour and nutmeg and mix everything together to form a soft dough. Wrap and chill in the refrigerator for 30 minutes.

● Preheat oven to 375°F. Grease several baking sheets or line with nonstick baking parchment.

● On a lightly floured work surface, divide the dough into 24 equal-sized pieces, roll each into a ball and flatten slightly. Place the chopped hazelnuts on a large plate, roll the flattened balls in the chopped hazelnuts and then lift onto the baking sheets spaced well apart. Bake the cookies for 15 to 18 minutes or until lightly golden. Transfer to a wire rack to cool. Dust with confectioners' sugar before serving. Store these cookies in an airtight container.

Cardamom Crisps

Preparation time: 25 minutes ● Cooking time:
15 minutes ● Makes: 20

These indulgent cookies flavored with cardamom and ginger are delicious. They will liven up anyone's nightcap.

INGREDIENTS

2¼ cups all-purpose flour, sifted

½ tsp ground cardamom

Pinch of salt

1 stick lightly salted butter, cut into small pieces

1 cup soft brown sugar

2 egg yolks

2 Tbsp finely chopped stem ginger or ginger preserves

Granulated sugar, for sprinkling

Preheat oven to 350°F. Grease several baking sheets or line with nonstick baking parchment.

● In a mixing bowl, place the flour, ground cardamom and salt. Blend in the butter, using your fingers, until the mixture resembles fine bread crumbs, stir in the sugar. Add the egg yolks and mix all the ingredients together to form a soft dough.

● On a lightly floured surface, roll out the dough to ¼-inch thick. Cut out the cookies using a 2½-inch shaped cutter, re-rolling the trimmings to make about 20, place on to the baking sheets.

● Sprinkle a little stem ginger or ginger preserves on the top of each cookie. Bake the cookies for 15 minutes or until lightly golden and crisp. Transfer the cookies to a wire rack and leave to cool. Sprinkle with granulated sugar before serving.

TIP

If using cardamom pods, crack open 7 pods, remove the black seeds and crush with a pestle and mortar.

Double Chocolate Mint Sandwiches

Preparation time: 1 hour + chilling ● Cooking time: 12 to 16 minutes ● Makes: About 24

A delicious combination of mint-flavored white chocolate ganache sandwiched between thin cocoa wafers, glazed with dark chocolate. These cookies are time-consuming to make, but make an excellent presentation gift.

INGREDIENTS

1 cup all-purpose flour

¾ cup unsweetened cocoa powder

1 stick butter

¼ cup superfine sugar

1 egg

1 tsp mint extract

FILLING

½ cup whipping cream

7 oz fine-quality white chocolate, chopped

GLAZE

5 oz semi-sweet chocolate, chopped

¾ stick butter, cut into pieces

Sift together the flour and cocoa. In a large bowl, beat the butter until creamy, add the sugar and continue beating until light and fluffy. Beat in the egg and mint extract until blended. Stir in the flour-cocoa mixture until a soft dough forms. Place the dough in plastic wrap and refrigerate for 1 to 2 hours until firm.

● Preheat oven to 350°F. Grease 2 baking sheets with nonstick baking parchment.

● On a lightly floured work surface, roll out half the dough to about ⅛ inch thick. Using a 2½-inch cutter, stamp out as many cookies as possible, re-rolling the dough as necessary and lift onto the baking sheets.

● Bake for 6 to 8 minutes or until the edges are set. Allow to cool and then transfer to a wire rack to cool completely. Repeat with the remaining dough.

● In a medium saucepan over a medium heat, bring the cream to a boil. Remove from the heat and add the white chocoate, stirring constantly until melted. Stir in mint extract and strain into a bowl. Cool until firm.

● Slightly beat white chocolate cream to lighten, then spread a little filling onto half of the cookies, pressing together gently. Allow to set for 24 hours.

● In a small saucepan over a low heat, melt the chocolate and butter for the glaze, stirring until smooth. Remove from the heat. Cool until thickened to spreading consistency, 20 to 30 minutes. Spread a small amount of glaze onto the top of each sandwiched cookie, smoothing tops. Refrigerate until set, 30 minutes or so. Store these cookies in an airtight container, refrigerated, with wax paper between the layers.

Strawberry Jam Sandwiches

Preparation time: 25 minutes + chilling ● *Cooking time: 8 to 10 minutes* ● *Makes: About 24*

Kids love strawberry jam sandwiches and these are the perfect cookies to take to a family party.

INGREDIENTS

⅔ cup blanched almonds

1½ cups all-purpose flour

1½ sticks lightly salted butter

½ cup superfine sugar

1 egg, separated

Grated rind of 1 lemon

1 tsp vanilla extract

½ tsp salt

½ cup slivered almonds, chopped

⅓ cup strawberry jam or preserve

1 Tbsp lemon juice

In a food processor fitted with a metal blade, process the blanched almonds and ¼ cup flour until the mixture becomes very fine. In a separate bowl, beat the butter until creamy, add the sugar, and continue beating until light and fluffy. Beat in the egg yolk, lemon rind, and vanilla until blended. Stir in the almond mixture and add the remaining flour and salt; process until combined. Wrap the dough in plastic wrap and refrigerate for 2 hours or overnight, until the dough is firm enough to handle.

● Preheat oven to 350°F. Grease or line two baking sheets with nonstick baking parchment.

● On a floured surface, roll half the dough into a 12-inch square; keep other half refrigerated. Cut the square crosswise and lengthwise into 6 strips to make 24 squares. Using a ¾-inch cutter, cut out centers from half the squares.

● Transfer the squares to baking sheets ½-inch apart. In a small bowl, whisk the egg white until frothy. Brush the top of cookies only with it and sprinkle with a few slivers of almond. Bake until just golden, 8 to 10 minutes. Allow the cookies to cool slightly, then transfer to wire racks to cool completely.

● In a saucepan over a low heat, melt the strawberry jam or preserve with the lemon juice. Spoon a little of the glaze over the cookie squares, then top with an almond-topped cookie, pressing the two gently together. Allow the jam to set before serving. These cookies are best eaten as soon as possible after baking as they will begin to go soft if kept for too long.

Real Vanilla Cookies

Preparation time: 30 minutes ● *Cooking time: 8 to 10 minutes* ● *Makes: About 24*

These cookies are a Danish Specialty. They use real vanilla seeds from a bean.

INGREDIENTS

2 cups all-purpose flour

2 Tbsp cornstarch

5 Tbsp superfine sugar

3 Tbsp fine chopped blanched almonds

½ vanilla bean or 1 tsp vanilla extract

2 sticks unsalted butter, cut into small pieces

1 egg, separated

Sugar, for sprinkling

Confectioners' sugar, for dusting

Preheat oven to 400°F. Grease two baking sheets, or line with nonstick baking parchment.

● Sift together the flour and cornstarch, stir in the sugar and almonds.

● Using a sharp knife, split the vanilla bean and scrape out the seeds. Add to the flour mixture and mix well. (If using vanilla extract, mix with the egg yolk and add later.) Blend the butter into the flour mixture until it resembles bread crumbs. In a separate bowl, beat the egg yolk (and vanilla extract) and add to the crumb mixture. Knead until a soft dough forms. (If the dough seems a little wet, add a little more flour.)

● Spoon the dough into a large piping bag fitted with a large plain tube and pipe "doughnut" shapes 1½ inches apart on the baking sheets. In a small bowl, beat the egg whites until foamy, then use to brush the shapes. Sprinkle with sugar.

● Bake until lightly golden and set, 8 to 10 minutes. Allow to cool slightly, then, using a metal spatula, transfer to wire racks to cool completely. Dust with confectioners' sugar. Store in an airtight container for up to one week.

Bitter Chocolate Discs

Preparation time: 25 minutes ● Cooking time: 15 minutes ● Makes: 16

These cookies have a crumbly melt-in-the-mouth texture with a rich chocolate flavor.

INGREDIENTS

1¾ sticks butter, softened

½ cup superfine sugar

2¼ cups all-purpose flour, sifted

Pinch of salt

½ cup unsweetened cocoa powder, sifted

DECORATION

3 oz white chocolate, melted

Preheat oven to 350°F. Grease several baking sheets or line with nonstick baking parchment.

● In a mixing bowl beat together the butter and sugar until light and fluffy. Add the flour, salt, and cocoa. Using your hands work these ingredients into the butter and sugar mixture until it comes together in a firm dough.

● On a lightly floured surface, roll out the dough to ¼-inch thick. Using a 3 inch fluted round cutter, stamp out 16 cookies, re-rolling as necessary and transfer on to the baking sheets. Prick with a fork and bake the cookies for 15 minutes. Transfer to a wire rack and leave to cool.

● Decorate the cookies by drizzling freestyle with melted white chocolate using a paper decorating bag. Leave on the wire rack until the chocolate icing becomes firm.

Chocolate Cookies

For many people, this will be their favorite chapter in the book. The appeal of chocolate just cannot be denied, even its Latin name acknowledges this, *Theobroma cacao* means "food of the gods" and who could doubt it. Chocoholics will find reading through these recipes alone will send them on a chocolate high.

When shopping for chocolate, be sure to buy real chocolate and not a synthetic chocolate-flavored candy or cooking bar. Different brands of the same type of chocolate can vary in taste, so to avoid disappointment, make sure that the chocolate that you cook with tastes the same as the one you most enjoy eating. If you are not sure, then have a nibble before you begin.

The biggest problem will be which recipe to cook first—maybe a purely chocolate cookie, or one with a hint of orange, or perhaps a chocolate cookie with a nutty crunch. One thing is guaranteed, and that is the enjoyment of tasting these rich and sumptuous cookies.

Lunch-box or Picnic Treats

No-cook Peanut Squares	154
Lunch-box Crunchies	154
Checkerboards	155
Chocolate Crackle-tops	156
Oat Jacks	159
Amaretti Drops	159
Apricot and Chocolate Cookies	160
Spiced Rum Chocolate Cookies	161
Cherry Chocolate Dreams	161
Chocolate Pinwheels	162

Cookies with Crunch

Orange Chocolate Cookies	164
Mocha Chunk Cookies	164
Chocolate Chip and Raisin Cookies	165
Coconut and Chocolate Crunch	167
White Chocolate Cashew Thins	167
White Chocolate Chunk and Pecan Cookies	168
Chocolate-dipped Macaroons	171
Granola and Choc-chip Cookies	171
Chocolate Cream-filled Hearts	172
Ultimate Chocolate Chip Cookies	173

Afternoon Tea

Chocolate Ginger Cookies	174
Red, White, and Blue Cookies	174
Chocolate Refrigerator Cookies	175
Chocolate and Orange Sandwiches	177
Chocolate-dipped Orange Shortbread	178
Marble Cookies	179
Sesame Chocolate Chewies	180
Chocolate Pistachio Cookies	180
Chocolate Pockets	181

Special Occasions

Chocolate-frosted Heart Cookies	182
Monkey Puzzles	184
Chocolate Dipped Cinnamon Meringues	185
Chocolate Wafers	186
Almond and Chocolate Clusters	187
Hazelnut Chocolate Crescents	188
Strawberry Cocoa Sandwich Stars	189
Chocolate and Chili Cookies	190
Chocolate Viennese Whirls	190

After-dinner Cookies

Chrunchy Chocolate Chip Cookies	192
Raspberry and White Chocolate Chunkies	193
Chocolate Fudge Cookies	195
Chocolate Mint Cookies	195
Chocolate Rugelach	196
Chocolate Crescents	197

No-cook Peanut Squares

Preparation time: 30 minutes + chilling ●
Cooking time: 5 minutes ● Makes: About 24

You do not even have to switch the oven on to make these chocolatey treats.

INGREDIENTS

1¼ cups corn syrup

1 cup peanut butter

2¼ cups All Bran breakfast cereal

1 cup chopped peanuts

7 oz milk chocolate

Grease or line a shallow 7 x 11-inch pan with nonstick baking parchment.

● Mix the syrup and peanut butter together in a large saucepan and cook over a medium heat stirring until the mixture begins to boil. Remove from the heat and stir in the breakfast cereal and chopped peanut until well blended. Spread the mixture into the baking pan. Press out evenly and chill for 1 hour in the refrigerator.

● Melt the chocolate in a small bowl set over a saucepan of simmering water and spread over the cookie base using a spatula. When set cut into squares and store in an airtight container.

TIP

All the cookies in this chapter will freeze for up to one month unless otherwise stated.

Lunch-box Crunchies

Preparation time: 20 minutes ● Cooking time: 15 minutes ● Makes: About 24

This is a small crunchy cookie, suitable for a lunch-box or picnic.

INGREDIENTS

1½ cups all-purpose flour

¼ stick slightly salted butter, softened

½ cup packed light brown sugar

1 egg

3 oz semi-sweet chocolate, chopped

Preheat oven to 350°F. Grease two baking sheets or line with nonstick baking parchment.

● Sift the flour into a bowl. Beat together the butter and sugar in a separate bowl. Beat in the egg. Mix the sifted flour into the butter with the chocolate pieces.

● Mold the mixture into 24 pieces. Place on baking sheets and press the top lightly with a fork. Bake for 15 minutes. Leave to cool on the baking sheet. Store in an airtight container.

Checkerboards

Preparation time: 25 minutes ● Cooking time: 15 to 20 minutes ● Makes: About 26

These cookies are good fun to make and look great for children's parties

INGREDIENTS

1½ sticks butter, softened
¾ cup superfine sugar
½ tsp vanilla extract
2 eggs
4½ cups all-purpose flour
2 tsp baking powder
1 tsp milk
1½ Tbsp unsweetened cocoa powder, sifted

Divide the butter and sugar evenly between 2 bowls. For the vanilla dough, beat butter and sugar until light and fluffy. Beat in the vanilla extract and one egg. Sift half the flour and baking powder into the bowl. Blend in with a spoon and then work by hand to form a smooth dough.

● Make the chocolate dough in the same way with the remaining butter, sugar and egg, adding milk and sifted cocoa along with the remaining flour and baking powder. Divide each portion of dough into 4 equal pieces.

● On a floured surface roll each piece into a rope 12 inches long. Place a chocolate rope next to a vanilla one. Place a chocolate one on top of the vanilla rope and a vanilla one on top of the chocolate. Press firmly together to form a square. Wrap in plastic wrap. Repeat with remaining dough. Chill for 1 hour in the refrigerator.

● Preheat oven to 350°F. Grease two baking sheets or line with nonstick baking parchment.

● Cut dough into 26 slices and place onto the baking sheets. Bake for 15 to 20 minutes until lightly browned. Transfer to a wire rack to cool. Once completely cool, store in an airtight container.

Chocolate Crackle-Tops

Preparation time: 25 minutes + chilling ● Cooking time: 10 to 15 minutes ● Makes: About 48

A simple chocolate cookie which is easy to make and will become a family favorite.

INGREDIENTS

7 oz semi-sweet chocolate, chopped

¾ stick slightly salted butter, softened

½ cup superfine sugar

3 eggs

1 tsp vanilla extract

1½ cups all-purpose flour

¼ cup unsweetened cocoa powder

½ tsp baking powder

1½ cups confectioners' sugar, for decoration

Heat the chocolate and butter in a saucepan over a low heat, stirring frequently. Remove from the heat and stir in the sugar. Continue stirring for 2 to 3 minutes until the sugar dissolves. Add the eggs one at a time, beating well. Add vanilla.

● Sift the flour, cocoa, and baking powder into a bowl. Gradually stir into the chocolate mixture in batches, until just blended. Cover dough and refrigerate for 1 hour or until cold.

● Preheat oven to 325°F. Grease two baking sheets or line with nonstick baking parchment.

● Place confectioners' sugar in a small bowl. Using a teaspoon, scoop dough into small balls and between palms of hand, roll into ½-inch balls. Drop balls one at a time into confectioners' sugar and roll until heavily coated. Remove ball with a slotted spoon and tap against the side of the bowl to remove excess sugar.

● Place the cookies on baking sheets spaced well apart. Bake for 10 to 15 minutes. Leave to cool on baking sheet for 3 minutes then remove to wire cooling rack. Eat within 2 days.

Oat Jacks

Preparation time: 15 minutes ● *Cooking time: 25 to 30 minutes* ● *Makes: 12*

A perfect lunch-box treat or a substantial afternoon snack. Try dipping them in white chocolate too.

INGREDIENTS

1 stick slightly salted butter, softened

½ cup packed light brown sugar

1¼ cups rolled oats

6 oz semi-sweet chocolate

Preheat oven to 325°F. Grease or line a shallow 8 x 8-inch pan with nonstick baking parchment.

● Melt the butter over a medium heat in a saucepan, then transfer to a bowl. Stir in the sugar and rolled oats.

● Spoon the mixture into the baking pan and bake for 25 to 30 minutes. Leave to cool in the pan for 5 minutes, then cut into squares.

● Melt the chocolate in a bowl over a saucepan of simmering water. When the oaty jacks are cold, dip each piece into melted chocolate and leave to set on waxed paper. Once the chocolate is set, store the cookies in an airtight container.

Amaretti Drops

Preparation time: 25 minutes ● *Cooking time: 12 to 15 minutes* ● *Makes: About 15*

This cookie is light and crispy on the outside, chewy on the inside and ideal as after-dinner treat.

INGREDIENTS

¼ cup amaretti cookies, crushed

1 Tbsp unsweetened cocoa powder

½ cup confectioners' sugar

2 egg whites

Preheat oven to 350°F. Grease or line a large baking sheet with nonstick paper.

● Place the cookies in a food processor and process briefly to produce coarse crumbs. Place in a bowl and sift in the unsweetened cocoa powder. Stir to blend.

● In a medium bowl beat the egg whites until stiff peaks form. Gradually beat in the confectioners' sugar a tablespoonful at a time. Then add the cookie mixture to the egg whites and fold the two together gently until just blended.

● Place rounded teaspoonfuls of the cookie mixture well apart on the prepared baking sheet and bake for 12 to 15 minutes. Cool the cookies on a baking sheet for about 10 minutes, then remove to a wire rack to cool completely. When cool, store cookies in an airtight container. Not suitable for freezing.

Apricot and Chocolate Cookies

Preparation time: 20 minutes ● *Cooking time: 12 minutes* ● *Makes: About 25*

A lovely chewy cookie with the unusual but delicious combination of chocolate and apricots.

INGREDIENTS

1½ sticks butter

½ cup packed light brown sugar

1 egg beaten

1½ cups all-purpose flour

Pinch of salt

1 tsp baking powder

⅔ cup chopped no-soak dried apricots

¼ cup semi-sweet chocolate chips

Preheat oven to 350°F. Grease two baking sheets or line with nonstick baking parchment.

● Beat the butter and sugar together until smooth and soft. Beat in the egg until fluffy. Sift the flour with the salt and baking powder into the butter mixture. Mix together until thoroughly blended. Beat in the apricots and chocolate chips.

● Roll the mixture into small balls and place well apart on baking sheets. Flatten with the prongs of a fork. Bake for 12 to 14 minutes until golden-brown. While hot, ease off the baking sheets and leave to cool on a wire rack. Once completely cool, store the cookies in an airtight container.

Spiced Rum Chocolate Cookies

Preparation time: 20 minutes ● Cooking time: 10 to 12 minutes ● Makes: About 18

A small, dark, and spicy cookie which is strictly for the adults.

INGREDIENTS

¾ cup packed light brown sugar

2 eggs, separated

1½ cups all-purpose flour

1 Tbsp unsweetened cocoa powder

1 tsp ground cinnamon

1 tsp pumpkin pie spice

⅓ cup superfine sugar

Grated rind of ½ orange

2 Tbsp rum

Preheat oven to 375°F. Grease two baking sheets or line with nonstick baking parchment.

● Beat together the brown sugar with the egg yolks until light and fluffy. Sift the flour and spices together, then stir in until the mixture resembles bread crumbs. Whisk the egg whites until they form stiff peaks and then beat in the superfine sugar until glossy. Fold into the mixture with the grated orange rind.

● Roll the mixture into walnut-sized pieces, place onto the baking sheets. Bake for 10 to 15 minutes. Brush with rum while still warm, then use a metal spatula to transfer to a wire cooling rack to cool completely. Store in an airtight container.

Cherry Chocolate Dreams

Preparation time: 15 minutes ● Cooking time: 12 to 15 minutes ● Makes: About 15

A winning combination of cherries and chocolate.

INGREDIENTS

1 stick slightly salted butter, softened

¼ cup superfine sugar

½ tsp vanilla extract

1¼ cups all-purpose flour, sifted

2 Tbsp candied cherries, fine chopped

2 Tbsp semi-sweet chocolate, fine chopped

Preheat oven to 375°F. Grease two baking sheets or line with nonstick baking parchment.

● Beat together the butter, sugar, and vanilla until light and fluffy. Stir in the flour until well combined. Add the cherries and chocolate and mix until blended. Place teaspoonfuls of the mixture on baking sheets.

● Bake for 12 to 15 minutes until lightly golden. Leave to cool for 2 minutes before transferring onto a wire cooling rack. Once cool, store in an airtight container.

TIP

It is easier to chop candied cherries if they have first been dipped in flour. Try using floured scissors instead of a knife.

Chocolate Pinwheels

Preparation time: 25 minutes + chilling ● *Cooking time: 8 to 10 minutes* ● *Makes: About 25*

A good, fun cookie, that is great for kid's parties.

INGREDIENTS

1 stick slightly salted butter, softened

⅓ cup superfine sugar

1 egg, beaten

1 tsp vanilla extract

1¼ cups all-purpose flour

Pinch of salt

1 oz semi-sweet chocolate

In a large bowl beat together the butter and sugar until light and fluffy. Beat in the egg and vanilla until blended. Sift the flour and salt onto the mixture and beat briefly until combined.

● Divide the dough in half and wrap one half in plastic wrap. Refrigerate until firm enough to roll. Melt the chocolate in a small bowl set over a saucepan of simmering water. Allow to cool slightly. Add the melted chocolate to remaining dough and mix until completely blended. Wrap chocolate dough in plastic wrap and refrigerate until firm enough to roll.

● On a lightly floured surface or between 2 sheets of plastic wrap, roll the vanilla dough to a rectangle. Repeat with the chocolate dough, rolling to the same size. If rolling between sheets of film, remove top sheet and place chocolate dough on top of plain dough. Roll up dough, from one short end as tightly as possible. Wrap tightly and refrigerate until very firm.

● Preheat oven to 375°F. Grease two baking sheets or line with nonstick baking parchment.

● Using a sharp knife, cut the dough roll into ¼-inch slices and place well apart onto the baking sheets. Bake for 7 to 10 minutes, until beginning to change color at the edges. Transfer to a wire rack and once completely cool, store in an airtight container.

TIP

The initial beating together of the butter and sugar is best done using an electric mixer. Beat for between 1 and 2 minutes, until light and fluffy. Reduce the speed to low to add any dry ingredients.

Orange Chocolate Cookies

Preparation time: 20 minutes ● Cooking time: 20 minutes ● Makes: About 18

Orange and chocolate are such a good combination. Try these with a cup of coffee anytime of the day.

INGREDIENTS

1½ cups all-purpose flour

¼ tsp baking powder

Pinch of salt

1 tsp grated orange rind

½ cup granulated sugar

¼ cup packed light brown sugar

1 stick slightly salted butter, softened

1 egg

½ tsp orange liqueur, optional

4 oz semi-sweet chocolate, coarse chopped

Preheat oven to 300°F. Grease two baking sheets or line with nonstick baking parchment.

● Sift the flour, baking powder, and salt into a bowl. In a large bowl blend the orange rind, sugars, and butter together until light and fluffy. Add the egg and orange liqueur and beat until light and well combined. Add the flour mixture and chopped chocolate. Mix together with a spoon to combine.

● Drop rounded tablespoons onto the baking sheet spaced 2 inches apart. Bake for 20 minutes until golden. Transfer cookies to a flat surface to cool completely. Once completely cool, store in an airtight container.

Mocha Chunk Cookies

Preparation time: 20 minutes ● Cooking time: 20 minutes ● Makes: About 16

A classic chunky style cookie with a rich coffee taste.

INGREDIENTS

1¼ cups all-purpose flour

2 Tbsp unsweetened cocoa powder

¼ tsp baking soda

Pinch of salt

2 tsp instant coffee granules

1 tsp coffee liqueur, optional

½ cup superfine sugar

¼ cup packed dark brown sugar

1 stick slightly salted butter, softened

1 egg

2 cups semi-sweet chocolate, coarse chopped

Preheat oven to 350°F. Grease 2 baking sheets or line with nonstick baking parchment.

● Into a medium sized bowl, sift the flour, cocoa, baking soda, and salt. In a small bowl dissolve coffee granules in coffee liqueur or hot water and set aside. In a large bowl, mix together the sugars. Add the butter and mix thoroughly until light. Add the eggs and coffee mixture and beat until smooth. Add the flour mixture and the chocolate chunks and mix gently with a spoon until well combined.

● Place rounded tablespoons of the mixture onto the baking sheets spaced 2 inches apart. Bake for 20 minutes until set. Transfer cookies to a flat surface to cool. Once completely cool, store in an airtight container.

Chocolate Chip and Raisin Cookies

Preparation time: 20 minutes ● *Cooking time: 18 to 20 minutes* ● *Makes: About 18*

A classic cookie jar cookie, moist, chewy, and delicious.

INGREDIENTS

1¼ cups all-purpose flour

¼ tsp baking powder

¼ cup packed light brown sugar

½ cup superfine sugar

1 stick slightly salted butter, softened

1 egg

1 tsp vanilla extract

1 cup raisins

1 cup semi-sweet chocolate chips

Preheat oven to 300°F. Grease two baking sheets or line with nonstick baking parchment.

● Combine the flour and baking powder in a medium-sized bowl. Place the sugars in a separate bowl, add the butter, then beat in the sugar until light and fluffy. Add the egg and vanilla and mix well. Add the flour mixture, raisins, and chocolate and blend well with a spoon.

● Drop rounded tablespoons of the mixture onto the baking sheet spaced 2 inches apart. Bake for 18 to 20 minutes until lightly golden. Remove cookies to a cool flat surface to cool completely. Store in an airtight container.

Coconut and Chocolate Crunch

Preparation time: 20 minutes • Cooking time: 20 minutes • Makes: About 28

The coconut in these cookies makes them really moist and chewy. This makes a good lunch-box cookie.

INGREDIENTS

1 stick slightly salted butter, softened

⅓ cup packed light brown sugar

1 egg, beaten

1 tsp vanilla extract

1 cup all-purpose flour

½ tsp baking powder

Pinch of salt

1 cup shredded coconut

¾ cup semi-sweet chocolate chips

¾ cup hazelnuts, fine chopped

Preheat oven to 300°F. Grease two baking sheets or line with nonstick baking parchment.

● In a medium bowl beat together the butter and sugar. Beat in the egg and vanilla extract. Mix thoroughly until light and fluffy. Sift in the flour, baking powder, and salt. Stir in the coconut, chocolate, and chopped nuts. Mix well with a spoon to combine.

● Drop rounded tablespoons of the cookie dough (spaced well apart) onto the baking sheets. Bake the cookies for 20 minutes until lightly golden, then transfer to a wire rack to cool. Once completely cool, store in an airtight container.

White Chocolate Cashew Thins

Preparation time: 20 minutes • Cooking time: 8 to 10 minutes • Makes: About 30

These cookies are really thin and crunchy, try eating them with ice cream.

INGREDIENTS

½ stick slightly salted butter, softened

¼ cup packed light brown sugar

¼ cup corn syrup

½ cup fine chopped salted cashews

⅓ cup all-purpose flour

1 tsp vanilla extract

6 oz white chocolate, coarse chopped

Preheat oven to 350°F. Grease two baking sheets or line with nonstick baking parchment.

● In a saucepan, melt the butter. Add the brown sugar and corn syrup, then bring to a boil stirring constantly for 3 to 4 minutes until the sugar dissolves. Remove from the heat. Stir in the cashews, flour, and vanilla.

● Drop half teaspoon mounds spaced well apart onto the baking sheet. Use the back of a spoon to spread each mound into a circle. Bake for 8 to 10 minutes or until golden-brown. Turn the baking sheet around halfway through cooking. Cool on the baking sheet for 1 minute, then transfer to a wire rack to cool completely.

● Melt the chocolate in a small bowl set over a saucepan of barely simmering water. Dip a fork into the melted chocolate and drizzle over the cookies. Return to cooling rack to set. Once set, store in an airtight container. Not suitable for freezing.

White Chocolate Chunk and Pecan Cookies

Preparation time: 20 minutes ● Cooking time: 20 minutes ● Makes: About 26

These cookies are really rich and chocolatey.

INGREDIENTS

2¾ cups all-purpose flour, sifted

½ tsp baking powder

Pinch of salt

1 cup packed light brown sugar

½ cup superfine sugar

1½ sticks butter, softened

2 eggs

1 tsp vanilla extract

1 cup pecans, coarse chopped

8 oz white chocolate, coarse chopped

Preheat oven to 300°F. Grease two baking sheets or line with nonstick baking parchment.

● Sift the flour, baking powder, and salt into a bowl. In a large bowl mix together the sugars and butter until well blended. Add the eggs and vanilla and beat until light and fluffy. Add the flour, pecans, and white chocolate and mix together with a spoon until combined.

● Drop rounded tablespoons of the mixture onto the greased or lined baking sheets spaced about 2 inches apart. Bake the cookies for 20 minutes until golden-brown. Transfer to a flat surface to cool. Once completely cool, store in an airtight container.

Chocolate Cream-filled Hearts

Preparation time: 40 minutes + chilling ● *Cooking time: 12 to 15 minutes Makes: About 18*

A special occasion cookie with a delicious chocolate-fudge filling.

INGREDIENTS

1½ sticks slightly salted butter, softened

1 cup confectioners' sugar

2 tsp vanilla extract

1¾ cups all-purpose flour

FILLING

⅓ cup heavy cream

½ cup semi-sweet chocolate chips

Beat the butter until soft and fluffy. Add the confectioners' sugar and vanilla and beat until smooth. Stir in the flour. Gather dough into 2 balls and flatten into discs. Wrap in plastic wrap. Refrigerate for 1 hour until firm.

● Preheat oven to 325°F. Grease two baking sheets or line with nonstick baking parchment.

● On a lightly floured surface, roll out the dough to ¼-inch thick. Cut out 2-inch hearts with a cutter. Repeat with all of the dough. Place the cookies on baking sheets spaced 1-inch apart. Bake for 12 to 15 minutes until firm. Transfer to a wire rack to cool.

● Place the cream in a small saucepan and warm briefly, add in the chocolate chips and stir until melted. Transfer to a small bowl. Set to one side and allow to cool at room temperature.

● To assemble, spread 1 teaspoon of the chocolate filling on the bottom side of half the cookies. Top with bottom side of another cookie to form a sandwich. Repeat with remaining cookies and cream. These cookies are best eaten soon after filling as they contain fresh cream; however, they may be stored for up to 2 days in an airtight container in the refrigerator.

Ultimate Chocolate Chip Cookies

Preparation time: 20 minutes ● *Cooking time: 18 to 20 minutes* ● *Makes: 10 to 12*

Huge cookies, the ultimate indulgence, a cookie packed with 3 types of chocolate. Make as large as you dare.

INGREDIENTS

1½ cups flour
½ tsp baking powder
Pinch of salt
1 stick slightly salted butter, softened
½ cup packed light brown sugar
½ Tbsp honey
1 egg
1 tsp vanilla extract
½ cup semi-sweet chocolate, chopped
½ cup milk chocolate, chopped
½ cup white chocolate, chopped

Preheat oven to 325°F. Grease two baking sheets or line with nonstick baking parchment.

● Sift the flour, baking powder, and salt together into a bowl. Beat together the softened butter and light brown sugar until light and fluffy. Gradually beat in the egg, vanilla, and honey. Stir in the flour mixture and all of the chocolate. Mix all the ingredients together until they are just combined.

● Drop about 2 tablespoonfuls of the dough spaced 2 to 3 inches apart on baking sheets. Bake the cookies for 18 to 22 minutes, depending on their size. Transfer them to a wire rack to cool. Once completely cool, store in an airtight container.

Chocolate Ginger Cookies

Preparation time: 25 minutes ● *Cooking time: 18 to 20 minutes* ● *Makes: About 20*

Ginger preserves give a lovely flavor without the harshness sometimes associated with ground ginger.

INGREDIENTS

½ cup packed dark brown sugar

¼ cup granulated sugar

1 stick slightly salted butter, softened

1 egg

1 tsp ginger or corn syrup

1½ cups all-purpose flour

½ tsp baking powder

Pinch of salt

½ cup semi-sweet chocolate chips

⅓ cup ginger preserves

Preheat oven to 300°F. Grease two baking sheets or line with nonstick baking parchment.

● In a large bowl blend the sugars together. Add the butter and beat together until light. Add the egg and ginger or corn syrup and mix well. Sift the flour, baking powder, and salt into the mixture. Add the chocolate chips and ginger preserve and mix thoroughly with a spoon.

● Drop rounded tablespoons onto a baking sheet spaced 2 inches apart. Bake the cookies for 18 to 20 minutes or until golden-brown. Transfer cookies to a flat surface to allow to cool completely. Store in an airtight container.

Red, White, and Blue Cookies

Preparation time: 20 minutes ● *Cooking time: 8 to 10 minutes* ● *Makes: About 36*

Dried sour cherries and blueberries make a lovely sweet sour contrast to the sweet white chocolate.

INGREDIENTS

1 cup all-purpose flour

¼ cup unsweetened cocoa powder

1 tsp baking powder

Pinch of salt

1 stick slightly salted butter, softened

1 cup granulated sugar

1 egg

½ tsp vanilla extract

1 cup white chocolate chips

¼ cup rough chopped dried sour cherries

¼ cup dried blueberries

Preheat oven to 350°F. Grease two baking sheets or line with nonstick baking parchment.

● Sift the flour, cocoa, baking powder, and salt into a medium bowl. Beat together the butter and sugar in a large bowl until light and fluffy. Beat in the egg and vanilla until blended. Beat in the flour mixture at low speed until just combined. Stir in the chocolate chips, sour cherries, and blueberries.

● Drop rounded teaspoonfuls of the dough onto the baking sheets. Bake for 8 to 10 minutes, until just firm. Transfer to a wire rack to cool. Once completely cool, store in airtight container.

Chocolate Refrigerator Cookies

Preparation time: 20 minutes + chilling ● Cooking time: 10 to 12 minutes ● Makes: About 45

This dough enables you to bake fresh cookies whenever you want them. It makes about 45 cookies altogether.

INGREDIENTS

1¾ cups all-purpose flour

1 tsp baking powder

1 stick slightly salted butter, softened

¾ cup superfine sugar

⅓ cup fine grated semi-sweet chocolate

1 tsp vanilla extract

1 egg, beaten

Sift together the flour and baking powder. Blend in the butter using the fingertips until mixture resembles fine bread crumbs. Add sugar and chocolate. Mix to form a dough with vanilla and beaten egg.

● Shape into a sausage. Transfer to a length of plastic wrap. Wrap plastic around dough and twist ends. Work backwards and forwards to form a roll about 2-inches in diameter. Refrigerate for one hour.

● When ready to make the cookies, preheat oven to 375°F. Grease two baking sheets or line with nonstick baking parchment.

● Cut very thin slices from the dough roll and place well apart onto the baking sheets. Bake for 10 to 12 minutes until pale gold. Cool on a wire cooling rack. The remaining roll can be returned to refrigerator and left for up to a week until required. Alternatively, freeze the dough for up to 1 month. Store the baked cookies in an airtight container.

TIP

A food processor can be used to blend the butter into the flour.

Chocolate and Orange Sandwiches

Preparation time: 45 minutes + chilling ● Cooking time: 8 minutes ● Makes: About 25

Orange cream is sandwiched between wafer cookies topped with melted chocolate.

INGREDIENTS

1 cup all-purpose flour

⅓ cup unsweetened cocoa powder

1 stick slightly salted butter, softened

¼ cup superfine sugar

1 egg

FILLING

½ cup whipping cream

7 oz white chocolate, chopped

1 tsp orange extract or liqueur

TOPPING

5 oz semi-sweet chocolate

¾ stick unsalted butter, chopped

Sift the flour and cocoa into a bowl. In a separate large bowl, beat the butter and sugar together until light and fluffy. Gradually beat in the egg until well combined; stir in the flour-cocoa mixture. Spoon the dough into a piece of plastic wrap and shape into a flat disc. Wrap well and refrigerate for 2 hours or overnight until firm.

● Preheat oven to 350°F. Grease two baking sheets or line with nonstick baking parchment.

● On a lightly floured surface roll out half of the cookie dough as thin as possible. Using a 2-inch heart-shaped cutter, cut out as many cookies as possible. Re-roll and cut out trimmings. Bake the cookies for 6 to 8 minutes until set. Cool on a wire rack and then repeat the process with remaining dough.

● Place the whipping cream in a saucepan over a medium heat and bring to a boil. Remove from the heat and add the white chocolate, stirring constantly until melted and smooth. Stir in orange extract or liqueur and pour into a bowl. Cool until firm but not hard, about 1 hour.

● Beat the orange filling with a wooden spoon until smooth. Spread a little filling onto half the cookies and immediately cover with another cookie pressing together very gently. Repeat with remaining cookies. Allow to set at room temperature.

● Melt the semi-sweet chocolate and butter in a small saucepan until smooth. Remove from the heat and cool until thickened slightly, about 20 to 30 minutes. Using a metal spatula, spread a small amount of chocolate onto the top of each cookie. Refrigerate until set. Once set, store in an airtight container in layers separated by waxed paper. These cookies are best eaten soon after filling as they contain fresh cream; however, they may be stored for up to 2 days in the refrigerator.

Chocolate-dipped Orange Shortbread

Preparation time: 30 minutes ● *Cooking time: 10 minutes* ● *Makes: About 35*

These elegant piped cookies make a great addition to a smart afternoon tea.

INGREDIENTS

2¼ cups all-purpose flour

Pinch of salt

1 tsp baking powder

2 sticks butter, softened

1 cup granulated sugar

1 egg

1 tsp grated orange rind

4 oz semi-sweet chocolate, chopped

Preheat oven to 350°F. Grease two baking sheets or line with nonstick baking parchment.

● Combine the flour, salt, and baking powder in a bowl. Beat the butter and sugar in a large bowl until light and fluffy. Beat in the egg and orange rind. Fold in the flour until just combined.

● Spoon the mixture into a pastry bag fitted with a large star tube. Pipe 1½-inch swirls, spaced 2 inches apart onto the baking sheets. Bake 10 to 12 minutes until just beginning to turn light gold around the edges. Transfer to a wire rack to cool completely.

● Melt the chocolate in a small bowl over a saucepan of barely simmering water. Dip the top of each cookie into the melted chocolate. Place cookies on a wire rack until the chocolate is set. Once completely cool, store in an airtight container.

Marble Cookies

Preparation time: 20 minutes ● *Cooking time: 18 minutes* ● *Makes: About 26*

A really unusual looking cookie with a rich velvety chocolate taste.

INGREDIENTS

2¼ cups all-purpose flour

½ tsp baking powder

Pinch of salt

½ cup packed light brown sugar

½ cup granulated sugar

1 stick slightly salted butter, softened

1 egg

½ cup sour cream

1 tsp vanilla extract

1 cup semi-sweet chocolate chips

Preheat oven to 300°F. Grease two baking sheets or line with nonstick baking parchment.

● Sift the flour, baking powder, and salt into a bowl. Beat together the butter and sugars in a large bowl until well blended. Add the egg, sour cream, and vanilla and beat until light and fluffy. Add the flour mixture and blend until just combined.

● Melt the chocolate chips in a bowl set over a saucepan of barely simmering water. Cool chocolate for a few minutes, then pour into the cookie mixture. Using a wooden spoon very lightly fold chocolate into the cookie mixture. Do not mix completely.

● Drop rounded tablespoonfuls of the mixture spaced 2 inches apart onto the baking sheets. Bake for 20 minutes. Transfer to a flat surface to cool. Once completely cool, store in an airtight container.

Sesame Chocolate Chewies

Preparation time: 20 minutes ●
Cooking time: 12 minutes ● Makes: About 12

A thin and crispy cookie great with ice cream.

INGREDIENTS

2 egg whites

1½ cups confectioners' sugar

⅓ cup unsweetened cocoa powder

2 Tbsp all-purpose flour

½ cup sesame seeds

Preheat oven to 350°F. Line a large baking sheet with nonstick baking parchment.

● Using an electric hand mixer whisk the egg whites together until frothy. Add the sugar, cocoa and flour to the bowl. Beat slowly firstly to incorporate the ingredients, then increase the speed of the hand mixer and beat until the cookie mixture thickens. Carefully fold in the sesame seeds.

● Place tablespoonfuls of the cookie mixture about 1 inch apart on the baking sheet. Bake the cookies for 12 minutes. Transfer the cookies using a spatula to a wire rack and allow to cool at room temperature. Once cool, store in an airtight container. Not suitable for freezing.

Chocolate Pistachio Cookies

Preparation time: 20 minutes ● Cooking time:
15 to 20 minutes ● Makes: About 12

Sweet pistachio nuts are lovely when combined with chocolate in this classic style cookie.

INGREDIENTS

1 stick slightly salted butter, softened

¼ cup superfine sugar

½ tsp vanilla extract

1 cup all-purpose flour

½ tsp baking powder

½ cup pistachio nuts, coarsely chopped

1 oz semi-sweet chocolate, chopped

Preheat oven to 375°F. Grease two baking sheets or line with nonstick baking parchment.

● Beat together the butter, sugar, and vanilla until light and creamy. Stir in the flour and baking powder, and then mix well. Add nuts and chocolate and mix to combine.

● Drop rounded teaspoonfuls of the mixture 1 inch apart onto the baking sheets. Bake for 15 to 20 minutes. Leave to cool onto the baking sheet for 2 minutes. Transfer to a wire rack to cool completely. Once completely cool, store in an airtight container.

Chocolate Pockets

Preparation time: 45 minutes + chilling ● *Cooking time: 15 minutes* ● *Makes: About 12*

These little pastry pockets are filled with a melt-in-the-mouth creamy chocolate filling

INGREDIENTS

1½ sticks slightly salted butter, softened

½ cup confectioners' sugar

3 Tbsp light brown sugar

2 egg yolks

1 tsp vanilla extract

1¾ cups all-purpose flour

FILLING

½ cup heavy cream

1 cup semi-sweet chocolate chips

In a medium bowl, beat together the butter and sugars until well blended. Add the egg yolks and vanilla and beat well until light and fluffy. Add the flour and stir until combined. Gather into a ball and flatten to a disk. Place between 2 sheets of plastic wrap and refrigerate for 1 hour.

● Meanwhile, heat the cream until just hot but not boiling. Remove pan from the heat and add the chocolate chips and stir well until melted.

● Preheat oven to 325°F. Grease two baking sheets or line with nonstick baking parchment.

● On a lightly floured surface, roll out half of the dough to ¼-inch thick. Cut out circles using a 2-inch round cutter. Place on baking sheets spaced 1 inch apart.

● Repeat with the remaining dough but set circles aside. Drop 1 teaspoon of the chocolate filling in the center of each circle onto the baking sheet, and then top with another circle. Use a fork to press down and completely seal the edges of the pockets. Bake for about 15 minutes or until golden-brown on the top. Transfer cookies with a spatula to a wire rack to cool. Once completely cool, store in an airtight container in a cool place. Not suitable for freezing.

Chocolate-frosted Heart Cookies

Preparation time: 1 hour + chilling ● *Cooking time: 8 to 10 minutes* ● *Makes: About 45*

Decorate these little cookies with sugar strands, sugar crystals, or silver and gold dragées, depending on the occasion.

INGREDIENTS

1 stick slightly salted butter, softened

⅓ cup brown sugar

¾ cup molasses

1 tsp ground ginger

1 tsp cinnamon

½ tsp ground cloves

1 tsp baking soda

1 egg, beaten

4 cups all-purpose flour

DECORATION

1 cup confectioners' sugar

2 Tbsp unsweetened cocoa powder

1 egg white

Sugar strands or dragées to decorate

Preheat oven to 325°F. Grease two baking sheets or line with nonstick baking parchment.

● Cut the butter into pieces and place in a large bowl. Place the sugar, molasses, and spices in a saucepan and bring to a boil. Add the baking soda and pour into the bowl with the butter. Stir until butter has melted, then stir in the egg. Sift in the flour and mix until thoroughly combined. Chill the dough until firm enough to roll out.

● Roll out on a lightly floured surface to ¼-inch thick. Cut into heart shapes with a 3-inch cutter. Place onto the baking sheets and bake in batches for 8 to 10 minutes. Transfer to a wire rack to cool completely.

● Sift the confectioners' sugar and cocoa into a bowl. Beat in the egg white and continue beating until soft peak consistency is reached. Spoon frosting onto cookies to cover and then decorate with sugar strands or dragées. Return the cookies to wire rack to set. Once set, store in an airtight container.

Monkey Puzzles

Preparation time: 45 minutes ● *Cooking time: 10 minutes* ● *Makes: About 14*

The cookies are really rich and chocolately, great with a cup of coffee.

INGREDIENTS

½ cup all-purpose flour

1½ Tbsp unsweetened cocoa powder

¼ tsp baking powder

¾ stick slightly salted butter, softened

6 Tbsp corn syrup

½ cup branflakes, coarsely crushed

6 oz semi-sweet chocolate, rough chopped

Preheat oven to 350°F. Grease two baking sheets or line with nonstick baking parchment.

● Sift the flour, cocoa, and baking powder into a bowl. Beat together the butter and syrup until soft. Stir in the flour mixture until combined. Blend in the branflakes.

● Place spoonfuls of the mixture spaced apart onto the baking sheets. Bake for 10 minutes. Transfer to a wire rack to cool.

● Melt the chocolate in a bowl set over a saucepan of barely simmering water. When the cookies are completely cold, spread spoonfuls of the melted chocolate over the surface of the cookies then return to the wire rack to allow the chocolate to set. Once set, store in an airtight container.

TIP

Decorate these cookies with white chocolate, if liked. Melt it as above and drizzle it over the cookies from the end of a spoon.

Chocolate-dipped Cinnamon Meringues

Preparation time: 30 minutes + cooling ● *Cooking time: 1 hour 15 minutes* ● *Makes: About 36*

These delicate little meringues are easy to make and are great for a special occasion.

INGREDIENTS

2 egg whites
¼ tsp cream of tartar
Pinch of salt
½ cup superfine sugar
½ tsp vanilla extract
3 Tbsp unsweetened cocoa powder
¼ tsp cinnamon
4 oz semi-sweet chocolate, rough chopped

Preheat oven to 225°F. Line two cookie sheets with aluminum foil.

● Beat the egg whites in a large mixing bowl with an electric hand mixer until foamy. Add the cream of tartar and salt and continue to beat until soft peaks form. Gradually beat in the sugar, 1 tablespoon at a time and then continue to beat until stiff.

● Gently fold in the vanilla, cocoa powder, and cinnamon with a large spoon until just blended. Spoon the meringue mixture into a large pastry bag fitted with a large star tube. Pipe into 3-inch lengths onto the baking sheets. Bake for 1 hour 15 minutes. Turn off oven and leave meringues in the oven to cool for 1½ hours or preferably overnight.

● Melt the chocolate in a bowl over a saucepan of barely simmering water. Gently peel the meringues away from the foil. Dip the tip of each meringue into the melted chocolate. Transfer the meringues to a wire rack and let stand until chocolate is set. Once set, store the meringues in an airtight container.

Chocolate Wafers

Preparation time: 20 minutes ● Cooking time: 15 minutes ● Makes: About 28

These nutty thins are great served with ice cream.

INGREDIENTS

1 stick slightly salted butter, softened
¼ cup superfine sugar
½ cup corn syrup
1 egg
½ tsp vanilla extract
1 cup all-purpose flour
1 Tbsp unsweetened cocoa powder
¼ tsp baking soda
¾ cup chopped mixed nuts

Preheat oven to 350°F. Line two baking sheets with nonstick baking parchment.

● Beat the butter, sugar, and syrup together until light and fluffy. Thoroughly beat in the egg and vanilla. Sift the flour, cocoa, and baking soda onto the butter mixture. Lightly stir into the mixture with the chopped mixed nuts.

● Place walnut-sized spoonfuls spaced 2 inches apart onto the baking sheets. Bake for 15 minutes. Lift from the baking sheet with a thin, metal spatula and lay over a lightly oiled rolling pin to produce a curved shape. Leave to cool on the rolling pin for a few minutes before transferring to a wire rack to cool completely. Once completely cool, store in an airtight container.

Almond and Chocolate Clusters

Preparation time: 25 minutes ● Cooking time: 15 minutes ● Makes: About 22

A light nutty cookie which you can either dip or drizzle with chocolate.

INGREDIENTS

1 stick slightly salted butter, softened

⅔ cup superfine sugar

1 egg

½ tsp almond extract

¼ cup ground blanched almonds

1 cup slivered almonds

1¼ cups all-purpose flour

TOPPING

¼ cup heavy cream

1 cup semi-sweet chocolate chips

2 tsp corn syrup

Preheat oven to 350°F. Grease two baking sheets or line with nonstick baking parchment.

● Beat together the butter and sugar until well blended. Add the egg and almond extract and beat until light and fluffy. Add the ground almonds and flour then stir until just combined. Form dough into walnut-sized balls and roll in the slivered almonds, pressing down slightly to coat each ball thoroughly.

● Place the balls onto the baking sheets spaced 2 inches apart. Bake for 15 minutes. Transfer cookies to a cool flat surface covered with waxed paper.

● Meanwhile, heat the cream, but do not allow to boil. Remove from the heat and stir in the chocolate chips and corn syrup. Cover and allow to stand for 10 minutes. Mix glaze gently with a wooden spoon until smooth.

● When cookies are cool, drizzle patterns on them with the warm chocolate or dip half each cookie into the chocolate. Return the cookies to the wax paper and place in the refrigerator until set. Once set, store in an airtight container. These cookies are best eaten soon after decorating as they contain fresh cream; however, they may be stored for up to 2 days in the refrigerator.

Hazelnut Chocolate Crescents

Preparation time: 30 minutes + chilling ● *Cooking time: 15 to 20 minutes* ● *Makes: 24*

These delicious nutty shortbread crescents can be dipped or drizzled with chocolate.

INGREDIENTS

¾ cup hazelnuts, unskinned

2 oz semi-sweet chocolate, coarsely chopped, then halved

4 Tbsp granulated sugar

1 cup all-purpose flour

Pinch of salt

1½ sticks plus 1 Tbsp slightly salted butter

Preheat oven to 350°F. Spread the hazelnuts on a baking sheet. Toast for 12 to 15 minutes until lightly browned. Leave to cool completely.

● Melt half the chocolate in a small bowl over a saucepan of barely simmering water. Remove and set aside to cool.

● Process the nuts and 1 tablespoon of sugar in a food processor until fine, do not overprocess. Transfer to a medium bowl with the flour and salt. Beat the butter and remaining sugar until light and fluffy. Beat in the melted chocolate and the nut mixture and mix well to combine. Cover and refrigerate for 2 hours.

● Preheat oven to 350°F. Grease 2 baking sheets or line with nonstick baking parchment.

● Shape teaspoonfuls of the dough into crescents and place onto the baking sheets spaced 2 inches apart. Bake for 15 to 20 minutes. Transfer to a wire rack to cool completely.

● Melt the remaining chocolate in a bowl set over a saucepan of barely simmering water. Remove from the heat. Dip one end of the cookie into the chocolate or drizzle the surface with a thin stream of chocolate. Return to wire rack and allow chocolate to set. Once set, store the cookies in airtight containers. Not suitable for freezing.

Strawberry Cocoa Sandwich Stars

Preparation time: 1 hour + chilling ● *Cooking time: 8 to 10 minutes* ● *Makes: About 20*

This makes a lovely special occasion cookie.

INGREDIENTS

1¾ cups all-purpose flour

⅓ cup unsweetened cocoa powder

1½ tsp baking powder

½ tsp ground cinnamon

Pinch of salt

1½ sticks lightly salted butter

½ cup superfine sugar

¼ cup light brown sugar

1 egg, beaten

2 tsp vanilla extract

Grated rind 1 lemon

FILLING

1 cup strawberry jam

1 Tbsp lemon juice

1 Tbsp superfine sugar

Confectioners' sugar for dusting

Sift the flour, cocoa, baking powder, cinnamon, and salt. In a separate bowl, beat together the butter and sugars until light and creamy. Gradually beat in the egg, vanilla, and lemon rind until well combined. Scrape the dough onto a piece of plastic film, cover with another sheet and press the dough into a disk. Refrigerate until firm enough to roll.

● Grease two baking sheets or line with nonstick baking parchment.

● On a lightly floured surface roll out half of the dough to ⅛-inch thick. Refrigerate remaining dough. Using a 3½-inch star-shaped cutter, cut out an even number of cookies. Using a 1-inch or 1½-inch star-shaped cutter, cut out the center of half of the cookies. Arrange cookies on baking sheets spaced 1 inch apart. Cover and refrigerate for 15 minutes.

● Preheat oven to 350°F.

● Bake cookies for 8 to 10 minutes. Cool onto the baking sheets for a couple of minutes then transfer to wire rack to cool completely. Repeat with remaining dough.

● Place the strawberry jam, sugar, and lemon juice in a small pan. Heat gently until runny. Sieve into a small bowl and allow to cool. Spread about 1 teaspoon of the strawberry mixture on each whole biscuit star to within ½-inch of the edge. Arrange cut out biscuit stars on a wire cooling rack. Dust liberally with confectioners' sugar. Carefully place cut out tops over whole stars, gently pressing together. Allow cookies to set for 1 hour at room temperature. Once set, store in an airtight container. Not suitable for freezing.

Chocolate and Chili Cookies

Preparation time: 20 minutes ● Cooking time: 10 to 12 minutes ● Makes: About 20

An unusual but fantastic combination.

1 stick of butter

¼ cup superfine sugar

¼ cup packed dark brown sugar

1 egg, beaten

½ tsp vanilla extract

1 cup all-purpose flour

½ tsp baking powder

½ to 1 tsp chili flakes

⅔ cup semi-sweet chocolate chips

Preheat oven to 350°F. Grease two baking sheets or line with nonstick baking parchment.

● Beat the butter and sugar together in a medium bowl, until light and fluffy. Gradually add the egg and vanilla and beat well. Stir the flour, baking powder, and chili flakes into the butter mixture and mix well to combine. Stir in the chocolate chips.

● Drop teaspoonfuls spaced 1 inch apart onto the baking sheets. Bake for 10 to 12 minutes. Remove with a spatula and place on a flat surface to cool. Once completely cool, store cookies in an airtight container.

Chocolate Viennese Whirls

Preparation time: 25 minutes ● Cooking time: 20 minutes ● Makes: About 20

A rich and attractive cookie, great for a smart afternoon tea party.

1½ sticks butter

½ cup confectioners' sugar

1½ cups all-purpose flour

½ tsp vanilla extract

10 candied cherries, halved

6 oz semi-sweet chocolate, coarse chopped

Preheat oven to 325°F. Grease two baking sheets or line with nonstick baking parchment.

● Beat together the butter and sugar until light and fluffy. Sift the flour into the bowl, add the vanilla and mix well to combine.

● Spoon the mixture into a pastry bag fitted with a large star-shaped tube. Pipe flat whirls onto the baking sheets. Put half a cherry on each one. Bake for 20 minutes until just golden. Leave to cool onto the baking sheet for 5 minutes then transfer to a wire rack to cool completely.

● Meanwhile, melt the chocolate in a small bowl set over a saucepan of simmering water. When the cookies are cold, dip into the melted chocolate. Return to the wire rack until the chocolate has set, then store in an airtight container.

Crunchy Chocolate Chip Cookies

Preparation time: 15 minutes ● Cooking time: 10 to 12 minutes ● Makes: About 20

A cookie jar classic with a twist, crisp on the outside and chewy on the inside.

INGREDIENTS

1 stick slightly salted butter, softened

¼ cup superfine sugar

⅓ cup packed dark brown sugar

1 egg, beaten

½ tsp vanilla extract

1 cup all-purpose flour

½ tsp baking powder

6 oz Dairy Crunch™ or other chocolate containing crisped rice, chopped

Preheat oven to 350°F. Grease two baking sheets or line with nonstick baking parchment.

● Beat the butter and sugar together in a medium bowl, until light and fluffy. Gradually add the egg and vanilla and beat well. Stir the flour and baking powder into the butter mixture and mix well to combine. Stir in the chocolate chunks.

● Drop teaspoons spaced 1 inch apart onto the baking sheets. Bake for 10 to 12 minutes. Remove with a spatula and place on a flat surface to cool. Once completely cool, store cookies in an airtight container.

TIP

Other flavored chocolates could be substituted. Dark chocolate orange is particularly good, so is rum and raisin, and mint-flavored chocolates that contain small pieces of crunchy mint are great too. The chunks should be left quite large to get the maximum effect from their flavors.

Raspberry and White Chocolate Chunkies

Preparation time: 20 minutes ● *Cooking time: 20 minutes* ● *Makes: About 16*

A sweet and fruity cookie, great served with vanilla ice cream.

INGREDIENTS

1½ cups all-purpose flour

¼ tsp baking soda

Pinch of salt

⅔ cup superfine sugar

1 stick slightly salted butter, softened

1 Tbsp beaten egg

⅓ cup sieved raspberry jam or preserve

6 oz white chocolate, coarse chopped

Preheat oven to 300°F. Grease two baking sheets or line with nonstick baking parchment.

● Sift the flour, baking soda, and salt and set aside. Beat together the sugar and butter until light and fluffy. Beat in the egg and then the raspberry jam. Add the flour mixture and white chocolate chunks and mix to combine.

● Drop tablespoonfuls onto the baking sheets spaced 2 inches apart. Bake for 20 minutes. Transfer to a cool surface. When cold, store in an airtight container.

Chocolate Fudge Cookies

Preparation time: 20 minutes ● *Cooking time: 18 to 20 minutes* ● *Makes: About 28*

These cookies have a pure chocolate taste.

INGREDIENTS

6 oz semi-sweet chocolate, fine chopped

1¼ cups all-purpose flour

¼ cup unsweetened cocoa powder

½ tsp baking powder

Pinch of salt

1 stick slightly salted butter, softened

1 cup packed dark brown sugar

2 eggs

1 tsp vanilla extract

3 oz white chocolate coarse chopped

Preheat oven to 300°F. Grease two baking sheets or line with nonstick baking parchment.

● Melt the chocolate in a bowl set over a saucepan of simmering water. Set aside to cool slightly.

● Sift the flour, cocoa, baking soda, and salt and set aside. In a separate bowl, beat the butter and sugar until light and fluffy. Beat in the eggs and vanilla. Mix in the cooled chocolate and fold in the flour until combined.

● Drop rounded tablespoonfuls of the dough spaced 2 inches apart onto the baking sheet. Bake for 18 to 20 minutes. Cool on the sheet for one minute then transfer to a wire rack to cool completely.

● Melt the white chocolate in a small bowl set over a saucepan of barely simmering water. When the cookies are cool, dip a fork into the melted chocolate and drizzle over the cookies. Leave to on wire racks to set the topping, then store the cookies in an airtight container.

Chocolate Mint Cookies

Preparation time: 20 minutes ● *Cooking time: 20 minutes* ● *Makes: About 18*

A nice late in the day cookie.

INGREDIENTS

1½ cups all-purpose flour

¼ tsp baking powder

Pinch of salt

¼ cup unsweetened cocoa powder

⅓ cup packed light brown sugar

⅓ cup granulated sugar

1 stick slightly salted butter, softened

1 egg

1 tsp mint extract

⅔ cup semi-sweet chocolate chips

Preheat oven to 300°F. Grease two baking sheets or line with nonstick baking parchment.

● Sift the flour, cocoa, baking powder, salt, and cocoa into a bowl and set aside. In a separate bowl, beat together the sugars and butter until light. Beat in the eggs and mint extract until thoroughly blended. Add the flour mixture and chocolate chips, mix well to combine. Do not over mix.

● Drop rounded tablespoonfuls of the mixture onto the baking sheets spaced 1½ inches apart. Bake 20 minutes apart. Bake 20 minutes until lightly golden. Transfer to a cool flat surface. When completely cool, store in an airtight container.

Chocolate Rugelach

Preparation time: 45 minutes + chilling ● *Cooking time: 20 minutes* ● *Makes: About 60*

A traditional Jewish cookie much loved by children.

INGREDIENTS

2 cups strong flour
Pinch of salt
1 stick slightly salted butter, softened
½ cup cream cheese
¼ cup soured cream
3 Tbsp superfine sugar
1 egg, separated
⅔ cup apricot jam
3 oz semi-sweet chocolate, finely chopped
2 Tbsp superfine sugar

Sift the flour and salt into a large bowl. Place the flour with the butter, cream cheese, sour cream, sugar, and egg yolk in a food processor. Process until a soft dough forms. Shape dough into a ball and flatten into a disk. Wrap in plastic wrap and refrigerate for 1 to 2 hours.

● Preheat oven to 350°F. Grease two baking sheets or line with nonstick baking parchment.

● On a lightly floured surface roll out one quarter of the dough to ⅛-inch thick. Using a plate as a guide, cut the dough into a 10- to 11-inch round. Spread with 3 tablespoons of apricot jam, leaving a small border around the edge. Sprinkle with the chopped chocolate.

● Cut this round into 12 equal-sized wedges. Starting the widest end, roll up each wedge jellyroll style. Place on the baking sheet spaced 1-inch apart. Beat the egg white with 1 tablespoon of water, and brush each roll with a little of the egg and water. Sprinkle each roll with a little sugar. Repeat with remaining dough.

● Bake until puffed and golden-brown. Turn the baking sheet around halfway through cooking. Cool onto the baking sheet for a few minutes then transfer to a wire cooling rack to cool completely.

Chocolate Crescents

Preparation time: 20 minutes ● Cooking time: 15 minutes ● Makes: About 30

Dusted with plenty of sugar, these make a great holiday cookie.

INGREDIENTS

2 cups all-purpose flour

¼ cup unsweetened cocoa powder

1 stick slightly salted butter, softened

¾ cup superfine sugar

1 tsp vanilla extract

1 egg

Confectioners' sugar to decorate

Preheat oven to 325°F. Grease two baking sheets or line with nonstick baking parchment.

● Combine the flour and cocoa in a small bowl. In a medium bowl, beat together the butter and sugar until creamy. Add the vanilla and egg and beat well until light and fluffy. Fold in the flour-cocoa mixture until just blended.

● Shape a tablespoonful of the mixture into a 3-inch long log. Bend into a crescent shape. Repeat with remaining dough. Place onto the baking sheets, spaced 1 inch apart. Bake for 15 minutes. Cool onto the baking sheet and then transfer to a wire rack. While still warm, roll the cookies in confectioners' sugar to coat. Once completely cool, store in an airtight container. Freeze for up to 1 month without the confectioners' sugar.

Children's Cookies

This part of the book has some creative ideas to make your snacks a bit more fun and they have all been specially written for children to make. Some of them are ideal to take in lunch boxes, like the jam ones, for example. Others are more for parties, such as the Chocolate Octopuses or the Snakes, and some are for when you just feel hungry.

I like making cookies because they are quick and easy, and most people eat them. If I make a batch of cookies on Monday I know that they will be gone by Friday. They are great to share—sometimes I take some Chocolate Chip Cookies to school and give them to my friends. I made cookies for my teachers at Christmas too and put them in pretty china bowls. They were really pleased with them.

A tip from an experienced cook (sure I am experienced): if you are quite slow at cooking (like me) or you don't have an electric mixer, then do not preheat the oven immediately—wait for a bit! Good Luck.

Katherine Gray, aged 11.

After-school Snacks

Alphabet Cookies	200
Teddy Bears Picnic	200
Balloon Cookies	203
Big White Chocolate and Apricot Cookies	204
Sunflower Cookies	205
Lemon-scented Peanut Butter Cookies	206
Strawberry Cookies	206
Stars and Moons	207
Tutti Frutti Faces	208

Cookies for Special Friends

Wholesome Hearts	210
Apple Cookies	211
Butterflies	211
Wiggly Sheep	213
Ice-cream Cone Cookies	214
Knots	215
Chocolate Speckled Cookies	215
Tic-tac Toe	216
Chocolate Chip Cookies	217

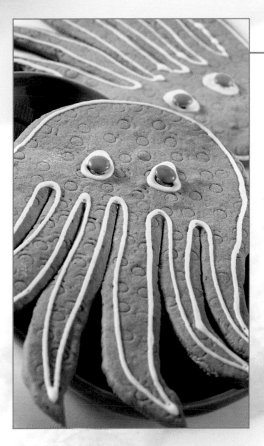

Birthday Parties

Jeweled Cookie Bars	218
Magical Mushrooms	219
Candy Eggs	221
Love Hearts	221
Peppermint Rings	222
Flower Cookies	223
Golden Circles	223
Mouse Cookies	224
Chicks	224
Children's Names Cookies	227
Chocolate Octopus	228

Lunch Box Favorites

Mandarin Flying Saucers	229
Treasure Coins	229
Chocolate Snakes	230
Fish	231
Gingerbread Selection	233
Jam Heart Cookies	234
Orange Carrot Shortbread	235
Poppy Seed Pinwheels	237
Number Cookies	237
Apple Cheese Cookies	238
Clock Cookies	238
Fruit Segments	239

Alphabet Cookies

Preparation time: 30 minutes ●
Cooking time: 20 minutes ● *Makes: 25*

These cookies have a full lemon flavor which melts in the mouth.

INGREDIENTS

½ stick butter, softened

⅓ cup superfine sugar

1 egg yolk

1½ cups all-purpose flour, sifted

½ tsp baking powder

2 Tbsp lemon juice

Grated rind from ½ a lemon

1 Tbsp milk

Confectioners' sugar, for dredging

Preheat oven to 325°F. Grease two baking sheets or line with nonstick baking parchment.

● In a mixing bowl, beat together the butter and superfine sugar until pale and fluffy, add the egg yolk, flour, baking powder, lemon juice, and lemon rind, then blend together.

● Add the milk, mix to a firm dough using your hands so that the dough comes together in a soft ball. Turn the dough out on to a lightly floured work surface and divide into about 25 equal-sized pieces. Roll each piece into a sausage shape with your hands and make letters of the alphabet, twisting the dough and trimming with a small knife if needed.

● Place the cookies on to the baking sheets and bake for 15 to 20 minutes. Lift them on to a wire rack to cool completely before dusting with confectioners' sugar. Store in an airtight container for up to 1 week.

Teddy Bears Picnic

Preparation time: 35 minutes ●
Cooking time: 10 to 12 minutes ● *Makes: 26*

These cookies are made with a spicy dough, you can use any other similar-sized cutter if you like.

INGREDIENTS

1½ cups all-purpose flour, sifted

½ tsp baking powder

1 tsp ground ginger

½ tsp ground cinnamon

1 cup confectioners' sugar

1¼ sticks butter, cut into small pieces

½ tsp vanilla extract

1 Tbsp water

DECORATION

1 cup confectioners' sugar

1 Tbsp water

Preheat oven to 375°F. Grease several baking sheets or line with nonstick baking parchment.

● Place the flour, baking powder, ground ginger, ground cinnamon, and confectioners' sugar in a bowl and combine. Blend in the butter using your fingertips, add the vanilla extract and 1 Tbsp cold water and, using your hands, bring the mixture together in a soft ball.

● Roll out the dough to about ¼-inch thick. Using a 3-inch teddy bear cutter, stamp out shapes and lift them on to the baking sheets, spacing them well apart. Gather up the remaining dough and roll it out again and cut into more shapes. Bake the cookies for 10 to 12 minutes or until evenly golden. Transfer to a wire rack to cool.

● To decorate the teddy bears, mix the confectioners' sugar with sufficient cold water to form a thin frosting. Using a decorating bag, pipe on the teddy bears' faces and patterns. Allow to set.

Balloon Cookies

Preparation time: 40 minutes + chilling ● Cooking time: 20 minutes ● Makes: 16

These cookies are thick and crunchy, you can really taste the coconut and orange flavors.

INGREDIENTS

½ stick butter, softened

½ cup superfine sugar

1 egg, beaten

1 cup plus 2 Tbsp self-rising flour

⅔ cup sweetened flaked coconut

Grated rind from 1 orange

DECORATION

1 cup confectioners' sugar, sifted

1 Tbsp water

4 food colorings

Colored ribbons

In a mixing bowl beat together the butter and sugar until pale and fluffy. Beat in the egg, sift in the flour and add the coconut and orange rind. Mix all the ingredients together with your hands, until they come together in a soft ball. Chill the dough in a plastic bag in the refrigerator for 30 minutes.

● Preheat oven to 325°F. Grease two baking sheets or line with nonstick baking parchment.

● On a lightly floured working surface, roll out the dough. Keep the dough quite thick when rolling out, if cracks appear gather up the dough, sprinkle more flour on the work surface and try again. Using a 2½-inch round cutter, cut out the cookies and lift on to the baking sheets. Using a metal skewer, make a hole at the top of each cookie for the ribbon. Bake the cookies for 15 to 20 minutes or until lightly golden. As soon as they come out of the oven re-shape the holes with a skewer. Lift them on to a wire rack to cool.

● To decorate the cookies, mix the confectioners' sugar with sufficient water to form a thin frosting. Divide into four bowls and color each one using a few drops of food color. Spread different colors onto each cookie and when the frosting has set, tie ribbons through the holes.

Big White Chocolate and Apricot Cookies

Preparation time: 5 minutes ● Cooking time: 12 to 15 minutes ● Makes: 12

These chewy cookies contain pieces of apricot that give a really juicy texture as well as pieces of chocolate.

INGREDIENTS

1 stick butter, softened

½ cup packed light brown sugar

1 egg, beaten

1¾ cups self-rising flour

⅔ cup white chocolate chips, or white chocolate, chopped

⅓ cup milk or semi-sweet chocolate chips

⅓ cup dried apricots, chopped

Preheat oven to 375°F. Grease two baking sheets or line with nonstick baking parchment.

● In a mixing bowl, beat together the butter and sugar until light and fluffy. Beat in the egg. Sift in the flour, both types of chocolate chips, and apricots, then stir everything together, until evenly mixed.

● Place mounds of the mixture on to the baking sheets, spaced well apart to allow for spreading. Bake the cookies for 12 to 15 minutes or until golden-brown. Lift onto wire racks to cool. These cookies are best eaten on the day they are baked, but once the cookies are completely cold, they may be stored in an airtight container.

Sunflower Cookies

Preparation time: 35 minutes ● Cooking time: 15 to 20 minutes ● Makes: 10

**These happy sunflowers will brighten up your day, the cookies taste great too, with crunchy
sunflower seeds mixed into the cookie dough.**

INGREDIENTS

¼ stick butter, softened

⅓ cup packed superfine sugar

1 cup all-purpose flour, sifted

1 egg, beaten

3 Tbsp sunflower seeds

2 Tbsp lemon juice

DECORATION

6 Tbsp confectioners' sugar, sifted

4 tsp water

Yellow and orange food colorings

Preheat oven to 350°F. Grease several baking sheets
or line with nonstick baking parchment.

● In a mixing bowl beat together the butter and sugar
until pale and fluffy. Add the flour, then the egg,
sunflower seeds, and lemon juice and mix everything
together to combine.

● Using two teaspoons, place mounds of dough on the
baking sheet about 4 inches apart to allow for the
cookies to spread, flatten slightly with a wet knife. Bake
the cookies for 15 to 20 minutes or until lightly golden
around the edges. Lift them on to a wire rack to cool. If
your rounds are not even after cooking, don't worry,
they will still make good faces.

● To decorate the sunflowers, mix the confectioners'
sugar with sufficient cold water to form a thin frosting,
color half yellow and half orange. Using decorating bags,
pipe on a happy face and then pipe a pattern around
each face.

Lemon-scented Peanut Butter Cookies

Preparation time: 25 minutes + chilling ●
Cooking time: 15 minutes ● Makes: 20

These popular cookies with their nutty taste will be enjoyed not only by children but adults as well.

INGREDIENTS

1 stick butter, softened

1 cup superfine sugar

½ cup chunky peanut butter

1 egg, beaten

1¼ cups all-purpose flour, sifted

½ tsp baking powder

⅓ cup unsalted natural peanuts, chopped

1 tsp grated lemon rind

Raw sugar for sprinkling

In a bowl beat together the butter and sugar until light and fluffy, add the peanut butter and beat again. Add the egg, a little at a time until it is mixed in, stir in the flour, baking powder, peanuts, and lemon rind and bring together to form a soft ball. Wrap the dough in a plastic bag and chill in the refrigerator for 30 minutes.

● Preheat oven to 375°F. Grease several baking sheets or line with nonstick baking parchment.

● On a lightly floured surface, divide the dough into 20 equal pieces and shape them into a ball, using the palms of your hands. Lift on to the baking sheets, spacing them apart to allow for spreading. Using the back of a fork flatten the balls slightly.

● Sprinkle with a little raw sugar and bake for 15 minutes or until golden. Transfer to a wire rack to cool.

Strawberry Cookies

Preparation time: 35 minutes + chilling ●
Cooking time: 15 minutes ● Makes: 12

Have fun decorating these strawberries, you can choose any colored frosting and pattern you like.

INGREDIENTS

1½ cups all-purpose flour, sifted

¾ stick butter, cut into small pieces

¾ cup superfine sugar

3 Tbsp strawberry jam or preserves

DECORATION

7 Tbsp confectioners' sugar

3 tsp water

Place the flour in a mixing bowl and blend in the butter using your fingertips until the mixture resembles fine bread crumbs. Stir in the sugar and strawberry jam and mix together, with your hands to form a soft ball. Wrap the dough in a plastic bag and chill in the refrigerator for 30 minutes.

● Preheat oven to 350°F, Grease several baking sheets or line with nonstick baking parchment. Roll out the dough to about ¼-inch thick. Using a 3½-inch cutter, stamp out hearts and lift on to the baking sheets. Gather up the remaining dough and roll it out again and cut out more shapes. With the trimmings, roll tiny balls into "sausage" shapes and attach these to the top of the hearts to look like the strawberry stalk.

● Bake the cookies for 15 minutes or until lightly golden at the edges. Transfer to a wire rack to cool.

● To decorate, mix the confectioners' sugar with sufficient water to form a thin frosting, add a few drops of green coloring. Using a decorating bag, pipe on little dots of frosting to look like a strawberry. Allow to set.

Stars and Moons

Preparation time: 40 minutes ● Cooking time: 15 minutes ● Makes: 20

These delicious cookies are really buttery with a crisp coconut texture.

INGREDIENTS

1 stick butter, softened

½ cup superfine sugar

1½ cups all-purpose flour, sifted

½ cup sweetened flaked coconut

2 Tbsp milk

DECORATION

6 Tbsp confectioners' sugar, sifted

About 4 tsp water

Preheat oven to 350°F. Grease two baking sheets or line with nonstick baking parchment.

● In a mixing bowl, beat together the butter and sugar until pale and fluffy. Add the flour to the mixture then add the coconut and milk; mix well. Using your hands bring the dough together to form a soft ball.

● Turn the dough out on to a lightly floured work surface and roll out to ¼-inch thick. Using a large star cutter, cut out shapes. To make the moon shape cut out rounds with an 3½-inch round cutter, cut away one-quarter of the round with the cutter to leave a crescent shape. Gather up the leftover dough, roll it out again and cut out more shapes. Lift the cookies on to the baking sheets. Bake the cookies for 15 to 20 minutes or until lightly golden and crisp, then lift them on to a wire rack to cool.

● To decorate the cookies, mix the confectioners' sugar with sufficient water to form a thin frosting. Fill a decorating bag with the frosting and pipe it carefully on to the cookies to make patterns.

Tutti Frutti Faces

Preparation time: 35 minutes ● Cooking time: 15 minutes ● Makes: 10

Adding chopped candied cherries to this recipe makes these cookies really tasty as well as pretty.

INGREDIENTS

½ cup soft tub margarine

⅓ cup packed superfine sugar

1 egg, beaten

1¾ cups all-purpose flour, sifted

½ cup multi colored candied cherries, chopped

DECORATION

⅓ cup confectioners' sugar, sifted

4 tsp water

Food colorings

Preheat oven to 350°F. Grease several baking sheets or line with nonstick baking parchment.

● In a mixing bowl beat together the margarine and sugar until pale and fluffy, beat in the egg. Stir in the flour and chopped cherries and mix everything together. Use your hands to bring the dough together to form a soft ball.

● Turn the dough out on to a lightly floured work surface and roll out to ¼-inch thick. Using a large 3 ½-inch round cutter, cut out your shapes. Gather up the leftover dough, roll it out again and cut out more shapes and lift the cookies on to the baking sheets. Bake the cookies for 15 minutes or until lightly golden. Lift them on to a wire rack to cool.

● To decorate the faces, mix the confectioners' sugar with about 4 teaspoons of cold water to make a thin frosting. Divide the frosting into three bowls and color one blue, one pink, and one yellow. Fill decorating bags with the frosting and pipe carefully on to the cookies to make different faces.

Wholesome Hearts

Preparation time: 25 minutes ● Cooking time: 20 minutes ● Makes: 10 Large cookies

These cookies are full of good things, so no extra frosting is needed for a change.

INGREDIENTS

1 stick butter, softened

½ cup superfine sugar

1 egg, beaten

1 tsp vanilla extract

2 cups self-rising flour, sifted

1 cup rolled oats

½ cup sweetened flaked coconut, plus 2 Tbsp extra for sprinkling

Preheat oven to 350°F. Grease several baking sheets or line with nonstick baking parchment.

● In a mixing bowl, beat together the butter and sugar until pale and fluffy. Beat in the egg with the vanilla, followed by the flour and mix well. Stir in the rolled oats and ½ cup coconut and knead the mixture together with your hands until it comes together in a soft ball.

● Turn the dough out on to a lightly floured work surface and roll out the dough to ¼-inch thick. Using a heart cutter, cut out your shapes and lift the cookies on to the baking sheets. Gather up the leftover dough, roll it out again, and cut out more shapes. Sprinkle each with the reserved coconut. Bake the cookies for 20 minutes or until lightly golden. Lift them on to a wire rack to cool.

Apple Cookies

Preparation time: 35 minutes + chilling ●
Cooking time: 18 to 20 minutes ● *Makes: 10*

**Using apple sauce in these cookies creates a smooth
texture as well as sweetness.**

INGREDIENTS

2 cups all-purpose flour, sifted

¾ cup confectioners' sugar

1¼ sticks butter, cut into small pieces

3 Tbsp apple sauce

DECORATION

7 Tbsp confectioners' sugar

3 tsp of cold water

Green food coloring

Place the flour and confectioners' sugar in a mixing
bowl and blend in the butter using your fingertips
until the mixture resembles fine bread crumbs. Add the
apple sauce and bring the mixture together in a soft ball.
Wrap in a plastic bag and chill in the refrigerator for
30 minutes.

● Preheat oven to 350°F. Grease several baking sheets or
line with nonstick baking parchment.

● On a lightly floured surface, roll out the dough to
about ¼-inch thick. Using a 3½-inch cutter, stamp out
rounds and lift on to the baking sheets. Roll out the
remaining dough again and cut out more shapes. Roll
the trimmings into "sausage" shapes and attach these to
the top of the circles to look like "stalks".

● Bake the cookies for about 18 to 20 minutes or until
lightly golden at the edges. Transfer to a wire rack.

● To decorate, mix the confectioners' sugar with cold
water to form a thin frosting, add a few drops of
coloring. Using a decorating bag, decorate each apple
with eyes and mouths.

Butterflies

Preparation time: 25 minutes + chilling ●
Cooking time: 15 minutes ● *Makes: 20*

**These cookies are made by mixing melted chocolate
through the dough, creating a marbled effect.**

INGREDIENTS

3 oz milk chocolate, broken into pieces

1 stick butter, softened

½ cup superfine sugar

1 egg, beaten

1½ cups all-purpose flour, sifted

Confectioners' sugar for dusting

Ask an adult to help you place a saucepan of water
to boil on the stove. When the water is simmering,
place the chocolate in a heatproof bowl on top of the
saucepan, gently melt the chocolate, stirring until
smooth. Remove from the heat and allow to cool.

● In a mixing bowl, beat together the butter and sugar
until light and fluffy. Beat in the egg. Stir in the flour
and combine all the ingredients to form a soft ball. Add
the chocolate and gently stir through to give a marbled
effect. Wrap the dough in a plastic bag and chill in the
refrigerator for 30 minutes.

● Preheat oven to 350°F. Grease several baking sheets or
line with nonstick baking parchment.

● On a lightly floured surface, roll out the dough to
about ¼-inch thick. Using a 3-inch butterfly cutter,
stamp out shapes and lift on to the baking sheets. Roll
out the remaining dough again and cut out more shapes.

● Bake the cookies for 15 minutes or until evenly
golden-brown. Transfer to a wire rack to cool. Just
before eating dust with confectioners' sugar.

Wiggly Sheep

Preparation time: 30 minutes ● *Cooking time: 15 minutes* ● *Makes: 18*

This lemon shortbread is delicious, so bake double the quantity!

INGREDIENTS

1¼ sticks butter, softened

¾ cup confectioners' sugar

2 cups all-purpose flour, sifted

Grated rind of 1 lemon

1 Tbsp milk

DECORATION

⅓ cup confectioners' sugar, sifted

4 tsp water

Preheat oven to 350°F. Grease several baking sheets or line with nonstick baking parchment.

● In a mixing bowl beat together the butter and confectioners' sugar until pale and fluffy. Stir in the flour, then add the lemon rind and milk. Mix everything together to form a soft dough using your hands.

● On a lightly floured work surface, roll out the dough to ¼-inch thick. Using your cutter, cut out your shapes and lift the cookies on to the baking sheets. Gather up the leftover dough, roll it out again and cut out more shapes. Bake the cookies for 15 minutes or until lightly golden. Lift them on to a wire rack to cool.

● To decorate the sheep, mix the confectioners' sugar with sufficient cold water to make a thin frosting. Fill a decorating bag with the frosting and pipe it in a wiggly pattern, on to the body of the sheep.

Ice-cream Cone Cookie

Preparation time: 40 minutes ● Cooking time: 15 minutes ● Makes: 18

Decorate these cookies with your favorite colored frosting to look like real frost cream cones with different toppings!

INGREDIENTS

1½ cups all-purpose flour, sifted

1 stick butter, cut into small pieces

½ cup superfine sugar

⅓ cup dried apricots, chopped

Grated rind from ½ orange

2 Tbsp orange juice

DECORATION

7 Tbsp confectioners' sugar

3 tsp water

Yellow or other food coloring

Preheat oven to 350°F. Grease several baking sheets or line with nonstick baking parchment.

● Place the flour in a mixing bowl and blend in the butter using your fingers, until the mixture resembles fine bread crumbs. Stir in the sugar, apricot, orange rind, and orange juice and mix everything together, bring the mixture together in a soft ball using your hands. On a lightly floured surface roll out the dough to about ¼-inch thick.

● Using a 4½-inch heart cutter, stamp out hearts, gather up the left over dough, roll it out again and cut out more hearts. Cut each heart in half lengthways and lift on to the baking sheets. Using the back of a knife, mark a line halfway across the top of the cookie, then below make criss-cross lines to resemble the sugar cone. Bake the cookies for 15 minutes or until golden-brown. Lift onto a wire rack to cool.

● To decorate the cookies, mix the confectioners' sugar with about 3 teaspoons of cold water to form a thin frosting, add a few drops of yellow or other coloring. Using a decorating bag, pipe the frosting on to the cookies to decorate. Allow to set.

Knots

Preparation time: 30 minutes ●
Cooking time: 30 minutes ● *Makes: 8*

**These knots are made by using two different colored
doughs, rolled together and tied into a "knot" shape.**

INGREDIENTS

½ stick butter, softened

¾ cup superfine sugar

1 egg yolk

1½ cups all-purpose flour, sifted

½ tsp baking powder

2 Tbsp milk

1 Tbsp unsweetened cocoa powder

Preheat oven to 325°F. Grease several baking sheets
or line with nonstick baking parchment.

● In a mixing bowl, beat together the butter and
superfine sugar until light and fluffy. Add the egg yolk,
flour, and baking powder and mix together. Add the
milk and mix to a firm dough using your hands, so that
the dough comes together in a soft ball. Transfer half the
mixture to another bowl and mix in the unsweetened
cocoa powder.

● On a lightly floured surface, divide the dough into 8
pieces each and roll into "sausage" shapes about 9 inches
long. Take 2 pieces of different coloured dough and lay
them together so they stick, very carefully wrap around
and tie through knot and lift on to the baking sheets.
Repeat with the remaining dough.

● Bake the cookies for 15 to 20 minutes, until evenly
golden and crispy. Transfer to a wire rack to cool.

Chocolate Speckled Cookies

Preparation time: 30 minutes ●
Cooking time: 15 minutes ● *Makes: 16*

**These tasty cookies combine condensed milk and
chocolate to give them a sweet flavor.**

INGREDIENTS

1 stick lightly salted butter, softened

2 Tbsp superfine sugar

½ cup sweetened condensed milk

2 cups self-rising flour

3 oz semi-sweet chocolate, grated

grated rind from ½ orange

Preheat oven to 325°F. Grease several baking sheets
or line with nonstick baking parchment.

● In a mixing bowl, beat together the butter and
superfine sugar until light and fluffy. Beat in the
condensed milk until well mixed.

● On a lightly floured surface, divide the dough into 16
equal-sized pieces.

● Using the palms of your hands, roll each piece into a
ball and lift on to the baking sheets, flatten them slightly
with the back of a fork.

● Bake the cookies for 15 minutes or until evenly golden
brown. Transfer to a wire rack to cool. Store these
cookies in an airtight container.

Tic-tac Toe

Preparation time: 30 minutes + chilling ● *Cooking time 10 to 15 minutes* ● *Makes: 24*

Have fun with these two colored cookies and see who can win!

INGREDIENTS

1 stick butter, softened

½ cup superfine sugar

1 egg, beaten

2 cups all-purpose flour

¼ tsp baking powder

Grated rind of 1 orange

2 Tbsp unsweetened cocoa powder, sifted

In a mixing bowl, beat the butter and sugar together until pale and fluffy, beat in the egg. Sift in the flour with the baking powder and stir in the grated orange rind. Mix everything together to form a soft dough.

● Divide the mixture in half, to one half fold in the cocoa powder thoroughly, so you are left with two mixtures. Chill the dough separately in plastic bags in the refrigerator for 30 minutes.

● Preheat oven to 375°F. Grease two baking sheets or line with nonstick baking parchment. On a lightly floured surface, roll out the chocolate dough and using a 2½-inch round cutter, stamp out rounds, then using a 1½-inch round cutter place in the middle of the cookie to create another circle, this becoming the "zero". Re-roll the dough to make 12 "zeros".

● Roll out the orange dough on a lightly floured surface and, using a cutter or a sharp knife, cut out 12 crosses and lift on to baking sheets. Bake the cookies for 15 minutes or until lightly golden and crisp. Lift the cookies on to a wire rack to cool. Store in an airtight container for up to 1 week.

Chocolate Chip Cookies

Preparation time: 25 minutes ● Cooking time: 12 minutes ● Makes: 18

These chocolate chip cookies are so easy to make; they are chewy and full of chocolate chunks in every mouth-watering bite.

INGREDIENTS

1 stick butter, softened

⅔ cup packed light brown sugar

1 egg, beaten

1 cup all-purpose flour, sifted

½ tsp baking soda

1 tsp vanilla extract

½ cup semi-sweet chocolate chips or ½ cup white chocolate chips

Preheat oven to 375°F. Grease two baking sheets or line with nonstick baking parchment.

● In a mixing bowl, beat together the butter and sugar until light and fluffy. Beat in the egg. Mix together the flour and baking soda. Add to the mixture with the vanilla and stir everything together well. Add the chocolate chips and stir them in until evenly spread.

● Spoon mounds of the mixture onto the baking sheets, leaving big spaces between each cookie as the mixture will spread during cooking. Bake the cookies for 10 to 12 minutes or until they are golden brown. Lift onto wire racks to cool.

Jeweled Cookie Bars

Preparation time: 25 minutes plus 4 hours to set (up to 24 hours) ● *Makes:16 bars*

**This a really easy recipe for children to use when they start cooking by themselves
as these cookies do not require baking.**

INGREDIENTS

10 oz milk or semi-sweet chocolate

9 oz Graham cookies

½ cup multi-colored candied cherries, chopped

½ cup raisins

½ cup dried apricots, chopped

½ cup white chocolate chips

½ cup slivered almonds

First, line a 9 x 9-inch shallow pan with nonstick baking parchment.

● Under adult supervision, melt the chocolate over a pan of simmering water. First, break the chocolate into pieces and place in a heatproof bowl and sit on top of the saucepan. Gently melt the chocolate, stirring until smooth.

● Using your fingers break up the Graham cookies into tiny pieces and place in a large mixing bowl. Keeping some of the remaining ingredients for the top of the cookies, add the remaining ingredients to the crushed cookies. Add the melted chocolate and mix well.

● Press the mixture into the pan, level the surface and sprinkle on the remaining ingredients and press gently down to set. Leave the pan in the refrigerator for 4 hours or overnight until it sets hard. Turn out of the pan onto a chopping board and cut into bars.

Magical Mushrooms

Preparation time: 35 minutes ● Cooking time: 20 minutes ● Makes: 16

The stalks of these mushrooms are made from ready-made marzipan, with a chocolate macaroon for the top!

INGREDIENTS

¾ cup confectioners' sugar

3 Tbsp ground almonds

2 tsp unsweetened cocoa powder

1 egg white

1½ tsp superfine sugar

10 oz white marzipan

DECORATION

Pink food coloring

3 Tbsp confectioners' sugar

2 tsp water

Preheat oven to 350°F. Line a baking sheet with a sheet of rice paper.

● Sift the confectioners' sugar, ground almonds, and cocoa together in a small bowl. In another mixing bowl, whisk the egg white until it forms soft peaks, then whisk in the superfine sugar. Fold in the sifted ingredients until combined.

● Spoon 16 small dots onto the rice paper spaced well apart. Bake for 20 minutes or until firm and cracking has appeared on the top of each cookie. Leave to go cold on the baking sheet, then neaten the edges of each cookie by trimming away the unwanted rice paper.

● Divide the marzipan into 17 equal-sized pieces. On a lightly floured work surface, roll 16 balls into a pear-shaped stalk. Color the remaining ball with the pink food coloring to make 16 small noses. To decorate the mushrooms, mix the confectioners' sugar with sufficient cold water to form a thin frosting and fill a decorating bag. Squeeze a small dot of frosting on the underside of each cookie and press on top of the marzipan stalk to complete the mushroom. Eyes and mouths can be pressed into the marzipan using the back of a sharp knife, pipe a small dot of frosting to attach the nose.

Candy Eggs

Preparation time: 30 minutes + chilling ●
Cooking time: 15 minutes ● *Makes: 13*

These brightly colored cookies bring enjoyment to any play time!

INGREDIENTS

6 Tbsp soft tub margarine

½ cup packed light brown sugar

1 egg, beaten

1½ cups self-rising flour, sifted

1 tsp ground cinnamon

2 packages chocolate candy buttons (about 100 M&Ms™)

In a mixing bowl, beat together the margarine and sugar until pale and fluffy. Beat in the egg, stir in the flour and ground cinnamon. Knead the mixture together with your hands until it comes together in a soft ball. Chill the dough in a plastic bag in the refrigerator for 30 minutes.

● Preheat oven to 350°F. Grease two baking sheets or line with nonstick baking parchment.

● Roll out the dough on a lightly floured surface, the dough will be quite soft so use extra dusting of flour if it begins to stick. Using a 3-inch oval or round cutter, stamp out the cookies. Gather up the leftover dough, roll it out again and cut out more shapes and lift on to baking sheets. Lightly press the candy buttons into the dough to decorate the egg shape. Bake the cookies for 15 minutes. Lift the cookies on to a wire rack to cool, then store an airtight container.

TIP

Make a hole in each cookie with a skewer so that you can hang them up with ribbon when they are cooked.

Love Hearts

Preparation time: 40 minutes + chilling ●
Cooking time: 15 minutes ● *Makes: 16*

Choose your favorite colors to decorate these heart shaped cookies.

INGREDIENTS

¾ stick butter, softened

⅔ cup superfine sugar

1 egg, beaten

1½ cups all-purpose flour, sifted

Grated rind from 1 lemon

DECORATION

1 cup confectioners' sugar

1 Tbsp of water

Pink, green, and yellow food coloring

In a mixing bowl beat together the butter and sugar until light and fluffy. Beat in the egg. Stir in the flour and lemon rind and using your hands bring the mixture together in a soft ball. Wrap the dough in a plastic bag and chill in the refrigerator for 30 minutes.

● Preheat oven to 350°F. Grease several baking sheets or line with nonstick baking parchment.

● On a lightly floured surface roll out the dough to about ¼-inch thick. Using a 3-inch heart cutter, stamp out hearts and lift on to the baking sheets. Gather up the remaining dough and roll it out again and cut out more shapes. Bake the cookies for 15 minutes or until lightly golden at the edges.

● To decorate the cookies, mix the confectioners' sugar with sufficient water to form a thin frosting. Transfer some of the frosting to two other bowls and add drops of food coloring to each bowl. Spread each cookie with different colored frosting and allow to set.

Peppermint Rings

Preparation time: 30 minutes + chilling ● *Cooking time: 15 minutes* ● *Makes: 20*

These cookies are for anyone who enjoys mint, they have peppermint extract in the dough with a mint-flavored boiled candy in the center.

INGREDIENTS

1½ cups all-purpose flour, sifted

½ cup confectioners' sugar

1 stick lightly salted butter, cut into small pieces

1 tsp peppermint extract

1 Tbsp water

20 sparkling clear mint candies

Place the flour and confectioners' sugar in a large mixing bowl and blend in the butter until the mixture resembles fine bread crumbs. Add the peppermint extract and water, using your hands bring the mixture together to form a dough. Wrap the dough in a plastic bag and chill in the refrigerator for 30 minutes or so.

● Line several baking sheets with nonstick baking parchment.

● On a lightly floured work surface, roll out the dough to about ¼-inch thick, using a 2½-inch round cutter, stamp out the middle of each cookie. Unwrap the candies and place in the gaps. Re-roll the trimmings and cut out more shapes. Chill the cookies in the refrigerator for 15 minutes.

● Preheat oven to 350°F. Bake the cookies for 15 minutes or until lightly golden. Allow to cool on the baking sheets and for the sweets to harden, before lifting onto a wire rack to cool. Store in an airtight container.

Flower Cookies

Preparation time: 40 minutes ●
Cooking time: 15 minutes ● *Makes: 20*

The children will love these cookies as they contain little pieces of M&M™ in the cooked dough.

INGREDIENTS

1½ cups all-purpose flour, sifted

1 stick butter, cut into small pieces

½ cup superfine sugar

3 Tbsp M&Ms™ broken into small pieces

2 Tbsp milk

DECORATION

7 Tbsp confectioners' sugar

3 tsp water

Yellow and pink food colorings

Preheat oven to 350°F. Grease several baking sheets or line with nonstick baking parchment.

● Place the flour in a mixing bowl and blend in the butter using your fingers until the mixture resembles fine bread crumbs. Stir in the sugar, M&Ms, and milk, bring the mixture together in a soft ball using your hands. On a lightly floured surface, roll out the dough to about ¼-inch thick.

● Using a 2½-inch fluted cutter, cut out your shapes and lift the cookies on to the baking sheets. Gather up the left over dough, roll it out again and cut more shapes. Bake for 15 minutes. Lift them on to a wire rack to cool.

● To decorate the flowers, mix the confectioners' sugar with the water and mix to a thin frosting. Transfer half the frosting to another bowl, add a few drops of yellow coloring to one bowl and pink coloring to the other bowl.

● Using decorating bags, pipe it carefully on to the flowers to make patterns. Allow to set.

Golden Circles

Preparation time: 25 minutes + chilling ●
Cooking time: 15 to 20 minutes ● *Makes: 18*

Crisp cookies with a hint of cheese and sesame seed will make the perfect snack.

INGREDIENTS

1 cup all-purpose flour, sifted

1 tsp mixed dried herbs

¾ stick butter, cut into small pieces

1 cup sharp Cheddar cheese, grated

1 egg beaten

3 Tbsp sesame seeds

Place the flour in a mixing bowl with the mixed dried herbs and blend in the butter using your fingertips until the mixture resembles fine bread crumbs. Add the cheese and bring the mixture together in a soft ball using your hands. On a lightly floured surface, shape the dough into a 9 x 1-inch "log" shape. Wrap in a plastic bag and chill in the refrigerator for 30 minutes.

● Brush the "log" shape dough with beaten egg, place the sesame seeds on a large plate and roll the dough in the sesame seeds until they evenly coat the log. Chill in the refrigerator for 15 minutes.

● Preheat oven to 375°F. Grease several baking sheets or line with nonstick baking parchment.

● Cut the dough into 18 equal slices and lift on to the baking sheets. Bake the cookies for 15 to 20 minutes or until lightly golden and crisp. Transfer to a wire rack to cool. These cookies are best eaten fresh.

Mouse Cookies

Preparation time: 30 minutes ●
Cooking time: 20 minutes ● *Makes: 14*

These cheeky little "mice" are flavored with cinnamon, if you like, you can dust them with extra cinnamon and confectioners' sugar after they have come out of the oven!

INGREDIENTS

1½ cups all-purpose flour, sifted

1 tsp ground cinnamon

1 stick butter, cut into small pieces

½ cup superfine sugar

2 Tbsp milk

DECORATION

7 currants, halved

Ground cinnamon for dusting

Confectioners' sugar, for dusting

Preheat oven to 350°F. Grease several baking sheets or line with nonstick baking parchment.

● Place the flour and ground cinnamon in a bowl and blend in the butter using your fingertips to form fine bread crumbs. Add the sugar and milk and using your hands bring the mixture together to form a soft dough.

● Divide the dough into 16 equal-sized pieces. Roll 14 pieces into balls using the palms of your hands, then flatten one side to look like the "nose" of a mouse.

● Divide the remaining 2 balls into 14 little balls and roll each one to a long "sausage" shape for the tail. Using a little water, attach each tail to the back of the mice. Position the currants to look like eyes, then using a pair of small scissors, snip into the dough to look like ears. Lift the mice onto the baking sheets.

● Bake the cookies for 20 minutes. Lift on to a wire rack to cool. Using a sieve, dust a little extra cinnamon and confectioners' sugar over the mice before eating.

Chicks

Preparation time: 25 minutes ● *Cooking time: 1 hour 30 minutes* ● *Makes: 30*

These cookies are made from meringue. If you do not want to use a decorating bag, make small blobs with teaspoons, they will be just as fun.

INGREDIENTS

3 egg whites

Pinch of salt

¾ cup superfine sugar

DECORATION

1 oz marzipan

Yellow food coloring

3 Tbsp confectioners' sugar, sifted

2 tsp water

Preheat oven to 250°F. Line several baking sheets with nonstick baking parchment.

● In a mixing bowl, whisk the egg whites with the salt until they form soft peaks. Whisk in the sugar, a little at a time, until the mixture is very thick and glossy. If you are using a decorating bag, fit it with a plain tube, pipe the meringue into small circles. Lift up and pipe a smaller circle to create a head. Allow a little space in between each chick.

● Bake the chicks for 1 hour and 30 minutes, until crisp and dried out so that the meringue lifts off the paper easily. Meanwhile, in a small bowl, color the marzipan yellow and shape into 60 small balls for the eyes and 30 bigger balls for the beak shape.

● Mix the confectioners' sugar with sufficient water to form a thin frosting and using a decorating bag, pipe little dots on each chick and place the eyes and beak in place. These meringues store well in an airtight container, if there are any left over!

Children's Names Cookies

Preparation time: 40 minutes + chilling ● Cooking time: 15 minutes ● Makes: 15

**Using a banana flavored pudding mix in these cookies gives them a real banana boost,
try using other flavors if you prefer.**

INGREDIENTS

6 Tbsp soft margarine

⅓ cup packed superfine sugar

1 egg, beaten

1½ cups self-rising flour, sifted

¼ cup banana flavored pudding mix

DECORATION

½ cup plus 1 Tbsp confectioners' sugar, sifted

2 Tbsp water

Pink and blue food coloring

In a mixing bowl, beat together the margarine and sugar until pale and fluffy. Beat in the egg, add the flour and banana pudding mix. Knead the mixture together with your hands until it comes together in a soft ball. Chill the dough in a plastic bag in the refrigerator for 30 minutes.

● Preheat oven to 350°F. Grease two baking sheets or line with nonstick baking parchment.

● Sprinkle some flour on the work surface and rolling pin. Roll out the dough to about ¼-inch thick. Using a 2½-inch square cutter, cut out your cookies and lift on to the baking sheets. Gather up the leftover dough, roll it out again and cut out more shapes. Bake the cookies for 15 minutes or until lightly golden, lift them on to a wire rack to cool.

● To decorate the squares, mix the confectioners' sugar with sufficient water to form a thin frosting. Keeping about 3 tablespoons of the frosting in the bowl, place the remaining frosting in two bowls and color one pink and one blue. Fill decorating bags with the frostings, pipe your favorite boy's names with the blue frosting on half the cookies and use the pink frosting to pipe girl's names onto the cookies. Use the white frosting to make a border around the names. Eat on the day frosted.

Chocolate Octopus

Preparation time: 35 minutes + chilling ● *Cooking time: 20 minutes* ● *Makes: 2 giant cookies*

This recipe makes two giant octopuses, if you prefer you can make lots of little ones!

INGREDIENTS

½ cup soft tub margarine

½ cup superfine sugar

1 egg, beaten

Scant 1 cup all-purpose flour

2 Tbsp unsweetened cocoa powder

DECORATION

3 Tbsp confectioners' sugar, sifted

2 tsp water

4 Chocolate candy buttons or chocolate chips

In a mixing bowl beat together the margarine and sugar until pale and fluffy. Add the egg. Sift together the flour and cocoa and mix everything together. Using your hands, bring the dough together until it forms a ball, chill the dough in a plastic bag in the refrigerator for 30 minutes.

● Preheat oven to 325°F. Grease two baking sheets or line with nonstick baking parchment. Divide the dough roughly in half to make two bodies for the octopus. Shape into a large oval and then cut five or six strips halfway up the oval to make the tentacles, push the dough apart and curl the edges of the strips. Transfer on to a baking sheet and make the second octopus. Bake the cookies for 20 minutes or until crisp, lift the two cookies on to wire racks to cool.

● To decorate mix the confectioners' sugar with sufficient water and mix to a thin frosting. Using a decorating bag pipe around the body with the frosting and pipe eyes on each octopus and top with the candies. Allow the frosting to set.

Treasure Coins

Preparation time: 30 minutes ●
Cooking time: 25 minutes ● *Makes: 24*

Small discs of vanilla shortbread are encrusted with candied cherries, candied citrus peel, and nuts to make these delicious edible coins!

INGREDIENTS

1½ cups all-purpose flour, sifted

½ cup superfine sugar

1 stick butter, cut into small pieces

2 tsp vanilla extract

¼ cup candied citrus peel

12 candied cherries, halved

24 whole blanched hazelnuts

Preheat oven to 350°F. Grease two baking sheets or line with nonstick baking parchment.

● Place the flour and sugar in a mixing bowl. Blend in the butter using your fingertips until the mixture resembles fine bread crumbs, add the vanilla and using your hands bring the mixture together in a soft ball.

● On a lightly floured surface, roll out the dough to about ¼-inch thick. Using a 2-inch round cutter, stamp out rounds and lift on to the baking sheets. Gather up the remaining dough and roll it out again and cut out more shapes.

● Press a little bit of candied citrus peel on to each cookie, then add half a cherry to each cookie, followed by a hazelnut. Bake the cookies for 25 minutes or until pale golden at the edges. Transfer to a wire rack to cool. Store these cookies in an airtight container and eat within one week.

Mandarin Flying Saucers

Preparation time: 30 minutes + chilling ●
Cooking time: 15 to 20 minutes ● *Makes: 10*

Canned mandarins are used in these cookies, they make a great flavor and color.

INGREDIENTS

1½ cups all-purpose flour, sifted

1 cup confectioner's sugar

1¼ sticks lightly salted butter, cut into small pieces

Grated rind from 1 orange

½ cup canned mandarin segments, drained well and dried

DECORATION

7 Tbsp confectioners' sugar

3 tsp reserved mandarin juice or water

A few mandarin segments, chopped

Place the flour and confectioners' sugar in a bowl, blend in the butter using your fingertips until the mixture resembles fine bread crumbs. Add the orange rind and mandarin segments, chopped, and using your hands bring together in a soft ball. Wrap the dough in a plastic bag and chill in the refrigerator for 30 minutes.

● Preheat oven to 350°F. Grease several baking sheets or line with nonstick baking parchment. Roll out the dough to about ¼-inch thick. Using a 4-inch round cutter, stamp out rounds and lift on to the baking sheets. Gather up the remaining dough and roll it out again and cut out more rounds.

● Bake the cookies for 15 to 20 minutes or until just golden at the edges. Transfer to a wire rack to cool.

● To decorate, mix the confectioners' sugar with sufficient juice or water to form a thin frosting. Place a dollop of frosting on each cookie and top with mandarin pieces.

Chocolate Snakes

Preparation time: 30 minutes ● *Cooking time: 15 minutes* ● *Makes: 8*

These crunchy chocolate cookies are fun to make, glazing them with egg white and sugar makes all the difference.

INGREDIENTS

4 Tbsp soft tub margarine

¼ cup superfine sugar

1 egg, separated

1 cup all-purpose flour

¼ tsp baking powder

2 Tbsp unsweetened cocoa powder, sifted

1 Tbsp milk

DECORATION

4 currants, halved

Granulated sugar, for sprinkling

Preheat oven to 375°F. Grease two baking sheets or line with nonstick baking parchment.

● In a mixing bowl beat together the margarine and sugar until pale and fluffy, add the egg yolk. Sift together the flour, baking powder, and unsweetened cocoa powder then add with the milk and mix thoroughly. The dough should come together in a soft ball.

● Turn the dough out on to a lightly floured work surface and divide into 8 equal-sized pieces. Roll each piece into a long sausage shape with your hands. Then make a spiral pattern with one piece of dough and overlap as you wind the dough up and around. Add 2 pieces of currants to make the eyes and place on to the baking sheets. Repeat with the remaining shapes.

● In a small bowl lightly beat the egg white and then, using a pastry brush, glaze the snakes all over and sprinkle with sugar. Bake for 15 minutes. Lift onto a wire rack to cool. Store in an airtight container.

Fish

Preparation time: 25 minutes + chilling ● *Cooking time: 10 to 15 minutes* ● *Makes: 40 small cookies*

Adding candied citrus peel to this creamed mixture gives these cookies a really fruity texture.

INGREDIENTS

¾ stick butter, softened or soft tub margarine

⅔ cup superfine sugar

1 egg, beaten

1½ cups all-purpose flour, sifted

6 Tbsp candied citrus peel

Grated rind of half a lemon

In a mixing bowl beat together the butter or margarine and sugar until light and fluffy. Beat in the egg. Stir in the flour, then stir in the candied citrus peel and lemon rind. Using your hands, bring the mixture together to form a soft dough. Place in a plastic bag and chill in the refrigerator for 20 minutes.

● Preheat oven to 350°F. Grease two baking sheets or line with nonstick baking parchment.

● On a lightly floured surface roll out the dough ¼-inch thick. Using a cutter, cut out as many fish shapes as possible (the exact number will depend on the size of your cutter) and lift onto the baking sheets. Gather up the remaining dough and roll it out again and cut out more fish shapes.

● Using the back of a teaspoon, decorate the fish with scales and make an eye with a metal skewer. Bake the cookies for 10 to 12 minutes until golden and crisp. Lift onto a wire rack to cool. Store in an airtight container.

Gingerbread Selection

Preparation time: 40 minutes + chilling ● *Cooking time: 8 to 10 minutes* ● *Makes: 24*

**These cookies are just as good as traditional gingerbread but with currants in the mixture.
You can use any cookie cutter you like.**

INGREDIENTS

¼ cup packed soft brown sugar

3 Tbsp corn syrup

½ tsp ground cinnamon

½ tsp ground ginger

1½ Tbsp butter

2 cups all-purpose flour, sifted

1 tsp baking powder

1 egg, beaten

½ cup currants, chopped

DECORATION

⅓ cup confectioners' sugar, sifted

4 tsp water

Green food coloring

Grease two baking sheets or line with nonstick baking parchment. Ask an adult to help you dissolve the sugar, syrup, spices, and butter together in a saucepan. Stir over low heat until they have melted.

● Sift the flour and baking powder into a mixing bowl add the syrup mixture, beaten egg and the currants. Mix everything together, then knead the mixture into a ball using your hands. Chill the dough in a plastic bag in the refrigerator for 30 minutes.

● Preheat oven to 325°F. Sprinkle some flour on the work surface and rolling pin. Roll out the dough thinly to about ¼ inch thick. Using the cutters, cut out your shapes and lift the cookies onto baking sheets. Gather up the leftover dough, roll it out again and cut out more shapes. Bake the cookies for 8 to10 minutes or until they are golden-brown, lift them on to a wire rack to cool.

● To decorate the gingerbread selection, mix the confectioners' sugar with sufficient water to make a thin frosting and add a few drops of green coloring. Using a decorating bag, pipe onto the cookies and decorate.

Jam Heart Cookies

Preparation time: 30 minutes + chilling ● *Cooking time: 20 minutes* ● *Makes: 12*

**Who can resist a crisp cookie base filled with lots of strawberry jam?
Use a different flavored preserve if you prefer.**

INGREDIENTS

1½ cups all-purpose flour, sifted
¼ cup ground almonds
1 stick butter, softened
¼ cup superfine sugar
2 Tbsp milk
1 egg, beaten
4 Tbsp strawberry jam or preserves

Place the flour and ground almonds in a mixing bowl, blend in the butter until the mixture resembles fine bread crumbs. Stir in the sugar and milk and using your hands work the mixture together to form a dough. Place in a plastic bag and chill in the refrigerator for 20 minutes.

● Preheat oven to 350°F. Grease two baking sheets or line with nonstick baking parchment.

● On a lightly floured surface, roll out the dough and cut out 3-inch hearts with a cutter. Place 12 of these heart cookies onto the baking sheets and prick with a fork. Cut out a heart shape from the center of the remaining hearts, using a 2-inch heart cutter. Gather up the remaining dough and roll it out again and cut out more 2-inch hearts so you have 12 lids for the cookies.

● Using a pastry brush, apply the beaten egg to the large heart cookies. Top with a heart "lid" and seal around the edges. Brush the whole cookie with more beaten egg. Bake the cookies for 20 minutes or until golden. Lift onto a wire rack to cool.

● Once the cookies have cooled spoon the jam or preserves onto each cookie keeping within the heart shape in the center.

Orange Carrot Shortbread

Preparation time: 35 minutes ● Cooking time: 15 to 20 minutes ● Makes: 16

**A rich buttery shortbread has been flavored with orange rind, with a drop of food coloring.
See how many people take a second look!**

INGREDIENTS

1¼ sticks butter, softened

⅓ cup packed superfine sugar

2 cups all-purpose flour, sifted

Grated rind of two oranges

2 Tbsp orange juice

Few drops of orange food coloring, optional

Preheat oven to 325°F. Grease two baking sheets or line with nonstick baking parchment.

● In a mixing bowl beat together the butter and sugar until light and fluffy. Add all the remaining ingredients and begin to mix well. Using your hands bring the mixture together to form a soft dough.

● On a lightly floured work surface, divide the dough into 16 equal pieces. Roll each piece of dough into a ball using the palms of your hands. Roll backwards and forwards so that one end begins to get thinner and you produce a "carrot" shape. Repeat with the remaining dough and lift onto the baking sheets. Using the back of a knife lightly score marks all over the carrots.

● Bake the cookies for 15 to 20 minutes or until lightly golden at the edges. Allow to cool slightly before lifting onto a wire rack.

TIP

If you prefer, cut the shortbread into your favorite shape.

235

Poppy Seed Pinwheels

Preparation time: 25 minutes + chilling ●
Cooking time: 15 to 20 minutes ● *Makes: About 20*

These crunchy cookies are sweet and sticky which comes from the jam as it oozes out during baking. We've used apricot, but you can use your favorite flavor of jam or preserve.

INGREDIENTS

1 stick butter, softened
¼ cup superfine sugar
1½ cups all-purpose flour, sifted
2 Tbsp milk
4 Tbsp apricot jam or preserves
1½ Tbsp poppy seeds

In a mixing bowl beat together the butter and sugar until light and fluffy. Stir in the flour and milk. Use your hands, bring the mixture together to form a dough. Place in a plastic bag and chill for 30 minutes.

● Preheat oven to 350°F. Line two baking sheets with nonstick baking parchment.

● On a lightly floured surface, roll out the dough to a 12 x 7-inch rectangle. Place the apricot jam or preserves in a small bowl and stir well with a wooden spoon so it becomes easier to spread. Spoon onto the dough and spread out evenly, sprinkle with poppy seeds.

● Starting from the longest edge, begin to roll up the dough tightly into a large sausage shape. Very carefully slice the dough so you have 20 even slices, lift onto the baking sheets. Bake the cookies for 15 to 20 minutes or until they are lightly golden. Allow to cool slightly on the sheets before lifting onto the wire rack to cool.

Number Cookies

Preparation time: 25 minutes + chilling ●
Cooking time: 10 to 15 minutes ● *Makes: 40*

These cookies are made from an orange dough, half of it is flavored with cocoa powder to create these two colors.

INGREDIENTS

1½ sticks butter, softened
⅓ cup superfine sugar
2¼ cups all-purpose flour, sifted
½ tsp grated orange rind
2 Tbsp unsweetened cocoa powder, sifted

In a mixing bowl beat together the butter and sugar until light and fluffy. Add the flour and orange rind and combine all the ingredients together in a soft ball. Transfer half the mixture to another bowl and fold in the cocoa powder until evenly mixed. Wrap the doughs separately in a plastic bag and chill in the refrigerator for 30 minutes.

● Preheat oven to 350°F. Grease several baking sheets or line with nonstick baking parchment.

● On a lightly floured surface, roll out the chocolate dough to about ¼-inch thick and stamp out numbers, lift on to the baking sheets. Gather up the remaining dough and roll it out again and cut out more numbers. Repeat with the orange dough.

● Bake the cookies for 10 to 15 minutes or until lightly golden at the edges. Lift on to a wire rack to cool. Store in an airtight container.

Apple Cheese Cookies

Preparation time: 20 minutes ●
Cooking time: 20 minutes ● Makes: 16

These are savory cookies with a hint of sweetness from the chopped apple.

INGREDIENTS

1¼ cups self-rising flour

Pinch of salt

1 stick butter, cut into small pieces

1 cup sharp Cheddar cheese, grated

1 apple, cored and fine chopped

Preheat oven to 350°F. Grease and line several baking sheets with nonstick baking parchment.

● Place the flour and salt in a mixing bowl and blend in the butter using your fingertips until the mixture resembles fine bread crumbs. Stir in the cheese and chopped apple and using your hands bring all the ingredients together to form a soft ball.

● On a lightly floured surface divide the dough into 16 equal-sized pieces and roll into balls using the palms of your hands and lift on to the baking sheets. Flatten slightly with the back of a fork.

● Bake the cookies for 20 minutes or until evenly golden-brown. Transfer to a wire rack to cool. These cookies are best eaten fresh.

Clock Cookies

Preparation time: 35 minutes + chilling ●
Cooking time: 15 to 20 minutes ● Makes: 10

These cookies are flavored with golden raisins and cut into circles to make big clock faces. Pipe the frosting to make different times on each cookie!

INGREDIENTS

6 Tbsp soft margarine

⅔ cup superfine sugar

1 egg, beaten

1½ cups all-purpose flour, sifted

Generous ½ cup golden raisins

DECORATION

1 cup confectioners' sugar

1 Tbsp cold water

In a mixing bowl beat together the margarine and sugar until light and fluffy. Beat in the egg. Stir in the flour and golden raisins and using your hands bring all the mixture together in a soft ball. Wrap the dough in a plastic bag and chill in the refrigerator for 30 minutes.

● Preheat oven to 350°F. Grease several baking sheets or line with nonstick baking parchment.

● On a lightly floured surface roll out the dough to about ¼-inch thick. Using a 4-inch round cutter, stamp out rounds and lift on to the baking sheets. Gather up the remaining dough and roll it again and cut out more shapes. Bake the cookies for 15 to 20 minutes or until evenly golden. Transfer to a wire rack to cool.

● To decorate the "clocks", mix the confectioners' sugar with about 1 tablespoon of cold water to form a thin frosting. Using a decorating bag, pipe the numbers 12, 3, 6, and 9 on to the circles in the correct clock positions. Then pipe an "hour" hand and "minute" hand to make different "times" on each cookie. Allow to set.

Fruit Segments

Preparation time: 25 minutes ● Cooking time: 15 minutes ● Makes: 16

These look just like a segment of fruit and they are full of citrus flavors.

INGREDIENTS

1 stick butter, softened

⅓ cup packed superfine sugar

1 egg, separated

1¾ cups all-purpose flour, sifted

Grated rind of 1 lemon

Grated rind of 1 orange

2 Tbsp orange juice

Granulated sugar, for sprinkling

Preheat oven to 350°F. Grease two baking sheets or line with nonstick baking parchment.

● In a mixing bowl, beat together the butter and sugar until pale and fluffy, beat in the egg yolk. Stir in the flour, grated rinds, and orange juice and mix everything together. Using your hands bring the dough together to form a ball.

● Turn the dough out on to a lightly floured work surface and roll out to ¼-inch thick. Using 3½-inch round cutter, cut out rounds, then cut each circle in half to make the segments. Gather up the leftover dough and roll it out again and cut out more circles. Lift the cookies onto the baking sheets, and using the back of a small knife, score marks across each segment.

● In a small bowl, whisk the egg white slightly with a fork and using a pastry brush, glaze each cookie and sprinkle with a little extra sugar. Bake the cookies for 15 minutes or until lightly golden and crisp. Lift them on to a wire rack to cool. When cold store them in an airtight container.

Cookies for Special Diets

Some people believe that being on a special diet puts an end to treats such as cookies. However, this need not be the case. This chapter is full of recipes specially created for those with specific dietary requirements. These cookies are so delicious that they will become firm favorites with the whole family.

Many of the recipes retain butter as the suggested fat because butter really does give the cookies a richness of flavor. However, margarines can be substituted for the butter, but be aware that the trans fats found in hard margarines are saturated like those in butter. Trans fats behave like saturated fats, increasing the risk of heart disease. Reduced and low-fat spreads have a high water content so cannot be substituted for butter. The butter content is kept as low as possible in these recipes and inventive techniques using prunes and apple sauce are used in some recipes to reduce the need for fat.

High Fiber

Increasing fiber is one of the basic tenets of healthy eating.

Coconut Crisps	242
Whole-wheat Shortbread	242
Peanut and Raisin Cookies	244
Banana and Date Cookies	245
Caribbean Lime Cookies	245
Apricot and Almond Cookies	246
Sesame Oat Crisps	247

Reduced Fat

Being placed on a low cholesterol diet does not have to mean total denial of cookies as these recipes show.

Ginger Thins	249
Molasses Cookies	249

Gluten Free/Wheat Free/Healthy

Lemon and Poppy Seed Cookies	250
Sour Cherry and Orange Oatmeal Cookies	251
Low Fat Chocolate Brownies	252
Muesli Cookies	252
Wheat-free Fruity Oat Bars	254
Simple Macaroons	255
Apple and Raisin Cookies	255

Coconut Crisps

Preparation time: 10 minutes ● *Cooking time:*
15 minutes ● *Makes: About 20*

**These delicious light crispy cookies are quick and easy to
make and simply melt in the mouth.**

INGREDIENTS

1 stick lightly salted butter

1 generous Tbsp corn syrup

½ cup raw sugar

1 cup rolled oats

⅔ cup sweetened flaked coconut

1 cup all-purpose flour

1 tsp baking soda

1 tsp hot water

Preheat oven to 350°F. Grease or line two baking
sheets with nonstick baking parchment.

● Place butter, syrup, and sugar in a large saucepan.
Heat the mixture gently until the butter has melted and
the sugar dissolved. Stir in the rolled oats and flour and
mix well. Dissolve the baking soda in the hot water and
stir into the mixture. Allow to cool slightly.

● Roll heaped teaspoonfuls of the mixture into balls the
size of a walnut. Then place on the baking sheets
allowing plenty of space for the mixture to spread. Bake
for 15 minutes or until evenly browned. Allow to cool
slightly, then use a thin metal spatula to transfer to a
wire rack to cool completely. Store for up to 1 week in
an airtight container.

Whole-wheat Shortbread

Preparation time: 15 minutes + chilling ●
Cooking time: 15 minutes ● *Makes: About 15*

**The fiber content of these shortbread cookies is
increased by substituting half the all-purpose flour
with whole-wheat.**

INGREDIENTS

¼ cup all-purpose flour

Pinch of salt

¼ cup plain whole-wheat flour

⅓ cup ground rice

1 stick lightly salted butter

¼ cup superfine sugar

Sift the all-purpose flour and salt together, stir in
the whole-wheat flour and ground rice.

● Beat the butter and sugar until light and fluffy. Mix in
the dry ingredients. When the mixture resembles bread
crumbs, gather the dough together with your hands and
turn on to a clean work surface. Knead lightly until it
forms a ball then roll into a sausage shape, about 2
inches in diameter. Wrap in plastic wrap and chill in the
refrigerator for at least 1 hour or until firm.

● Preheat oven to 375°F. Grease or line two baking
sheets with nonstick baking parchment.

● Using a sharp knife slice the dough into ⅓-inch thick
slices. Transfer to the baking sheets and bake for 15
minutes. Allow to cool slightly then, using a thin metal
spatula, transfer to a wire rack to cool completely. Store
in an airtight container for up to 1 week.

Peanut and Raisin Cookies

Preparation time: 15 minutes cooling ● *Cooking time: 15 minutes* ● *Makes: About 20*

Diets which contain a daily intake of peanuts, peanut butter, or peanut oil may help protect against heart disease.

INGREDIENTS

1 stick lightly salted butter, melted

⅔ cup superfine sugar

1 egg, beaten

5 tsp baking powder

Scant cup crunchy peanut butter

¾ cup all-purpose flour

¾ cup whole-wheat flour

1 cup raisins

Preheat oven to 375°F. Grease or line two baking sheets with nonstick baking parchment.

● Place all the ingredients except the raisins into a bowl and beat together until well blended. Stir in the raisins. Spoon heaping teaspoonfuls of the mixture onto baking sheets spaced well apart to allow the mixture to spread. Bake for 15 to 20 minutes or until brown around the edges.

● Allow to cool slightly, then using a thin metal spatula, transfer to a wire rack to cool completely. Store for up to 1 week, in an airtight container.

Banana and Date Cookies

Preparation time: 15 minutes ● Cooking time: 15 to 20 minutes ● Makes: About 15

Dates are a rich in fiber, potassium, and the B vitamin niacin. Bananas are an excellent source of potassium and rich in vitamin B6.

INGREDIENTS

1 stick lightly salted butter or margarine

⅓ cup superfine sugar

1 egg, beaten

¾ cup all-purpose flour

1 tsp baking powder

½ cup plain whole-wheat flour

½ cup rough chopped banana chips

¾ cup rough chopped dates

Preheat oven to 375°F. Grease or line two baking sheets with nonstick baking parchment.

● Beat together the butter and sugar until light and fluffy. Beat in the egg. Sift the all-purpose flour and baking powder. Stir in both flours, the banana chips, and dates.

● With floured hands, roll the dough into balls the size of walnuts. Place on baking sheets, allowing enough space for the mixture to spread. Bake for 15 to 20 minutes or until brown around the edges. Allow to cool slightly, then use a thin, metal spatula, to transfer to a wire rack to cool completely. Store for up to 1 week in an airtight container.

Caribbean Lime Cookies

Preparation time: 15 minutes ● Cooking time: 15 to 20 minutes ● Makes: About 15

Dried tropical fruits are readily available and make a good alternative to dried apricots.

INGREDIENTS

1 stick lightly salted butter

¾ cup superfine sugar

1 egg, beaten

¾ cup all-purpose flour

1 level tsp baking powder

½ cup whole-wheat flour

⅔ cup chopped dried mango

⅔ cup sweetened flaked coconut

Grated rind of 2 limes

Preheat oven to 375°F. Grease or line two baking sheets with nonstick baking parchment.

● Beat together the butter and sugar until soft. Beat in the egg. Sift the all-purpose flour and the baking powder. Stir in both flours, mango, coconut, and grated lime rind.

● With floured hands roll the dough into balls the size of walnuts. Place on the baking sheets, allowing enough space for the mixture to spread. Bake in the oven for 15 to 20 minutes or until brown around the edges. Allow to cool slightly, then use a thin metal spatula to transfer to a wire rack to cool completely. Store for up to 1 week in an airtight container.

Apricot and Almond Cookies

Preparation time: 15 minutes + cooling ● *Cooking time: 15 minutes* ● *Makes: 15 to 20*

**Dried apricots provide good amounts of betacarotene, potassium, and soluble fiber.
They are also a useful source of iron.**

INGREDIENTS

1 stick lightly salted butter

⅓ cup superfine sugar

1 egg, beaten

¾ cup all-purpose flour

1 tsp baking powder

¾ cup whole-wheat flour

½ cup rough chopped ready-to-eat dried apricots

¾ cup slivered almonds

1 tsp almond extract

Preheat oven to 375°F. Grease or line two baking sheets with nonstick baking parchment.

● Beat together the butter and sugar until soft. Beat in the egg. Sift the all-purpose flour together with the baking powder. Stir in the both types of flour, apricots, almonds, and almond extract.

● With floured hands roll the dough into balls the size of walnuts. Place on the baking sheets, allowing enough space for the mixture to spread. Bake for 15 to 20 minutes or until brown around the edges. Allow to cool slightly, then transfer to a wire rack to cool completely. Store for up to 1 week in an airtight container.

Sesame Oat Crisps

Preparation time: 10 minutes ● Cooking time: 15 minutes ● Makes: About 20

Sesame seeds are a good source of calcium and vitamin E and add a delicious nutty flavor to these cookies.

INGREDIENTS

1 stick lightly salted butter

1¼ Tbsp corn syrup

½ cup raw sugar

¾ cup rolled oats

⅓ cup sesame seeds

1 cup all-purpose flour

1 tsp baking soda

1 tsp hot water

Preheat oven to 350°F. Grease or line two baking sheets with nonstick baking parchment.

● Place butter, syrup, and sugar in a large saucepan. Heat the mixture gently until the butter has melted and the sugar dissolved. Stir in rolled oats, sesame seeds, and flour and mix well. Dissolve the baking soda in the hot water and stir into the mixture. Allow to cool slightly.

● Roll heaped teaspoonfuls of the mixture into balls the size of walnuts. Place on the baking sheets allowing plenty of space for the mixture to spread as it bakes. Bake for 15 minutes or until evenly browned. Remove from the oven and allow to cool slightly, then using a thin metal spatula transfer to a wire rack to cool completely. Store for up to 1 week in an airtight container.

Ginger Thins

Preparation time: 10 minutes ● Cooking time: 7 minutes ● Makes: About 10

These cookies contain just 1.3g fat each. Serve them with frozen yogurt or reduced fat ice cream.

INGREDIENTS

1 Tbsp unsalted butter
1 Tbsp confectioners' sugar
3 Tbsp corn syrup
2 Tbsp all-purpose flour
1 level tsp ground ginger
Pinch of salt

Preheat oven to 375°F. Grease or line two baking sheets with nonstick baking parchment.

● Place the butter, confectioners' sugar, and syrup in a small saucepan and gently heat until the sugar has dissolved. Remove from the heat and allow to cool slightly.

● Sift together the flour, ginger, and salt and stir into the butter mixture.

● Place small spoonfuls of the mixture on to the prepared baking sheets, allowing plenty of space for the mixture to spread. Bake for 7 minutes or until golden brown. Allow the cookies to cool on the tray for about 30 seconds. Using a thin, metal spatula carefully lift the cookies off the baking sheet and while they are still warm and pliable, shape them over a rolling pin or tall glass. Once set, transfer to a wire rack to cool completely. Store for up to 1 week in an airtight container.

Molasses Cookies

Preparation time: 10 minutes ● Cooking time: 20 minutes ● Makes: About 15

These cookies contain just 1.7g fat. Oatmeal is rich in soluble fiber, which can help reduce high blood cholesterol levels.

INGREDIENTS

1 cup self-rising flour
½ cup fine oatmeal
3 Tbsp superfine sugar
¼ cup molasses
¼ stick lightly salted butter
2 Tbsp skim milk

Preheat oven to 375°F. Grease or line two baking sheets with nonstick baking parchment.

● Mix all the dry ingredients in a bowl. Place the butter and molasses in a small saucepan and gently heat until the butter has melted. Pour the molasses mixture onto the dry ingredients, add the milk and mix to make smooth dough.

● Knead the dough on a lightly floured surface then roll out to about ⅛-inch thick. Using a 2-inch round cutter, cut out the cookies and transfer to baking sheet. Using a sharp knife make shallow cuts across the surface and bake for 20 minutes or until firm to the touch. Transfer to wire rack to cool. Store for up to 1 week in an airtight container.

Lemon and Poppy Seed Cookies

Preparation time: 15 minutes ● *Cooking time: 15 to 20 minutes* ● *Makes: About 36*

Poppy seeds give these healthy gluten-free cookies an added crunch.

INGREDIENTS

1 stick lightly salted butter or margarine

½ cup superfine sugar

1 egg, beaten

1½ cups gluten-free flour

Grated rind of 2 lemons

2 Tbsp poppy seeds

Preheat oven to 350°F. Grease or line two baking sheets with nonstick baking parchment.

● Beat together the butter and sugar until light and fluffy. Gradually beat in the egg. Add in the gluten-free flour, lemon rind, and poppy seeds and mix well.

● On a lightly floured surface roll the dough out ¼ inch thick. Using a 2-inch round cutter, cut out the cookies and transfer to the baking sheets and bake for 15 to 20 minutes. Allow to cool slightly on the baking sheets then, using a thin metal spatula carefully transfer to a wire rack to cool completely.

Sour Cherry and Orange Oatmeal Cookies

Preparation time: 15 minutes ● *Cooking time: 15 to 20 minutes* ● *Makes: 15 to 20*

Oats are an excellent source of soluble fiber which can help reduce high blood cholesterol levels, thereby lessening the risk of heart disease.

INGREDIENTS

1 cup all-purpose flour

½ tsp baking soda

½ tsp baking powder

½ tsp salt

1 stick unsalted butter

½ cup packed dark brown sugar

1 egg, beaten

1 tsp vanilla extract

1 Tbsp milk

Grated rind of 1 large orange

1¾ cups rolled oats

¾ cup sour cherries, rough chopped

Preheat oven to 350°F. Grease or line two baking sheets with nonstick baking parchment.

● Sift together the flour, baking soda, baking powder, and salt. Beat together the butter and sugar. Gradually add the egg, vanilla, and milk and beat until smooth. Stir in the sifted ingredients and mix well. Stir in the grated orange rind, oats, and sour cherries.

● Scoop up balls of cookie dough with a tablespoon and place them spaced well apart on the baking sheets to allow the mixture to spread. Bake for 15 to 20 minutes or until just brown. Remove from the oven and allow the cookies to cool slightly, then using a thin metal spatula, transfer to a wire rack to cool completely. Store for up to 1 week in an airtight container.

Low Fat Chocolate Brownies

Preparation time: 15 minutes ● Cooking time: 50 to 60 minutes ● Makes: 9

These brownies contain a fraction of the fat in traditional brownies.

INGREDIENTS

1 cup ready-to-eat prunes
3 Tbsp water
4 oz semi-sweet chocolate
3 egg whites
1 cup packed light brown sugar
1 tsp salt
1 tsp vanilla extract
½ cup all-purpose flour, sifted
¼ cup pecans, chopped

Preheat oven to 350°F. Grease and line the base of an 8 x 8-inch shallow cake pan with nonstick baking parchment.

● Using a blender, blend the prunes with the water until they make a smooth purée. Break the chocolate into a bowl and place over a saucepan of simmering water. Stir occasionally until the chocolate has melted. Remove from the heat and set aside to cool slightly.

● In a bowl mix together the prune purée, melted chocolate, egg whites, sugar, salt, and vanilla extract. Fold in sifted flour.

● Spread the mixture into the prepared pan, sprinkle with pecans and bake for about 50 to 60 minutes or until firm to the touch. Leave in the pan to cool completely. Store, covered in the pan, for 3 days.

Muesli Cookies

Preparation time: 10 minutes ● Cooking time: 15 to 20 minutes ● Makes: About 15

Muesli is high in fiber and rich in vitamins.

INGREDIENTS

1 stick lightly salted butter or margarine
⅓ cup raw sugar
1 egg, beaten
1 cup sugar free muesli
½ cup whole-wheat flour
1¼ tsp baking powder

Preheat oven to 375°F. Grease or line two baking sheets with nonstick baking parchment.

● Beat together the butter and sugar until light and fluffy. Gradually beat in the egg. Stir in the muesli and flour and mix well. Roll into balls the size of a walnut and place on the baking sheets, allowing space for the cookies to spread. Using the palm of your hand flatten the cookies slightly.

● Bake the cookies for 15 to 20 minutes. Allow to cool slightly on the baking sheets then use a thin metal spatula to transfer to a wire rack to cool completely. Store in an airtight container.

Wheat-free Fruity Oat Bars

Preparation time: 10 minutes ● *Cooking time: 30 to 35 minutes* ● *Makes: 9*

Sunflower seeds are a rich source of vitamin E, the B vitamins thiamin and niacin, and the mineral zinc.

INGREDIENTS

1 stick unsalted butter or margarine
½ cup packed light brown sugar
1 Tbsp corn syrup
1¾ cup rolled oats
⅓ cup golden raisins
⅓ cup rough chopped ready-to-eat dried apricots
⅓ cup plus 1 Tbsp sunflower seeds

Preheat oven to 350°F. Lightly grease and base-line a shallow 8 x 8-inch baking pan.

● Heat the butter, sugar, and syrup in a saucepan until dissolved. Remove from the heat, add the remaining ingredients, and mix well. Spoon the mixture into the prepared pan, level the surface and bake in the oven for about 30 minutes or until golden brown.

● Leave to cool for 5 minutes in the pan, then cut into 9 pieces. When cold, transfer to an airtight container. Don't try to remove the bars from the pan while they are still warm because they will break.

Simple Macaroons

Preparation time: 10 minutes ● Cooking time: 25 minutes ● Makes: About 24

These classic cookies use no flour whatsoever, so are both gluten and wheat free. They are low in saturated fat too.

INGREDIENTS

1½ cups ground almonds

1 cup confectioners' sugar, sifted

1 egg white

12 blanched almonds, split in half

Preheat oven to 300°F. Line two baking sheets with nonstick baking parchment.

● Whisk the egg whites in a bowl until stiff but not dry. Gently fold in the confectioners' sugar and almonds until the mixture becomes a sticky dough.

● Spoon walnut-sized balls of mixture onto the baking sheets leaving plenty of space in between. Press half an almond onto the top of each macaroon. Bake for about 25 minutes; the outer crust should be golden and the inside soft. Transfer to a wire rack to cool. Store for up to 1 week in an airtight container.

Apple and Raisin Cookies

Preparation time: 15 minutes ● Cooking time: 15 to 20 minutes ● Makes: 16 to 18

Apple sauce has been used to replace some of the fat in these cookies.

INGREDIENTS

½ stick lightly salted butter or margarine

½ cup superfine sugar

½ cup unsweetened apple sauce

1 egg yolk

1¼ cup all-purpose flour

⅔ cup rolled oats

½ tsp baking soda

½ tsp baking powder

⅓ cup raisins

⅓ cup chopped walnuts

Preheat oven to 375°F. Line two baking sheets with nonstick baking parchment.

● Beat together the butter and sugar until light and fluffy. Beat in the apple sauce and egg yolk. Add the flour, oats, baking soda, baking powder, raisins, and walnuts and beat to make a soft dough.

● With lightly floured hands roll the mixture into balls the size of a walnut and place on the baking sheets, allowing space for the cookies to spread. Using the palm of your hand flatten the cookies slightly and bake for 15 to 20 minutes until set. Allow to cool slightly on the baking sheet, then transfer to a wire rack to cool. Store for up to 1 week in an airtight container.

Cookies for Festive Occasions

Cookies are treats and treats are for enjoying on special occasions. It is no wonder that there are cookies associated with holidays throughout the world. The very best ingredients are always reserved for these special times, so the cookies are packed with dried fruit, nuts, and exotic spices. Most of us are familiar with the cookies made in our own country for Christmas, Valentine's Day, or Easter, but here are a number of cookies from different parts of the world that would make an interesting addition to the table.

Children love being involved in the preparation for these events, so have them help make the cookies and maybe decorate some too. Their childish cookies will have a special appeal and would make a lovely, personalized gift.

Christmas

The rich scent of warm cinnamon and spice is one of the first smells of Christmas. Some recipes can be cooked in advance and frozen.

Cinnamon Candy Trees	258
Spiced Christmas Cookies	259
Tipsy Christmas Puddings	261
Stained-glass Windows	261
Snowballs	262
White Chocolate Slice	263
Cherry Garlands	264
Walnut Macaroons	264
Rum-glazed Wreaths	266
Sugar and Spice Stars	267
Winter Logs	267
Maple Moons	268
Catherine Wheels	269
Praline Sparklers	271
Vanilla Fudge Crumbles	272
Triple Ginger Cookies	274
Kourambiedes	274
Cookie Candy Canes	275
Brandied Shortbread	275

Thanksgiving

The food-lover's holiday of the year. Be sure to make plenty of delicious cookies to offer the family as they catch up on news over cups of steaming coffee.

Cranberry and Orange Clusters	277
Pumpkin Fingers	277
Sticky Toffee Apple Treats	278

Independence Day

Cookies are the perfect treat to take on picnics in the park, or to take along to a cookout. Be patriotic and make cookies to celebrate the stars and stripes.

Shooting Stars	279
Celebration Cookies	280
Coffee Mergingues	283

Passover and Hanukkah

Home-cooked treats are a must for Jewish holidays.

Cinnamon Balls	283
Hanukkah Sugar Cookies	284

Valentine's Day

These cookies are perfect gifts for loved ones. They are light and airy, pink and fancy, sentimental and kitsch—and fun to make.

Sweethearts	285
Honeyed Hearts	287
Rose Petal Cookies	287
Lovers' Knots	288
Soft Centers	288

Saints' Days and Special Days

Many saints and even some poets have a special day with accompanying customs and traditional foods. The following are just a few.

Shamrocks	289
Sedgemoor Easter Cookies	290
Frosted Easter Ovals	291
Maypole Twists	293
Honey and Oat Bites	294
Cattern Cakes	294
Whiskey and Ginger Shortbreads	295

Cinnamon Candy Trees

Preparation time: 30 minutes ● Cooking time: 15 minutes ● Makes: About 20

These crisp cinnamon Christmas cookies are decorated with sparkling jelly candies.

INGREDIENTS

1 stick unsalted butter

¼ cup superfine sugar

1¼ cups all-purpose flour

½ tsp ground cinnamon

⅓ cup rice flour

FROSTING

¼ cup confectioners' sugar

1 tsp lemon juice

2 x 1½ oz packets small jelly candies

Preheat oven to 350°F. Line two large baking sheets with nonstick baking parchment.

● Beat the butter in a bowl until soft, then gradually mix in the sugar. Stir in the flour, cinnamon, and rice flour until well mix, then knead lightly. Roll out on a lightly floured surface to ¼ inch thick. Cut out twenty 3-inch tree shapes. Lift onto the baking sheets, spacing slightly apart.

● Bake for 15 minutes, until lightly golden. Leave on the baking sheets for a few minutes, then remove and cool on wire racks. Sift the confectioners' sugar into a small bowl and stir in the lemon juice to make a smooth frosting. Dip the bases of the jelly candies into the frosting and stick onto the trees. Leave to set.

VARIATION

● Make chocolate candy trees by substituting ¼ cup unsweetened cocoa powder for the same amount of flour, and make up as above.

Spiced Christmas Cookies

Preparation time: 30 minutes ● *Cooking time: 15 minutes* ● *Makes: About 20*

With their crunchy, sugary topping and warm spicy flavoring, these cookies taste equally good served with steaming hot punch or for afternoon tea.

INGREDIENTS

1 stick unsalted butter, softened

⅓ cup packed light brown sugar

1 egg, separated

1 ¼ cups all-purpose flour, sifted

1 tsp ground cinnamon

½ tsp ground ginger

¼ tsp freshly grated nutmeg

¼ tsp ground cloves

2 Tbsp granulated sugar

Preheat oven to 350°F. Line two baking sheets with nonstick baking parchment.

● Beat the butter and sugar together until light and fluffy. Reserve 2 teaspoons egg white. Add the remaining white and yolk to the mixture and mix well. Stir in the flour and spices to make a soft dough. Wrap in plastic wrap and chill in the refrigerator for 1 hour.

● Roll out the dough about ¼ inch thick on a lightly floured surface. Cut into Christmas shapes with floured 2½-inch cutters.

● Transfer the cookies to baking sheets. Brush with the reserved egg white and sprinkle with sugar. Bake for 10 to 12 minutes. Leave for 1 or 2 minutes before lifting off the baking sheets and cooling on wire racks.

TIP

If you want to hang the cookies on the Christmas tree, make a small hole in each with a skewer before baking to allow a ribbon to be threaded through.

Tipsy Christmas Puddings

Preparation time: 30 minutes ●
Cooking time: 15 minutes ● *Makes: About 20*

These spice and fruit cookies are half-coated in a rich rum frosting to look like Christmas puddings.

INGREDIENTS

1 stick lightly salted butter
½ cup packed dark brown sugar
2 egg yolks
2 cups all-purpose flour
½ tsp ground mixed spice
¼ cup candied cherries, chopped
½ cup dried mixed fruit

FROSTING

1 cup confectioners' sugar
2 tsp white rum or lemon juice
Candied cherries and angelica, to decorate

Preheat oven to 350°F. Lightly grease two baking sheets or line with nonstick baking parchment.

● Beat the butter and sugar together until light and fluffy. Add the egg yolks and beat well. Work the flour into the mixture with the mixed spice, cherries, and mixed fruit to make a fairly firm dough. Lightly knead until smooth, then roll out on a lightly floured surface to a thickness of ¼ inch. Cut into rounds, using a plain 2¾-inch cutter. Transfer to the baking sheets.

● Bake for about 15 minutes, until lightly browned. Then transfer to wire racks to cool.

● Sift the confectioners' sugar into a bowl. Stir in enough rum or lemon juice to make a thick frosting. Frost the top half of each cookie and decorate with a piece of candied cherry and angelica.

Stained-glass Windows

Preparation time: 45 minutes ●
Cooking time: 8 to 10 minutes ● *Makes: About 20*

These cookies look wonderful hanging on the Christmas tree with light shining through.

INGREDIENTS

2 cups all-purpose flour
1¼ sticks lightly salted butter
¾ cup superfine sugar
Grated rind 1 orange
1 egg yolk
Boiled candies, preferably clear with bright colors

Preheat oven to 375°F. Line two large baking sheets with nonstick baking parchment.

● Sift the flour into a bowl. Blend in the butter until the mixture resembles bread crumbs. Stir in the sugar and orange rind. Add the egg yolk and mix to a dough.

● Knead on a lightly floured surface for a few seconds, then roll out to ⅛ inch thick. With floured cutters, cut out various Christmas shapes. Cut out the centers leaving a border at least ¼ inch all round. Cut a hole in each to hold a ribbon. Transfer to the baking sheets.

● Put the boiled candies into plastic bags and coarsely crush with a rolling pin. Sprinkle the crushed candies in the cut-out centers of the cookies. Bake for 8 to 10 minutes, until the cookies are golden and the candies have melted. Leave to cool completely on the baking sheets. Thread ribbon through the holes in the top of the cookies. Eat within 10 days.

Snowballs

Preparation time: 35 minutes ● Cooking time: 18 minutes ● Makes: About 12

These little coconut cookies are sandwiched together in pairs, then coated in even more coconut to look like snowballs.

INGREDIENTS

1½ sticks lightly salted butter

1 cup superfine sugar

2 egg yolks

3 cups all-purpose flour

½ tsp baking soda

1 cup loose packed sweetened flaked coconut

2 Tbsp milk

DECORATION

4 oz white chocolate

1 cup apricot jam or preserve

3 cups loose packed sweetened flaked coconut

Confectioners' sugar, to dust (optional)

Preheat oven to 375°F. Lightly grease two baking sheets or line with nonstick baking parchment.

● Beat the butter and sugar together until light and fluffy. Add the egg yolks and beat well. Sift the flour and baking soda together, then work into the butter mixture, with the sweetened flaked coconut and milk. Divide the mixture into 24 pieces and shape into balls. Place on the baking sheets, allowing 1½ inches for them to spread. Bake for 18 to 20 minutes, or until golden-brown. Remove from the baking sheets and cool on a wire rack.

● Break the white chocolate into squares and put in a small bowl over a pan of near-boiling water. Stir occasionally until melted. Dip one cookie into the chocolate and sandwich together with a second cookie to make 12 pairs. Leave to set for 20 minutes.

● Heat the apricot jam or preserve in a small pan until melted, then sift. Brush over the cookies, then roll in the sweetened flaked coconut to coat. If desired, pile up the snowballs on a plate and lightly dust with confectioners' sugar before serving.

White Chocolate Slice

Preparation time: 30 minutes ● *Cook time: 40 minutes* ● *Makes: 14 slices*

These slices are covered in coconut that looks like snow, to give them a really festive feel.

INGREDIENTS

½ cup pitted dates

Grated rind and juice of two oranges

½ stick lightly salted butter

½ cup light brown sugar

1 egg, beaten

½ cup self-rising flour

1 cup all-purpose flour

TOPPING

5 Tbsp clear honey

2 cups unpacked sweetened flaked coconut

2 eggs, beaten

2 Tbsp sweetened flaked coconut, for sprinkling

Preheat oven to 350°F. Grease and line a 7 x 11-inch shallow pan with nonstick parchment.

● Put the dates, orange rind, and orange juice into a small pan and heat gently for about 15 minutes, until soft and pulpy. Leave to cool.

● Beat the butter and sugar together until mixed. Gradually add the egg, beating between each addition. Sift the flours together and stir into the mixture. Spread over the base of the prepared pan.

● Spread the date mixture over the base. For the topping, mix the honey, coconut, and eggs together. Spread evenly over the date mixture. Bake for 40 minutes until pale golden. Leave to cool in the pan then cut into slices.

● Sprinkle with the coconut flakes and serve.

Cherry Garlands

Preparation time: 40 minutes ●
Cooking time: 15 to 20 minutes ● *Makes: About 20*

These pretty piped cookies are decorated with candied cherries and angelica.

INGREDIENTS

½ cup confectioners' sugar

1 cup soft margarine

2 cups all-purpose flour

½ cup cornstarch

½ tsp almond extract

¼ cup candied cherries, chopped very fine

Candied cherries and angelica, to decorate

1 Tbsp confectioners' sugar, to dredge

Preheat oven to 375°F. Lightly grease two baking sheets or line with nonstick baking parchment.
● Sift the confectioners' sugar into a bowl. Add the margarine and cream together until light and fluffy. Sift the flour and cornstarch together and beat into the mixture with the almond extract and the chopped candied cherries.
● Spoon half the mixture into a decorating bag fitted with a ½-inch star tube. Pipe 2-inch rings onto the baking sheet, spacing apart. Decorate each cookie with quartered candied cherries and pieces of angelica. Bake for 15 to 20 minutes until pale golden. Leave on the baking sheets for a few minutes, then transfer to a wire rack and allow to cool. Dredge with confectioners' sugar before serving. Store cooled cookies in an airtight container with nonstick paper between the layers.

Walnut Macaroons

Preparation time: 20 minutes ● *Cooking time: 15 to 20 minutes* ● *Makes: About 20*

Classic macaroons are made with ground almonds, but here walnuts are used instead. Lightly roasting the nuts before grinding intensifies their flavor. Try a batch using hazelnuts or a mixture of almonds and walnuts.

INGREDIENTS

1 cup walnut pieces

½ cup superfine sugar

1 egg white

1 Tbsp superfine sugar, for sprinkling

Preheat oven to 350°F. Put the walnuts on a baking sheet and roast for 10 minutes, until lightly browned. Allow to cool then put in a food processor or blender and process until finely ground.
● Mix the ground walnuts with the sugar and enough egg white to make a fairly stiff paste. Spoon into a decorating bag fitted with a ½ inch plain tube and pipe small rounds onto a baking sheet lined with rice paper, spacing slightly apart.
● Lightly sprinkle the cookies with superfine sugar. Bake for 15 to 20 minutes, until lightly browned. Transfer to a wire rack and carefully remove excess rice paper when the cookies are completely cool. Store in an airtight container.

Rum-glazed Wreaths

Preparation time: 35 minutes ● *Cooking time: 15 minutes* ● *Makes: About 16*

These cookies look impressive, but are very simple to make.

INGREDIENTS

¾ stick lightly salted butter

⅓ cup packed light brown sugar

1½ cups all-purpose flour

½ tsp vanilla extract

1 Tbsp milk

RUM GLAZE

1 cup confectioners' sugar

4 tsp dark rum, orange liqueur, or lemon juice

Preheat oven to 375°F. Lightly grease two baking sheets or line with nonstick baking parchment.

● Beat the butter and sugar until light and fluffy. Sift the flour and work into the mixture along with the vanilla extract and milk. On a floured surface, lightly knead the dough for a few seconds.

● Divide the dough into 16 pieces, then divide each piece into 8, and roll into balls. Arrange the balls in rings on the baking sheets, touching each other. Bake for 15 minutes until golden. Leave the balls to cool on the baking sheets.

● For the glaze, sift the confectioners' sugar into a bowl and stir in the rum, orange liqueur, or lemon juice. Brush over the cookies and leave to set on a wire rack before serving.

Sugar and Spice Stars

Preparation time: 10 minutes ●
Cooking time: 12 to 15 minutes ● *Makes: About 12*

These crisp spicy cookies are given a festive finish with a dusting of confectioners' sugar and cinnamon.

INGREDIENTS

3 Tbsp unsalted butter

¼ cup superfine sugar

Grated rind of ½ lemon

½ egg, beaten

⅓ cup ground almonds

1 cup all-purpose flour

½ tsp ground mixed spice

3 Tbsp raspberry jam or preserve

2 Tbsp confectioners' sugar, to dust

½ tsp ground cinnamon, to dust

Preheat oven to 350°F. Lightly grease two baking sheets or line with nonstick baking parchment.

● Beat the butter, sugar, and lemon rind together until light and fluffy. Add the egg, a little at a time, beating well after each addition. Stir in the ground almonds, then sift in the flour and spice and mix to a dough. Lightly knead for a few seconds, then wrap in plastic wrap and chill in the refrigerator for 30 minutes.

● Roll out the dough to about ⅛ inch thick on a lightly floured surface. Using a floured 3-inch star-shaped cutter, cut out about 20 cookies and transfer to the baking sheets.

● Bake for 10 minutes, or until golden. Transfer to a wire rack to cool. Warm the raspberry jam or preserve and use to sandwich the cookies together in pairs. Dust the cookies with confectioners' sugar, then with ground cinnamon before serving.

Winter Logs

Preparation time: 35 minutes ●
Cooking time: 12 minutes ● *Makes: About 35*

Dipping these meltingly light chocolate cookies in chocolate makes them twice as nice.

INGREDIENTS

1½ sticks unsalted butter, softened

⅓ cup confectioners' sugar

½ tsp vanilla extract

1¼ cups all-purpose flour

¼ cup unsweetened cocoa powder

⅓ cup cornstarch

4 oz semi-sweet chocolate

1 Tbsp confectioners' sugar, for dusting

Preheat oven to 350°F. Line two baking sheets with nonstick baking parchment.

● Beat the butter, sugar, and vanilla extract together until light and fluffy. Sift the flour, cocoa powder, and cornstarch together and fold in.

● Spoon the mixture into a decorating bag fitted with a ½-inch star tube. Pipe 2½-inch lengths onto the baking sheets, spacing well apart. Bake the logs for 12 minutes, then remove from the baking sheets and transfer to wire racks to cool.

● Melt the chocolate in a bowl over a pan of near-boiling water. Dip both ends of the logs into the chocolate and leave to set on nonstick baking parchment. Dust with confectioners' sugar before serving.

Maple Moons

Preparation time: 25 minutes + chilling ● *Cooking time: 10 minutes* ● *Makes: 40*

Use real maple syrup in these cookies; its taste is vastly superior to synthetic flavorings.

INGREDIENTS

¾ stick lightly salted butter
3 Tbsp light brown sugar
3 Tbsp maple syrup
1 egg yolk
1 cup all-purpose flour
½ cup self-rising flour

Lightly grease two baking sheets or line with nonstick baking parchment.

● Beat together the butter and sugar until light and fluffy. Beat in the maple syrup and egg yolk. Sift the flours together and work into the mixture to make a soft dough. Wrap the dough in plastic wrap and then chill for 2 hours until firm.

● Preheat oven to 350°F.

● Roll out the dough on a lightly floured surface to ⅛ inch thick. Cut out moon shapes using a 2½-inch cutter and place on the baking sheets. Bake for 10 minutes, until light golden-brown. Leave on the baking sheets for a few minutes to harden, then transfer to a wire rack and leave to cool.

VARIATION

● Sandwich the moons together in pairs with coffee butter cream. Dissolve 2 teaspoons instant coffee in 2 teaspoons near-boiling water. Cream with 1 stick unsalted butter and 4 tablespoons sifted confectioners' sugar until light and fluffy. Chill in the refrigerator for 15 minutes to firm slightly before serving.

Catherine Wheels

Preparation time: 40 minutes + chilling ● *Cooking time: 10 to 12 minutes* ● *Makes: 40*

Whirls of orange and chocolate dough make these cookies doubly delicious.

INGREDIENTS

1 stick lightly salted butter

½ cup superfine sugar

2 eggs, beaten

Grated rind 1 orange

3¼ cups all-purpose flour

¼ cup unsweetened cocoa powder

Lightly grease two baking sheets or line with nonstick baking parchment.

● Beat the butter and sugar until very light and fluffy. Divide the butter mixture in two. Work 1¾ cups flour and the orange rind into one half of the butter mixture and the remaining 1½ cups flour and the unsweetened cocoa powder into the other. Lightly knead each piece of dough for a few minutes.

● Roll out on a lightly floured surface to a rectangle measuring 10 x 6 inches. Lift the sheet of chocolate dough on top of the orange, then roll up like a jellyroll. Wrap in plastic wrap and chill for 2 hours.

● Preheat oven to 400°F.

● Cut the roll into ¼-inch slices and put on the baking sheets. Bake for 10 to 12 minutes, until darkened. Leave to cool on the baking sheets for a few minutes, then remove and cool on a wire rack.

VARIATION

● For licorice and vanilla wheels, omit the orange rind and add 1 teaspoon vanilla extract to one half of the dough and omit the unsweetened cocoa powder and add an extra ¼ cup all-purpose flour and 1 teaspoon black licorice flavoring and coloring to the other half.

Praline Sparklers

Preparation time: 50 minutes ● *Cooking time: 20 minutes* ● *Makes: 14*

**Sandwich these short almond cookies together in pairs with a creamy coffee filling,
then sprinkle with crushed praline, for the ultimate cookie.**

INGREDIENTS

1¼ cups all-purpose flour

¾ cup ground almonds

1 stick lightly salted butter

1 Tbsp confectioners' sugar

1 egg yolk

FILLING AND TOPPING

2 Tbsp all-purpose flour

2 Tbsp superfine sugar

1 egg yolk

¼ cup milk

3 Tbsp confectioners' sugar

½ stick unsalted butter

1 tsp coffee extract

PRALINE

½ cup granulated sugar

⅓ cup slivered almonds

Preheat oven to 350°F. Lightly grease two baking sheets or line with nonstick baking parchment.

● Sift the flour into a bowl. Stir in the ground almonds, then blend in the butter until the mixture resembles bread crumbs. Sift the confectioners' sugar and stir in. Add the egg yolk and mix to a dough.

● Lightly knead for a few seconds, then roll out on a lightly floured surface to ⅛ inch thick. Cut into rounds using a 2½-inch plain or fluted cutter. Place on the baking sheets. Bake for 10 minutes, until lightly browned. Transfer to a wire rack to cool.

● For the filling, put the flour and sugar in a small saucepan. Gradually blend in the egg yolk and milk to make a smooth paste. Bring to a boil and cook for 1 to 2 minutes until thick, stirring all the time. Leave to cool. Sift the confectioners' sugar into a bowl. Add the butter and beat until light. Add the coffee extract and mix well. Beat in the cooled custard, a little at a time. Chill in the refrigerator for 30 minutes.

● For the praline, put the sugar and 2 tablespoons water in a heavy-bottomed saucepan and heat gently until the sugar has completely dissolved. Bring to a boil and cook until a rich golden-brown. Add the nuts and pour onto an oiled baking sheet. Leave until cold, then crush the praline coarsely.

● Sandwich pairs of cookies together with coffee cream. Spread the top cookie with coffee cream and sprinkle with crushed praline.

Vanilla Fudge Crumbles

Preparation time: 30 minutes + chilling ● *Cooking time: 12 minutes* ● *Makes: About 20*

Chunks of creamy fudge contrast beautifully with the crunchy texture of these substantial cookies.

INGREDIENTS

3 oz vanilla fudge

2 cups all-purpose flour

½ tsp baking soda

1 stick unsalted butter

½ cup light brown sugar

1 egg

1 tsp vanilla extract

Confectioners' sugar, for dusting

Preheat oven to 375°F. Lightly grease two baking sheets or line with nonstick baking parchment.

● Finely chop the fudge. Sift the flour and baking soda into a bowl. Blend in the butter until the mixture resembles fine bread crumbs. Stir in the sugar. Mix the egg and vanilla extract together and add to the dry ingredients with the chopped fudge. Mix to a firm dough.

● Turn out onto a lightly floured surface and shape into a cylinder 9 inches long. Wrap and chill in the refrigerator for 30 minutes. Cut into 20 slices and put the slices on the baking sheets, spaced slightly apart.

● Bake for 12 minutes, until golden-brown. Leave on the baking sheets for 5 minutes, then transfer to a wire rack to cool. Lightly dust with confectioners' sugar before serving.

VARIATIONS

● Try different flavored fudges in the cookies for a change; chocolate, coffee, or rum and raisin fudge all taste delicious.

Triple Ginger Cookies

Preparation time: 30 minutes + chilling ●
Cooking time: 10 minutes ● *Makes: About 36*

These festive cookies are packed with ginger—ground, crystallized, and fresh—not for the faint-hearted.

INGREDIENTS

2¼ cups all-purpose flour
1 Tbsp ground ginger
2 Tbsp baking soda
½ tsp salt
1½ sticks unsalted butter, softened
¾ cup dark brown sugar
½ cup molasses
1 egg
2 Tbsp fine chopped fresh ginger root
½ cup chopped crystallized ginger, plus extra for decoration

Into a medium bowl, sift together the flour, ground ginger, baking soda, and salt.

● In a large bowl, beat the butter until soft, beat in the sugar until the mixture is light and fluffy. Beat in the molasses and egg until combined. Stir in the flour-spice mixture followed by the fresh and crystallized ginger.

● Form the dough into a ball, wrap in plastic wrap and refrigerate for 2 to 3 hours, or overnight until chilled.

● Preheat oven to 350°F. Grease or line two baking sheets with nonstick baking parchment.

● Using a tablespoon to scoop up the mixture, form into ½-inch balls. Place 2 inches apart on baking sheets and press a few pieces of crystallized ginger into each. Bake until golden-brown, about 10 minutes. Allow the cookies to cool for 2 minutes, then transfer to wire racks to cool completely. Store in an airtight container.

Kourambiedes

Preparation time: 25 minutes + chilling ●
Cooking time: 15 to 20 minutes ● *Makes: About 30*

These rich, tender almond cookies are served at all festive occasions in Greece. At Christmas they often bury a whole clove in the cookies to symbolize the gifts the three wise men brought to the Christ child.

INGREDIENTS

½ cup blanched almonds, lightly toasted and cooled
2 sticks unsalted butter
2 Tbsp confectioners' sugar
¼ tsp salt
1 small egg yolk
1 Tbsp brandy or orange-flavored liqueur
2 cups all-purpose flour
Confectioners' sugar, for dusting

In a food processor fitted with a metal blade, process the cooled toasted almonds until very fine crumbs are formed.

● In a medium bowl, beat the butter until soft, beat in the sugar until the mixture becomes light and fluffy. Beat in the salt, egg yolk, and brandy until combined. Stir in the flour and ground almonds until a soft dough forms. Refrigerate, covered, until firm, about 1 hour.

● Preheat oven to 450°F.

● Use a tablespoon to scoop out dough, and form into 1-inch balls. Place on ungreased baking sheets, and bake until set and just golden, about 15 to 20 minutes. Allow to cool slightly, then transfer the cookies onto wire racks to cool completely. Dust with confectioners' sugar. Store in an airtight container.

Cookie Candy Canes

Preparation time: 20 minutes + chilling ●
Cooking time: 15 to 17 minutes ● *Makes: About 24*

This cane dough can be shaped into candy canes or Christmas wreaths, then tinted whatever color you like.

INGREDIENTS

2 sticks unsalted butter, softened
1½ cups confectioners' sugar
½ tsp vanilla extract
¼ tsp peppermint extract
2½ cups all-purpose flour, sifted
¼ tsp salt
¼ tsp red food coloring, optional
2 oz crushed peppermint candies

In a large bowl, beat the butter until soft, beat in the sugar until the mixture becomes light and fluffy. Beat in the egg, vanilla, and peppermint extract until combined. Stir in the flour and salt until well blended.

● Place half the dough in plastic wrap and seal. Add food coloring and crushed peppermint candies to the remaining dough and beat until mixed. Wrap tightly in plastic wrap and refrigerate both doughs for 1 hour.

● Preheat oven to 350°F. Grease two baking sheets or line with nonstick baking parchment.

● To form canes, use a teaspoon to scoop out a piece of plain dough then roll into a 4-inch long log shape. Repeat with the red-colored dough. Twist the two logs together, and bend the top end to form into a cane shape. Set canes 2 inches apart on baking sheets.

● Bake until firm, about 8 to 10 minutes; do not allow to brown. Cool for a few minutes then place on wire racks to cool completely. Store in an airtight container.

Brandied Shortbread

Preparation time: 25 minutes ●
Cooking time: 25 minutes ● *Makes: 8 wedges*

This buttery brandy-flavored shortbread is enhanced by the addition of rice flour, giving it a lighter and crunchier texture.

INGREDIENTS

1 stick unsalted butter, softened
½ cup superfine sugar
1 Tbsp brandy
Few drops of brandy extract
1 cup all-purpose flour
⅓ cup fine rice flour
4 Tbsp candied cherries
Few pieces candied angelica
1 Tbsp superfine sugar, for sprinkling

Preheat oven to 350°F. Beat the butter in a mixing bowl, then gradually add the sugar, brandy, and brandy essence. Add the flour and rice flour and stir with a thin metal spatula until blended.

● Press the mixture into a 7-inch round shallow pan with a removable base and level the top. Prick all over with a fork. Mark into eight equal wedges and decorate each with small pieces of candied cherry angelica. Sprinkle with superfine sugar and bake for 25 minutes, or until pale golden.

● While the shortbread is still hot, carefully remove from the pan, but leave on the base. Cut into eight wedges, but do not separate the pieces, or they will dry out. Cool on a wire rack. Stored in an airtight pan or wrapped in foil, the shortbread will keep for up to a week.

Cranberry and Orange Clusters

Preparation time: 20 minutes ●
Cooking time: 15 minutes ● *Makes: 20*

The tartness of dried cranberries adds a certain bite to these soft-textured drop cookies.

INGREDIENTS

1 stick unsalted butter
½ cup superfine sugar
Grated rind of 1 orange
1 egg
1¼ cup rolled oats
½ cup dried cranberries
1¼ cups all-purpose flour
½ tsp baking powder

Preheat oven to 350°F. Lightly grease two baking sheets or line with nonstick baking parchment.

● Beat the butter, sugar, and orange rind in a bowl until creamy. Gradually add the egg, beating well between each addition. Stir in the oats and cranberries. Sift the flour and baking powder into the bowl and mix until evenly combined.

● Place small tablespoons of the mixture on the prepared baking sheets, spacing them well apart. Flatten slightly with the back of a fork. Bake for 15 minutes until risen and light golden-brown. Leave on the baking sheets for 5 minutes, then transfer to a wire rack to cool. The cookies will still be soft when you take them out of the oven, but will become firm as they cool.

Pumpkin Fingers

Preparation time: 30 minutes ●
Cooking time: 50 minutes ● *Makes: 18*

These buttery shortbread fingers with a pumpkin topping make a great alternative to pumpkin pie for a Thanksgiving supper.

INGREDIENTS

1 cup all-purpose flour
½ cup confectioners' sugar
½ stick unsalted butter
1 egg yolk

TOPPING

2 cups cooked pumpkin
1 cup light cream
2 eggs, beaten
1 cup packed light brown sugar
1 tsp ground cinnamon
1 Tbsp confectioners' sugar, for dusting

Preheat oven to 350°F. Grease a shallow 7 x 11-inch pan and line with nonstick baking parchment.

● Sift the flour and confectioners' sugar into a bowl. Blend in the butter until the mixture resembles fine bread crumbs. Add the egg yolk and mix to a dough. Lightly knead on a floured surface until smooth, then press into the base of the prepared pan. Prick all over with a fork, then bake for 10 minutes, until golden.

● For the filling, sift the cooked pumpkin to make a smooth purée. Stir in the cream, eggs, sugar, and cinnamon. Pour over the base and bake for 40 to 45 minutes more, or until a skewer inserted into the middle comes out clean.

● Leave to cool in the pan, then cut into 18 fingers. Remove from the pan and lightly dust with confectioners' sugar before serving.

Sticky Toffee Apple Treats

Preparation time: 25 minutes ● *Cooking time: 10 minutes* ● *Makes: 20*

These fall cookies are packed with chunks of apple and drizzled with toffee frosting.

INGREDIENTS

1 stick lightly salted butter

½ cup packed light brown sugar

1 egg, beaten

1¼ cups self-rising flour

Pinch of salt

1 cup dried apples, chopped

FROSTING

3 Tbsp butter

⅓ cup packed light brown sugar

3 Tbsp milk

¾ cup confectioners' sugar

Preheat oven to 375°F. Lightly grease two baking sheets or line with nonstick baking parchment.

● Beat the butter and sugar until light and fluffy. Gradually add the egg, beating well each time. Sift the flour and salt into the mixture and mix in the apples.

● Place heaping teaspoonfuls of the mixture onto the prepared baking sheets, spacing well apart to allow the cookies to spread. Bake for 10 minutes or until just golden-brown. Leave on the baking sheets for 3 minutes, then remove and cool on a wire rack.

● For the toffee frosting, melt the butter over a gentle heat. Add the brown sugar and milk and stir gently until dissolved. Boil for 1 minute. Remove from the heat, then sift the confectioners' sugar and beat in. Spoon into a decorating bag while still warm, snip off the end and drizzle over the cookies. Frost the cookies quickly before the frosting cools and starts to harden. Leave the frosting to set.

Shooting Stars

Preparation time: 40 minutes ● *Cooking time: 10 to 12 minutes* ● *Makes: 30*

Cut these cookies into stars of several sizes and sprinkle with colored sugar crystals before baking, for a sparkling effect.

INGREDIENTS

1 stick lightly salted butter

½ cup superfine sugar

Grated rind of 1 lemon

1 egg, beaten

2¼ cups all-purpose flour

¼ cup cornstarch

½ tsp vanilla extract

¼ cup colored sugar crystals

Preheat oven to 350°F. Lightly grease two baking sheets or line with nonstick baking parchment.

● Beat the butter, sugar, and lemon rind together until pale and fluffy. Gradually add the egg, beating well after each addition.

● Sift the flour and cornstarch together and blend into the butter mixture with the vanilla. Lightly knead for a few seconds until smooth. Roll out on a floured surface to ¼ inch thick, then cut into large and small star shapes using 2½ inch, 1½ inch and 1 inch floured cutters. Place on the prepared baking sheets, separating the largest stars.

● Sprinkle the tops with colored sugar crystals, then press down gently. Bake the smaller cookies for 10 minutes and the larger ones for 12 minutes, until golden. Leave to cool on the baking sheets for 3 minutes, then transfer to a wire rack to cool.

Celebration Cookies

Preparation time: 35 minutes ● *Cooking time: 15 minutes* ● *Makes: 8*

These giant all-American cookies are drizzled with frosting in the colors of the flag—red, white, and blue.

INGREDIENTS

½ stick lightly salted butter

½ cup shortening

⅓ cup light brown sugar

1 egg, beaten

½ tsp vanilla extract

1¼ cups self-rising flour

FROSTING

1 cup confectioners' sugar

1 Tbsp hot water

red and blue food coloring

Preheat oven to 375°F. Lightly grease two baking sheets or line with nonstick baking parchment.

● Beat the butter, shortening, and sugar together until light and fluffy. Gradually add the egg and vanilla, beating well between each addition. Sift the flour and stir into the mixture.

● Drop tablespoonfuls of the mixture onto the baking sheets, spacing well apart. Flatten to about ¾ inch thick. Bake for 15 minutes until golden. Leave on the baking sheets for 2 to 3 minutes, then remove and cool on a wire rack.

● Sift the confectioners' sugar into a bowl and stir in enough water to make a thick piping consistency. Divide the frosting into three. Leave one white, color one red, and one blue. Spoon into separate decorating bags, snip off the ends, and drizzle over the cookies. Leave to set before serving.

TIP

Unbaked, the cookie mixture will keep in a sealed container in the refrigerator for up to a week. The cookies are best eaten on the day they are frosted.

Coffee Meringues

Preparation time: 20 minutes ●
Cooking time: 2 hours ● *Makes: 50*

**Light as air crisp meringues with just a hint of coffee, are
dipped in smooth chocolate for bite-sized treats.**

INGREDIENTS

4 egg whites

1 cup superfine sugar

1 tsp coffee extract

8 oz semi-sweet chocolate

Preheat oven to 275°F. Lightly grease two baking
sheets or line with nonstick baking parchment.

● Put the egg whites and sugar into a large bowl over a
pan of very hot water and whisk until stiff and shiny,
making sure that the water does not boil, or the mixture
will get too hot. Remove the bowl from the heat, add the
coffee extract and continue whisking until the mixture
will hold stiff peaks.

● Spoon the mixture into a decorator's bag fitted with a
large star tube and pipe swirls of meringue on the
baking sheets. Bake for 2 hours or until completely
dried out, switching the baking sheets around halfway
through cooking. Allow the meringues to cool on the
baking sheets.

● Melt the chocolate in a bowl over very hot water. Dip
the base of the meringues into the chocolate and leave
to set on nonstick paper before serving, or if prefered,
sandwich the meringues together in pairs.

Cinnamon Balls

Preparation time: 20 minutes ●
Cooking time: 25 to 30 minutes ● *Makes: About 20*

**These are very popular Passover cookies,
as they contain no flour.**

INGREDIENTS

2 cups blanched and ground almonds, walnuts, or pecans

¼ cup superfine sugar

1 Tbsp ground cinnamon

2 egg whites

¼ tsp cream of tartar

Scant 1 cup confectioners' sugar

1 Tbsp ground cinnamon

Preheat oven to 325°F. Grease or line two baking
sheets with nonstick baking parchment.

● In a medium bowl, combine the nuts, half the sugar,
and the cinnamon. In a separate bowl, beat the egg
whites until foamy. Add the cream of tartar, and
continue beating until soft peaks form. Gradually add
the remaining sugar, a tablespoon at a time, beating well
after each addition, until the whites are stiff and glossy.
Gently fold in the nut mixture.

● With moistened hands, shape mixture into walnut-
size balls. Place on baking sheets 1 inch apart. Bake until
set and golden, 25 to 30 minutes, turning baking sheets
halfway through cooking. Allow the cookies to cool
slightly.

● Combine the confectioners' sugar and cinnamon. Roll
each warm cinnamon ball in the mixture to coat
completely, then set on a wire rack to cool. Roll balls in
the cinnamon-sugar again when cold. Store in an
airtight container.

Hanukkah Sugar Cookies

Preparation time: 45 minutes + chilling ● *Cooking time: 20 to 24 minutes* ● *Makes: About 40*

**Search out some unusual cutters for this special joyous holiday, or make your own
Jewish star template from a piece of cardboard.**

INGREDIENTS

2 ¼ cups all-purpose flour

½ tsp baking powder

½ tsp salt

1½ sticks unsalted butter, softened

⅔ cup superfine sugar

1 egg, beaten

Grated rind of 1 lemon

1 Tbsp fresh lemon juice

1 tsp vanilla extract

½ tsp lemon extract

FROSTING

4½ cups confectioners' sugar

2-3 Tbsp milk

1 Tbsp lemon juice

Blue food coloring

Into a medium bowl, sift together the flour, baking powder, and salt. In a large bowl beat the butter, until creamy, then add the sugar and beat until light and fluffy. Gradually beat in the egg, lemon rind and juice, vanilla, and lemon extract until well blended. Little by little add the flour mixture until a soft dough forms. Wrap in plastic wrap and refrigerate for several hours or overnight until firm enough to roll (the dough can be made up to 2 days ahead).

● Preheat oven to 350°F. Grease or line two baking sheets with nonstick baking parchment.

● On a lightly floured surface, roll out half the dough to ¼ inch thick (keep the remaining dough refrigerated). Using a floured cutter or template, cut out as many shapes as possible. Place 1 inch apart on the baking sheets. Bake until golden, 10 to 12 minutes. Allow the cookies to cool slightly, then transfer to wire racks to cool completely. Repeat with remaining dough.

● In a medium bowl, sift the confectioners' sugar. Stir in 2 tablespoons of milk and the lemon juice, adding a little more milk if the mixture is too thick. Spoon half of the frosting into a separate bowl and add a few drops of food coloring mixing to the desired shade. Spoon the frostings into two decorating bags and pipe designs or decorations onto each cookie shape. Leave frosting to set for 2 hours. Store in an airtight container with a layer of waxed paper between each of the cookie layers.

Sweethearts

Preparation time: 45 minutes ● *Cooking time: 10 minutes* ● *Makes: 20*

Use gingerbread men and women cutters to make these cute cookies with tiny hearts.

INGREDIENTS

1 Tbsp corn syrup	1 egg yolk
½ stick butter	2 oz pink or red boiled candies
¼ cup superfine sugar	FROSTING
2 cups all-purpose flour	2 cups confectioners' sugar
½ tsp baking soda	1 egg white
3 Tbsp milk	¼ tsp lemon juice

Preheat oven to 350°F. Line two baking sheets with nonstick baking parchment.

● Put the syrup, butter, and sugar in a small saucepan and heat gently until melted, stirring occasionally. Remove from the heat and leave to cool for 2 to 3 minutes. Sift the flour and baking soda into a mixing bowl and make a well in the middle. Pour in the syrup mixture, milk, and egg yolk. Mix to form a soft smooth dough.

● Roll out the warm dough between two sheets of nonstick baking parchment or plastic wrap until ⅛ inch thick. Cut into men and women using 3-inch cutters.

Transfer to the baking sheets. Cut a small heart shape from the center of each.

● Roughly crush the boiled candies and sprinkle about a quarter of a candy in each cutout section. Bake for 10 minutes, until lightly browned and firm. Leave to cool on the baking sheets.

● Sift the confectioners' sugar twice. Put the egg white in a bowl and whisk lightly. Gradually beat in enough confectioners' sugar until the mixture stands in soft peaks and is a pipeable consistency. Spoon into a decorating bag fitted with a number 1 tube and pipe faces, buttons, and bows on the people. Leave to set.

Honeyed Hearts

Preparation time: 20 minutes + chilling ●
Cooking time: 15 minutes ● *Makes: 30*

These honey cookies with a crunchy sugar topping will melt even the hardest heart.

INGREDIENTS

¾ stick lightly salted butter

½ cup superfine sugar

1 Tbsp set honey

1 egg, beaten

1½ cups all-purpose flour

2 Tbsp cornstarch

1 Tbsp egg white

2 Tbsp brown sugar coffee crystals

Preheat oven to 350°F. Lightly grease two baking sheets or line with nonstick baking parchment.
● Beat the butter, sugar, and honey until very soft, light and fluffy. Gradually add the egg. Sift the flour and cornstarch together and work into the butter mixture to make a soft dough. Lightly knead on a floured surface for a few seconds until smooth, then wrap in plastic wrap and chill in the refrigerator for 30 minutes.
● Roll out on a lightly floured surface to a thickness of ¼ inch. Cut into heart shapes using a floured 2-inch cutter. Place on the baking sheets, spacing slightly apart. Brush the cookies with egg white and sprinkle each with a few sugar crystals. Bake for 15 minutes, or until lightly browned. Leave the cookies on the baking sheets for 2 to 3 minutes, then remove and cool on a wire rack.

Rose Petal Cookies

Preparation time: 25 minutes + chilling ●
Cooking time: 10 minutes ● *Makes: 16*

Make these fragrant cookies using red or yellow perfumed rose petals.

INGREDIENTS

2¼ cups all-purpose flour

1 cup confectioners' sugar

1¾ sticks unsalted butter

Petals of 2 roses

Lightly grease two baking sheets or line with nonstick baking parchment. Sift the flour and confectioners' sugar into a bowl. Blend in the butter until the mixture resembles fine bread crumbs.
● Snip the rose petals into small pieces with scissors and stir into the mixture. Continue to blend with the fingers until a dough forms. Lightly knead for a few seconds on a floured surface until smooth. Roll the dough into a cylinder about 8 inches long. Wrap in plastic wrap and chill in the refrigerator for 1 hour.
● Preheat oven to 325°F. Cut the dough into ½-inch slices and arrange on the baking sheets, spacing slightly apart. Bake for 8 to 10 minutes until light golden-brown. Leave on the baking sheets for 2 minutes, then remove and cool on a wire rack.

TIP

Make sure you use unsprayed freshly picked roses for these cookies.

Lovers' Knots

Preparation time: 45 minutes + chilling ●
Cooking time: 10 minutes ● *Makes: 20*

Rich, dark, and handsome, chocolate cookie dough is twisted into knots, then dipped into yet more chocolate.

INGREDIENTS

¼ cup unsweetened cocoa powder
2 Tbsp boiling water
1 tsp vanilla extract
1 stick lightly salted butter
½ cup superfine sugar
1 egg, beaten
2 cups all-purpose flour
12 oz semi-sweet chocolate

Lightly grease two baking sheets or line with nonstick baking parchment. Sift the unsweetened cocoa powder into a small bowl and pour on the boiling water. Stir to form a smooth paste, then stir in the vanilla extract.

● Beat the butter and sugar until light and fluffy. Gradually add the egg, beating well after each addition. Beat in the cocoa mixture until well mixed. Sift the flour and work into the mixture to make a soft dough. Wrap in plastic wrap and chill for 1 hour.

● Preheat oven to 325°F. Divide the dough into 20 pieces. Roll each piece into a sausage shape about 6 inches long, then tie in a loose knot, tucking the ends under. Arrange on the prepared baking sheets and bake for 10 minutes until firm. Allow to cool on the sheets.

● Break the chocolate into pieces and melt, stirring, in a bain-marie. Coat the knots, one at a time, with the chocolate. Leave to set on a wire rack.

Soft Centers

Preparation time: 25 minutes + chilling ●
Cooking time: 10 minutes ● *Makes: 20*

A crisp coffee case conceals a melted chocolate center. Serve these cookies freshly baked while still warm.

INGREDIENTS

1¼ sticks unsalted butter
¾ cup superfine sugar
2 tsp coffee extract
1 egg yolk
2½ cups self-rising flour
2 oz semi-sweet chocolate
2 oz white chocolate
1 Tbsp unsweetened cocoa powder, for dusting

Lightly grease a large baking sheet or line with nonstick baking parchment. Beat the butter and sugar until light and fluffy. Beat in the coffee extract and egg yolk. Sift the flour into the bowl and mix to a firm dough. Wrap and chill in the refrigerator for 20 minutes.

● Preheat oven to 350°F.

● Roll out about a third of the dough on a lightly floured surface to ⅛ inch thick and cut out 20 circles with a 2-inch cutter. Transfer to the prepared baking sheet. Place a square of chocolate in the middle of each circle. Roll out the remaining dough and cut out 20 circles with a 2½-inch cutter. Lay these over the chocolate-topped bases, pressing the edges together to seal and enclose the filling.

● Bake for 10 minutes, until darkened and risen. Leave on the baking sheets for 5 minutes, then remove and cool on a wire rack. Dust with cocoa powder before serving.

Shamrocks

Preparation time: 25 minutes + chilling ● *Cooking time: 15 minutes* ● *Makes: 20*

The emblem of Ireland is the shamrock and these cookies are ideal to serve on St Patrick's day.

INGREDIENTS

2 oz mint-flavored chocolate sticks

1½ sticks butter

1 cup superfine sugar

1 egg

3 cups all-purpose flour

FROSTING

2 cups confectioners' sugar

¼ tsp mint extract

2 Tbsp hot water

Green food coloring

Lightly grease two baking sheets or line with nonstick baking parchment. Finely chop the mint-flavored chocolate sticks. Beat the butter and sugar until light and fluffy. Gradually add the egg, beating well after each addition. Sift the flour into the bowl, add the chocolate pieces, and mix to a soft dough. Lightly knead for a few seconds until smooth, then wrap in plastic wrap and chill in the refrigerator for 30 minutes.

● Preheat oven to 350°F. Roll out the dough on a lightly floured surface until ¼ inch thick and cut into shamrock shapes with a 2½-inch cutter. Transfer to the baking sheets. Bake for 15 minutes, until light golden-brown. Leave on the baking sheets for 2 to 3 minutes, then remove and cool on a wire rack.

● Sift the confectioners' sugar into a bowl. Add the mint extract and enough water to make a thick frosting. Stir in a drop of green food coloring. Use to ice the cookies. Leave the frosting to set before serving.

Sedgemoor Easter Cookies

Preparation time: 15 minutes ● *Cooking time: 20 minutes* ● *Makes: 16*

Legend tells that when the Duke of Monmouth was fleeing the Battle of Sedgemoor, he fell into a ditch. A local woman thought he was an unfortunate peasant down on his luck and baked him these cookies.

INGREDIENTS

2 cups all-purpose flour

1 tsp ground cinnamon

1 stick lightly salted butter

½ cup superfine sugar

½ cup currants

1 egg, beaten

2 Tbsp brandy

1 Tbsp milk

1 Tbsp granulated sugar, for sprinkling

Preheat oven to 350°F. Lightly grease two baking sheets or line with nonstick baking parchment.

● Sift the flour and cinnamon into a bowl and blend in the butter until the mixture resembles bread crumbs. Stir in the sugar and currants. Mix the egg, brandy, and milk together and stir into the dry mixture to produce a soft dropping consistency.

● Drop tablespoonfuls of the mixture onto the baking sheet and sprinkle with granulated sugar. Bake for 20 minutes, until lightly browned and firm. Leave on the baking sheets for a few minutes, then remove and cool on a wire rack.

VARIATION

Mixed dried fruit or quartered candied cherries can be added to the mixture instead of currants.

Frosted Easter Ovals

Preparation time: 25 minutes ● *Cooking time: 15 minutes* ● *Makes: 20*

These chocolate chip cookies with pastel ribbon and bow frosting make great Easter treats.

INGREDIENTS

½ stick butter

1 cup superfine sugar

1 egg, beaten

3 cups all-purpose flour

2 Tbsp cornstarch

⅓ cup semi-sweet chocolate chips

FROSTING

2 cups confectioners' sugar

2 Tbsp hot water

Pink, green, and yellow food coloring

Preheat oven to 350°F. Lightly grease two baking sheets or line with nonstick baking parchment.

● Beat the butter and sugar until light and fluffy. Gradually add the egg. Sift the flour with the cornstarch and work into the butter mixgture with the chocolate chips to make a stiff dough. Lightly knead the dough for a few seconds until smooth.

● Roll out on a floured surface to a thickness of ¼ inch. Cut into 20 ovals with a plain or fluted 3-inch oval cutter. Bake in the oven for 15 minutes, until light golden-brown. Leave the cookies to cool on the baking sheets for a few minutes, then remove to a wire rack to cool completely.

● For the frosting, sift the confectioners' sugar into a bowl and stir in enough hot water to make a smooth frosting. Divide the frosting into three and color one pale pink, one pale green, and one yellow. Spoon into decorating bags, snip off the ends and pipe a ribbon and bow design on each cookie. Leave to set before serving.

291

Maypole Twists

Preparation time: 40 minutes + chilling ● *Cooking time: 10 minutes* ● *Makes: 12*

Strands of dough, one coated in colored sugar crystals are twisted together to make these cookies.

INGREDIENTS

2 cups all-purpose flour
1 tsp baking powder
½ stick unsalted butter
½ cup superfine sugar
Grated rind of 1 lemon
1 Tbsp lemon juice
1 egg, beaten
2 Tbsp yellow and orange sugar crystals

Line two baking sheets with nonstick baking parchment. Sift the flour and baking powder into a bowl. Blend in the butter until the mixture resembles fine bread crumbs. Stir in the sugar and lemon rind. Add the lemon juice and beaten egg and mix to a soft dough. Lightly knead for a few seconds until smooth. Wrap in plastic wrap and chill in the refrigerator for 30 minutes.

● Preheat oven to 350°F. Divide the dough into 24 pieces. Roll each into a 4-inch length, then roll 12 of the lengths in the sugar crystals. Place 2 lengths side by side, one sugar-coated and one plain, and press the top ends together. Twist the two lengths together, pressing the ends to join again at the finish and trimming.

● Place on the prepared baking sheets, spacing slightly apart, and bake for 10 minutes until light golden-brown. Leave on the baking sheets for 2 minutes, then remove and cool on a wire rack.

VARIATION

● If preferred the twists can be glazed with a lemon frosting instead of using the sugar crystals. Sift 1 cup confectioners' sugar into a bowl. Stir in 5 teaspoons lemon juice to make a thin frosting. Lightly brush over the twists while still warm. Leave the cookies to cool and the frosting to set before serving.

Fruit Cookies

This chapter is full of unusual cookies using the wide range of fruits now on the market. Everyday fruits, such as apples, oranges, and bananas, make an appearance along with exotic star fruits, papayas, and papaws. Some recipes use fresh fruit, but many more exploit the rich, intense flavors of dried fruits. A number of cookies contrast the sharp flavor of candied fruits with the sweetness of the cookie with stunning effect.

There are several bar cookies in this section that would be excellent in lunch-boxes and many of the chunky fruit cookies would travel well. Next time you plan a hike or take a trip to the beach, make up a batch of cookies to nibble when hunger pangs strike.

Quick Bites

Dates and Cinnamon Cookies	298
Orange and Cardamom Filled Thins	298
Cherry Rings	301
The Ultimate Banana Cookies	302
Spicy Mixed Fruit Bars	303

Combined Flavors

Blackberry and Orange Cookies	304
Lemon and Lime Thins	305
Strawberry Pinwheels	306
Tropical Papaya Drops	307
Cherry and Vanilla Squares	309
Banana and Cointreau Temptations	309
Carrot and Date Drops	310

Fruity Treats

Passion Fruit Shortbread	311
Chewy Pineapple Drops	312
Mango and Ginger Delights	312
Honeyed Apricot Cookies	313
Prune and Grapefuit Marmalade Drops	313
Cherry Chocolate Cookies	315
Fruit Salad and Brazil Nuts	315
Exotic Fruit and Coconut Treats	316
Tangerine Fingers	317
Banana Chocolate Squares	319
Cranberry and White Chocolate Cookies	320
Chunky Mixed Fruit Squares	321

Fresh and Dried Fruits

Truly Blueberry Cookies	322
Pear Bars	324
Candied Cherry Florentines	325
Candied Peel and Dark Chocolate Squares	327
Apricot Wheels	328
Rum and Raisin Cookies	330
Brandy and Fresh Apple Cookies	330
Crumbly Pineapple Cookies	331
Star Fruit Cookies	332
Chewy Peach and Cherry Thins	332
Pineapple and Ginger Cookies	333
Winter Fruit Cookies	334
Pear and Walnut Cookies	334

Dates and Cinnamon Cookies

Preparation time: 15 minutes + chilling ●
Cooking time: 15 to 18 minutes ● *Makes: About 30*

Dates are soft and chewy and keep these cookies really moist.

INGREDIENTS

2 sticks butter, softened

¾ cup packed light brown sugar

3 Tbsp corn syrup

2 eggs, beaten

3 cups all-purpose flour

1 tsp ground cinnamon

1½ cups chopped dates

Put butter, sugar, and corn syrup in a bowl. Beat until light and fluffy. Gradually add the eggs; mix well between additions. Sift in the flour and cinnamon; mix well. Stir in the dates. Chill for 2 hours.

● Preheat oven to 350°F. Grease two baking sheets or line with nonstick baking parchment.

● Roll teaspoons of the mixture into balls and flatten slightly. Arrange on the baking sheets at least 2 inches apart and bake for 15 to 18 minutes. Allow to cool for 5 minutes then transfer to wire racks to cool completely. Store in an airtight container.

Orange and Cardamom Filled Thins

Preparation time: 40 minutes + chilling ● *Cooking time: 12 minutes* ● *Makes: About 20 filled cookies*

These are delicate sandwich cookies, but they are also great fun for kids to make.

INGREDIENTS

1 stick butter, softened

⅔ cup superfine sugar

2 medium eggs, beaten

Grated rind of 1 large orange

1 cup all-purpose flour

2 tsp ground cardamom

FILLING

1¼ cups confectioners' sugar

3 Tbsp butter, softened

1 Tbsp orange juice

Put the butter and sugar in a bowl and beat until light and fluffy. Gradually beat in the eggs and orange rind. Sift in the flour and ground cardamom and mix well. Form into a ball and chill for 30 minutes.

● Meanwhile, beat together the filling ingredients, adding the orange juice gradually.

● Preheat oven to 375°F. Grease two baking sheets or line with nonstick baking parchment.

● Roll out the dough thinly and stamp out 2-inch rounds using a straight edged cutter. Place the cookies on the baking sheets spaced about 1 inch apart. Bake for about 12 minutes until golden. Cool for 5 minutes on the sheet then transfer to wire racks to cool completely.

● Sandwich the cookies together with the filling.

Cherry Rings

Preparation time: 40 minutes + chilling ● *Cooking time: 20 minutes* ● *Makes: About 30*

These are crispy cookies with a chewy cherry topping.

INGREDIENTS

1¼ sticks butter, softened

½ cup superfine sugar

⅔ cup packed light brown sugar

1 tsp vanilla extract

2½ cups all-purpose flour

1 cup dried cherries, roughly chopped

GLAZE

1 small egg, beaten

3 tsp milk

2 tsp superfine sugar

Put the butter, sugars, and vanilla in a mixing bowl and beat with an electric mixer until light and fluffy. Sift in the flour, mix well, and form into a soft dough and chill for 30 minutes in the refrigerator.

● Preheat oven to 325°F. Grease two large baking sheets or line with nonstick baking parchment.

● Mix the glaze ingredients together.

● Dust work surface with flour and roll out dough to ½-inch thick. Stamp out 2½-inch rounds with a fluted cutter. Then, cut out the center with a ½-inch cutter. Transfer to the baking sheets and brush with the glaze. Decorate with the cherries, covering the entire surface.

● Bake for about 20 minutes until light brown. Cool for 5 minutes then transfer to wire racks to cool completely. Store in an airtight container.

VARIATION

● Substitute 1 cup of dried blueberries for the cherries.

The Ultimate Banana Cookies

Preparation time: 15 minutes + chilling ● *Cooking time: 18 to 20 minutes* ● *Makes: About 35*

You simply can't fit any more bananas into these banana coconut cookies!

INGREDIENTS

1½ sticks butter, softened

½ cup superfine sugar

½ cup packed soft brown sugar

1 egg, beaten

3 medium bananas, mashed

1 tsp vanilla extract

2¼ cups all-purpose flour

1 tsp baking powder

1½ cups dried banana chips, broken up

½ cup shredded sweetened coconut

Put the butter and sugars in a bowl and beat until light and fluffy. Gradually beat in the egg ensuring each addition is well incorporated. Stir in the mashed bananas and vanilla extract. Sift in the flour and baking powder. Then stir in the banana chips and coconut. Chill for at least 2 hours in the refrigerator.

● Preheat oven to 375°F. Grease two baking sheets or line with nonstick baking parchment.

● Take tablespoons of the mixture and roll into balls. Flatten slightly then place on the baking sheets at least 2 inches apart. Bake for 18 to 20 minutes until golden. Chill for 5 minutes then transfer to wire cooling racks. Store in an airtight container.

Spicy Mixed Fruit Bars

Preparation time: 30 minutes ● *Cooking time: 40 minutes* ● *Makes: 12 bars*

These are substantial bars of moist fruit and coconut, well worth the effort.

INGREDIENTS

TOPPING

⅓ cup fine chopped dried apricots

⅓ cup golden raisins

⅓ cup fine chopped dried peaches

⅓ cup dried blueberries

3 Tbsp brandy

3 eggs, beaten

½ cup packed light brown sugar

½ cup all-purpose flour

1 tsp baking powder

½ cup shredded sweetened coconut, packed

BASE

½ cup butter, softened

⅓ cup superfine sugar

1¼ cups all-purpose flour

1 tsp ground ginger

1 tsp ground cinnamon

Put the apricots, golden raisins, peaches and blueberries in a bowl and add the brandy. Leave to soak for 20 minutes.

● Preheat oven to 350°F. Grease and line the base of a 13 x 9-inch pan with nonstick baking parchment.

● Prepare the base. Place the butter and sugar in a bowl and beat until light and fluffy. Sift in the flour, ginger, and cinnamon and mix to a dough. Spread over the base of the pan and bake for 8 to 10 minutes.

● While the base is cooking, finish making the topping. Beat the eggs and sugar together for about 5 minutes until thick and creamy. Sift in the flour and baking powder. Stir in the coconut and soaked fruit. Pour over the baked base and bake for a further 30 to 35 minutes until firm to the touch. Cool in the sheet before cutting into 12 bars. Store in an airtight container.

Blackberry and Orange Cookies

Preparation time: 20 minutes + chilling ● *Cooking time: 15 to 17 minutes* ● *Makes: About 35*

These plump, purplish-black berries give a wonderful flavor to these simple butter cookies. If they are not in season when you want to bake these cookies, you can use dried fruits, such as blueberries or cranberries instead—readily available from supermarkets and whole food stores.

INGREDIENTS

2 sticks butter, softened

¾ cup superfine sugar

¾ cup packed light brown sugar

2 eggs, beaten

Grated rind of 1 orange

2¼ cups all-purpose flour

1 tsp salt

1 tsp baking powder

1¼ cups whole blackberries

Beat together butter and sugars until soft and creamy. Gradually beat in the eggs and orange rind. The mixture may look like it is curdling, but it will be fine when cooked. Sift in flour, salt, and baking powder and mix to combine. Add blackberries and mix well. Chill the mixture for at least one hour in the refrigerator.

● Preheat oven to 350°F. Grease two large baking sheets or line with nonstick baking parchment.

● Roll tablespoons of the mixture into balls and place on the baking sheets at least 3 inches apart. Flatten slightly with the back of a spoon. Bake for 15 to 17 minutes until golden. Leave to cool for 5 minutes then transfer to wire racks to cool completely. Store in an airtight container.

TIP

Dried apricots, papaya, mango, or peach also work well in these cookies.

Lemon and Lime Thins

Preparation time: 15 minutes + chilling ● *Cooking time: 15 to 18 minutes* ● *Makes: About 20*

The frosted lemon rind garnish is an effective way of jazzing up simple cookies.

INGREDIENTS

2 lemons
1 lime
1 stick butter, softened
5 Tbsp superfine sugar
1¼ cups all-purpose flour
1 egg white
Confectioners' sugar, to decorate

Pare the rind from one lemon and place in a bowl. Grate the rind from the lime and other lemon into a separate bowl and squeeze 2 tablespoons of juice from the lemon.

● Put butter, 3 tablespoons of the sugar and grated rinds in a bowl and beat until light and fluffy. Add lemon juice gradually. Sift in the flour and mix to a soft dough. Place on a piece of waxed paper and form into a log. Chill for one hour.

● Meanwhile, place the lemon rind in a pan of boiling water for one minute. Drain and pat dry. Lightly beat the egg white until frothy. Dip the rind into the egg white then into the remaining sugar to frost. Leave to dry on waxed paper.

● Preheat oven to 350°F. Grease two baking sheets or line with nonstick baking parchment.

● Slice the dough log into ½-inch slices and place on the baking sheets. Bake for 15 to 18 minutes. Leave to cool for 5 minutes then transfer to wire cooling racks. Top with the frosted rind and dust lightly with confectioners' sugar to serve, if liked.

Strawberry Pinwheels

Preparation time: 35 minutes + chilling ● *Cooking time: 11 to 13 minutes* ● *Makes: About 16*

Adults and kids alike will have great fun making these festive cookies.

INGREDIENTS

1 stick butter, softened

1 Tbsp superfine sugar

1 tsp vanilla extract

1¼ cups all-purpose flour

3 Tbsp strawberry jam

Put butter, sugar, and vanilla extract in a bowl and beat until light and creamy. Sift in the flour. Mix to a dough by hand then chill for 30 minutes.

● Preheat oven to 350°F. Grease two baking sheets or line with nonstick baking parchment.

● Roll out half the dough on a piece of floured waxed paper to a 10-inch square. Trim to these dimensions. Cut into 16 equal-sized squares with a blunt knife or fluted pastry cutter. Cut a 1-inch slice from each corner towards the center. If the dough sticks to the knife dip it in flour.

● Put half a teaspoon of jam into the center of each cookie. Fold over every other corner to the center to form a pinwheel, lightly sticking the dough to the jam. Transfer to the baking sheets and bake for 11 to 13 minutes.

● Cool for 5 minutes on the baking sheets then transfer to wire cooling racks. Store in an airtight container.

Tropical Papaya Drops

Preparation time: 20 minutes + cooling ● *Cooking time: 15 to 18 minutes* ● *Makes: About 30 drops*

Dried papaya has a more intense flavor than fresh, so a little gives a strong flavor.

INGREDIENTS

1¾ cups all-purpose flour

1 tsp baking powder

1 Tbsp superfine sugar

1 cup fine chopped, dried papaya

1 stick butter

½ cup corn syrup

1 tsp vanilla extract

Preheat oven to 350°F. Grease two baking sheets or line with nonstick baking parchment.

● Sift the flour and baking powder into a large bowl. Stir in the sugar and chopped papaya and make a well in the center. Put the butter, corn syrup, and vanilla extract in a small saucepan and stir over a gentle heat until the butter has melted. Pour into the dry ingredients and mix to a soft dough. Cool for 10 minutes.

● Take teaspoons of the mixture and roll into balls. Place on the baking sheets at least 2 inches apart and flatten slightly with the back of a spoon. Bake for 15 to 18 minutes. Cool for 5 minutes, then transfer to wire cooling racks. Store in an airtight container.

VARIATION

You can substitute papaws for the papaya or try using a combination of mango and papaya for truly tropical cookie treats.

Cherry and Vanilla Squares

Preparation time: 20 minutes •
Cooking time: 30 to 35 minutes • Makes: 16

Use dried Morello or sour cherries, rather than candied cherries for these moist squares.

INGREDIENTS

1¼ cups all-purpose flour

⅓ cup confectioners' sugar

1¾ sticks cold butter

2 tsp vanilla extract

1 cup dried cherries

Preheat oven to 350°F. Grease or line an 8 x 8-inch pan with nonstick baking parchment.

● Sift flour and confectioners' sugar together into a bowl. Add butter and vanilla and blend in with your fingertips until the mixture resembles coarse bread crumbs. Stir in the cherries and form into a soft dough.

● Transfer to the pan and press to fit. Bake for 30 to 35 minutes. Leave to cool then cut into 16 bars. Store, covered in the pan or in an airtight container.

TIP

For extra flavor and stickiness, brush the cooked dough with cherry or strawberry preserve when it comes out of the oven.

Banana and Cointreau Temptations

Preparation time: 20 minutes + chilling •
Cooking time: 15 to18 minutes • Makes: About 30

Cointreau is delicately flavored with orange which is the perfect partner for bananas.

INGREDIENTS

1¼ cups honeyed banana chips

2 sticks butter, softened

¾ cup superfine sugar

¼ cup packed light brown sugar

2 eggs, beaten

2 Tbsp Cointreau

2¼ cups all-purpose flour

1 tsp salt

1 tsp baking powder

Place the banana chips in a bag and smash with a rolling pin or wooden spoon to break them up.

● Beat together butter and sugars until soft and creamy. Gradually beat in eggs and Cointreau. Sift in flour, salt, and baking powder and mix to combine. Add bananas and mix well. Chill the mixture for at least one hour in the refrigerator.

● Preheat oven to 350°F. Grease two large baking sheets or line with nonstick baking parchment.

● Roll tablespoons of the mixture into balls and place on the baking sheets at least 3 inches apart. Flatten slightly with the back of a spoon. Bake for 15 to 18 minutes until golden.

● Leave to cool for 5 minutes then transfer to wire racks to cool completely. Store in an airtight container.

Carrot and Date Drops

Preparation time: 15 minutes + chilling ● *Cooking time: 10 to 12 minutes* ● *Makes: About 25*

These are unusual, delicious, and moist—maybe more like a cake than a cookie.

INGREDIENTS

1 stick butter, softened
½ cup packed light brown sugar
1 egg, beaten
¾ cup all-purpose flour
1 tsp baking powder
1 tsp salt
1 tsp ground nutmeg
½ tsp ground ginger
¾ cup grated carrot
1 cup chopped dates

Put butter and sugar in a bowl and beat until light and fluffy. Gradually beat in the egg. Sift in the flour, baking powder, salt, nutmeg, and ginger and stir until combined. Then stir in the carrots and dates. Chill for at least 2 hours.

● Preheat oven to 375°F. Grease two baking sheets or line with nonstick baking parchment.

● Take small tablespoons of the mixture and roll into balls, then flatten slightly. Place at least 2 inches apart on the baking sheets and bake for 10 to 12 minutes. Cool for 5 minutes on the baking sheets then transfer to wire racks to cool completely. Store the cookies in an airtight container.

Passionfruit Shortbread

Preparation time: 25 minutes + chilling ● Cooking time: 20 minutes ● Makes: About 20

Sometimes called purple granadillas, the passion fruit pulp contains masses of small seeds that are left in the dough for an added crunch.

INGREDIENTS

1½ sticks butter, softened

¼ cup superfine sugar

1 ½ cups all-purpose flour

½ cup cornstarch

Pulp of 3 passion fruit

Confectioners' sugar to decorate, optional

Put butter and sugar in a bowl and beat until light and fluffy. Sift in the flour and cornstarch and mix to a dough by hand. Stir in the passion fruit pulp.

● Transfer to a piece of waxed paper and form the dough into a log. Then chill for at least one hour in the refrigerator.

● Preheat oven to 350°F. Grease two baking sheets or line with nonstick baking parchment.

● Cut ½-inch slices from the log and place on the baking sheets. Bake for about 20 minutes until golden-brown. Cool for 5 minutes on the baking sheets then transfer to wire racks to cool completely. Dust with confectioners' sugar to serve, if liked. Store in an airtight container and eat within 4 days.

Chewy Pineapple Drops

Preparation time: 20 minutes + chilling ●
Cooking time: 15 minutes ● *Makes: About 30*

These are very sweet cookies.

INGREDIENTS

2 sticks butter, softened

¾ cup superfine sugar

¾ cup packed light brown sugar

2 eggs, beaten

2 Tbsp honey

2¼ cups all-purpose flour

1 tsp salt

1 tsp baking powder

1⅓ cups chopped dried pineapple

Beat together butter and sugars until light and fluffy. Gradually beat in the egg and honey. The mixture may look like it is curdling, but it will be fine when cooked. Sift in flour, salt, and baking powder and mix to combine. Add pineapple and mix well. Chill the mixture for at least one hour in the refrigerator.

● Preheat oven to 350°F. Grease two large baking sheets or line with nonstick baking parchment.

● Roll heaped teaspoons of the mixture into balls and place on the baking sheets at least 3 inches apart. Flatten slightly with the back of a spoon. Bake for 15 minutes until golden. Leave to cool for 5 minutes then transfer the cookies to wire racks to cool completely. Store in an airtight container.

Dried Mango and Ginger Delights

Preparation time: 20 minutes ●
Cooking time: 15 minutes ● *Makes: About 40*

Using cream cheese makes this cookie dough really soft and pliable.

INGREDIENTS

¾ stick butter, softened

⅓ cup cream cheese, softened

⅔ cup superfine sugar

1 tsp baking powder

1 egg, beaten

1 Tbsp ginger preserve or stem ginger syrup

2¼ cups all-purpose flour

1 cup fine chopped dried mango

2 tsp finely chopped crystallized or stem ginger

Put butter and cream cheese in a bowl and beat for 30 seconds. Add sugar and beat until light and fluffy. Add the baking powder, egg, and syrup and beat again. Sift in the flour and beat for 30 seconds.

● Stir in the mango and chopped stem or preserved ginger and form the mixture into a soft dough. Form into a ball, wrap in plastic wrap and chill for 30 minutes in the refrigerator.

● Preheat oven to 350°F. Grease two baking sheets or line with nonstick baking parchment.

● Roll out dough to about ⅓-inch thick and stamp out shapes with cutters. Reroll as necessary. Transfer to the baking sheets and bake for about 15 minutes until lightly golden. Chill for 5 minutes on the baking sheets then transfer to wire cooling racks. Store the cookies in an airtight container.

Honeyed Apricot Cookies

Preparation time: 15 minutes + chilling ●
Cooking time: 15 minutes ● *Makes: About 30*

If you can find honeyed apricots, use these and omit the honey from this recipe.

INGREDIENTS

2 sticks butter, softened
¾ cup superfine sugar
¾ cup packed light brown sugar
2 eggs, beaten
2 Tbsp honey
1 tsp ground ginger
2 cups plus 3 Tbsp all-purpose flour
1 tsp salt
1 tsp baking powder
1 cup chopped apricots

Beat together butter and sugars until soft and creamy. Gradually beat in the eggs and honey. The mixture may look like it is curdling, but it will be fine when cooked. Sift in ginger, flour, salt, and baking powder and mix to combine. Add diced apricots and mix well. Chill the mixture for at least one hour in the refrigerator.

● Preheat oven to 350°F. Grease two large baking sheets or line with nonstick baking parchment.

● Roll tablespoons of the mixture into balls and place on the baking sheets at least 3 inches apart. Flatten slightly with the back of a spoon. Bake for 15 minutes until golden. Leave to cool for 5 minutes on the sheets then transfer to wire racks to cool completely. Store in an airtight container.

Prune and Grapefruit Marmalade Drops

Preparation time: 15 minutes + chilling ●
Cooking time: 15 to 17 minutes ● *Makes: About 30*

These are quite dry, chunky cookies.

INGREDIENTS

2 sticks butter, softened
¾ cup packed light brown sugar
2 Tbsp corn syrup
2 eggs, beaten
4 Tbsp grapefruit marmalade
2½ cups all-purpose flour
1 tsp salt
1 tsp baking powder
1 cup fine chopped pitted prunes
Confectioners' sugar, optional

Put the butter, sugar and syrup in a bowl and beat until light and fluffy. Gradually beat in eggs and grapefruit marmalade. The mixture may look like it is curdling, but it will be fine when cooked. Sift in flour, salt, and baking powder and mix to combine. Add prunes and mix well. Chill the mixture for at least one hour in the refrigerator.

● Preheat oven to 350°F. Grease two large baking sheets or line with nonstick baking parchment.

● Roll tablespoons of the mixture into balls, then flatten between your palms. Place on the baking sheets at least 1 inch apart. Bake for 15 to 17 minutes until golden. Leave to cool for 5 minutes then transfer to wire racks to cool completely.

● Dust lightly with confectioners' sugar to serve, if liked. Store in an airtight container.

Cherry Chocolate Cookies

Preparation time: 20 minutes + chilling ●
Cooking time: 15 to 18 minutes ● *Makes: About 18*

Chunky and chewy—great feel good cookies!

INGREDIENTS

1¼ sticks butter
⅔ cup superfine sugar
1 egg yolk
1¾ cups all-purpose flour
1 cup rough chopped candied cherries
⅔ cup semi-sweet chocolate chips

Put butter and sugar in a bowl and mix well until light and fluffy. Add the egg yolk and beat. Sift in flour and mix well then stir in the cherries and chocolate chips. Chill for at least 2 hours.

● Preheat oven to 375°F. Grease two baking sheets or line with nonstick baking parchment.

● Take tablespoons of the mixture and roll into balls, then flatten slightly. Place onto the baking sheets at least 1 inch apart. Bake for 15 to 18 minutes. Cool for 5 minutes on the baking sheets then transfer to wire racks to cool completely. Store in an airtight container.

Fruit Salad and Brazil Nuts

Preparation time: 20 minutes + chilling ●
Cooking time: 17 minutes ● *Makes: About 35*

Chewy fruit and crunchy nuts give you everything you desire from a cookie.

INGREDIENTS

2 sticks butter, softened
¾ cup superfine sugar
¾ cup packed light brown sugar
2 eggs, beaten
2¼ cups all-purpose flour
1 tsp salt
1 tsp baking powder
⅔ cup chopped dried fruit salad
⅔ cup chopped Brazil nuts

Beat together the butter and sugars until soft and creamy. Gradually beat in the eggs. The mixture may look like it is curdling, but it will be fine when cooked. Sift in flour, salt, and baking powder and mix to combine. Add the fruit salad and Brazil nuts and mix together well. Chill the mixture for at least one hour in the refrigerator.

● Preheat oven to 350°F. Grease two large baking sheets or line with nonstick baking parchment.

● Roll tablespoons of the mixture into balls and place on the baking sheets at least 3 inches apart. Flatten slightly with the back of a spoon. Bake for 15 to 17 minutes until golden. Leave to cool for 5 minutes then transfer to wire racks to cool completely. Store in an airtight container.

Exotic Fruit and Coconut Treats

Preparation time: 20 minutes + chilling ● *Cooking time: 15 to 18 minutes* ● *Makes: About 30*

Look for packets of assorted tropical fruits, or experiment with your own combinations.

INGREDIENTS

2 sticks butter, softened

¾ cup superfine sugar

¾ cup packed light brown sugar

2 eggs, beaten

Grated rind of 1 orange

2¼ cups all-purpose flour

1 tsp salt

1 tsp baking powder

1 cup chopped mixed tropical dried fruit or fruit salad

2 cups shredded sweetened coconut, unpacked

Beat together butter and sugars until soft and creamy. Gradually beat in the eggs and orange rind. The mixture may look like it is curdling, but it will be fine when cooked. Sift in flour, salt, and baking powder and mix to combine. Add tropical fruits and coconut and mix well. Chill the mixture for at least one hour in the refrigerator.

● Preheat oven to 350°F. Grease two large baking sheets or line with nonstick baking parchment.

● Roll tablespoons of the mixture into balls and place on the baking sheets at least 3 inches apart. Flatten slightly with the back of a spoon. Bake for 15 to 18 minutes until golden. Leave to cool for 5 minutes then transfer to wire racks to cool completely. Store in an airtight container.

Tangerine Fingers

Preparation time: 30 minutes + chilling ● *Cooking time: 40 to 45 minutes* ● *Makes: About 30*

Scrumptious shortbread with a tangy tangerine orange topping.

INGREDIENTS

BASE

2 sticks butter

⅓ cup superfine sugar

Grated rind of 1 tangerine orange

2 cups all-purpose flour

½ cup cornstarch

TOPPING

Grated rind of 2 tangerine oranges

3 Tbsp fresh squeezed tangerine orange juice

1 cup superfine sugar

3 eggs, beaten

Scant ½ cup all-purpose flour

½ tsp baking powder

Grease a 9 x 13-inch pan or line with nonstick baking parchment.

● Put butter, sugar, and tangerine rind in a bowl and beat together until light and fluffy. Sift in flour and cornstarch; mix well then form into a soft dough. Press into the prepared pan and smooth with a knife. Chill for 30 minutes in the refrigerator.

● Preheat oven to 350°F.

● Bake for 15 to 20 minutes until lightly golden. Remove from the oven, leaving the oven switched on.

● Beat together the tangerine rind, sugar, and eggs until creamy. Sift in the flour and baking powder and fold in. Beat in the tangerine juice. Pour over the shortbread and bake for a further 25 minutes. Cool in the pan. Cut into 30 bars. Dust with confectioners' sugar to serve, if liked.

Banana Chocolate Squares

Preparation time: 30 minutes ● Cooking time: 25 to 30 minutes ● Makes: 18

These delicious cookies are like shortbread with a dark and white chocolate topping.

INGREDIENTS

1¼ cups all-purpose flour
Pinch salt
8 tsp cornstarch
¼ cup superfine sugar
1½ sticks cold butter, chopped
⅔ cup banana chips, roughly chopped
⅓ cup semi-sweet chocolate chips
⅓ cup white chocolate chips

Preheat oven to 350°F. Grease and line a shallow 11 x 7-inch pan with nonstick baking parchment.
● Sift flour, salt, and cornstarch into a bowl then stir in the sugar. Add the butter and blend in with your fingertips until it resembles coarse bread crumbs. Stir in the banana chips and form into a soft dough.
● Roll out to just under the size of the pan. Transfer to the pan and press to fit. Bake for 25 to 30 minutes until lightly browned. Allow to cool for a few minutes then mark out 18 squares (3 rows of 6 squares across). Cool in the pan.
● Cut the squares out of the pan and place on a sheet of waxed paper. Melt the dark and white chocolate in 2 separate bowls in the microwave or in a bowl over a saucepan of simmering water. Pipe lines of semi-sweet and white chocolate over each square. Allow to set before serving. Store in an airtight container.

TIP

If you do not have a decorating bag, place the chocolate into one corner of a small plastic bag, snip off the end and drizzle lines over each cookie.

Cranberry and White Chocolate Cookies

Preparation time: 30 minutes + chilling ● Cooking time: 15 to 20 minutes ● Makes: About 30

Dried cranberries are not as tart as fresh ones and the cookies are made even sweeter by the addition of chocolate.

INGREDIENTS

2 sticks butter, softened

¼ cup superfine sugar

¼ cup packed light brown sugar

2 eggs, beaten

2¼ cups all-purpose flour

1 tsp salt

1 tsp baking powder

1 cup dried cranberries

1½ cups white chocolate chips, or white chocolate, chopped

Beat together butter and sugars until soft and creamy. Gradually beat in the eggs. The mixture may look like it is curdling, but it will be fine when cooked. Sift in flour, salt, and baking powder and mix to combine. Add cranberries and ⅔ cup of the white chocolate chips and mix well. Chill the mixture for at least one hour in the refrigerator.

● Preheat oven to 350°F. Grease two large baking sheets or line with nonstick baking parchment.

● Roll tablespoons of the mixture into balls and place on the baking sheets at least 3 inches apart. Flatten slightly with the back of a spoon. Bake for 15 to 20 minutes until golden.

● Leave to cool for 5 minutes then transfer to wire racks to cool completely. Melt the white chocolate and drizzle it over the cookies. Leave to cool before serving. Store in an airtight container.

Chunky Mixed Fruit Squares

Preparation time: 20 minutes ● *Cooking time: 60 to 70 minutes* ● *Makes: 16*

These are moist, spongy squares baked just like a cake and each square is packed full of fruit.

INGREDIENTS

1 stick butter, softened

¾ cup superfine sugar

1 tsp vanilla extract

2 medium eggs, beaten

½ cup milk

1½ cups all-purpose flour

2⅔ cups mixed fruit (see Tip)

2 Tbsp raw sugar

Preheat oven to 350°F. Grease and line a 7 x 7-inch square pan with nonstick baking parchment.

● Put butter, sugar, vanilla, and eggs in a bowl and beat together for 2 minutes. Beat in the milk, then sift in the flour and mix until smooth.

● Pour half the batter into the prepared pan then scatter over half the mixed fruit. Spoon over the remaining mixture, smooth with a blunt knife and scatter over the remaining fruit and the raw sugar.

● Bake for 60 to 70 minutes until the cake is cooked through. To test if the cake is cooked, stick a skewer into the center of the cake and leave it for 5 seconds. When the skewer is removed it should be dry with no soggy cake mixture attached. Cool in the pan for 10 minutes, then cut into 16 squares.

TIP

Just about any mixed fruit can be used in this recipe. Try apricots, blueberries, banana chips, pineapple, and mango, depending on seasonal availability. Chop the fruits well before adding.

Truly Blueberry Cookies

Preparation time: 20 minutes + chilling ● *Cooking time: 15 to 18 minutes* ● *Makes: About 30*

Macerating (soaking) the blueberries in orange and brandy makes the cookies even moister and more delicious. Omit the brandy and increase the orange juice if you want to make these cookies for kids.

INGREDIENTS

1 cup dried blueberries

4 Tbsp orange juice

2 Tbsp brandy

2 sticks butter, softened

¾ cup superfine sugar

¾ cup packed light brown sugar

2 eggs, beaten

2¼ cups all-purpose flour

1 tsp baking powder

Place blueberries, orange juice, and brandy in a small pan and simmer for 5 minutes. Remove from the heat and leave to cool. Beat together butter and sugars until soft and creamy. Gradually beat in eggs. The mixture may look like it is curdling, but it will be fine when cooked.

● Sift in flour and baking powder and mix to combine. Strain the blueberries, discarding any liquid and add to cookie mixture. Mix well. Chill the mixture for at least one hour in the refrigerator.

● Preheat oven to 350°F. Grease two large baking sheets or line with nonstick baking parchment.

● Roll tablespoons of the mixture into balls and place on the baking sheets at least 3 inches apart. Flatten slightly with the back of a spoon. Bake for 15 to 18 minutes until golden. Leave to cool for 5 minutes then transfer to wire racks to cool completely.

● Store in an airtight container.

Pear Bars

Preparation time: 15 minutes ● *Cooking time: 20 to 25 minutes* ● *Makes: About 16*

Dried pears make these cookies all sticky and chewy.

INGREDIENTS

1 stick butter

⅔ cup soft brown sugar

2 Tbsp corn syrup

3 cups rolled oats

1 cup chopped dried pears

⅓ cup currants

Preheat oven to 375°F. Lightly grease a shallow 11 x 7-inch pan.

● Put butter, sugar, and corn syrup in a pan and cook over a gentle heat until the butter has melted. Combine the dry ingredients and add to the pan; stir well.

● Spoon into the prepared pan and press down with the back of a spoon. Bake for 20 to 25 minutes until lightly golden. Cool for 5 minutes in the pan then mark into 6 bars; leave to cool completely in the pan. Store in an airtight container.

Candied Cherry Florentines

Preparation time: 20 minutes ● Cooking time: 8 to 10 minutes ● Makes: About 12

This is the best recipe to use when you want a quick, but impressive cookie.

INGREDIENTS

½ stick lightly salted butter

2 Tbsp corn syrup

¼ cup superfine sugar

⅓ cup all-purpose flour

¾ cup fine chopped candied cherries

Grated rind of 1 orange

Preheat oven to 350°F. Grease two large baking sheets or line with nonstick baking parchment.
● Put the butter, corn syrup, and sugar in a saucepan over a medium heat and stir until the sugar dissolves. Remove from the heat and cool for 5 minutes, stirring frequently. Sift in the flour, then stir in the cherries and orange rind. Mix well.
● Drop heaped teaspoons onto the baking sheets, at least 3 inches apart. Shape them into neat rounds. Bake for 8 to 10 minutes. Reshape into rounds while hot, if necessary. Cool for 5 minutes, then transfer to wire racks to cool completely. Store in an airtight container.

Candied Peel and Dark Chocolate Squares

Preparation time: 45 minutes ● *Cooking time: 30 to 35 minutes* ● *Makes: 24*

For a special occasion these bitter treats are perfect. Make up a batch then place in gift box and take to a dinner party.

INGREDIENTS

2 cups plus 2 Tbsp all-purpose flour

¼ cup superfine sugar

1½ sticks cold butter, diced

¾ cup chopped candied peel

4 squares (1 oz each) good quality semi-sweet chocolate

Preheat oven to 350°F. Grease and line the base of a shallow 11 x 7-inch pan.

● Sift flour into a bowl and stir in the sugar. Add the butter and blend in with your fingertips until the mixture resembles coarse bread crumbs. Stir in ½ cup of the mixed peel and form into a soft dough.

● Roll out to just under the size of the pan. Transfer to the pan and press to fit. Prick all over with a fork. Bake for 25 to 30 minutes until lightly browned. Cool for 5 minutes then mark into 24 bars. Cool in the pan.

● Melt chocolate in a microwave or in a glass bowl over a saucepan of simmering water. Cut dough into the squares and remove from the pan. Dip each bar into the chocolate to coat the top and sides and place on waxed paper. While the chocolate is still warm, sprinkle over a few pieces of candied peel. Leave to harden before serving. Store in an airtight container with layers of waxed paper.

Apricot Wheels

Preparation time: 40 minutes + chilling • Cooking time: 10 to 12 minutes • Makes: About 40

These wheels are cut from a log of dough filled with a sweet apricot filling.

INGREDIENTS

FILLING

1⅓ cups dried apricots, finely chopped (see Tip)

½ cup superfine sugar

1 tsp ground nutmeg

½ cup orange juice

DOUGH

1½ sticks butter, softened

¾ cup packed light brown sugar

1 medium egg, beaten

1 tsp almond extract

3 cups all-purpose flour

1 tsp baking powder

Place all the filling ingredients in a small saucepan and bring to a boil. Simmer for 3 minutes until most of the orange juice has evaporated and the mixture is thick. Set aside and cool.

● Put the butter and sugar in a bowl and mix until light and fluffy. Gradually add the egg; mixing well between each addition. Stir in the almond extract. Sift in the flour and baking powder and form into a dough. Wrap in plastic wrap and chill for at least 30 minutes.

● Divide the dough in half, then place one half on a piece of floured waxed paper. Roll out the dough on the paper to a 8 x 10-inch rectangle. Slide a thin, metal spatula between the paper and the dough so that it does not stick to the paper when rolled up. Cover dough with half the filling and roll up from a long side using the paper to help you roll. Rewrap in plastic wrap and chill for about 20 minutes. Repeat with remaining dough and filling.

● Preheat oven to 350°F. Grease two baking sheets or line with nonstick baking parchment.

● Cut ½-inch slices from the log and place on the baking sheets. Bake for 10 to 12 minutes. Cool on baking sheets for 5 minutes then transfer to wire cooling racks. Store in an airtight container.

TIP

It's important to chop the apricots finely, otherwise it will be difficult to roll up the dough.

Rum and Raisin Cookies

Preparation time: 20 minutes + chilling ●
Cooking time: 15 to 17 minutes ● *Makes: About 35*

The traditional combination of rum and raisins is perfect for cookies as it makes them moist and chewy.

INGREDIENTS

2 sticks butter, softened

¾ cup superfine sugar

¾ cup packed light brown sugar

1 egg, beaten

3 Tbsp rum

2¼ cups all-purpose flour

1 tsp salt

1 tsp baking powder

1⅓ cups seedless raisins

Beat together the butter and sugars until soft and creamy. Gradually beat in the egg and rum. The mixture may look like it is curdling, but it will be fine when cooked. Sift in the flour, salt, and baking powder and mix to combine. Add the raisins and mix well. Chill for at least one hour in the refrigerator.

● Preheat oven to 350°F. Grease two large baking sheets or line with nonstick baking parchment.

● Roll tablespoons of the mixture into balls and place on the baking sheets at least 3-inches apart. Flatten slightly with the back of a spoon. Bake for 15 to 17 minutes until golden. Leave to cool for 5 minutes then transfer to wire racks to cool completely. Store in an airtight container.

Brandy and Fresh Apple Cookies

Preparation time: 20 minutes ●
Cooking time: 15 minutes ● *Makes: About 10 to 12*

Fresh apples add texture and a sweet flavor.

INGREDIENTS

¾ cup grated apple

1 Tbsp lemon juice

½ stick butter

2 Tbsp corn syrup

¼ cup superfine sugar

2 Tbsp brandy

½ cup all-purpose flour

½ cup chopped almonds

Preheat oven to 350°F. Grease two large baking sheets or line with nonstick baking parchment.

● Squeeze the grated apples in your hand to extract the juice. Discard the juice then toss the apple in the lemon juice to coat.

● Put butter, corn syrup, sugar, and brandy in a saucepan over a medium heat and stir until the sugar dissolves. Remove from the heat and cool for 5 minutes, stirring frequently. Sift in the flour, then stir in the almonds and apple. Mix well.

● Drop heaped teaspoons onto the baking sheets, at least 3 inches apart. Shape them into neat rounds. Bake for about 15 minutes. Cool for 5 minutes, then transfer to wire racks to cool completely. Store in an airtight container.

Crumbly Pineapple Cookies

Preparation time: 30 minutes + chilling ● *Cooking time: 20 to 25 minutes* ● *Makes: About 24*

These cookies are different as they have a pineapple crumble on top of sweet cookie bases.

INGREDIENTS

1 stick butter
3 Tbsp superfine sugar
1 tsp vanilla extract
1¼ cups all-purpose flour
¾ cup ground almonds
1 egg yolk

TOPPING

1 cup all-purpose flour
¼ cup superfine sugar
½ stick cold butter, chopped
1 cup dried pineapple, finely chopped

Grease two large baking sheets or line with nonstick baking parchment.

● Put the butter and sugar in a bowl and beat until light and fluffy. Stir in the vanilla. Sift in flour then stir in the almonds. Mix to a soft dough. Chill for 30 minutes in the refrigerator.

● Dust the work surface with a little flour, then roll out dough to about ⅓-inch thick. Stamp out 3-inch rounds with a cutter, rerolling and stamping out the trimmings. Place the cookies on the baking sheets and chill for at least 30 minutes in the refrigerator.

● Meanwhile, combine the flour and sugar for the topping. Add the butter and mix with your finger tips to the consistency of coarse bread crumbs. Stir in the chopped pineapple.

● Preheat oven to 325°F.

● Brush the cookies with the egg yolk then sprinkle a little crumble onto each. Bake cookies for 20 to 25 minutes until lightly golden. Allow to cool slightly, then transfer to wire racks to cool completely. Store in an airtight container.

Star Fruit Cookies

Preparation time: 20 minutes + chilling ●
Cooking time: 15 to 17 minutes ● *Makes: About 35*

Dried star fruit has a slightly perfumed flavor and make these most unusual cookies really special.

INGREDIENTS

2 sticks butter, softened
¾ cup superfine sugar
¾ cup packed light brown sugar
2 eggs, beaten
Grated rind of 1 lemon
2¼ cups all-purpose flour
1 tsp salt
1 tsp baking powder
3 cups dried star fruit, roughly chopped

Beat together the butter and sugars until soft and creamy. Gradually beat in the eggs and lemon rind. The mixture may look like it is curdling, but it will be fine when cooked. Sift in the flour, salt, and baking powder and mix to combine. Stir in chopped star fruit and mix well. Chill the mixture for at least one hour in the refrigerator.

● Preheat oven to 350°F. Grease two large baking sheets or line with nonstick baking parchment.

● Roll tablespoons of the mixture into balls and place on the baking sheets at least 3 inches apart. Flatten slightly with the back of a spoon. Bake for 15 to 17 minutes until golden. Leave to cool for 5 minutes then transfer to wire racks to cool completely. Store in an airtight container.

TIP

Dried star fruit is quite difficult to find. Look for it in whole food shops and specialty food stores.

Chewy Peach and Cherry Thins

Preparation time: 15 minutes ●
Cooking time: 10 minutes ● *Makes: About 10*

These cookies are packed full of fruit with just a little dough to hold them together.

INGREDIENTS

½ stick butter
2 Tbsp corn syrup
¼ cup superfine sugar
⅓ cup all-purpose flour
½ cup chopped dried peach
⅔ cup dried Morello or sour cherries

Preheat oven to 350°F. Grease two large baking sheets or line with nonstick baking parchment.

● Put butter, corn syrup, and sugar in a saucepan over a medium heat and stir until the sugar dissolves. Remove from the heat and cool for 5 minutes, stirring frequently. Stir in the flour, followed by the dried peach and cherries. Mix well.

● Drop heaped teaspoons onto the baking sheets, at least 1½ inches apart. Shape them into neat rounds. Bake for about 10 minutes. Reshape into rounds while hot, if necessary. Cool for 5 minutes, then transfer to wire racks to cool. Store in an airtight container.

Pineapple and Ginger Cookies

Preparation time: 15 minutes + chilling ● Cooking time: 15 to 17 minutes ● Makes: About 25

Chewy cookies with a hint of ginger.

INGREDIENTS

2 sticks butter, softened

¾ cup packed light brown sugar

¾ cup superfine sugar

2 eggs, beaten

1 Tbsp fine chopped stem ginger or ginger preserve

3 tsp stem ginger syrup from the stem ginger jar or corn syrup

2¼ cups all-purpose flour

1 tsp baking powder

1 tsp salt

1 cup diced dried pineapple

Put the butter and sugars in a bowl and beat together until pale and creamy. Gradually beat in the eggs, stem ginger and ginger syrup. Do not worry if it looks like it is curdling it will be fine when cooked. Sift in the flour, baking powder and salt and mix. Stir in the pineapple and mix well. Chill for at least one hour in the refrigerator.

● Preheat oven to 350°F. Grease two baking sheets or line with nonstick baking parchment.

● Roll tablespoons of the mixture into balls and place onto the baking sheets, at least 3 inches apart. Flatten with the back of a spoon. Bake for 15 to 17 minutes until golden, but still soft. Cool for 5 minutes on the baking sheets then transfer to wire cooling racks. Store in an airtight container.

Winter Fruit Cookies

Preparation time: 20 minutes + chilling ●
Cooking time: 15 to 17 minutes ● *Makes: About 30*

These cookies are full of the flavor of Christmas as they are packed with the dried fruits associated with the festive season.

INGREDIENTS

2 sticks butter, softened

¾ cup superfine sugar

¾ cup packed light brown sugar

2 eggs, beaten

Generous 2 cups all-purpose flour

1 tsp salt

1 tsp baking powder

⅔ cup chopped dates

⅔ cup dried cherries

⅔ cup diced candied citrus peel

12 whole candied cherries, halved

Put the butter and sugars in a bowl and beat until light and fluffy. Gradually beat in the eggs. The mixture may look like it is curdling but it will be fine when cooked. Sift in the flour, salt, and baking powder and mix. Add dates, cherries, and candied peel and mix well. Chill for 1 hour in the refrigerator.

● Preheat oven to 350°F. Grease two large baking sheets or line with nonstick baking parchment.

● Roll tablespoons of the mixture into balls and place on the baking sheets at least 3 inches apart. Flatten slightly between your palms and push half a cherry into the center of each cookie. Bake for 15 to 17 minutes until golden. Leave to cool for 5 minutes then transfer to wire racks to cool completely. Store in an airtight container.

Pear and Walnut Cookies

Preparation time: 15 minutes + chilling ●
Cooking time: 15 to 17 minutes ● *Makes: About 30*

These cookies ring the changes and use whole-wheat flour. It gives the cookies a really rich flavor.

INGREDIENTS

2 sticks butter, softened

¾ cup packed light brown sugar

¾ cup superfine sugar

2 eggs, beaten

1 tsp vanilla extract

2¼ cups whole-wheat flour

1 tsp baking powder

1 tsp salt

1 cup fine chopped dried pears

1 cup chopped walnut pieces

Put the butter and sugars in a bowl and beat together until pale and creamy. Gradually beat in the eggs and almond extract. Do not worry if it looks like it is curdling it will be fine when cooked. Sift in the flour, baking powder, and salt and mix. Stir in the pears and walnuts and mix well. Chill for at least one hour in the refrigerator.

● Preheat oven to 350°F. Grease two baking sheets or line with nonstick baking parchment.

● Roll tablespoons of the mixture into balls and place onto the baking sheets, at least 3-inches apart. Flatten with the back of a spoon. Bake for 15 to 17 minutes until golden, but still soft. Cool for 5 minutes on the baking sheets then transfer to wire cooling racks. Store in an airtight container.

Nut Cookies

Nuts are a central feature in many of the most successful cookies. They add an additional crunch to already crunchy cookies or a contrasting bite to soft, chewy cookies. Some cookies substitute ground nuts for flour, giving the resulting cookies a rich, dense flavor. The subtle flavors and textures of pecans, macadamia, almonds, and cashew nuts, for instance, can be savored alone or in crafty combinations that show each off to its best advantage. Combined with fragrant spices or delectable chocolate, nut-based cookies are simply wonderful.

Anyone who loves nutty cookies will be pleased to learn that the latest health findings are in favor of nuts. Nuts are high in proteins, monounsaturated fats, (the same fats found in olive oil), and polyunsaturated fats (which help lower cholesterol levels), and masses of micronutrients including vitamin E and folic acid. Of course, these cookies still contain butter and sugar so it's not all good news, but eaten in moderation they make a truly satisfying treat.

Traditional Classics

Almond Brittle Cookies	338
Chunky Pistachio Drops	338
Almond and Ginger Hearts	339
Peanut Butter Cookies	341
Pecan and Cinnamon Cookies	341
White Chocolate and Macadamia Nut Treats	342
Walnut Crescents	343
Hazelnut and Orange Cookies	344

Family Favorites

Almond and Peach Chews	344
Pecan and Semi-sweet Chocolate Pebbles	345
Coconut and Chocolate Swirls	347
Orange and Macadamia Half Moons	348
Toasted Cashew and Raisin Cookies	348
Banoffee Squares	350
Walnut and Banana Cookies	351

Clever Combinations

Pistachio and Orange Thins	352
Chunky Pine Nut and Lemon Cookies	353
Coffee Brazil Cookies	354
Coconut and Walnut Cookies	354
Hazelnut and Cinnamon Rounds with Vanilla Glaze	355
Double Almond Cookies	355
Drizzled Chocolate and Brazil Nut Cookies	356
Pistachio and Apricot Cookies	357
Flaky Chocolate and Peanut Cookies	359
Coffee and Walnut Cookies	359
Almond and Orange Sandwich Cookies	360
Coconut and Lime Crunchies	363
Crunchy Nut Cookies	363
Double Ginger Pecan Cookies	364

Exotic Delights

Pistachio and Mint Creams	364
Chocolate and Hazelnut Treats	365
Nuts and Cherry Cookies	365
Pecan and Marshmallow Cookies	367
Walnut and Marmalade Cookies	367
Walnut and Carrot Cookies	368
Syrupy Macadamia Nut Cookies	368
Macadamia Chocolate Bars	371
Hazelnut Molasses Cookies	371
Coconut Macaroons	372
Coconut and Rum Cookies	373
Mocha Mixed Nut Drops	374
Brazil and Orange Chocolate Treats	374
Almond and Ginger Florentines	375

Almond Brittle Cookies

Preparation time: 25 minutes + chilling ●
Cooking time: 15 to 20 minutes ● Makes: About 20

Almond brittle is simple to make and gives these cookies an unusual twist.

INGREDIENTS

ALMOND BRITTLE

1¼ cups blanched almonds

½ cup superfine sugar

COOKIE DOUGH

2 sticks butter, softened

1 cup superfine sugar

2 eggs, beaten

2 cups all-purpose flour

1 tsp baking powder

1 tsp salt

For the almond brittle, preheat oven to 425°F. Place almonds on a baking sheet and toast for 3 to 4 minutes. Melt sugar in a small saucepan over medium heat without stirring. Add the almonds, mix quickly then remove from the heat. Quickly spread onto a baking sheet and cool. Chop fine.

● To make the cookies, put the butter and sugars in a bowl and beat until pale and creamy. Gradually beat in the eggs. Sift in flour, baking powder, and salt; mix well. Stir in the almond brittle and mix. Chill for 1 hour.

● Preheat oven to 350°F. Grease or line two baking sheets with nonstick baking parchment.

● Drop teaspoons of the mixture onto the baking sheets, at least 3 inches apart. Flatten with the back of a spoon. Bake for 15 to 18 minutes until golden. Cool on wire racks. Store in an airtight container.

Chunky Pistachio Drops

Preparation time: 20 minutes + chilling ●
Cooking time: 15 to 18 minutes ● Makes: About 25

The green of the pistachios gives these cookies an exotic appeal.

INGREDIENTS

2 sticks butter, softened

¾ cup superfine sugar

¾ cup packed light brown sugar

2 eggs, beaten

2 cups plus 3 Tbsp all-purpose flour

1 tsp salt

1 tsp baking powder

1½ cups chopped unsalted, pistachios

1 tsp vanilla extract

Beat together butter and sugars until soft and creamy. Gradually beat in eggs. The mixture may look like it is curdling, but it will be fine when cooked. Sift in flour, salt, and baking powder; mix to combine. Stir in pistachios and vanilla. Chill mixture for at least 1 hour in the refrigerator.

● Preheat oven to 350°F. Grease two baking sheets or line with nonstick baking parchment.

● Roll tablespoons of the mixture into balls and place on the sheets at least 3 inches apart. Flatten slightly with the back of a spoon. Bake for 15 to 18 minutes until golden. Leave to cool for 5 minutes then transfer to wire racks to cool. Store in an airtight container for up to 1 week.

Almond and Ginger Hearts

Preparation time: 30 minutes + chilling ● *Cooking time: 20 to 25 minutes* ● *Makes: About 24*

These delicate hearts are perfect for an afternoon treat.

INGREDIENTS

1 stick butter

3 Tbsp superfine sugar

1¼ cups all-purpose flour, plus extra for rolling

¾ cup ground almonds

2 tsp fine chopped stem ginger or ginger preserve

2 tsp stem ginger syrup or corn syrup

Confectioners' sugar to serve, optional

Grease two baking sheets or line with nonstick baking parchment.

● Put the butter and sugar in a bowl and beat until light and fluffy. Sift in flour then stir in almonds, chopped ginger or ginger preserve, and syrup. Mix to a soft dough. Chill for 30 minutes.

● Roll out dough on a floured surface to a thickness of about ⅓ inch. Stamp out heart shapes with a pastry cutter, re-rolling and stamping out the trimmings. Transfer to the baking sheets and chill for at least 30 minutes in the refrigerator.

● Preheat oven to 325°F. Bake cookies for 20 to 25 minutes until lightly golden. Transfer to wire racks to cool. Dust with confectioners' sugar to serve, if liked. Store in an airtight container for up to 1 week.

Peanut Butter Cookies

Preparation time: 30 minutes + chilling ●
Cooking time: 15 to 20 minutes ● *Makes: About 20*

These are really chunky, perfect for brown bag lunches and picnics.

INGREDIENTS

¾ stick butter, softened

⅓ cup crunchy peanut butter

⅓ cup dark brown sugar

½ cup superfine sugar

1 egg, beaten

1¼ cups all-purpose flour

1 tsp baking powder

Put the butter, peanut butter, and sugars in a bowl and beat until light and fluffy. Gradually beat in the egg. Don't worry if it looks like it is curdling, it will be fine once cooked. Sift in the flour and baking powder. Chill mixture for 1 hour.

● Preheat oven to 350°F. Grease two baking sheets or line with nonstick baking parchment.

● Place spoonfuls of the dough onto the baking sheets at least 3 inches apart. Flatten slightly with the back of a spoon. Bake for 15 to 20 minutes until golden. Cool for 5 minutes on the baking sheet then transfer to wire racks to cool. Store in an airtight container for up to 1 week.

Pecan and Cinnamon Cookies

Preparation time: 20 minutes + chilling ●
Cooking time: 12 to 15 minutes ● *Makes: 25*

Pecans and cinnamon are a classic fall combination.

INGREDIENTS

2 sticks butter, softened

¾ cup superfine sugar

¾ cup packed light brown sugar

2 eggs, beaten

2¼ cups all-purpose flour

1 tsp salt

2 tsp ground cinnamon

1 tsp baking powder

2 cups chopped pecans

Beat together butter and sugars in a mixing bowl until soft and creamy. Gradually beat in eggs. The mixture may look like it is curdling, but it will be fine when cooked. Sift in flour, salt, ground cinnamon, and baking powder and mix to combine. Stir in pecans and ground cinnamon. Chill mixture for at least 1 hour in the refrigerator.

● Preheat oven to 350°F. Grease two baking sheets or line with nonstick baking parchment.

● Roll tablespoons of the mixture into balls and place on the sheets at least 3 inches apart. Flatten slightly with the back of a spoon. Bake for 12 to 15 minutes until golden. Leave to cool for 5 minutes then transfer to wire racks to cool. Store in an airtight container for up to 1 week.

White Chocolate and Macadamia Nut Treats

Preparation time: 15 minutes + chilling ● *Cooking time: 10 to 15 minutes* ● *Makes: About 20*

You can really get your teeth into these chunky cookies.

INGREDIENTS

2 sticks butter, softened
¼ cup superfine sugar
¼ cup packed light brown sugar
2 eggs, beaten
2 cups plus 3 Tbsp all-purpose flour
1 tsp salt
1 tsp baking powder
1 cup chopped macadamia nuts
1 cup white chocolate chips

Beat together butter and sugars until soft and creamy. Gradually beat in eggs. The mixture may look like it is curdling, but it will be fine when cooked. Sift in flour, salt, and baking powder; mix to combine. Add macadamia nuts and white chocolate chips and mix together well. Chill mixture for at least 1 hour in the refrigerator.

● Preheat oven to 350°F. Grease two baking sheets or line with nonstick baking parchment.

● Roll tablespoons of the mixture into balls and place on the sheets at least 3 inches apart. Flatten slightly with the back of a spoon. Bake for 10 to 15 minutes until golden. Leave to cool for 5 minutes then transfer to wire racks to cool. Store in an airtight container for up to 1 week.

Walnut Crescents

Preparation time: 30 minutes + chilling ● *Cooking time: 20 to 25 minutes* ● *Makes: About 25*

These cookies are light, crumbly, and nutty.

INGREDIENTS

1 stick butter
3 Tbsp superfine sugar
1¼ cups all-purpose flour
½ cup finely chopped walnuts

Put the butter and sugar in a bowl and beat until light and fluffy. Sift in the flour then stir in the walnuts. Mix to form a soft dough. Chill 30 minutes in the refrigerator.

● Grease two baking sheets or line with nonstick baking parchment. Dust work surface with a little flour, then roll out dough to a thickness of about ⅓ inch. Stamp out crescent shapes with a cutter, re-rolling and stamping out the trimmings. Transfer to the baking sheets and, if you have time, chill for a further 30 minutes.

● Preheat oven to 325°F. Bake cookies for 20 to 25 minutes until lightly golden. Transfer to wire racks to cool. Store in an airtight container for up to 1 week.

Hazelnut and Orange Cookies

Preparation time: 20 minutes + chilling •
Cooking time: 18 to 20 minutes • *Makes: 40*

The combination of hazelnut and orange works really well in these cutout cookies. Use Christmas cutters and serve during the holidays.

INGREDIENTS

2 sticks butter, softened

½ cup superfine sugar

½ cup light brown sugar

2½ cups all-purpose flour, plus extra for rolling

1¼ cups chopped hazelnuts

Grated rind of 1 orange

Put the butter and sugars in a mixing bowl and beat with an electric beater until light and fluffy. Sift in the flour and mix to a dough. Stir in the chopped hazelnuts and orange rind. Mix well. Chill for 30 minutes.

• Preheat oven to 325°F. Grease two baking sheets or line with nonstick baking parchment.

• Dust work surface with flour and roll out dough to ½ inch thick. Stamp out 2-inch rounds with a cutter. Transfer to the baking sheets. Bake for 18 to 20 minutes until golden. Cool for 5 minutes then transfer to wire racks to cool. Store in an airtight container.

Almond and Peach Chews

Preparation time: 20 minutes + chilling •
Cooking time: 12 to 15 minutes • *Makes: About 25*

The candied peaches in these cookies give them a great chewy texture.

INGREDIENTS

2 sticks butter, softened

¾ cup packed light brown sugar

¾ cup superfine sugar

2 eggs, beaten

2 cups all-purpose flour

1 tsp baking powder

1 tsp salt

1¼ cups chopped almonds

¾ cup candied peaches, rough chopped

Put the butter and sugars in a bowl and beat together until pale and creamy. Gradually beat in the eggs. Don't worry if it looks like it is curdling, it will be fine when cooked. Sift in flour, baking powder, and salt; stir to combine. Stir in the almonds and candied peaches and mix well. Chill for 1 hour.

• Preheat oven to 350°F. Grease two baking sheets or line with nonstick baking parchment.

• Roll tablespoons of the mixture into balls and place onto the baking sheets, at least 3 inches apart. Flatten with the back of a spoon. Bake for 12 to 15 minutes until golden, but still soft. Cool for 5 minutes on the baking sheets then transfer to wire racks. Store in an airtight container for up to 1 week.

Pecan and Semi-sweet Chocolate Pebbles

Preparation time: 30 minutes • Cooking time: 10 to 12 minutes • Makes: 15

**These are very rich meringue-style cookies that look just like beach pebbles!
They are filled with a delicious chocolate ganache.**

INGREDIENTS

1½ cups pecans

1¼ cups superfine sugar

3 egg whites

1 tsp vanilla extract

GANACHE FILLING

7 oz good quality semi-sweet chocolate, broken up

¼ stick unsalted butter

¼ cup heavy cream

Preheat oven to 325°F. Grease two baking sheets or line with nonstick baking parchment.

● Place pecans in a food processor and grind until fine chopped but not into a paste. Add 1 cup of the sugar and grind for 10 seconds more.

● Beat the egg whites until stiff peaks form. Beat in the remaining sugar a little at a time, beating well after each addition. Beat in the vanilla. Gradually beat in the pecan mixture a little at a time until it is all incorporated.

● Fit a decorating bag with a ½-inch tube and fill with the mixture. Pipe 2-inch fingers about 1 inch apart on the baking sheets. Bake for 10 to 12 minutes until pale golden. Allow to cool completely on the baking sheets before adding the ganache.

● To make the ganache, melt the chocolate in a bowl in the microwave or in a double boiler over simmering water. Heat the butter and cream in a small saucepan, add to the chocolate and stir until smooth and glossy. Cool, stirring occasionally, until a spreadable consistency is reached. Carefully spread half the fingers with the ganache and sandwich with another finger. Because these cookies contain fresh cream they should be eaten on the day they are made.

Coconut and Chocolate Swirls

Preparation time: 40 minutes + chilling ● Cooking time: 10 to 15 minutes ● Makes: About 25

These are very delicate pinwheel cookies, ideal for a child's party.

INGREDIENTS

1 stick butter, softened

⅔ cup packed light brown sugar

1 cup all-purpose flour

¼ cup unsweetened cocoa powder

½ tsp salt

½ tsp baking powder

COCONUT FILLING

2 heaping Tbsp apricot jam or preserve

⅔ cup sweetened flaked coconut

Beat butter and sugar together in a mixing bowl until light and fluffy. Sift in flour, cocoa powder, salt, and baking powder. Gradually mix to a soft dough using your fingertips. Roll out on a piece of waxed paper to a 9 x 10-inch rectangle, cutting the dough to shape. Do not flour the waxed paper as it will change the color of the dough. Carefully slide a thin metal spatula under the dough to release it from the paper, but leave it on the paper.

● Gently warm the jam or preserve then brush all over the cookie dough. Sprinkle over the coconut, patting it into the jam or preserve. Roll up the dough from a long side using the paper to help, but ensuring that it does not go inside the rolled dough. Do not allow the dough to crack. If it does, gently warm a knife and seal the crack. Roll up in the paper and chill for at least 30 minutes.

● Preheat oven to 350°F. Grease or line a baking sheet with nonstick baking parchment

● Allow the rolled dough to sit at room temperature for 5 minutes then, using a thin-bladed knife, cut the log into ½-inch slices and place on baking sheet. Bake for 10 to 15 minutes. Cool for 5 minutes then transfer to wire racks to cool. Store in an airtight container for up to 1 week.

Toasted Cashew and Raisin Cookies

Preparation time: 20 minutes + chilling ●
Cooking time: 12 to 15 minutes ● *Makes: About 20*

Toasting the cashews makes them crisper, so the cookies are crunchier.

INGREDIENTS

1¼ cups cashew nuts

1 stick butter, softened

⅔ cup packed light brown sugar

1 egg, beaten

2 tsp almond extract

1 cup all-purpose flour

2 tsp baking powder

1 tsp of salt

1¼ cups raisins

Preheat oven to 375°F. Place cashew nuts on a baking sheet and toast for 5 minutes. Cool then rough chop.

● Put butter and sugars in a bowl and beat until light and fluffy. Beat in the egg and almond extract. Sift in the flour, baking powder, and salt; mix well. Add the chopped cashew nuts and raisins. Mix to a dough. Chill for 30 minutes if the dough is really soft.

● Preheat oven to 350°F. Grease two baking sheets or line with nonstick baking parchment.

● Drop heaping teaspoons of the mixture onto the sheets at least 2 inches apart and flatten slightly. Bake for 12 to 15 minutes until lightly golden. Cool for 5 minutes on the baking sheets then transfer to wire racks. Store in an airtight container for up to 1 week.

Orange and Macadamia Half Moons

Preparation time: 30 minutes + chilling ●
Cooking time: 20 to 25 minutes ● *Makes: 25*

Orange flower water gives the cookies a subtle orange flavor.

INGREDIENTS

1 stick butter, softened

3 Tbsp superfine sugar

1½ cups all-purpose flour, plus extra for rolling

¾ cup chopped macadamia nuts

1 Tbsp orange flower water

3 oz good quality semi-sweet chocolate, broken up

Grease two baking sheets or line with nonstick baking parchment.

● Put the butter and sugar in a bowl and beat until light and fluffy. Sift in flour, then stir in macadamia nuts and orange flower water. Mix to a soft dough. Chill for 30 minutes.

● Dust work surface with a little flour, then roll out dough to about ⅓ inch thick. Stamp out half moon shapes with a cutter, re-rolling and stamping out the trimmings. Transfer to the baking sheets and chill for at least 30 minutes in the refrigerator.

● Preheat oven to 325°F. Bake cookies for 20 to 25 minutes until lightly golden. Cool on wire racks.

● Meanwhile, melt the chocolate in a bowl in the microwave or in a double boiler over simmering water. Once the cookies have cooled, dip one half of each crescent into the melted chocolate. Place on nonstick paper to set. Store in an airtight container.

Banoffee Squares

Preparation time: 35 minutes + chilling ● *Cooking time: 35 minutes* ● *Makes: 24*

**These cookies are packed full of chewy banana chips and topped with a rich
toffee and pecan sauce—truly scrumptious!**

INGREDIENTS

BANANA BASE

1 stick butter, softened

½ cup superfine sugar

1 medium egg, beaten

1½ cups all-purpose flour

½ tsp baking powder

Scant 1 cup dried banana chips

PECAN TOPPING

½ stick unsalted butter

¾ light brown soft sugar

¼ cup heavy cream

½ cup corn syrup

1¼ cups rough chopped pecans

Grease and line the base and sides of a 11 x 8-inch baking pan with nonstick baking parchment.

● Put the butter and sugar in a bowl and beat until light and fluffy. Beat in the egg. Sift in the flour and baking powder and mix well. Stir the banana chips into the mixture. Spoon the mixture into the pan, spreading it evenly. This takes a little time and is easiest with a small spatula or blunt knife. Chill for 30 minutes.

● Preheat oven to 375°F. Cover dough with a piece of waxed paper and bake for 5 minutes. Remove paper and bake for a further 5 minutes. Cool while making the topping. (Leave the oven turned on.)

● To make the topping, put the butter, sugar, cream, and corn syrup in a saucepan and melt gently over low heat until the sugar dissolves, stirring frequently. Boil hard for 1 minute. Remove from the heat and stir in the pecans. Pour over the baked crust and bake for a further 10 minutes until the top is bubbling. Leave to cool completely in the pan on a wire rack.

● Run a knife around the edges, between the pan and waxed paper and lift out onto a board. Cut into 24 pieces, 6 across and 4 down. Store in an airtight container for up to 1 week.

Walnut and Banana Cookies

Preparation time: 20 minutes + chilling ● *Cooking time: 10 to 15 minutes* ● *Makes: 25*

These are quite sweet cookies with a soft consistency.

INGREDIENTS

1½ sticks butter, softened

¾ cup packed light brown sugar

¾ cup superfine sugar

2 large ripe bananas, mashed

2½ cups all-purpose flour

1 tsp salt

1 tsp baking powder

1 cup chopped walnuts

Put the butter and sugars in a bowl and beat until light and fluffy. Mix in the bananas. Sift in the flour, salt, and baking powder and mix well. Stir in the walnuts. Chill for about 2 hours.

● Preheat oven to 350°F. Grease two baking sheets or line with nonstick baking parchment.

● Drop heaping teaspoons of the mixture onto the baking sheets and flatten with the back of a spoon. Bake for 10 to 15 minutes until golden. Cool for 5 minutes on the baking sheets then transfer to wire racks. Store in an airtight container for up to 1 week.

Pistachio and Orange Thins

Preparation time: 30 minutes + chilling ● *Cooking time: 15 minutes* ● *Makes: About 25*

Look out for shelled pistachios which will save you lots of time shelling them!

INGREDIENTS

1 stick butter, softened
3 Tbsp superfine sugar
3 Tbsp light brown sugar
3 Tbsp Grand Marnier
1½ cups all-purpose flour
½ cup shelled, unsalted pistachios

Put butter and sugars in a mixing bowl and beat until pale and creamy. Beat in Grand Marnier. Sift in the flour and mix to a firm dough. Transfer to a piece of waxed paper and roll into a log 2 inches in diameter. Chill for 30 minutes.

● Meanwhile, grind or fine chop the pistachios and transfer to a sheet of waxed paper. Roll log in the pistachios several times, ensuring the whole log is covered in nuts. Rewrap in the waxed paper and chill for a further 30 minutes.

● Preheat oven to 325°F. Grease two baking sheets or line with nonstick baking parchment.

● Cut the log into ⅓-inch thick slices and place on the baking sheets 2 inches apart. Bake for 15 minutes. Cool for 5 minutes then transfer to wire racks to cool. Store in an airtight container for up to 1 week.

Chunky Pine Nut and Lemon Cookies

Preparation time: 15 minutes + chilling • Cooking time: 10 to 15 minutes • Makes: 20

Toasting pine nuts brings out their flavor and gives them a slightly smoky taste.

INGREDIENTS

COOKIES

1¾ cups pine nuts

1 stick butter, softened

¾ cup packed light brown sugar

¾ cup superfine sugar

2 eggs, beaten

Grated rind of 1 lemon

2¼ cups all-purpose flour

1 tsp baking powder

1 tsp salt

GLAZE (OPTIONAL)

⅓ cup granulated sugar

2 Tbsp water

1 Tbsp fresh lemon juice

Pared rind from 1 lemon

Preheat oven to 375°F. Place pine nuts on a baking sheet and toast for 5 minutes. Cool.

● Put the butter and sugars in a bowl and beat together until pale and creamy. Gradually beat in the eggs. Don't worry if it looks like it is curdling, it will be fine when cooked. Stir in the lemon rind. Sift in flour, baking powder, and salt and mix. Stir in the nuts and mix well. Chill for 1 hour.

● Preheat oven to 350°F. Line two baking sheets with nonstick baking parchment.

● Roll tablespoons of the mixture into balls and place onto the baking sheets at least 3 inches apart. Flatten with the back of a spoon. Bake for 10 to 15 minutes until golden, but still soft. Cool for 5 minutes on the baking sheets then transfer to wire racks.

● If making the glaze, gently dissolve the sugar in the water and lemon juice. Boil for 5 minutes. Remove from the heat and stir in the lemon rind. Cool then drizzle a little over each cookie. Eat within a day or two, otherwise the cookies will go soft due to the glaze.

TIP

For a special occasion, omit 1 tablespoon of the water and stir in one tablespoon of liqueur into the glaze once it has cooled.

Coffee Brazil Cookies

Preparation time: 30 minutes + chilling ●
Cooking time: 15 to 20 minutes ● *Makes: About 25*

These elegant cookies are subtly flavored with coffee.

INGREDIENTS

1 Tbsp strong coffee granules
2 Tbsp boiling water
½ cup Brazil nuts
1 stick butter, softened
¼ cup packed light brown sugar
1½ cups all-purpose flour, plus extra for dusting

Dissolve the coffee in the boiling water and cool. Put the Brazil nuts in a food processor and fine grind, but take care not to grind to a paste.

● Place butter and sugar in a mixing bowl and beat together until light and fluffy. Beat in the coffee, then sift in the flour. Stir in the ground Brazil nuts and mix to a stiff dough. Chill for at least 30 minutes.

● Grease two baking sheets or line with nonstick baking parchment. Dust work surface with flour and roll out the dough to ⅓ inch thick. Stamp out shapes using cookie cutters, re-rolling and stamping out the trimmings. Transfer to the baking sheets and chill for about 15 minutes.

● Preheat oven to 350°F. Bake for 15 to 20 minutes. Cool for 5 minutes then transfer to wire racks. Store in an airtight container for up to 1 week.

Coconut and Walnut Cookies

Preparation time: 15 minutes + chilling ●
Cooking time: 12 minutes ● *Makes: About 40*

The coconut gives these cookies a delicious chewy texture.

INGREDIENTS

2 sticks butter, softened
1 cup granulated sugar
2 eggs, beaten
1 tsp vanilla extract
2 cups all-purpose flour
1 tsp baking powder
1 tsp salt
1¼ cups sweetened flaked coconut
About 40 walnut halves

Put butter and sugar in a bowl and beat until pale and creamy. Gradually add the eggs and vanilla extract. Sift in the flour, baking powder, and salt and stir in the sweetened flaked coconut. Divide the dough into two pieces, transfer to two pieces of waxed paper and form each piece into a log about 2 inches in diameter. Chill for at least 2 hours and preferably overnight.

● Preheat oven to 350°F. Grease two baking sheets or line with nonstick baking parchment.

● Unwrap one log and slice into ½ inch slices. Transfer to the baking sheets and press a walnut half into the center of each cookie. Bake for about 12 minutes until lightly golden around the edges. Cool for 5 minutes then transfer to wire cooling racks. Repeat with the second log. Store in an airtight container for up to 1 week.

Hazelnut and Cinnamon Rounds with Vanilla Glaze

Preparation time: 25 minutes + chilling •
Cooking time: 15 minutes • *Makes: About 40*

Have fun with these cookies stamping out all different shapes and sizes.

INGREDIENTS

1 stick butter, softened
3 Tbsp superfine sugar
1 cup all-purpose flour
2 tsp ground cinnamon
1¼ cups ground hazelnuts

GLAZE

¾ cup confectioners' sugar, sifted
1 tsp vanilla extract
2-3 tsp water

Put butter and sugar in a bowl and beat until light and creamy. Sift in the flour and cinnamon, then stir in the ground hazelnuts. Mix to a dough. Transfer to nonstick baking parchment and roll into a log about 2 inches in diameter. Chill for 2 hours.

● Grease two baking sheets or line with nonstick baking parchment. Cut slices of about ⅓ inch thick from the log. Transfer to the baking sheets.

● Preheat oven to 350°F. Bake cookies for about 15 minutes until lightly browned. Cool for 5 minutes on the baking sheets then transfer to wire racks.

● To make the glaze, place the confectioners' sugar and vanilla in a small bowl and add sufficient water to make a pourable frosting. Drizzle over the cookies. Allow glaze to set before serving.

Double Almond Cookies

Preparation time: 15 minutes + chilling •
Cooking time: 15 to 17 minutes • *Makes: About 30*

If you like almonds, you'll love these cookies! You simply couldn't fit any more almonds in the batter.

INGREDIENTS

2 sticks butter, softened
¾ cup superfine sugar
¾ cup packed light brown sugar
2 large eggs, beaten
2 cups plain flour
1 tsp salt
1 tsp baking powder
1½ cups chopped blanched almonds
1 cup slivered almonds

Beat together butter and sugars until soft and creamy. Gradually beat in the eggs. The mixture may look like it is curdling, but it will be fine when cooked. Sift in flour, salt, and baking powder and mix to combine. Add all the almonds and mix well. Chill mixture for at least 1 hour in the refrigerator.

● Preheat oven to 350°F. Line two large baking sheets with nonstick baking parchment.

● Roll tablespoons of the mixture into balls and place on the baking sheets at least 3 inches apart. Flatten slightly with the back of a spoon. Bake for about 15 to 17 minutes until golden. Leave to cool for five minutes then transfer to wire racks to cool. Store in an airtight container.

Drizzled Chocolate and Brazil Nut Cookies

Preparation time: 35 minutes + chilling ● Cooking time: 10 to 15 minutes ● Makes: About 25

The swirled chocolate makes these cookies a bit special.

INGREDIENTS

2 sticks butter, softened

¾ cup packed light brown sugar

¾ cup superfine sugar

2 eggs, beaten

2¼ cups all-purpose flour

1 tsp baking powder

1 tsp salt

1 cup fine chopped Brazil nuts

2 oz semi-sweet chocolate, chopped

Put the butter and sugars in a bowl and beat together until pale and creamy. Gradually beat in the eggs. Don't worry if it looks like it is curdling, it will be fine when cooked. Sift in flour, baking powder, and salt and mix. Stir in the Brazil nuts and mix well. Chill for 1 hour.

● Preheat oven to 350°F. Grease two baking sheets or line with nonstick baking parchment.

● Roll tablespoons of the mixture into balls and place onto the baking sheets, at least 3 inches apart to allow for speading. Flatten with the back of a spoon. Bake for 10 to 15 minutes until golden, but still soft. Cool for 5 minutes on the baking sheets then transfer to wire cooling racks.

● Melt the chocolate in a microwave or in a bowl over a pan of simmering water. Using a teaspoon, drizzle the chocolate over the cookies. Allow to set before serving. Best eaten on the day made, but may be stored in an airtight container.

Pistachio and Apricot Cookies

Preparation time: 25 minutes + chilling ● *Cooking time: 15 to 20 minutes* ● *Makes: 20*

These are very buttery cookies and need a little care in cooking.

INGREDIENTS

1½ sticks butter, softened

⅔ cup superfine sugar

2 medium egg yolks

Grated rind of 1 orange

1 tsp vanilla extract

1½ cups all-purpose flour

3 Tbsp shelled pistachios, fine chopped

3 Tbsp apricot jam or preserve

Place butter and sugar in a bowl and beat until pale and fluffy. Beat in the egg yolks, orange rind, and vanilla. Sift in the flour and mix to a soft dough. Chill for at least 1 hour.

● Preheat oven to 350°F. Grease two baking sheets or line with nonstick baking parchment.

● Roll tablespoons of the dough into balls then flatten between your palms. Place on the baking sheets, at least 1 inch apart. Bake for 15 to 20 minutes.

● Meanwhile, place the pistachios in a food processor and fine grind. Take care not to overgrind them, otherwise a paste will form. Warm the jam or preserve over low heat until melted. As soon as the cookies come out of the oven, brush with the melted jam or preserves and sprinkle with the nuts. Cool for 5 minutes then transfer to wire racks. Store in airtight containers.

TIP

If you don't have a food processor, chop the nuts finely, or buy them ready-chopped.

Flaky Chocolate and Peanut Cookies

Preparation time: 15 minutes + chilling ●
Cooking time: 10 to 15 minutes ● *Makes: 25*

Chocolate flakes in the dough give these cookies a crazy speckled appearance.

INGREDIENTS

¾ cup blanched, unsalted peanuts, fine chopped

2 sticks butter, softened

¾ cup packed light brown sugar

¾ cup superfine sugar

2 eggs, beaten

2¼ cups all-purpose flour

1 tsp baking powder

1 tsp salt

½ cup chocolate flakes

Preheat oven to 375°F. Place peanuts on a baking sheet and toast for 5 to 8 minutes. Cool.

● Put the butter and sugars in a bowl and beat together until pale and creamy. Gradually beat in the eggs. Don't worry if it looks like it is curdling, it will be fine when cooked. Sift in flour, baking powder, and salt and mix. Stir in the peanuts and chocolate flakes and mix well. Chill for 1 hour.

● Preheat oven to 350°F. Grease two baking sheets or line with nonstick baking parchment.

● Roll tablespoons of the mixture into balls and place onto the baking sheets, at least 3 inches apart. Flatten with the back of a spoon. Bake for 10 to 15 minutes until golden, but still soft. Cool for 5 minutes on the baking sheets then transfer to wire racks.

Coffee and Walnut Cookies

Preparation time: 20 minutes + chilling ●
Cooking time: 15 to 18 minutes ● *Makes: 35*

Chocolate-covered coffee beans give you the best of both worlds—dreamy chocolate and strong coffee.

INGREDIENTS

2 sticks butter, softened

¾ cup packed light brown sugar

¾ cup superfine sugar

2 eggs, beaten

2¼ cups all-purpose flour

1 tsp baking powder

1 cup fine chopped walnuts

⅔ cup chocolate-covered coffee beans, fine chopped (see tip)

Put the butter and sugar in a bowl and beat until light and fluffy. Gradually beat in the eggs. Don't worry if it looks like it is curdling, it will be fine when cooked. Sift in flour and baking powder and mix. Stir in the walnuts and chocolate-covered coffee beans and mix well. Chill for 1 hour.

● Preheat oven to 350°F. Grease two baking sheets or line with nonstick baking parchment.

● Roll tablespoons of the mixture into balls and place onto the baking sheets, at least 3 inches apart. Flatten with the back of a spoon. Bake for 15 to 18 minutes until golden, but still soft. Cool for 5 minutes on the baking sheets then transfer to wire racks. Store in an airtight container for up to 1 week.

TIP

You can find chocolate-covered coffee beans in good supermarkets, gourmet food stores, and some coffee bars.

Almond and Orange Sandwich Cookies

Preparation time: 35 to 40 minutes ● *Cooking time: 10 minutes* ● *Makes: About 15*

Crunchy almond cookies sandwiched together with an orange butter cream filling.

INGREDIENTS

1¼ cups all-purpose flour

1 tsp baking powder

1 Tbsp superfine sugar

¾ cup ground almonds

7 Tbsp butter

½ cup corn syrup

FILLING

½ stick unsalted butter, softened

1 cup confectioners' sugar

Grated rind of 1 orange

1 Tbsp fresh orange juice

Preheat oven to 375°F. Grease two baking sheets or line with nonstick baking parchment.

● Sift the flour and baking powder into a large bowl. Stir in the sugar and ground almonds and make a well in the center. Put the butter and corn syrup in a small saucepan and stir over gentle heat until the butter has melted. Pour into the dry ingredients and mix to a soft dough. Cool slightly.

● Take teaspoons of the mixture and roll into balls. Place on the baking sheets at least 2 inches apart and flatten slightly with the back of a spoon. Bake for 10 minutes. Cool for 5 minutes then transfer to wire racks.

● To make the filling, beat the butter until very soft and creamy, then gradually beat in the confectioners' sugar. Slowly beat in the orange rind and juice. Leave it to harden slightly, then use to sandwich the cookies together. Best eaten soon after filling but may be stored in an airtight container.

Coconut and Lime Crunchies

Preparation time: 20 minutes + chilling ●
Cooking time: 7 minutes ● *Makes: About 12*

**These are light and crispy cookies with a
hint of tangy lime.**

INGREDIENTS

¾ cup sweetened flaked coconut

1 stick butter, softened

⅓ cup superfine sugar

Pinch of salt

Grated rind of 1 lime

1 Tbsp fresh lime juice

Heat a skillet over medium to high heat. Add sweetened flaked coconut a little at a time and dry fry for about 30 seconds, stirring continuously until lightly golden. Transfer to a mixing bowl.

● In a separate bowl beat the butter and sugar together until pale and fluffy. Beat in salt, lime rind, and lime juice. Stir in toasted coconut and form a soft dough. Cover and chill for at least 2 hours.

● Preheat oven to 375°F. Grease two baking sheets or line with nonstick baking parchment.

● Take teaspoons of the mixture, roll into balls then squash flat. Place on baking sheets at least 1 inch apart. Bake for about 7 minutes. Cool on the baking sheets. Store in an airtight container for up to 1 week.

TIP

Toasting coconut before using it really improves the flavor and gives it a chewy texture.

Crunchy Nut Cookies

Preparation time: 15 minutes + chilling ●
Cooking time: 10 to 15 minutes ● *Makes: 30*

Crunchy nut cereals are great for adding to cookie dough because they already contain nuts and the cereal makes the cookies really crunchy.

INGREDIENTS

2 sticks butter, softened

¾ cup packed light brown sugar

¾ cup superfine sugar

2 eggs, beaten

2¼ cups all-purpose flour

1 tsp baking powder

1 tsp salt

2½ cups crunchy nut cereal

Put the butter and sugars in a bowl and beat together until pale and creamy. Gradually beat in the eggs. Don't worry if it looks like it is curdling it will be fine when cooked. Sift in flour, baking powder, and salt; fold into the mixture. Stir in the crunchy nut cereal and mix well. Chill for 1 hour.

● Preheat oven to 350°F. Grease two baking sheets or line with nonstick baking parchment.

● Roll tablespoons of the mixture into balls and place onto the baking sheets, at least 3 inches apart. Flatten with the back of a spoon. Bake for 10 to 15 minutes until golden, but still soft. Cool for 5 minutes on the baking sheets then transfer to wire racks. Store in an airtight container for up to 1 week.

Double Ginger Pecan Cookies

Preparation time: 20 minutes ●
Cooking time: 12 minutes ● *Makes: 25*

These cookies are for real ginger lovers, they contain both ground ginger and stem or preserved ginger.

INGREDIENTS

1¾ cups all-purpose flour

1 tsp baking powder

2 tsp ground ginger

1 Tbsp superfine sugar

¾ cup chopped pecans

1 stick butter

½ cup corn syrup

1 Tbsp fine chopped stem ginger or ginger preserve

2 tsp stem ginger syrup or additional corn syrup

Preheat oven to 375°F. Grease two baking sheets or line with nonstick baking parchment.

● Sift the flour, baking powder, and ground ginger into a large bowl. Stir in the sugar and pecans and make a well in the center.

● Put butter, syrup, stem ginger, and stem ginger syrup, if using, in a small saucepan and stir over gentle heat until the butter has melted. Pour into the dry ingredients and mix to a soft dough. Cool for 10 minutes.

● Take teaspoons of the mixture and roll into balls. Place on the baking sheets at least 2 inches apart and flatten slightly with the back of a spoon. Bake for 15 to 20 minutes until golden. Cool for 5 minutes then transfer to wire racks. Store in an airtight container for up to 1 week.

Pistachio and Mint Creams

Preparation time: 30 minutes + chilling ● *Cooking time: 10 to 15 minutes* ● *Makes: About 20*

Delicate pistachio cookies sandwiched together with a rich, dark chocolate and mint ganache

INGREDIENTS

¾ cup pistachios

1 stick butter, softened

3 Tbsp superfine sugar

1¼ cups all-purpose flour

MINT GANACHE

¼ stick butter

4 oz semi-sweet chocolate

1 tsp mint extract

2 Tbsp whipping cream, at room temperature

Put pistachios in a food processor and fine grind. Put butter and sugar in a bowl and beat until light and fluffy. Sift in the flour, add the ground pistachios, and mix to a dough. Scrape onto a piece of waxed paper and form into a log 2 inches in diameter. Chill for 1 hour.

● Preheat oven to 350°F. Grease two baking sheets or line with nonstick baking parchment.

● Slice ½-inch thick cookies from the dough and put on the baking sheets at least 1 inch apart. Bake for 10 to 15 minutes. Cool for 5 minutes then transfer to wire racks.

● To make the ganache, place the butter, chocolate, and mint extract and cream in a double boiler over simmering water. Stir until melted and smooth. Remove from the heat and cool for 5 minutes. Then stir until thick. Spread over the base of half the cookies and gently stick to the base of the remaining cookies. These are best eaten on the day they are made.

Chocolate and Hazelnut Treats

Preparation time: 25 minutes ●
Cooking time: 10 to 15 minutes ●
Makes: 30 double cookies

These are deliciously crumbly and you get twice the amount of cookie!

INGREDIENTS

2 sticks butter, softened

¾ cup packed light brown sugar

¾ cup superfine sugar

2 eggs, beaten

2¼ cups all-purpose flour

1 tsp baking powder

1 tsp salt

1½ cups fine chopped hazelnuts

¾ cup chocolate and hazelnut spread

Put the butter and sugars in a bowl and beat together until pale and creamy. Gradually beat in the eggs. Don't worry if it looks like it is curdling, it will be fine when cooked. Sift in flour, baking powder, and salt and mix. Stir in the hazelnuts and mix well. Chill for 1 hour.

● Preheat oven to 350°F. Grease two baking sheets or line with nonstick baking parchment.

● Roll level teaspoons of the mixture into balls and place onto the baking sheets, at least 2 inches apart. Flatten with the back of a spoon. Bake for 10 to 15 minutes until golden, but still soft. Cool for 5 minutes on the sheets then transfer to wire cooling racks. Once cooled, sandwich together with the chocolate spread. Best eaten soon after filling but may be stored in an airtight container.

Nuts and Cherry Cookies

Preparation time: 30 minutes + chilling ●
Cooking time: 13 to 15 minutes ● *Makes: About 30*

Any combination of nuts can be used, or buy a packet of ready mixed nuts.

INGREDIENTS

2 sticks butter, softened

½ cup packed light brown sugar

¾ cup superfine sugar

2 eggs, beaten

2¼ cups all-purpose flour

1 tsp baking powder

1 tsp salt

1 cup fine chopped mixed nuts

1 cup dried Morello or sour cherries

Put the butter and sugars in a bowl and beat together until pale and creamy. Gradually beat in the eggs. Don't worry if it looks like it is curdling, it will be fine when cooked. Sift in flour and baking powder and mix. Stir in the chopped nuts and dried cherries mix well. Chill for 1 hour.

● Preheat oven to 350°F. Grease two baking sheets or line with nonstick baking parchment.

● Roll tablespoons of the mixture into balls and place onto the baking sheets, at least 3 inches apart. Flatten with the back of a spoon. Bake for 13 to 15 minutes until golden, but still soft. Cool for 5 minutes on the sheets then transfer to wire cooling racks.

● These cookies are best eaten on the day made, but may be stored in an airtight container.

Pecan and Marshmallow Cookies

Preparation time: 15 minutes + chilling ●
Cooking time: 12 to 15 minutes ● *Makes: About 25*

These chewy cookies are simply irresistible! The marshmallows melt in little patches of each cookie giving an unexpected change of flavor.

INGREDIENTS

1½ cups butter, softened
½ cup packed light brown sugar
¾ cup superfine sugar
2 eggs, beaten
3 Tbsp clear honey
2¼ cups all-purpose flour
1 tsp baking powder
1 tsp salt
1 cup fine chopped pecans
2 cups mini marshmallows

Put the butter and sugars in a bowl and beat together until pale and creamy. Gradually beat in the eggs and honey. Sift in flour, baking powder, and salt; mix well. Stir in the pecans and marshmallows until well combined. Chill for at least 1 hour.

● Preheat oven to 350°F. Grease two baking sheets or line with nonstick baking parchment.

● Roll tablespoons of the mixture into balls and place onto the baking sheets, at least 3 inches apart. Flatten with the back of a spoon. Bake for 12 to 15 minutes until golden, but still soft. Cool for 5 minutes on the baking sheets then transfer to wire racks. Store in an airtight container for up to 1 week.

Walnut and Marmalade Cookies

Preparation time: 15 minutes + chilling ●
Cooking time: 15 to 18 minutes ● *Makes: About 30*

Adding marmalade to cookies gives them a toffee-like flavor and texture.

INGREDIENTS

2 sticks butter, softened
¾ cup packed light brown sugar
¾ cup superfine sugar
2 eggs, beaten
¼ cup orange marmalade
2¼ cups all-purpose flour
1 tsp baking powder
1 tsp salt
1 cup fine chopped walnuts

Put the butter and sugars in a bowl and beat together until pale and creamy. Gradually beat in the eggs and marmalade. Don't worry if it looks like it is curdling, it will be fine when cooked. Sift in flour, baking powder, and salt and mix. Stir in the walnuts and mix well. Chill for 1 hour.

● Preheat oven to 350F. Grease two baking sheets or line with nonstick baking parchment.

● Roll tablespoons of the mixture into balls and place onto the baking sheets, at least 3 inches apart. Flatten with the back of a spoon. Bake for 15 to 18 minutes until golden, but still soft. Cool for 5 minutes on the baking sheets then transfer to wire racks. Store in an airtight container for up to 1 week.

Walnut and Carrot Cookies

Preparation time: 30 minutes + chilling ●
Cooking time: 10 to 12 minutes ● *Makes: About 20*

Carrots have a sweet flavor and make the perfect match for walnuts.

INGREDIENTS

1½ sticks butter, softened

1 cup plus 2 Tbsp superfine sugar

2 eggs, beaten

1¼ cups chopped walnuts

⅔ cup grated carrot

3¼ cups all-purpose flour

1 tsp baking powder

Put butter and sugar in a mixing bowl and beat until pale and fluffy. Gradually beat in the eggs. Don't worry if the mixture looks like it is curdling, it will be fine once cooked. Stir in the walnuts and grated carrot. Sift in the flour and baking powder and form into a dough. Chill for 1 hour.

● Preheat oven to 350°F. Grease two baking sheets or line with nonstick baking parchment.

● Take tablespoonfuls of the dough and form into balls. Place on the baking sheets at least 1 inch apart and flatten with the back of a spoon. Bake for 10 to 12 minutes. Cool on the baking sheets. Store the cookies in an airtight container.

Syrupy Macadamia Nut Cookies

Preparation time: 30 minutes + chilling ●
Cooking time: 20 minutes ● *Makes: About 16*

Macadamia nuts are very rich so not many are required to give a strong, nutty flavor.

INGREDIENTS

1 stick butter, softened

⅔ cup packed light brown sugar

4 tsp corn syrup

1 medium egg yolk

1 Tbsp fresh orange juice

1½ cups all-purpose flour

½ tsp baking powder

½ cup macadamia nuts, rough chopped

½ cup white chocolate chips

Put butter and sugar in a bowl and beat until pale and fluffy. Beat in the corn syrup, egg yolk, and orange juice. Sift in the flour and baking powder; mix well. Stir in the macadamia nuts and mix to a soft dough.

● Press into a greased 8-inch square pan and chill for 30 minutes.

● Preheat oven to 350°F. Bake the mixture for about 20 minutes until cooked through.

● Meanwhile melt the chocolate in a microwave or in a double boiler over simmering water. Drizzle the baked dough with the chocolate. Allow to harden before slicing into 16 squares. Store in an airtight container for up to 1 week.

Macadamia Chocolate Bars

Preparation time: 35 minutes ●
Cooking time: 25 minutes ● *Makes: 21*

The easy way to make a chocolate topping—just use whole bars of chocolate and let them melt over the warm cookie dough!

INGREDIENTS

1½ sticks butter, softened

½ cup superfine sugar

3 Tbsp milk

1 tsp almond extract

1½ cups all-purpose flour

Pinch of salt

1 cup macadamia nuts, rough chopped

10 oz good quality milk or semi-sweet chocolate bars

Preheat oven to 350°F. Grease and base line a 13 x 9-inch baking pan.

● Put the butter and sugar in a bowl and beat until light and fluffy. Beat in the milk and almond extract. Sift in the flour and salt and form into a dough. Add half the nuts and mix well. Spread into the prepared pan and bake for 20 to 25 minutes until lightly browned around the edges.

● As soon as it is out of the oven, cover with the chocolate bars, then return to the oven for 2 minutes. Once out of the oven leave for 1 minute to let the chocolate melt. Once melted spread the chocolate evenly over the baked dough. Scatter over the remaining nuts and leave to cool completely. Cut into 21 bars, 7 across and 3 down. Store in an airtight container for up to 1 week.

Hazelnut and Molasses Cookies

Preparation time: 15 minutes + chilling ●
Cooking time: 15 minutes ● *Makes: About 25*

Some of the sugar is replaced by molasses in this drop cookie. It makes the cookies rich, rather than intensely sweet.

INGREDIENTS

1½ sticks butter, softened

¾ cup packed light brown sugar

¼ cup molasses

1 egg, beaten

2¼ cups all-purpose flour

1 tsp baking powder

1 tsp grated nutmeg

1 tsp salt

1 cup chopped hazelnuts

Put the butter and sugar in a bowl and beat until light and fluffy. Gradually beat in the molasses and egg. Sift in the flour, baking powder, nutmeg, and salt; then mix. Stir in the nuts and form into a dough. Chill for at least 1 hour or overnight.

● Preheat oven to 350°F. Grease two baking sheets or line with nonstick baking parchment.

● Take heaping teaspoons of the dough, form into balls, and flatten slightly between your palms. Place on the baking sheets at least 2 inches apart and bake for 15 minutes. Cool for 5 minutes and then transfer to wire racks.

Coconut Macaroons

Preparation time: 10 minutes ● *Cooking time: 20 minutes* ● *Makes: 20*

These are so simple to make, you'll never buy shop-bought macaroons again!

INGREDIENTS

4 egg whites

4 tsp cornstarch

1 cup superfine sugar

Scant 3 cups sweetened flaked coconut

20 whole blanched almonds

Rice paper (optional)

Preheat oven to 350°F. Grease two baking sheets or line with rice paper or nonstick baking parchment.
● Beat the egg whites until foamy but not holding their shape. Stir in the remaining ingredients and mix well. Place 2 teaspoons of the mixture on the baking sheets about 2 inches in diameter, spaced well apart. Flatten slightly and place an almond in the center of each.
● Bake for 20 minutes until just turning golden. Cool on the baking sheets. If using rice paper, tear from around each macaroon once cooled.

Coconut and Rum Cookies

Preparation time: 30 minutes + chilling ● *Cooking time: 15 to 20 minutes* ● *Makes: About 20*

These are delicate, crisp, and crumbly cookies.

INGREDIENTS

1¼ cups sweetened flaked coconut

2 sticks butter, softened

¾ cup packed light brown sugar

2 Tbsp dark rum

1¼ cup all-purpose flour

Pinch of salt

½ cup chopped slivered almonds

Heat a skillet over high heat. Add half the coconut and dry fry for about 30 seconds, stirring continuously until lightly golden. Place in a bowl and repeat with remaining coconut.

● Place the butter and sugar in a separate bowl and beat until light and fluffy. Beat in the rum. Sift in the flour and salt and mix well. Stir in the almonds and half the toasted coconut; mix well. Lightly flour the work surface and knead dough until soft.

● Divide mixture in two. Place each piece in a piece of waxed paper and shape each into a log about 2 inches in diameter and wrap each piece in waxed paper. Chill for at least 2 hours or overnight.

● Preheat oven to 350°F. Grease two baking sheets or line with nonstick baking parchment.

● Cut dough into ½-inch slices and arrange on the baking sheets at least 2 inches apart. Cook for 15 to 20 minutes until very lightly browned. As soon as the cookies are out of the oven, sprinkle over the remaining toasted coconut. Cool for 5 minutes on the baking sheets then transfer to wire racks. Store in an airtight container for up to 1 week.

Bar Cookies

A cross between a cookie and a cake, bar cookies make a satisfying treat. This selection includes some old favorites as well as some new ideas that draw on the new ingredients on the market. There is even a short-cut recipe for making delicious chewy brownies in the microwave. So whether you're making bar cookies for dessert, or to pack in the lunchbox, whether you want them crispy or crunchy, healthy or indulgent, you'll find plenty of inspiration in this chapter.

Family Favorites

Grasmere Gingerbread	378
Coconut and Prune Triangles	378
Double Pear Treats	381
Simnel Bars	382
Coconut and Sesame Crunch	384
Boston Brownies	384
Rocky Road Pizza	385
Brazil Nut Blondies	386

Special Treats

Chocolate and Raspberry Macaroon Bars	387
Cherry and Cinnamon Candy Bars	389
Chocolate Chip and Pecan Shortbread	390
Chocolate and Orange Slices	391
Date and Oat Crumb Squares	391
Cranberry and Golden Raisin Bars	393
Easy Apricot Squares	393
Double Chocolate and Mango Brownies	394

Quick Bites

Fig and Oat Slices	394
Exotic Fruit and Almond Slices	396
Cranberry Bars	397
Fruit and Brandy Sticks	399
Oat Bars	400
Hazelnut Bars	400
Lemon Cheesecake Fingers	401
Fruit and Nut Bars	403
Lemon and Hazelnut Fingers	404
Melting Almond Shortbread	404
Linzer Bake	406

Portable Snacks

Mango and Pistachio Slices	407
Microwave Brownies	409
Prune and Two Chocolate Pieces	410
Orange and Raisin Shortbread	410
Spanish Date Meringue Slices	413
Munch	413
Stollen Bars	414
Toffee Bars	416
Double Ginger Bars	416
Chocolate Orange Dream Bars	417

Grasmere Gingerbread

Preparation time: 20 minutes ●
Cooking time: 30 minutes ● Makes: 16 pieces

Grasmere, one of the prettiest lakes in the English Lake District, is famous for a ginger shortbread. The gingerbread shop in Grasmere jealously guards their recipe but this family recipe is as good, if not better!

INGREDIENTS

2 cups all-purpose flour

1½ teaspoons ground ginger

1 stick lightly salted butter

¾ cup lightly packed light brown sugar

1 Tbsp corn syrup

1 Tbsp chopped candied orange peel or candied citrus peel

1 Tbsp chopped crystallized ginger

Preheat oven to 350°F. Grease and base-line a 7 x 11-inch shallow pan and line with waxed paper or nonstick baking parchment.

● Beat the butter, sugar, and corn syrup until light and well blended. Beat in the remaining ingredients and press into the prepared pan.

● Bake for 25 to 30 minutes or until pale golden. Cut into 16 pieces while still hot but leave in the pan to cool. Store in an airtight container.

TIP

Try to find candied orange peel rather than candied citrus peel as the flavor and texture is superior.

Coconut and Prune Triangles

Preparation time: 30 minutes ●
Cooking time: 35 to 40 minutes ● Makes: 18 triangles

This recipe is a delicious mixture of basic store cupboard ingredients.

INGREDIENTS

½ cup pitted prunes

Juice and rind of 1 lemon

4 Tbsp water

1 Tbsp sugar

½ cup whole-wheat flour

¾ tsp baking powder

1 cup all-purpose flour

6 Tbsp soft tub margarine

¾ cup packed soft brown sugar

1 egg, beaten

TOPPING

2 cups sweetened flaked coconut

4 Tbsp honey

2 eggs

Preheat oven to 350°F. Grease and base line a 7 x 11-inch shallow pan.

● Chop the prunes and place in a pan with the lemon rind and juice, water, and sugar. Cook until soft

● Sift the two flours and baking powder retaining the bran. Beat the margarine and sugar and beat in the egg. Work in the flours to form a dough and press into the pan. Spread the prune mixture over the dough.

● Beat the remaining 2 eggs, then beat in the honey and stir in the coconut. Spread over the prune mixture.

● Bake for 30 to 35 minutes. Cool in the pan, then cut into squares and across into triangles.

Double Pear Treats

Preparation time: 1 hour ● Cooking time: 40 to 45 minutes ● Makes: 15 pieces

These are delicious served hot with cream or yogurt as a dessert. Part of the bake could be used served hot with cream or yogurt as a dessert. The remainder can be quickly cooled to store in the cake pan.

INGREDIENTS

BASIC SHORTBREAD

¾ cup all-purpose flour

½ stick lightly salted butter

2 Tbsp superfine sugar

BASIC TOPPING

½ stick lightly salted butter or margarine

¼ cup packed soft brown sugar

1 egg, beaten

½ cup whole-wheat flour

¾ tsp baking powder

¼ tsp pumpkin pie spice

¼ tsp nutmeg

Grated rind of ½ orange

½ Tbsp milk

FILLING

3 pear halves from a can of pears in natural juice

4 dried pear halves

2 Tbsp semi-sweet chocolate chips

To make the shortbread, preheat oven to 350°F. Grease an 8-inch pan and line with nonstick baking parchment, so it stands 1-inch above the sides.

● Sift the flour into a bowl and blend in the butter until it resembles bread crumbs, then stir in the sugar. Press the crumb mixture into the pan, making sure it is smooth and level.

● Bake for 10 to 15 minutes or until the center is pale golden. Remove from the oven and cool while the filling is prepared.

● For the topping, beat the butter and sugar until light and fluffy. Gradually beat in the egg. Sift the spices and flour and fold into the mixture, together with the bran left in the sifter, the orange rind, and the milk.

● Thoroughly drain the pear halves and chop. Scatter over the shortbread. Dice the dried pears and mix into a bowl of basic topping together with the chocolate chips. Pour over the chopped pears and level.

● Bake for 40 to 45 minutes or until the centers are firm. Cool in the pan for 15 minutes. Turn onto a cooling rack and when cool, cut into portions. Store in an airtight container, or freeze for up to 3 months.

Simnel Bars

Preparation time: 1 hour ● Cooking time: 40 to 45 minutes ● Makes: 15 pieces

This recipe is ideal for Easter entertaining. However, if you wish to make it less seasonal, leave out the marzipan and replace it with a simple frosting on the top.

INGREDIENTS

BASIC SHORTBREAD

¾ cup all-purpose flour

½ stick lightly salted butter

2 Tbsp superfine sugar

BASIC TOPPING

½ stick lightly salted butter or margarine

¼ cup packed soft brown sugar

1 egg, beaten

½ cup whole-wheat flour

¾ tsp baking powder

¼ tsp pumpkin pie spice

¼ tsp nutmeg

Grated rind of ½ orange

½ Tbsp milk

FILLING

1 cup mixed dried fruit

6 candied cherries

2 tsp brandy

6 oz marzipan

1 Tbsp apricot jam or preserves

Make the shortbread as for the previous recipe on page 381 and bake as instructed. Then prepare the topping, also following the instructions on page 381.

● Now chop the cherries and lightly mix into a bowl of basic topping together with the brandy and mixed dried fruit. Pour over the shortbread and level the surface.

● Bake for 40 to 45 minutes or until the centers are firm and the sides coming away from the edge of the pan. Cool in the pan for 15 minutes.

● Meanwhile roll out the marzipan to fit the sheet, using confectioners' sugar to prevent it sticking to the work surface. Preheat the broiler for 5 minutes.

● Warm the apricot jam and brush over the top. Carefully lift the marzipan over and press lightly to fit. Using a sharp knife, mark diagonal lines across the top, making diamonds.

● Place under the broiler and turn the heat down to medium. Leave until the marzipan has started to brown, checking constantly. Leave to cool until the marzipan is firm. Then gently turn onto a cooling rack covered with a folded dish towel.

● Slip onto a board and cut into portions with a sharp knife. Cool completely before storing or freezing for up to 3 months.

Coconut and Sesame Crunch

Preparation time: 15 minutes ●
Cooking time: 20 minutes ● *Makes: 12 pieces*

A delicious crunch bar with a distinctive nutty flavor. It is a great favorite, with a quick and easy method.

INGREDIENTS

1 stick margarine or butter

¼ cup superfine sugar

½ Tbsp corn syrup

¾ cup self-rising flour

½ cup rolled oats

⅓ cup sweetened flaked coconut

2 Tbsp sesame seeds

Preheat oven to 350°F. Grease and base-line an 8 x 8-inch shallow pan.

● Melt the fat, sugar, and syrup over a low heat in a large saucepan. Remove from the heat and stir in the remaining ingredients. Press into the pan. Do not worry if it looks very greasy at this stage, it is dry when cooked. Bake for 15 to 20 minutes until golden. Leave to cool for 10 minutes then cut into 12 pieces but leave to cool completely in the pan. Store in an airtight container for up to 1 week.

Boston Brownies

Preparation time: 20 minutes ●
Cooking time: 30 to 35 minutes ●
Makes: 9 large squares

Brownies are quite irresistible gooey squares of chocolate heaven and crunchy nuts. This recipe uses only cocoa which gives it a rich, full flavor—and is useful when the chocolate has disappeared from the cupboard.

INGREDIENTS

⅔ cup unsweetened cocoa powder

5 Tbsp water

¾ stick margarine or lightly salted butter

2 eggs

1 cup granulated sugar

¾ cup all-purpose flour

¾ cup rough chopped pecan nuts

Preheat oven to 350°F. Grease and base-line an 8 x 8-inch pan.

● Place the cocoa in a small saucepan and gradually blend in the water. Briefly stir over a low heat to make a smooth paste. Add the butter or margarine and heat until it has melted.

● Beat the eggs and sugar until light and fluffy, then beat in the cocoa mixture.

● Sift the flour and fold in, then stir in the nuts. Spread in to the pan.

● Bake for 25 to 30 minutes until risen and firm in the center. It is normal for the mixture to sink a little in the center on cooling. Cool for 15 minutes, then cut into squares. Store in an airtight container.

Rocky Road Pizza

Preparation time: 40 minutes ● *Cooking time: 20 minutes + 10 minutes* ● *Makes: 8 wedges*

The rocky road cookie appears in many guises. In this version, a very traditional, lemon-flavored, Shrewsbury cookie mixture is used to make a pizza base.

INGREDIENTS

SHREWSBURY COOKIE BASE

2 cups all-purpose flour

1 stick lightly salted butter or margarine

½ cup superfine sugar

Grated rind of 1 lemon

1 egg

Milk, if required

TOPPING

¼ cup mixed chopped nuts

1¼ cups mini marshmallows

½ cup milk or semi-sweet chocolate chips

2 Tbsp caramel topping

Preheat oven to 350°F. Grease or line a baking sheet with nonstick baking parchment.

● Prepare the pizza base. Sift the flour into a bowl and blend in the butter or margarine to make fine bread crumbs. Stir in the sugar and lemon rind. Beat the egg and use it, together with milk if needed, to make a firm but soft dough. It must not be sticky.

● To make an 8-inch base, take three quarters of the dough and roll out in a circle. Lift onto the baking sheet and use a tart ring or plate as a guide to the correct shape, alternatively use a pizza pan.

● Bake for about 20 minutes until pale golden and cooked in the center. Five minutes before the end of the cooking time, place the mixed chopped nuts on a baking sheet and slip into the oven to toast. Leave there for about 10 minutes, until just starting to color.

● Allow the pizza base to cool slightly, then scatter the marshmallows over the surface, followed by the nuts and the chocolate chips. Drizzle the caramel topping over and return to the oven for about 10 minutes until the pizza edges are a deeper color and the marshmallows are just starting to melt. Serve hot or cold.

Brazil Nut Blondies

Preparation time: 15 minutes ● Cooking time: 20 minutes ● Makes: 12 pieces

Blondies are brownies without chocolate. To make up for the disappointment, there are plenty of nuts in this sweet, chewy mixture and the color is quite dark due to the dark sugar and baking soda.

INGREDIENTS

1 egg

1½ cups packed dark brown sugar

1 tsp vanilla extract

¾ cup all-purpose flour

¼ tsp baking soda

1 cup chopped Brazil nuts

2 tsp milk

Preheat oven to 350°F. Grease and base-line an 8 x 8-inch pan.

● Beat the egg and stir in the sugar and vanilla extract. Sift the flour and baking soda into the mixture and stir in, together with the nuts and milk. The mixture will be very stiff.

● Spread into the pan and bake for 15 to 20 minutes. Mark into squares before completely cold and leave to cool in the pan. Store in an airtight container.

Chocolate and Raspberry Macaroon Bars

Preparation time: 25 minutes ● *Cooking time: 20 to 25 minutes* ● *Makes: 25*

These are small, rich bars with an intense chocolate flavor. Use homemade raspberry jam or preserve if possible as the flavor mingles deliciously with the chocolate.

INGREDIENTS

CHOCOLATE SHORTBREAD

¾ cup all-purpose flour

⅓ cup unsweetened cocoa powder

¼ stick lightly salted butter

2 egg yolks

3 Tbsp superfine sugar

4-5 Tbsp good quality raspberry jam or preserve

MACAROON MIXTURE

¾ cup ground almonds

1½ Tbsp ground rice

2 egg whites

3 drops almond extract

1½ tsp unsweetened cocoa powder

Preheat oven to 350°F. Grease and base-line a 7 x 11-inch pan.

● Sift the flour and cocoa, blend in the butter, stir in the egg yolks and sugar. Work together to form a dough and press into the pan. Lightly spread the raspberry jam over the shortbread.

● Place the sugar, ground almonds, and ground rice in a bowl and gently mix. Whisk the egg white and almond extract until it stands in stiff peaks. Gradually fold in the dry ingredients to a stiff mixture. Spoon over the jam and spread roughly with a fork dipped in water.

● Bake for 25 to 35 minutes until dry but not colored. Mark into pieces while still warm and leave in the pan until cold. Lightly dust with sifted cocoa powder. Store in an airtight container.

Cherry and Cinnamon Candy Bars

Preparation time: 45 minutes ● *Cooking time: 25 minutes* ● *Makes: 10 bars*

These ever-popular caramel fingers are combined with powdered cinnamon and dried cherries to give a new slant to a favorite recipe.

INGREDIENTS

SHORTBREAD BASE

¾ stick butter or margarine

2 Tbsp granulated sugar

1 tsp powdered cinnamon

1 cup all-purpose flour

FILLING

1 stick lightly salted butter

¼ cup superfine sugar

2 Tbsp corn syrup

1 cup condensed milk

½ tsp almond extract

1 tsp powdered cinnamon

½ cup dried cherries, halved

TOPPING

3 oz semi-sweet chocolate

1 Tbsp unsalted butter

Preheat oven to 350°F. Grease and base-line an 8 x 8-inch pan.

● Prepare the base first by beating together the butter and sugar. Sift the flour and cinnamon and work into the mixture. Evenly press into the pan. Prick well and bake for about 20 to 25 minutes until golden. Allow to cool.

● To make the filling, place the butter, sugar, syrup, and condensed milk in a heavy-bottomed saucepan and stir over gentle heat to dissolve. Slowly bring to a boil and cook, stirring constantly, for about 7 minutes until thick and a pale toffee color. Remove from the heat and beat in the almond extract and cinnamon. Pour half the mixture over the shortbread, sprinkle the cherries over, then the remaining filling. Allow to cool to room temperature and then place in the refrigerator.

● When this layer is cold, melt the chocolate and butter together, either over a bowl of hot water or in the microwave for 1 to 2 minutes. Stir gently and pour over the cherry caramel. Spread evenly over and leave to set. Cut into bars when cold and then store in an airtight container.

Chocolate Chip and Pecan Shortbread

Preparation time: 25 minutes ● *Cooking time: 50 to 60 minutes* ● *Makes: 8 pieces*

This pale, traditional shortbread is made even more tempting by the addition of nuts and chocolate. It would make a welcome gift at any time of year but especially for Christmas.

INGREDIENTS

⅓ cup chocolate chips

2 cups all-purpose flour

⅔ cup ground rice

½ cup superfine sugar

Pinch of salt

2 sticks lightly salted butter

⅔ cup chopped pecan nuts

Grease a two piece 8-inch tart pan. Place the chocolate chips in the freezer for at least 30 minutes.

● Sift the flour and ground rice into a large bowl, mix in the sugar and salt, then blend in the butter. Stir in the nuts and the chilled chocolate and bring together to form a crumbly dough. Transfer this to the prepared pan and press down firmly using a knife. Prick the surface evenly with a skewer and mark a pattern round the edge using the flat point of a vegetable peeler. Chill for one hour. Mark into 8 portions.

● Preheat oven to 300°F. Bake for 50 to 60 minutes. The shortbread must look pale but be cooked in the center. Return to the oven if necessary for up to 10 minutes longer. Score into portions again and leave to cool in the pan.

TIP

It is not necessary to have an 8-inch two-piece pie pan as the shortbread can be shaped using a plate or saucepan lid and cooked on a baking sheet.

Chocolate and Orange Slices

Preparation time: 30 minutes ●
Cooking time: 20 minutes ● *Makes: 12 slices*

These easy slices are another example of the versatility of rolled oats. The orange flavor is only in the frosting, so make sure it tastes strong enough before you pour it on.

INGREDIENTS

1 stick margarine
1 cup self-rising flour
1 Tbsp unsweetened cocoa powder
1 cup rolled oats
¼ cup superfine sugar

TOPPING

3 Tbsp confectioners' sugar
1 tsp unsweetened cocoa powder
Grated rind and juice of ½ an orange
Candied orange pieces, to decorate

Preheat oven to 350°F. Grease and base-line an 8 x 8-inch pan.

● Melt the margarine gently in a large saucepan. Sift the flour and cocoa and stir into the margarine with the oats and sugar.

● Press into the pan and level the surface. Bake for 15 to 20 minutes until shrinking from the sides of the pan. Allow to cool while preparing the topping.

● Sift the confectioners' sugar and cocoa together and mix with sufficient orange juice to make a thin frosting. Stir in the orange rind and pour over the cookies while still warm.

● It will look more like a glaze than a thick frosting. Cut each one into slices and decorate with a small piece of candied orange slice.

Date and Oat Crumb Squares

Preparation time: 30 minutes ●
Cooking time: 25 to 30 minutes ● *Makes: 18*

This recipe can be utilized to use up dates left after Christmas and provide snacks in the dark weeks of the New Year. The sharpness of lemon contrasts well with the dates but orange could be used instead.

INGREDIENTS

2½ cups rolled oats
1 cup whole-wheat flour
1½ sticks margarine
¼ cup packed soft brown sugar
2 cups pitted dates
8 Tbsp water
2 Tbsp lemon juice
2 tsp grated lemon rind

Preheat oven to 375°F. Grease and base line a 7 x 11-inch shallow pan.

● Mix the oats and flour in a large bowl and blend in the margarine. Stir in the sugar.

● Chop the dates and place in a saucepan with the remaining ingredients. Heat gently until they form a pulp.

● Press half the crumble mixture firmly into the base of the pan. Gently spread the date mixture over, then the remaining crumb mixture. Press and level the mixture. Bake for about 25 minutes until golden and the mixture is starting to shrink from the sides of the pan.

● Cool in the pan but cut into squares while still warm. Store in an airtight container.

Cranberry and Golden Raisin Bars

Preparation time: 20 minutes ●
Cooking time: 25 to 30 minutes ● *Makes: 16 pieces*

Cranberries give a vivid color and sharp flavor in contrast to the sweet base mixture. They are most widely available in the Fall, in preparation for Christmas and freeze well. In this recipe they can be used from frozen if they are free flowing.

INGREDIENTS

1 stick margarine or butter
½ cup packed soft brown sugar
2 eggs
1 cup self-rising flour
¼ cup ground almonds
1 cup cranberries
⅔ cup golden raisins

Preheat oven to 350°F. Grease and base-line an 8 x 8-inch pan.

● Beat the margarine and sugar until light and fluffy. Beat the eggs and beat in gradually. Sift the flour and gently fold in, together with the ground almonds, whole cranberries, and golden raisins.

● Pour into the pan and bake for 25 to 35 minutes until well risen, firm in the center and the cake shrinking slightly from the sides of the pan. Turn out onto a wire sheet to cool, then cut into slices. These bars are best stored in the refrigerator.

Easy Apricot Squares

Preparation time: 15 minutes ●
Cooking time: 20 to 30 minutes ● *Makes: 9 pieces*

These are easy as only five ingredients are quickly combined into a soft, succulent bar. Do leave the apricots in large pieces to make the squares more unusual.

INGREDIENTS

½ stick lightly salted butter
3 Tbsp creamed honey
3 Tbsp corn syrup
¼ cup ready to eat dried apricots, halved
2⅔ cups muesli or granola

Preheat oven to 325°F. Grease and base-line an 8 x 8-inch pan.

● Soften the butter, beat until light, then beat in the honey and syrup. Stir in the remaining ingredients thoroughly and press into the pan. Bake for 20 to 30 minutes. Cool for 5 minutes, then cut into 9 squares. Leave to cool completely before removing from the pan. Store in an airtight container.

Double Chocolate and Mango Brownies

Preparation time: 30 minutes ●
Cooking time: 30 minutes ● *Makes: 12 pieces*

A luscious brownie with white chocolate pieces inside. The mango contrasts well with the traditional rich chocolate and pecan mixture. This version is firmer than the other brownie recipes, to hold up all these exciting textures.

INGREDIENTS

4 oz semi-sweet chocolate
½ stick lightly salted butter
2 eggs
½ cup packed soft brown sugar
1 cup self-rising flour
½ cup chopped candied mango
½ cup chopped pecan nuts
⅓ cup white chocolate chips
⅓ cup semi-sweet chocolate chips

Preheat oven to 375°F. Grease and base-line an 8 x 8-inch pan.

● Melt the chocolate over a bowl of hot water or in the microwave for 1½ to 2 minutes. Slice the butter into the chocolate and stir to melt, re-heating briefly if necessary.

● Beat the eggs and sugar until thick and stir into the chocolate mixture. Beat again, then gently fold in the flour, nuts, mango and two types of chocolate. Pour the mixture into the pan. Bake for 25 to 30 minutes or until the center appears stable. Cool in the pan and cut into 12 pieces.

Fig and Oat Slices

Preparation time: 20 minutes ●
Cooking time: 30 to 35 minutes ● *Makes: 12 pieces*

This is a useful and economical recipe. It freezes well for up to three months, it is a welcome addition to lunchboxes and may be served warm with yogurt for a winter dessert.

INGREDIENTS

1 cup figs
5 Tbsp water
Grated rind of ½ orange
1½ cups whole-wheat flour
2 cups rolled oats
⅓ cup packed soft brown sugar
1½ sticks margarine

Preheat oven to 350°F. Meanwhile, grease and base-line an 8 x 8-inch pan.

● Chop the figs, discarding the stalks and place in a pan with the water and orange rind. Bring to a boil and simmer for 5 minutes until very soft.

● Mix the flour and oats in a large bowl. Melt the sugar and margarine gently and stir into the oat mixture. Thoroughly combine and press half into the pan. Level the top and press well in.

● Spread the fig mixture on top and cover with the remaining oat mixture, leveling and pressing it as much as possible. Bake for 30 to 35 minutes until golden and the mixture is shrinking from the sides of the pan. Cool, cut into pieces and store in an airtight container.

TIP

● Try to find unwaxed lemons, oranges, and limes for grating, as even a good wash does not remove all the waxes from the skins.

Exotic Fruit and Almond Slices

Preparation time: 45 minutes ● *Cooking time: 35 minutes* ● *Makes: 16 slices*

This is another opportunity to use up small quantities of fruit and nuts including some of the more recent additions to the dried fruit range.

INGREDIENTS

BASE

¾ stick lightly salted butter or margarine

⅓ cup superfine sugar

¾ cup whole-wheat flour

1 tsp baking powder

¾ cup ground rice or semolina

3 Tbsp superfine sugar

TOPPING

⅓ cup raisins

⅓ cup candied cherries

⅓ cup dried mango

⅓ cup candied pineapple

⅓ cup ready to eat dried apricots

⅓ cup chopped walnuts

1 stick lightly salted butter or margarine

1 cup superfine sugar

1 egg, beaten

½ cup ground almonds

½ cup ground rice or semolina

2 Tbsp slivered almonds

Preheat oven to 350°F. Grease and base-line a 7 x 11-inch shallow pan.

● Make the base by beating the sugar and butter together until light and stirring in the flour, ground rice or semolina, and sugar. Press firmly into the pan.

● Coarse chop the fruit and nuts.

● Beat the remaining butter and sugar, then beat in the egg. Fold in the ground almonds and ground rice. Stir in the chopped fruit and nuts and pour over the base. Sprinkle with the slivered almonds. Bake for about 35 minutes until the mixture and the almonds are golden-brown. Leave in the pan to cool and cut in slices. Store in an airtight container.

Cranberry Bars

Preparation time: 15 minutes ● *Cooking time: 25 to 35 minutes* ● *Makes: 24*

This recipe has a high percentage of fat, but it is worth using butter for the flavor and reserving them for special occasions. Dried cranberries are widely available, but try to find a variety that is not too sweet.

INGREDIENTS

1½ sticks butter

¾ cup packed soft brown sugar

2 Tbsp corn syrup

3 cups rolled oats

¾ cup dried cranberries

Preheat oven to 325°F. Grease and base-line a 7 x 11-inch shallow pan.

● Melt the butter, sugar and syrup until the sugar is dissolved. Stir in the oats and cranberries and press into the pan.

● Bake for 25 to 35 minutes until set. Cool in the pan and cut into pieces while still warm. Store in an airtight container.

Fruit and Brandy Sticks

Preparation time: 30 minutes ● *Cooking time: none* ● *Makes: 25 small sticks*

This recipe is an excellent way of preserving leftover fruit cake. If much of it is still remaining in the cake box after New Year, use some of it in this recipe, freeze and use to accompany vanilla ice cream.

INGREDIENTS

TO MAKE 1 CUP OF CAKE WITHOUT FROSTING TAKE:

½ stick lightly salted butter

2 Tbsp corn syrup

2 oz semi-sweet chocolate

1 Tbsp brandy

6 Tbsp confectioners' sugar

Rose water or water

Pink coloring

Grease a 8 x 8-inch pan and then line the base of the pan as well.

● Crumble the cake into a bowl and chop any large pieces of fruit or nuts. Melt the butter, syrup, and chocolate very gently and combine with the cake crumbs and brandy.

● Press, into the pan. Level and firm the mixture and chill for at least a day before completing. The cookies may be frozen at this stage.

● Remove the mixture from the pan and place on a board. To make the frosting, sift the confectioners' sugar and mix to a thick consistency with sufficient water and/or rose water to make a thin frosting. However, add the rose water cautiously and taste the strength before use and mix with water if too strong. Add a drop or two of pink food coloring, beat well and add a few drops more of water if the frosting is too stiff. Pour evenly over the cake.

● Before the frosting sets completely, cut into pieces with a sharp knife dipped into hot water. Allow to dry before storing the pieces in an airtight container.

Oat Bars

Preparation time: 15 minutes ●
Cooking time: 30 minutes ● *Makes: 18*

**This is a delicious, simple recipe , suitable for everyday
packed lunches and snacks.
So easy to make, young members of the family
will soon be making them for you.**

INGREDIENTS

1 stick margarine or lightly salted butter

3 Tbsp corn syrup

⅓ cup packed soft brown sugar

2¾ cups rolled oats

Preheat oven to 325°F. Grease and base line a
7 x 11-inch shallow pan.

● Place margarine, syrup, and sugar in a large pan and
heat gently, stirring from time to time until the sugar
has melted. Stir in the oats and press into the pan. Bake
about 30 minutes until golden. Cool slightly before
cutting into 18 pieces. Allow to cool completely before
removing from the pan. Store in an airtight container
for up to 1 week.

Hazelnut Bars

Preparation time: 15 minutes ●
Cooking time: 25 to 30 minutes ● *Makes: 18*

**Cooks sometimes avoid hazelnuts because they need
roasting and rubbing to remove their skins. In this recipe
that is not necessary, all you do is chop them.**

INGREDIENTS

1 stick margarine or lightly salted butter

8 Tbsp honey

⅓ cup packed light brown sugar

2½ cups rolled oats

½ cup chopped hazelnuts

Preheat oven to 350°F. Grease and base-line a
7 x 11-inch shallow pan.

● Melt the margarine or butter, honey, and sugar in a
large heavy-bottomed saucepan. Stir in the oats and
nuts. Press in the pan and level the top. Bake for 25 to
30 minutes. Cool in the pan and cut into bars when still
slightly warm. Store in an airtight container.

Lemon Cheesecake Fingers

Preparation time: 50 minutes ● *Cooking time: 40 minutes* ● *Makes: 12 fingers*

These fingers would be excellent taken on a summer picnic to round off a sumptuous meal with friends. The cream cheese makes them a little more substantial to withstand any knocks en route.

INGREDIENTS

PASTRY BASE

1½ cups all-purpose flour

¾ stick block margarine or lightly salted butter

1 egg, separated

1 Tbsp water

CHEESECAKE MIXTURE

1 cup plus 2 Tbsp cream cheese

1 egg, separated

½ cup superfine sugar

Grated rind and juice of 1 lemon

1 Tbsp all-purpose flour

⅓ cup golden raisins

1 Tbsp rum, optional

Preheat oven to 375°F. Grease, base- and side-line a 7 x 11-inch shallow pan.

● Make the pastry by lightly blending the margarine or butter into the flour. Beat together the egg yolk (reserve the white for cheesecake mixture) and water, add to the mixture to make a soft dough. Use a little more water if necessary as the dough must be pliable. Reserve one-quarter of the pastry.

● Roll out the remaining pastry and line the base of the pan. Press a piece of foil on top of the pastry. Bake for about 20 minutes. Remove the foil and cool. Increase oven temperature to 400°F.

● Beat the cream cheese, egg yolk, sugar, lemon rind, and juice to thoroughly combine and stir in flour, golden raisins, and rum, if using.

● Beat the 2 egg whites to a firm peak and beat 2 tablespoons into the cheese mixture, then fold in the rest. Pour over the cooled pastry base and level gently.

● Roll out the remaining pastry and either cut strips to make a lattice or cut leaves to decorate the top. Bake for 15 minutes, then reduce temperature to 350°F and bake for 15 minutes longer. Cool in the pan and cut into fingers. Store in an airtight container in the refrigerator for 2 to 3 days.

Fruit and Nut Bars

Preparation time: 45 minutes ● *Cooking time: 30 minutes* ● *Makes: 24 bars*

The name of this recipe could be "spring cleaning bars" because the topping is excellent for using up ends of packets of nuts and dried fruit discovered when sorting out cupboards.

INGREDIENTS

SHORTBREAD BASE

2 cups all-purpose flour
2 Tbsp cornstarch
½ cup confectioners' sugar
2¼ sticks butter

TOPPING

1¼ cups nuts to include at least half the volume in almonds
1 cup chopped dried fruit, at least half to be candied cherries
2 Tbsp lightly salted butter
3 Tbsp superfine sugar
1 Tbsp milk
2 tsp vanilla extract

Preheat oven to 400°F. Grease and base-line a 7 x 11-inch shallow pan.

● Prepare the base by sifting the flour, cornstarch, and confectioners' sugar into a bowl and blending in the butter to look like bread crumbs. Press the crumbs into the pan. Level and firm down, then bake for 15 to 20 minutes. Leave in the pan to cool.

● Prepare and chop the nuts, leaving them in large pieces. Whole almonds must first be blanched, then halved. Cut the cherries into quarters and other fruit to a similar size.

● Place the topping in a heavy-bottomed saucepan and heat gently to dissolve. Try to avoid stirring too much. Add the nuts and leave to cool.

● Stir in the fruit and pour over the base. Return to the oven and bake at the same temperature for about 15 minutes or until the nuts are browning. Cool in the pan and cut into bars when cold. Store in an airtight container.

TIP

Suitable fruits to use in this recipe include candied pineapple, ginger, angelica, ready to eat prunes and apricots, dried raisins, and golden raisins.

Lemon and Hazelnut Fingers

Preparation time: 20 minutes ●
Cooking time: 25 minutes ● *Makes: 16 fingers*

These are truly heavenly. They are also incredibly easy to make and are perfect for a celebration picnic dessert.

INGREDIENTS

PASTRY

1 cup all-purpose flour

¾ stick lightly salted butter

3 tsp confectioners' sugar

LEMON CURD FILLING

2 eggs, beaten

1 cup confectioners' sugar

2 small lemons

½ stick unsalted butter

¾ cup ground hazelnuts

Preheat oven to 375°F. Grease, base- and side-line a 7 x 11-inch shallow pan.

● Place all the ingredients for the pastry in a food processor and process until they resemble fine bread crumbs. Tip the pastry mixture into the pan and press into the base. Bake for 5 minutes.

● Meanwhile make the filling. Soften the butter to the consistency of tub margarine and place in a large bowl with the remaining ingredients. Whisk well to combine. Pour the filling over the pastry and return to the oven for 15 to 20 minutes until golden and set. Allow to get cold in the pan before cutting into pieces. Best eaten when freshly made.

Melting Almond Shortbread

Preparation time: 10 minutes ● *Cooking time: 45 to 50 minutes* ● *Makes: 16 bars*

This is called "melting" for two reasons. Firstly because it melts in the mouth. Secondly because the butter and it must be butter, is melted and the other ingredients are simply stirred in.

INGREDIENTS

2 sticks butter

1½ cups self-rising flour

½ cup all-purpose flour

2 Tbsp cornstarch

¼ cup superfine sugar

4 drops almond extract

½ cup slivered almonds

Preheat oven to 350°F. Grease and base-line a 7 x 11-inch shallow pan.

● Gently melt the butter. Meanwhile, sift the flours and cornstarch together into a bowl and stir in the superfine sugar. Add all but 2 tablespoons of slivered almonds.

● Make a well in the center and stir in the melted butter.

● Turn into the pan, press in place, and sprinkle the remaining slivered almonds over. Do not worry if the mixture seems rather sparse in the pan as the mixture will increase in volume while cooking. Bake for 45 to 50 minutes until very pale golden but the center looks cooked and the shortbread is beginning to shrink away from the sides of the pan. Leave in the pan to cool, then cut into pieces.

Linzer Bake

Preparation time: 40 minutes ● Cooking time: 30 to 35 minutes ● Makes: 9 dessert portions

Linzer Torte is a traditional Austrian dessert of raspberries and a light, spiced pastry which is a cross between cake and pastry. This version would be perfect to pack for a special picnic.

INGREDIENTS

1½ cups self-rising flour

½ tsp ground cloves

½ tsp pumpkin pie spice

5 Tbsp lightly salted butter

½ cup superfine sugar

⅓ cup ground almonds or hazelnuts

Grated rind of ½ lemon

½ tsp vanilla extract

1 egg

1–2 Tbsp milk

1½ cups raspberry jam or preserves

Preheat oven to 350°F. Grease and base-line an 8 x 8-inch pan.

● Sift the flour and spices and blend in the butter. Stir in the sugar, ground almonds, and lemon rind. Beat together the egg and vanilla extract and stir in, followed by sufficient milk to make up to a firm but slightly soft dough. Gently knead to remove any cracks, wrap in plastic and chill for 30 minutes.

● Roll out the pastry and use to line the pan. Trim the pastry level with the top of the pan. Fill the center with raspberry jam or preserves.

● Roll out the trimmings and cut into lattice strips. Place two or three in each direction, over the jam to make an even lattice. Do not try weaving the strips as this pastry is too fragile.

● Bake in the oven for 25 to 30 minutes until the pastry is barely colored.

Mango and Pistachio Slices

Preparation time: 20 minutes ● Cooking time: 30 minutes ● Makes: 16 slices

Lightly spiced and slightly chewy, these slices look and taste glorious, with the golden mango contrasting beautifully with the lime green nuts.

INGREDIENTS

1 stick lightly salted butter

½ cup superfine sugar

1 egg

½ tsp vanilla extract

1 cup self-rising flour

½ tsp grated nutmeg

½ cup dried mango pieces

¾ cup pistachio nuts

1 Tbsp sherry

4 Tbsp confectioners' sugar

Preheat oven to 350°F. Grease and base-line a 7 x 11-inch shallow pan.

● Check the dried mango packet for directions and, if necessary, soak in boiling water for 10 minutes. Drain and dry on paper towels and rough chop.

● Grind half the pistachio nuts to powder and rough chop the rest.

● Beat the butter and sugar until light and beat in the egg, vanilla, and mango pieces.

● Stir in the nut, flour, and sherry. The mixture should be quite stiff. Spread the pan and bake 30 minutes. Allow to cool in the pan.

● Sift the confectioners' sugar and mix with a little water until sufficiently runny to drizzle over the bars. When set cut into pieces with a sharp knife. Store in an airtight container.

Microwave Brownies

Preparation time: 10 minutes ● *Cooking time: 7 minutes* ● *Makes: 8 wedges*

These microwaved Brownies are amazingly good and well worth a try. Eat them fresh from the microwave or at least the same day they are baked.

INGREDIENTS

Scant 2 oz semi-sweet chocolate, chopped

¼ stick butter or margarine

¾ cup packed dark brown sugar

2 eggs

1 cup all-purpose flour

¼ cup unsweetened cocoa powder

¼ tsp baking powder

1 tsp vanilla extract

⅓ cup chopped walnuts

2 Tbsp milk

Cook in a 10 x 6 x 2-inch heatproof glass or pottery dish lined with lightly greased waxed paper.

● Melt the chocolate and butter or margarine in the microwave on HIGH for 2 minutes. Beat in the sugar and egg until smooth. Stir in the remaining ingredients to form a smooth batter. Spread in the prepared dish.

● Microwave on HIGH for about 7 minutes until the mixture is slightly risen and a few broken bubbles break the surface. The center will probably look damp but will set during standing time. Cool the brownies in the dish for 10 minutes then cut in16 wedges.

TIP

Check the brownies after 5½ minutes, then check every 30 seconds until cooked to prevent overcooking.

409

the top

Prune and Two Chocolate Pieces

Preparation time: 40 minutes ●
Cooking time: 15 minutes ● *Makes: 25*

These delectable pieces can be served with after dinner coffee or arranged in an attractive box as a gift. Choose the ready to eat type of prune to avoid having to soak them.

INGREDIENTS

1 cup prunes

1 Tbsp sweet sherry or orange juice

2 Tbsp water

½ cup self-rising flour

1 tsp powdered cinnamon

1 cup rolled oats

¾ stick lightly salted butter

¼ cup packed soft brown sugar

½ cup white chocolate chips

2 oz milk or semi-sweet chocolate

Preheat oven to 375°F. Grease and base-line an 8 x 8-inch pan.

● Chop the prunes and place in a saucepan with the sherry or orange juice and water. Bring to a boil and cook for 2 minutes, stirring all the time. Leave to cool.

● Mix the flour, cinnamon, and oats, blend in the butter and stir in the sugar.

● Stir in the white chocolate chips, lastly the prune mixture. Press into the pan and bake for 12 to 15 minutes or until just starting to turn golden. Leave in the pan to cool.

● Melt the remaining chocolate and pour over the bake. Using a sharp knife, cut into squares while still warm. Drizzle with more melted white chocolate, if liked. Store in an airtight container.

Orange and Raisin Shortbread

Preparation time: 30 minutes + chilling ●
Cooking time: 30 to 40 minutes ● *Makes: 8 pieces*

This is a delicious alternative to traditional shortbread. If you can find them, use the pale dessert raisins that are available at Christmas.

INGREDIENTS

¾ cup all-purpose flour

½ cup cornstarch

1 stick lightly salted butter

¼ cup superfine sugar

¼ cup ground almonds

Grated rind of one small orange

¼ cup raisins

1 teaspoon superfine sugar

Start by lightly greasing the base and sides of an 8-inch two-piece tart pan.

● Sift the flour and cornstarch and blend in the butter. Stir in the sugar, ground almonds, and orange rind. Press the mixture together and incorporate the raisins before the dough is fully formed. Knead lightly to evenly distribute the ingredients and ensure the dough is free from cracks.

● Lift onto the base of the pan and roll or press out to form an 8-inch circle. Leave the ring in place and smooth the surface. Half cut through to mark 8 portions and prick evenly with a fork. Chill for 1 hour.

● Preheat oven to 325°F and bake for 30 to 40 minutes or until very pale apricot-colored. Dust with the remaining superfine sugar. Remove the ring from the pan and cut into the portions. Leave on the sheet to cool and harden. Store in an airtight container.

Spanish Date Meringue Slices

Preparation time: 45 minutes ●
Cooking time: 40 minutes ● Makes: 16 slices

This traditional recipe uses a delicious combination of dates and oranges.

INGREDIENTS

PASTRY BASE

½ stick lightly salted butter or margarine

2 Tbsp superfine sugar

1 Tbsp beaten egg

Grated rind of ½ an orange

1 cup all-purpose flour

FILLING

1 cup pitted dates

1 Tbsp rum or orange juice

3 egg whites

½ cup ground almonds

2 Tbsp cornstarch

⅓ cup superfine sugar

Preheat oven to 350°F. Grease and base-line a 7 x 11-inch shallow pan.

● Make the pastry base. Beat the butter or margarine and sugar together until light and fluffy. Beat in the egg and orange rind, then work in the flour. Press into the base of the pan.

● Chop the dates and pour over the rum or orange juice. Mix the ground almonds, cornstarch, and sugar.

● Beat the egg whites to a stiff peak, fold in the soaked dates and the dry ingredients. Spread over the pastry. Bake for about 40 minutes or until the center is firm. Leave to cool in the pan, then cut into slices. Store in an airtight container.

Munch

Preparation time: 15 minutes ●
Cooking time: 20 to 30 minutes ● Makes: 12 pieces

A simple, traditional recipe, evocative of childhood. Munch used to be prepared during the morning, ready to slip in the hot oven when lunch came out.

INGREDIENTS

2 sticks margarine

1 cup packed soft brown sugar

2½ cups rolled oats

Preheat oven to 350°F. Grease and base-line an 8 x 8-inch pan.

● Beat the butter until soft and gradually beat in the sugar until light and fluffy. Stir in the oats. Press into the pan and bake for 25 to 30 minutes or until golden. Cut into pieces. Store in an airtight container.

Stollen Bars

Preparation time: 1 hour + rising time ● *Cooking time: 25 to 30 minutes* ● *Makes: 30 bars*

**Here, stollen, the traditional flat, oval German Christmas cake, is converted into bars.
Try them warmed for a special Christmas breakfast.**

INGREDIENTS

2 cups white bread flour

2 tsp easy-blend dried yeast

1 Tbsp lukewarm water

2 Tbsp sugar

¼ stick lightly salted butter

1 egg

5 Tbsp lukewarm milk

Grated rind of half a lemon

1 Tbsp chopped almonds

⅓ cup chopped candied citrus peel

¼ cup candied cherries

¼ cup golden raisins

6 oz cup marzipan

1 Tbsp melted butter

2 Tbsp confectioners' sugar

Grease the base of a 7 x 11-inch shallow pan and then line it.

● Take 1 tsp of flour from the measured amount and place in a small bowl with the yeast, warm water, and a pinch of the measured sugar. Blend and leave about 10 minutes in a warm place until the mixture froths.

● Meanwhile, blend the butter into the remaining flour and stir in the sugar.

● Beat the egg. Slightly warm the milk.

● Make a well in the center of the flour and work in the yeast mixture, egg, and milk to make a pliable dough which is slightly stiffer than bread dough. Add a little more milk or flour as necessary. Turn out and knead for about 10 minutes until silky. Place in a lightly greased bowl, cover the bowl with a dish towel or plastic wrap and leave in a warm, draught-free place until doubled in size.

● Punch back the dough, then knead lightly. Knead in the lemon rind, candied citrus peel, chopped candied cherries, and golden raisins.

● Divide the dough in half and roll a piece to fit the base of the pan. Slice the marzipan thinly in an even layer over the top. Roll the second piece of dough to fit over.

● Cover with lightly greased plastic wrap and leave in a warm draught-free place for about 20 minutes until risen and slightly puffy.

● Preheat oven to 450°F and bake for about 20 minutes until golden-brown and firm in the center. Immediately brush with melted butter. When cold dredge heavily with confectioners' sugar and cut into 30 pieces. Store in an airtight container.

Toffee Bars

Preparation time: 45 minutes ●
Cooking time: 20 minutes ● *Makes: 16*

These bars hide under a multitude of recipe names but the three layers of shortbread, caramel, and chocolate are universally popular with people of all ages.

INGREDIENTS

SHORTBREAD BASE

1¼ cups all-purpose flour

¼ cup superfine sugar

1 stick lightly salted butter

FILLING

1 stick lightly salted butter

1 cup superfine sugar

1 cup evaporated milk

Few drops vanilla essence

TOPPING

3 oz semi-sweet chocolate

2 Tbsp unsalted butter

Preheat oven to 350°F. Grease and base-line a 7 x 11-inch shallow pan.

● Make the base by beating the butter and sugar together until light, then working in the flour. Press the dough into the pan and bake for 20 minutes or until firm in the center and lightly golden. Cool in the pan.

● Put the butter, sugar, and evaporated milk into a heavy-bottomed saucepan and stir over a gentle heat until the sugar has dissolved. Bring to a boil and, stirring constantly, cook for about 15 minutes until thick and caramel in color. Remove from the heat and beat in the vanilla and pour over the shortbread. Allow to cool.

● Gently melt the butter and chocolate together. Pour over the caramel and cut into pieces when set. Store in an airtight container.

Double Ginger Bars

Preparation time: 20 minutes ●
Cooking time: 20 to 25 minutes ● *Makes: 8 to 16 slices*

These bars have a strong gingery taste with succulent pieces of candied ginger hidden in the sweet, chewy cookie base.

INGREDIENTS

½ stick butter

1½ Tbsp molasses

¼ cup packed dark brown sugar

1 tsp ground ginger

2 cups rolled oats

⅓ cup chopped crystallized ginger

½ cup chopped pecans

¼ tsp salt

Preheat oven to 350°F. Line an 8 x 8-inch baking pan. Lightly oil parchment or foil.

● In a medium saucepan, cook the butter, syrup, sugar, and ground ginger over a medium heat until well blended. Remove from the heat and stir in the oats, crystallized ginger, pecans, and salt. Pour into prepared pan and level.

● Bake until crisp and golden-brown, 20 to 25 minutes. Remove the pan to a wire rack to cool slightly, 5 to 10 minutes. Invert onto a board and peel off paper. While still warm, cut into 8 or 16 slices. Return to wire rack to cool completely. Store in an airtight container.

Chocolate Orange Dream Bars

Preparation time: 30 minutes ● Cooking time: 35 to 40 minutes ● Makes: 18

These bars are made with the magical combination of chocolate and orange. They are really rich—a little goes a long way.

INGREDIENTS

BASE

1 cup all-purpose flour

¼ cup unsweetened cocoa powder

¼ tsp salt

1¼ sticks unsalted butter, softened

⅓ cup superfine sugar

½ cup confectioners' sugar

ORANGE TOPPING

Grated rind of 1 orange

½ cup fresh orange juice

¼ cup water

4 tsp cornstarch

1 tsp lemon juice

1 Tbsp butter

3 Tbsp orange marmalade

CHOCOLATE GLAZE

3 Tbsp heavy cream

½ tsp corn syrup

3 oz bittersweet or semi-sweet chocolate, chopped

Preheat oven to 325°F. Grease and line an 8 x 8-inch baking pan.

● Sift together the flour, cocoa, and salt. In a separate bowl beat the butter until creamy, add the sugars and continue beating until light and fluffy. Beat in the flour mixture in 2 or 3 batches until a dough forms. If necessary, turn the dough out onto a lightly floured surface and knead until blended.

● Pat down the dough into the base of the baking pan in an even layer. Prick the dough bottom all over with a fork. Bake crust until set and golden, 30 to 35 minutes. Remove to a wire rack while preparing topping.

● In a medium saucepan, whisk together the orange rind, juice, water, cornstarch, and lemon juice. Over a medium heat, bring to a boil whisking constantly until mixture thickens, about 1 minute. Remove from the heat and whisk in butter and marmalade until melted and smooth. Pour over warm crust and return to the oven. Bake for 5 minutes more. Remove to a wire cooling rack to cool completely, then refrigerate until the topping is set, about 1 hour.

● In a small saucepan, bring the cream and corn syrup to a boil. Remove from the heat and all at once, stir in the chocolate until melted and smooth. Cool chocolate slightly until thickened, stirring occasionally.

● Using the paper to help, remove the cookies from the pan. Peel off the paper and cut into bars. Spoon the cooled, thickened chocolate into a decorating bag and drizzle the chocolate over the bars. Refrigerate until set, about 30 minutes. Store in the refrigerator in an airtight container.

Savory Cookies

Some of these cookies are served fresh from the oven, others are eaten cold. Either way this fabulous selection of savory cookies will liven up any occasion. Unless otherwise stated, most of the cookies can be prepared ahead of the party and frozen for up to three months.

Cheese Cookies

Cheese cookies make a wonderful addition to any lunch-box, picnic, buffet, or even formal meal. Once you start producing home baked cheese cookies, you will never want to buy them again.

Parmesan, Almond, and Paprika Crisps	420
Quattro Formaggi	420
Feta, Olive, and Sun-dried Tomato Bites	422
Blue Cheese Shortbread	423
Cheese and Relish Puffs	423
Smoked Cheese Twists	425
Hot Cheese Melts	425
Cream Cheese and Chive Cornbread Cakes	426
Red Cheese and Fruity Relish Palmiers	427
Oat Clusters with Cheese Crumble Top	428
Hot Pizza Snacks	428
Halloumi Cookies	430

Meat and Fish

A selection of tangy cookies that would be perfect for brunch or cocktail parties. Most would be good served with soft cheeses or pâtés.

Smoked Ham Rings	430
Ham Pineapple Corn Cakes	432
Thai Shrimp Crackers	432
Smoked Salmon and Sour Cream Snacks	433
Crispy Bacon and Blue Cheese Melts	434
Pepperoni and Peppercorn Shortbreads	435
Anchovy, Olive, and Basil Spirals	437
Curried Shrimp Diamond Oatcakes	437
Smoked Salmon and Lemon Kisses	438
Honeyed Ham and Onion Cookies	439

Nuts and Seeds

Peanut, Sesame, Carrot, and Raisin Pinwheels	440
Mixed Nut Clusters with Cajun Spices	442
Pine Tree Shillings	442
Poppy Seed Spirals	443
Roasted Pecan Snacks	444
Mixed Seed Crunchies	445
Whole-Wheat Pumpkin Shortbread	445
Apricot and Pecan Rye Cookies	446
Buttery Hazelnut Hoops	447
Middle Eastern Almond Rolls	448
Hot Cashew Crumbles	449
Brazil Nut Bakes	450

Vegetable Cookies

A bright and tasty selection of vegetable-based cookies that are great to serve with drinks as an informal appetizer and wonderful to take to ball games and other outdoor events. They are so delicious that the kids won't object to eating vegetables.

Roast Pepper Cookies	450
Herb Crackers	452
Fried Onion and Thyme Crackers	453
Hot Herbed Mushroom Bites	454
Zucchini Triangles	454
Soft Bake Artichoke and Olive Fingers	457
Carrot, Cumin, and Orange Phyllo Crisps	457
Soft Bake Buckwheat Beet Snacks	458
Mexican Potato and Chili Bean Corn Cakes	459

Quattro Formaggi

Preparation time: 20 minutes ● Cooking time:
25 minutes ● Makes: 15

Just like the familiar pizza topping, these cookies are flavored with 4 different cheeses.

INGREDIENTS

1 Tbsp fresh grated Parmesan cheese
1 Tbsp crumbled blue cheese such as Roquefort, Danish, or Stilton
1 Tbsp grated Swiss or Edam cheese
1 Tbsp grated sharp Cheddar cheese
1 cup all-purpose flour
Pinch of salt
1 stick lightly salted butter or margarine, softened
1 tsp dried oregano

Preheat oven to 350°F. Grease or line two baking sheets with nonstick baking parchment.

● Mix all the cheeses together and sift in the flour and salt. Make a well in the center, and add the butter or margarine and oregano. Using a round bladed knife, or fingertips blend the mixture together, and shape it into a soft dough.

● Divide into 15 walnut-sized balls and place on baking sheets, spaced about 2 inches apart. Flatten slightly with a fork, and bake for 20 to 25 minutes until lightly golden and firm to the touch. Cool on the sheets. Best served slightly warmed. Store in an airtight container for 3 to 4 days, or freeze for up to 3 months.

Parmesan, Paprika Crisps

Preparation time: 15 minutes ● Cooking time:
10 minutes ● Makes: 18

These thin nutty, cheese morsels are delicious served as a snack on their own or to accompany a fine wine.

INGREDIENTS

7 Tbsp lightly salted butter or margarine
⅔ cup slivered almonds
½ cup ground almonds
1 cup fresh grated Parmesan cheese
¼ tsp cayenne pepper
1 tsp paprika

Preheat oven to 350°F. Line three baking sheets with waxed paper or baking parchment.

● Melt the butter or margarine in a small saucepan. Remove from the heat and stir in the slivered and ground almonds. Stir in the Parmesan cheese, cayenne, and paprika.

● Drop the mixture, well spaced apart, in 18 small, well-rounded heaps on to the baking sheets. Bake in the oven for 10 minutes until golden-brown. Remove from the oven and push around the edges of the cookies with the blade of a knife to neaten the shape. Leave on the sheets to cool completely. Carefully lift off using a thin, metal spatula. Store between sheets of waxed paper in an airtight container for 3 to 4 days, or freeze in the same way for up to 3 months.

Smoked Cheese Twists

Preparation time: 25 minutes + chilling ●
Cooking time: 20 minutes ● *Makes: 30*

**Long, thin twisting pastries are just the thing for parties.
Serve on their own or use as delicious dippers.**

INGREDIENTS

5 Tbsp lightly salted butter or margarine, softened

3 Tbsp full-fat soft cheese

1 egg yolk

1½ cups all-purpose flour

Pinch of salt

2 garlic cloves, crushed

1 cup fine grated smoked cheese

2 Tbsp cold water

In a bowl, beat the butter or margarine with the soft cheese and egg yolk. Sift in the flour and salt. Add the garlic, ½ cup of the cheese, and 2 tablespoons cold water. Stir the mixture to bring the mixture together. Turn on to a lightly floured surface and knead lightly to form a smooth dough. Wrap and chill for 30 minutes.

● Preheat oven to 350°F. Line two baking sheets with nonstick baking parchment.

● Roll out the dough to ¼-inch thick, and cut into ½-inch wide strips, about 6 inches long. Twist the strips and place on baking sheets, pressing down the edges well to prevent them untwisting. Sprinkle lightly with the remaining cheese. Bake for about 20 minutes until lightly golden. Transfer to wire racks and cool for about 15 minutes before serving. Cool completely and place in an airtight container for 1 week.

Hot Cheese Melts

Preparation time: 20 minutes + chilling ●
Cooking time: 15 minutes ● *Makes: 16*

**For easy eating, spear each hot cookie on a toothpick or
small skewer before arranging them on a serving platter.**

INGREDIENTS

1 cup fine grated sharp Cheddar cheese

½ cup all-purpose flour

1 tsp dry mustard powder

Pinch of salt

½ stick lightly salted butter or margarine, softened

1 Tbsp wholegrain mustard

1 tsp black mustard seeds

Place all the ingredients together in a large bowl and work the mixture until a firm dough is formed.

● Divide the mixture into 16 equal portions, and shape it into balls. Arrange the balls on a large ungreased baking sheet. Cover and chill for 1 hour until they become firm.

● Preheat oven to 375°F. Just prior to serving, uncover and bake in the oven for about 10 to 15 minutes until golden. Cool for 10 minutes and then serve hot.

Cream Cheese and Chive Cornbread Cakes

Preparation time: 20 minutes ● *Cooking time: 20 minutes* ● *Makes: 20*

A cross between biscuit and a cookie, these cakes can be served with soups and stews, or as part of lunch box.

INGREDIENTS

⅔ cup cornmeal

¼ cup all-purpose flour

2 tsp baking powder

3 Tbsp lightly salted butter or margarine

1 egg, beaten

3 Tbsp fresh chopped chives

6-7 Tbsp milk

1 cup full fat soft cheese

Preheat oven to 375°F. Grease or line two baking sheets with nonstick baking parchment.

● Sift the cornmeal, flour, baking powder, and salt into a mixing bowl and blend in the butter or margarine until well mixed. Make a well in the center and gradually mix in the egg, 2 tablespoons chives, and milk, to form a thick batter.

● Using a teaspoon, spoon 20 small mounds of the mixture, about 2 inches apart, on baking sheets, and bake for 15 to 20 minutes until lightly golden and firm to the touch. Transfer to wire racks to cool completely.

● Beat the soft cheese to soften and spread gently on the tops of the cookies. Then top with the remaining chives to serve. Best eaten on same day as topped. Store, before topping with soft cheese and chives, in airtight container for up to 1 week.

Red Cheese and Fruity Relish Palmiers

Preparation time: 20 minutes ● Cooking time: 12 minutes ● Makes: 16

Small, heart-shaped puffs of pastry filled with tasty red cheese and tangy relish make attractive canapés.

INGREDIENTS

6 oz puff pastry, thawed if frozen

3 Tbsp savory fruit relish, chopped fine

¾ cup fine grated Colby or similar red cheese

Fresh ground black pepper

Preheat oven to 425°F. Grease or line a large baking sheet with nonstick baking parchment

● Roll the pastry into a 16 x 8-inch rectangle. Spread thinly with 2 tablespoons of the relish and then sprinkle with two thirds of the cheese. Season with pepper.

● Fold the pastry two ends up and over the filling, equally from each side, to meet in the middle. Spread the pastry top with remaining relish and sprinkle with the cheese. Season with pepper. Fold the pastry ends as before, turn over and press together firmly.

● Using a sharp knife, cut the folded pastry into 16 slices and transfer to the baking sheet, leaving a small space between each. Bake for 10 to 12 minutes until lightly golden. Cool for 10 minutes then transfer to a wire rack to cool. Best served warm.

TIP

These can be made 24 hours in advance, store in an airtight container and re-crisp them in a hot oven for a few minutes just before serving.

Hot Pizza Snacks

Preparation time: 25 minutes ● Cooking time: 20 minutes ● Makes: 12

Best served warm, these tomato snacks contain the familiar ingredients you would find on a pizza, and have a soft cheese Mozzarella cheese center.

INGREDIENTS

1 Tbsp all-purpose flour

Pinch of salt

1 tsp dried oregano

1 stick lightly salted butter or margarine, softened

2 Tbsp fresh grated Parmesan cheese

2 Tbsp tomato paste

1 oz piece block Mozzarella cheese, cut into 12 small cubes

6 pitted black olives, halved

Preheat oven to 375°F. Grease or line a baking sheet with nonstick baking parchment.

● Sift the flour and salt into a bowl and stir in the oregano, butter or margarine, Parmesan, and tomato paste using a round bladed knife, and bring together with the hands to form a firm dough. Divide the mixture into 12 portions, and form into balls. Press a piece of cheese into the center of each and reform the dough over it to enclose the cheese.

● Place on the baking sheet and lightly press an olive half on top of each. Sprinkle with a little Parmesan cheese and bake for 20 minutes until lightly golden and firm. Cool for 10 minutes before serving.

Oat Clusters with Cheese Crumble Top

Preparation time: 20 minutes ● Cooking time: 20 minutes ● Makes: 18

Easy to make and delicious, these crackers have a crisp and chewy texture, with a lightly spiced, topping.

INGREDIENTS

1½ sticks lightly salted butter or margarine

Scant 2 cups rolled oats

½ cup whole-wheat flour

1 tsp salt

TOPPING

1 Tbsp fresh grated Parmesan cheese

6 Tbsp whole-wheat flour

¼ stick lightly salted butter or margarine

1 tsp cumin seeds, crushed

1 tsp dried thyme

Preheat oven to 375°F. Grease or line two baking sheets with nonstick baking parchment.

● Melt the butter or margarine for the cookies in a saucepan. Remove from the heat and stir in the oats, flour, and salt. Set aside.

● Now make the crumble. Mix the cheese and flour together and blend in the butter or margarine until well mixed, and it resembles large fresh bread crumbs.

● Drop the oat mixture on to baking sheets to form 18 walnut-sized mounds. Space them about 1 inch apart. Press them down lightly with a fork and then sprinkle each with a little of the crumble topping, a few cumin seeds, and some thyme. Bake in the oven for 20 minutes until rich golden-brown. Leave to cool on the baking sheets. Store in airtight containers between sheets of waxed paper for up to 1 week.

Halloumi Cookies

Preparation time: 15 minutes ● Cooking time: 25 minutes ● Makes: 14

Halloumi cheese is mild tasting, slightly salty, and perfect for baking as it holds its shape well.

INGREDIENTS

1 cup all-purpose flour

3 oz Halloumi cheese, cut into small pieces

¼ cup pitted black olives, drained and chopped

2 Tbsp fresh chopped cilantro

5 Tbsp good quality olive oil

Preheat oven to 350°F. Grease or line a large baking sheet with nonstick baking parchment.

● Sift the flour into a bowl and mix in the cheese, olives, and cilantro. Bind together with the olive oil to form a dough. Turn on to a lightly floured surface and knead gently until smooth.

● Using a teaspoon, pile 14 small mounds on to the baking sheet, and press down lightly using a fork. Bake in the oven for 20 to 25 minutes until lightly golden and firm. Cool for 10 minutes, then transfer to a wire rack. Best served slightly warmed.

Smoked Ham Rings

Preparation time: 20 minutes ● Cooking time: 20 minutes ● Makes: 24

These cookies are good to serve with dips, or try sandwiching them together with cream cheese.

INGREDIENTS

1½ sticks butter or margarine, softened

2 oz lean smoked ham, very fine chopped

¼ cup fine grated smoked cheese

1 cup all-purpose flour

½ cup cornstarch

Pinch of salt

½ tsp dry mustard powder

Preheat oven to 350°F. Line two baking sheets with waxed paper or nonstick baking parchment.

● In a bowl, beat the butter or margarine, ham, and cheese together until well mixed.

● Sift the remaining ingredients into the bowl, mix well.

● Place the dough in a decorating bag fitted with a ½-inch all-purpose tube. Pipe 24 x 2½-inch rings, spaced well apart, on the baking sheets. Bake in the oven for 20 minutes until lightly golden. Cool for 5 minutes then transfer to a wire rack to cool completely. Store in an airtight container for up to 4 days or freeze for up to 3 months.

Ham Pineapple Corn Cakes

Preparation time: 15 minutes ● Cooking time: 20 minutes ● Makes: 15

Serve these soft cookies to accompany soups, stews, and casseroles.

INGREDIENTS

⅔ cup cornmeal
½ cup all-purpose flour
2 tsp baking powder
3 Tbsp lightly salted butter or margarine
2 oz lean ham, chopped fine
⅓ cup fine chopped fresh or canned pineapple
2 Tbsp fresh chopped parsley
1 egg, beaten
6 Tbsp milk

Preheat oven to 375°F. Line two baking sheets with waxed paper or nonstick baking parchment.

● Sift the cornmeal, flour, baking powder, and salt into a bowl. Blend in the butter or margarine. Stir in the ham and pineapple. Make a well in the center and add the egg, then gradually pour in the milk, stirring to form a thick batter.

● Using a teaspoon, drop 15 mounds, spaced about 2 inches apart on the baking sheets. Bake for 15 to 20 minutes until lightly golden and firm. Cool for 10 minutes, then transfer to a wire rack. Store in an airtight container for up to 5 days or freeze for up to 3 months.

Thai Shrimp Crackers

Preparation time: 30 minutes + chilling ● Cooking time: 25 minutes ● Makes: 16

These light and flaky wafer cookies are flavored with Oriental ingredients. Serve with satay sauce.

INGREDIENTS

2 cups self-rising flour
1 tsp salt
½ tsp ground white pepper
½ tsp hot chili powder
¼ stick lightly salted butter or margarine
2 Tbsp crunchy peanut butter
7-8 Tbsp cold water
4 scallions, trimmed and chopped fine
2 oz (⅓ cup) peeled shrimp, thawed if frozen, ground or fine chopped

Sift the flour, salt, pepper, and chili powder into a bowl. Blend in the butter or margarine until well mixed, and stir in the peanut butter. Mix in sufficient cold water to form a firm dough. Turn on to a lightly floured surface and knead until smooth.

● Roll out into a 15 x 6-inch rectangle. Score lightly into three. Mix the scallions and shrimp and place one third in the middle section. Fold up the bottom third, bring the top third down over it, seal the edges and give the pastry a half-turn. Repeat twice more, sprinkling the scallion and shrimp mixture each time. Re-roll and fold the dough again. Wrap and chill for 30 minutes.

● Preheat oven to 350°F. Grease and flour a baking sheet. Roll the dough out on a floured surface to form a 12-inch square. Trim the edges and divide into 16 squares. Transfer to the baking sheet, prick all over and bake for 20 to 25 minutes until golden. Cool on wire racks.

Smoked Salmon and Sour Cream Snacks

Preparation time: 25 minutes + chilling ● Cooking time: 15 minutes ● Makes: 15

Try these luxurious cookies at a brunch-time buffet.

INGREDIENTS

5 Tbsp lightly salted butter or margarine, softened

3 Tbsp full-fat soft cheese

1 egg yolk

1½ cups all-purpose flour

Pinch salt

4 Tbsp fresh chopped dill

2 Tbsp cold water

FILLING

1 cup full-fat soft cheese

4 oz smoked salmon pieces, shredded fine

In a bowl, beat the butter or margarine with the soft cheese and egg yolk. Sift in the flour and salt and add the dill, then stir until evenly mixed. Stir in sufficient cold water to form a dough.

● Turn on to a floured surface and knead until smooth; place in plastic wrap and chill for 30 minutes.

● Preheat oven to 350°F. Line two baking sheets with waxed or baking parchment paper.

● Roll out the pastry thinly and stamp out 30 circles using a 2½-inch cutter, re-rolling as necessary. Place on the prepared baking sheets, score lightly with a knife in diagonal lines, and then bake in the oven for about 15 minutes until lightly golden. Leave to cool on the sheets.

● To serve, beat the soft cheese until smooth and spread over half the cookies. Sprinkle with a few strips of smoked salmon and then top with the remaining cookies. Serve immediately.

● Store, unfilled, in an airtight container for up to 1 week, or freeze unfilled for up to 3 months.

Crispy Bacon and Blue Cheese Melts

Preparation time: 25 minutes • Cooking time: 30 minutes • Makes: 15

Basic cookie dough is transformed into a melting mixture by adding cheese. Serve these tasty snacks as an accompaniment to other cheeses and fruits, soups, and salads.

INGREDIENTS

6 slices rindless bacon

½ cup crumbled blue cheese

1 cup all-purpose flour

1 stick lightly salted butter or margarine, softened

Pinch of cayenne pepper

Preheat oven to 350°F. Grease or line two baking sheets with nonstick baking parchment.

● Preheat the broiler to a hot setting and cook the bacon for 2 to 3 minutes on each side until golden and crispy. Drain on paper towels and allow to cool. Then mince or chop fine.

● Mix all the ingredients and the chopped bacon together using a round bladed knife, and bring together with the hands to form a dough.

● Divide the dough into 15 portions and shape each one into a small disk. Prick the surfaces with a fork and bake in the oven for 20 to 25 minutes until lightly golden and firm to the touch. Leave to cool for 15 minutes and then serve warm. Store in an airtight container for up to 4 days.

Pepperoni and Peppercorn Shortbreads

Preparation time: 15 minutes + chilling ● Cooking time: 25 minutes ● Makes: 14

You can make and freeze these tasty pre-dinner nibbles ahead of time, and you may want to double the recipe as they will be very popular.

INGREDIENTS

1 cup all-purpose flour

Pinch of salt

¾ stick unsalted butter

2 oz sliced pepperoni sausage, chopped fine

1 Tbsp pickled green peppercorns, drained

1 egg, beaten

Fresh ground black pepper

Sift the flour and salt into a bowl, then blend in the butter until you have fine crumbs. Stir in the pepperoni and peppercorns, and add enough egg to bring together to form a dough; reserve the rest for glazing.

● Turn onto a lightly floured surface and knead until smooth. Wrap and chill for 20 minutes.

● Preheat oven to 325°F. Line two baking sheets with waxed paper or nonstick baking parchment.

● Roll out to ½-inch thick. Using a 1½ inch round cutter, stamp out 14 rounds, re-rolling as necessary. Transfer to the baking sheet, brush with reserved egg and then dust with ground black pepper. Bake in the oven for 20 to 25 minutes until firm to the touch and golden. Cool for 5 minutes and then transfer to a wire rack to cool completely. To make ahead, pack into an airtight container and freeze for up to 3 months.

Anchovy, Olive, and Basil Spirals

Preparation time: 20 minutes ● Cooking time: 12 minutes ● Makes: 24

A sophisticated puff pastry snack with a delicious fishy flavor. They are best eaten on the day they are made, and served slightly warmed.

INGREDIENTS

6 oz puff pastry, thawed if frozen

1 egg, beaten

2 oz anchovy fillets, drained

¼ cup chopped fine pitted black olives

¼ cup pimiento stuffed green olives, chopped fine

½ oz fresh basil leaves

Preheat oven to 425°F. Line two baking sheets with waxed or nonstick baking parchment.

● Roll out the pastry on a lightly floured surface to a 12 x 8-inch rectangle. Brush the pastry with beaten egg and lay the anchovy fillets, lengthwise, over the pastry. Sprinkle with the olives and lay the basil leaves on top. Starting from the long side, roll up the pastry tightly, like a jelly roll. Press lightly to seal the end, and then slice into 24 pieces.

● Lay the pastry pieces, spaced a little apart, on the baking sheets, and brush with more egg. Bake for 10 to 12 minutes until golden and crisp. Cool for 10 minutes before serving. These are best eaten on the day they are made, and served slightly warmed.

Curried Shrimp Diamond Oatcakes

Preparation time: 20 minutes ● Cooking time: 15 minutes ● Makes: 18

These crisp oatcakes are flavored with Chinese curry spices and chopped shrimp. Try serving with fish pâté.

INGREDIENTS

¾ cup all-purpose flour

1½ cups medium oatmeal

½ tsp baking powder

½ tsp salt

1½ tsp Chinese curry powder

5 Tbsp shortening

2 oz (⅓ cup) peeled shrimp, thawed if frozen, very fine chopped

1 to 2 tsp cold water

1 egg, beaten

2 Tbsp sesame seeds

Preheat oven to 400°F. Grease or line a baking sheet with nonstick baking parchment.

● Sieve the flour, oatmeal, baking powder, salt, and curry powder into a bowl. Blend in the shortening with the fingertips until the mixture is crumbly, then stir in the shrimp and mix with sufficient water to form a firm dough.

● Roll out the dough to ¼-inch thick on a lightly floured surface. Slice the dough into 1½-inch strips, and then cut each strip on the diagonal into diamond shapes; you should make about 18.

● Transfer to the baking sheet. Brush with egg and sprinkle with sesame seeds. Bake for about 15 minutes until firm and lightly golden. Allow to cool.

Smoked Salmon and Lemon Kisses

Preparation time: 20 minutes • Cooking time: 25 minutes • Makes: 12

These delicate flavored melt-in-the-mouth soft bake cookies are good served with cream cheese. This would work well with ham in place of the salmon if preferred.

INGREDIENTS

1 cup all-purpose flour

Pinch of salt

2 Tbsp fresh chopped parsley

4 oz smoked salmon pieces, shredded fine

½ tsp finely grated lemon rind

1 stick lightly salted butter or margarine, softened

Preheat oven to 350°F. Grease or line two baking sheets with nonstick baking parchment.

● Sift the flour and salt into a bowl. Stir in the parsley, smoked salmon, lemon rind, and butter or margarine using a round bladed knife. Bring together with the hands to form a dough.

● Divide the dough into 12 pieces and form them into walnut-sized balls. Place on baking sheets, spaced about 2 inches apart. Flatten slightly and bake for 20 to 25 minutes until lightly golden and firm to the touch. Leave to cool on the sheets for 15 minutes. These cookies are best served slightly warm, and on the same day as baking. These cookies can be frozen, once baked and cooled, for up to 3 months.

Honeyed Ham and Onion Cookies

Preparation time: 25 minutes + chilling ● *Cooking time: 30 minutes* ● *Makes: 16*

With a little advance preparation, these cookies make truly delicious snacks. They'll be popular as a snack, or as an interesting accompaniments to salads or soups.

INGREDIENTS

¾ stick lightly salted butter or margarine

1 medium onion, sliced fine

2 tsp honey

1 cup all-purpose flour

Pinch of salt

1 Tbsp fresh chopped sage or 1 tsp dried sage

3 oz lean honey roast ham, fine chopped

2-3 tsp cold water

1 small egg, beaten

A bunch small sage leaves, optional

Melt ¼ stick of butter in a small skillet and gently fry the onion for 5 minutes, stirring, until just softened. Add the honey, raise the heat, and cook for a further 2 to 3 minutes until lightly golden. Set the mixture aside to cool.

● Sift the flour, salt, and sage together into a bowl. Blend in the remaining butter and stir in the ham and prepared onion. Bind together with sufficient cold water to form a soft dough. Turn on to a lightly floured surface and knead until smooth. Wrap and chill the dough for 30 minutes.

● Preheat oven to 350°F. Line a large baking sheet with waxed paper or nonstick baking parchment.

● Divide the dough into 16 and form into small round disks. Place on the baking sheet, brush with beaten egg and press a sage leaf on to each, if using. Bake for 20 to 25 minutes until lightly golden and firm. Cool for 10 minutes and then serve warm.

Peanut, Sesame, Carrot, and Raisin Pinwheels

Preparation time: 25 minutes + chilling ● Cooking time: 20 minutes ● Makes: 24

A healthful combination of ingredients make these cookies an excellent addition to the lunch box—the peanut flavor will make them popular with children.

INGREDIENTS

5 Tbsp lightly salted butter or margarine, softened
3 Tbsp full-fat soft cheese
1 egg yolk
1⅔ cups whole-wheat flour
Pinch of salt
2 Tbsp cold water
4 Tbsp crunchy peanut butter
½ cup fine grated carrot
3 Tbsp fine chopped raisins
1 Tbsp toasted sesame seeds

In a bowl, beat together the butter, soft cheese, and egg yolk. Sift the flour and salt into the bowl, adding any husks which remain in the strainer, then stir in the water until evenly mixed. Stir in to form a dough. Turn on to a lightly floured surface and knead lightly until smooth. Wrap and chill for 30 minutes.

● Preheat oven to 350°F. Line two baking sheets with waxed paper or nonstick baking parchment.

● Roll out the dough to a 12 x 9-inch rectangle. Soften the peanut butter by heating it gently and then thinly spread over the dough. Sprinkle with the carrot, raisins, and sesame seeds.

● Starting at the longest side, roll up the dough tightly, like a jelly roll, and press gently to seal the edge. Slice the roll into 24 pieces and place the pinwheels on lined baking sheets with waxed paper. Bake in the oven for about 20 minutes until firm and lightly golden. Cool for 10 minutes then transfer to a wire rack to cool completely. Store in an airtight container for up to 3 days. Will not freeze.

Mixed Nut Clusters with Cajun Spices

Preparation time: 20 minutes ●
Cooking time: 25 minutes ● *Makes: 15*

These cookies are for the real nut lover. You can use any combination of nuts for this recipe, but choose a good spread of flavors, and use unsalted varieties.

INGREDIENTS

3 Tbsp walnut pieces

3 Tbsp slivered whole almonds

3 Tbsp macadamia nuts, lightly crushed

3 Tbsp shelled unsalted pistachios, lightly crushed

1 cup all-purpose flour

Pinch of celery salt

Pinch of onion salt

1 tsp paprika

¼ tsp cayenne pepper

1 tsp dried thyme

1 stick lightly salted butter or margarine, softened

Preheat oven to 350°F. Grease or line two baking sheets with nonstick baking parchment.

● Mix all the nuts together and place in a bowl. Sift in the flour, salts, paprika, and cayenne. Add the thyme, butter or margarine, and mix together with a round bladed knife. Bring together with the hands to form a dough.

● Divide into 15 and form into walnut-sized balls. Place on baking sheets, spaced about 2 inches apart. Flatten slightly, and bake in the oven for 20 to 25 minutes until lightly golden and firm to the touch. Leave to cool on the baking sheets. Excellent served slightly warm. Store in an airtight container for up to 1 week, or freeze for up to 3 months.

Pine Tree Shillings

Preparation time: 15 minutes ●
Cooking time: 25 minutes ● *Makes: 14*

Pine nuts have a fragrant, resinous flavor which goes very well with the woodiness of rosemary and olives. A very Mediterranean cocktail nibble.

INGREDIENTS

1 cup all-purpose flour

1 tsp salt

1 Tbsp fresh chopped rosemary or 1 tsp dried

½ cup pine nuts

¼ cup fine, chopped, pitted black olives

5 Tbsp good quality olive oil

Preheat oven to 350°F. Line two baking sheets with waxed paper or nonstick baking parchment.

● Sift the flour and salt into a bowl and stir in the rosemary, pine nuts, and olives. Add the olive oil and stir to mix into a dough.

● Drop 14 teaspoonfuls of the mixture on to baking sheets and bake for 20 to 25 minutes. Cool for 10 minutes and then transfer to a rack to cool completely.

● Store in an airtight container for up to 1 week, or freeze for up to 3 months.

Poppy Seed Spirals

Preparation time: 25 minutes ● *Cooking time: 27 minutes* ● *Makes: 16*

The small black seeds in these crisp pastry rolls have a nutty flavor and crunchy texture. Substitute with sesame seeds or crushed pumpkin seeds if preferred.

INGREDIENTS

1¼ sticks lightly salted butter or margarine

1 medium red onion, sliced fine

1 Tbsp lemon juice

1 tsp coriander seeds, crushed

2 tsp honey

9 large sheets of phyllo pastry (18 x 12 inches)

6 Tbsp poppy seeds

4 Tbsp fresh chopped cilantro

Preheat oven to 400°F. Line a baking sheet with waxed or nonstick baking parchment.

● Melt ¼ stick lightly salted butter or margarine in a small skillet and gently fry the onion with the lemon juice and coriander seeds for 5 minutes until softened. Add the honey and cook, stirring, over a high heat for a further 2 minutes. Set aside to cool.

● In a small saucepan, gently melt the remaining butter or margarine.

● To assemble the spirals, lay a sheet of phyllo pastry on the work surface and brush with melted fat. Lay two more sheets on top, brushing with fat as you go. Sprinkle over 2 tablespoons poppy seeds and 1 tablespoon chopped cilantro.

● Prepare three more sheets of phyllo as before and place on top of the seeds. Sprinkle with 2 tablespoons poppy seeds and another 1 tablespoon cilantro. Spread over the cooked onion mixture. Finally, prepare the remaining three sheets of phyllo as before and lay over the onion layer. Sprinkle with remaining seeds and cilantro. From the shortest side, carefully roll up the pastry like a jelly roll, pressing the roll gently to seal the edge.

● Slice into 16 pieces and arrange on a baking sheet lined with waxed paper. Brush with the remaining melted fat and bake in the oven for 15 to 20 minutes until richly golden. Cool for 10 minutes and then serve. These pastries can be made up to 24 hours in advance of baking, and stored in the fridge.

Roasted Pecan Snacks

Preparation time: 30 minutes + chilling ● *Cooking time: 25 minutes* ● *Makes: 24*

Use ready roasted pecan halves in this recipe for a more intense flavor. Try experimenting with honey roast or barbecue smoke flavored pecans as an alternative.

INGREDIENTS

2 cups self-rising flour

1 tsp salt

½ stick lightly salted butter or margarine

7-8 Tbsp cold water

Scant ⅔ cup roasted pecan nuts, chopped fine

Sift the flour and salt into a bowl and blend in the fat. Add sufficient water to form a pliable dough. Turn on to a lightly floured surface and knead until smooth.

● Roll into a 15 x 6-inch rectangle. Mark lightly into three equal portions, and sprinkle the middle portion with one third of the nuts. Fold up the bottom third, bring the top third down over it, seal the edges and give the pastry a half turn. Repeat this rolling and folding twice more, sprinkling with the nuts each time. Re-roll and fold once more. Wrap and chill for 30 minutes.

● Preheat oven to 350°F. Grease and flour a baking sheet.

● Roll out the pastry thinly and evenly to form a square slightly bigger 12 inches. Trim away the edges to neaten, and then cut into 1 x 6-inch thin fingers; you should make about 24 fingers. Transfer to the baking sheet, prick all over with a fork and baken for 20 to 25 minutes until lightly golden and puffed up. Transfer to a wire rack to cool. Store in an airtight container for up to 1 week.

Mixed Seed Crunchies

Preparation time: 10 minutes + standing ●
Cooking time: 15 minutes ● *Makes: 18*

Use small seeds in this recipe to give a very crisp texture. The oats in this recipe add a healthful taste, making them an ideal wholesome snack.

INGREDIENTS

1⅓ cups rolled oats
⅔ cup medium oatmeal
2 Tbsp poppy seeds
2 Tbsp sesame seeds
1 tsp celery seeds
1 tsp fennel seeds, lightly crushed
½ cup sunflower oil
1 tsp salt
1 egg, beaten

Place the oats, oatmeal, and seeds in a bowl, and mix in the oil. Leave to stand for 1 hour.

● Preheat oven to 325°F. Line a baking sheet with waxed paper or nonstick baking parchment.

● Add the salt and egg to the oat mixture and beat together thoroughly. Place 18 teaspoonfuls of the mixture, spaced a little apart on a baking sheet lined with waxed paper, and press flat with a wetted fork. Bake in the oven for about 15 minutes until golden-brown. Leave to cool on the sheets. Store in an airtight container for up to 1 week.

Whole-wheat Pumpkin Shortbread

Preparation time: 15 minutes + chilling ●
Cooking time: 20 to 25 minutes ● *Makes: 14*

Green pumpkin seeds have a nutty flavor, and they add texture to a rich, crumbly whole-wheat shortbread mixture. Use white all-purpose flour if preferred.

INGREDIENTS

1 cup whole-wheat flour
Pinch of salt
¾ stick unsalted butter
7 Tbsp pumpkin seeds, lightly crushed
1 egg yolk
2 Tbsp milk

Preheat oven to 325°F. Line two baking sheets with waxed paper or nonstick baking parchment.

● Sift the flour and salt into a bowl and blend in the butter until you have fine crumbs. Stir in the pumpkin seeds and egg yolk. Bring together with your hands to form a dough. Turn on to a lightly floured surface and knead lightly until smooth. Wrap and chill for 20 minutes.

● Roll out to ½-inch thick and cut into fourteen ½-inch squares, re-rolling as necessary. Place on baking sheets lined with waxed paper and score the tops lightly with a knife. Brush lightly with the milk and bake for 20 to 25 minutes until firm and golden. Cool on the baking sheet for 5 minutes and then transfer to a wire rack to cool completely. Store in an airtight container for up to 1 week.

Apricot and Pecan Rye Cookies

Preparation time: 20 minutes ● Cooking time: 20 minutes ● Makes: 18

Rye flour has a distinctive nutty flavor and makes an interesting cookie. The addition of dried apricot gives a delicate sweetness; chopped dates or raisins could also be used.

INGREDIENTS

1 cup dark rye flour

Pinch of salt

½ cup pecan halves, lightly crushed

3 Tbsp fine chopped dried apricots

1 stick lightly salted butter or margarine, softened

2 Tbsp fresh chopped parsley

Preheat oven to 350°F. Grease or line two baking sheets with nonstick baking parchment.

● Mix all the ingredients together with a round bladed knife to form into a dough.

● Divide into 18 portions and form into small balls. Place about 1 inch apart on the baking sheets and flatten slightly with a fork. Bake for 20 minutes until lightly golden and firm to the touch. Cool on the baking sheets. Store in an airtight container for 3 to 4 days.

Buttery Hazelnut Hoops

Preparation time: 20 minutes ● Cooking time: 15 minutes ● Makes: 24

Toasted hazelnuts have a rich roasted flavor and are perfect for baking. These piped cookies look good on a platter of canapés, and taste excellent with blue cheese and grapes.

INGREDIENTS

1½ sticks lightly salted butter or margarine, softened

½ cup ground toasted hazelnuts

1 cup all-purpose flour

½ cup cornstarch

Pinch of salt

3 Tbsp lightly crushed hazelnuts

Preheat oven to 350°F. Line two baking sheets with waxed paper or nonstick baking parchment.

● Beat the butter or margarine and ground hazelnuts together. Sift in the flour, cornstarch, and salt, and beat well. Place in a decorating bag fitted with all-purpose ½-inch round tube, and pipe 24 x 2½-inch rings, spaced well apart on baking sheets. Sprinkle the rings with the crushed hazelnuts.

● Bake in the oven for 15 minutes until lightly golden. Cool for 5 minutes and then transfer to wire rack to cool completely. Store between layers of waxed paper in an airtight container for up to 5 days.

Middle Eastern Almond Rolls

Preparation time: 30 minutes + chilling ● *Cooking time: 25 minutes* ● *Makes: 18*

Mild tasting buttery almonds combine well with sweet Middle Eastern spices and sweet red onion in this filling.

INGREDIENTS

5 Tbsp lightly salted butter or margarine, softened

3 Tbsp full-fat soft cheese

1 egg yolk

1 cup all-purpose flour

½ cup ground almonds

Pinch of salt

2 Tbsp cold water

FILLING

½ stick lightly salted butter or margarine

1 small red onion, chopped fine

1 Tbsp lemon juice

½ cup fine chopped blanched almonds

1 tsp ground coriander

1 tsp ground cumin

3 Tbsp golden raisins

2 Tbsp fresh chopped cilantro

1 egg, beaten

In a bowl, beat the butter or margarine, soft cheese, and egg yolk. Sift the flour and add the ground almonds and salt. Stir until evenly mixed. Add sufficient water to form a dough. Turn on to a lightly floured surface and knead lightly until smooth. Wrap and chill for 30 minutes.

● Meanwhile, make the filling. Melt the butter or margarine and gently fry the onion with the lemon juice, chopped almonds, and spices, stirring, for 5 minutes until the onion is softened. Remove from the heat and add the golden raisins and cilantro. Set the filling aside to cool.

● Preheat oven to 350°F. Line a baking sheet with waxed paper or nonstick baking parchment.

● Roll out the dough thinly to an approximate 10½-inch square. Trim away the edges to neaten and divide into 9 smaller squares. Divide the mixture between each square, and form a mound down the center of each. Brush the edges with beaten egg and carefully roll each square up. Press the edge gently to seal. Cut each roll in half.

● Transfer the rolls to a baking sheet lined with waxed paper. Score the tops lightly with a sharp knife, then brush with beaten egg to glaze and bake in the oven for 20 minutes until lightly golden. Leave to cool on the baking sheet. Store in an airtight container for up to 1 week.

Hot Cashew Crumbles

Preparation time: 10 minutes + chilling ● Cooking time: 15 minutes ● Makes: 16

Cashews have a nutty sweetness, and are delicious flavored with Indian spices. Serve these crumbly cookies while still warm. Replace the garbanzo bean flour with white all-purpose flour if preferred.

INGREDIENTS

½ cup ground unsalted cashew nuts

¼ cup lightly chopped, roasted cashew nuts

½ cup garbanzo bean (gram) flour

1 tsp mild curry powder

1 stick lightly salted butter or margarine, softened

2 Tbsp fresh chopped cilantro

16 unsalted cashew halves

Place the ground and chopped cashews together in a bowl and sift in the garbanzo flour and curry powder. Add the butter or margarine and chopped cilantro and mix all the ingredients together to form a dough.

● Use your hands to roll the dough out into 16 balls and arrange on a large ungreased baking sheet. Press a cashew half on to the top of each. Cover and chill for 1 hour until firm.

● Preheat oven to 375°F. To serve, uncover the cookies and bake in the oven for about 15 minutes until golden. Leave to stand for 10 minutes and then carefully lift the cookies off the sheets and serve them while they are still warm.

● The uncooked dough will keep covered in the refrigerator for 24 hours.

Brazil Nut Bakes

Preparation time: 15 minutes ●
Cooking time: 10 minutes ● *Makes: 18*

Here chips of creamy tasting Brazil nuts combine with cheese to make crisp and slightly chewy cookies. Serve as cocktail nibbles.

INGREDIENTS

7 Tbsp lightly salted butter or margarine

Scant ½ cup Brazil nuts, chipped or flaked

½ cup ground Brazil nuts

1 cup fresh grated Parmesan cheese

Salt and pepper

2 Tbsp fresh chopped parsley

Preheat oven to 350°F. Line a baking sheet with waxed paper or nonstick baking parchment.

● Melt the butter or margarine in a saucepan. Remove from the heat and stir in the remaining ingredients.

● Drop spoonfuls of cookie mixture, well spaced apart, in 18 small mounds on the baking sheets. Flatten with a fork and bake in the oven for 10 minutes until golden-brown. Remove from the oven and push in the edges using a knife, to neaten. Cool for 5 minutes on the sheets, and then transfer to a wire rack to cool completely. Store in an airtight container between layers of waxed paper for 3 to 4 days.

Roast Pepper Cookies

Preparation time: 25 minutes ●
Cooking time: 25 minutes ● *Makes: 12*

These colorful cookies use three different colored bell peppers, but you can use just one or two varieties if you prefer.

INGREDIENTS

½ small red bell pepper, seeded

½ small orange bell pepper, seeded

½ small green bell pepper, seeded

1 cup all-purpose flour

Pinch of salt

½ tsp hot chili powder

1 stick lightly salted butter or margarine, softened

2 tsp dried chile flakes, optional

Preheat the broiler to a high setting and place the bell peppers on the rack. Cook the bell peppers for 5 minutes on each side until softened and lightly charred. Cool for 10 minutes. Peel if preferred, and then chop the flesh fine. Allow to cool completely.

● Preheat oven to 350°F. Grease or line two baking sheets with nonstick baking parchment.

● Sift the flour, salt, and chili powder into a bowl. Stir in the peppers and butter or margarine. Using a round bladed knife, mix to form a dough. Divide into 12, and form into walnut-sized balls. Place on lightly greased baking sheets, spaced about 2 inches apart. Flatten slightly and sprinkle each with a few chile flakes, if using. Bake in the oven for 20 minutes until lightly golden and firm. Cool on the sheets. Best served slightly warm. Store in an airtight container for 3 to 4 days.

Herb Crackers

Preparation time: 25 minutes + chilling ●
Cooking time: 25 minutes ● Makes: 16

These crisp cookies can be made in any shape. They are ideal for serving with cheese, or could be crumbled into small pieces and used as croutons for soups and salads.

INGREDIENTS

2 cups self-rising cake flour

1 tsp salt

½ tsp ground white pepper

¼ cup shortening

¾ cup grated hard cheese such as Cheddar, Swiss, or Colby

3 Tbsp fresh chopped parsley

3 Tbsp fresh chopped chives

Sift the flour, salt, and pepper into a bowl and blend in the shortening. Mix to form a pliable dough by adding 7 to 8 tablespoons cold water.

● On a lightly floured surface, roll the dough into a 15 x 6-inch rectangle. Mark lightly into three equal segments. Mix the cheese and herbs together and sprinkle the middle section of pastry with one third of the herbed cheese. Fold up the bottom third, bring the top third down over it, seal the edges and give the pastry a half-turn. Repeat the rolling and folding twice more, to use up the herbed cheese. Re-roll and fold once more, then wrap and chill for 30 minutes.

● Preheat oven to 350°F. Lightly grease and flour a baking sheet.

● Roll out the pastry to a square slightly larger than 12 inches. Trim the edge to neaten and then divide into 16 equal square portions. Transfer to the prepared baking sheet and prick all over with a fork. Bake for 20 to 25 minutes until lightly golden and puffed up. Transfer to a wire rack to cool. Store in an airtight container for up to 1 week.

Fried Onion and Thyme Crackers

Preparation time: 30 minutes + chilling ● *Cooking time: 33 minutes* ● *Makes: 16*

These puffed wheat crackers are interlaced with a rich mixture of buttery fried onion and fresh thyme.

INGREDIENTS

1 stick lightly salted butter or margarine

1 large onion, chopped fine

1 Tbsp fresh chopped thyme or 1 tsp dried

2 cups self-rising flour

1 tsp salt

7-8 Tbsp cold water

Melt half of the fat in a small skillet and gently cook the onion and thyme, stirring occasionally, for 7 to 8 minutes until lightly golden. Set aside to cool.
● Sift the flour and salt into a bowl. Blend in the remaining butter or margarine, and mix in sufficient water to form a firm dough. Turn on to a lightly floured surface and knead until smooth.

● Roll into a 15 x 6-inch rectangle. Mark lightly into three equal portions. Place one third of the cooked onion mixture in the middle section and fold up the bottom third. Bring the top third down over it, seal the edges and give the pastry a half-turn. Repeat this rolling and folding twice, adding the onion mixture each time. Re-roll and fold once more. Wrap and chill for 30 minutes.
● Preheat oven to 350°F. Grease and flour a baking sheet.
● Roll the dough out thinly on a lightly floured surface to form a square slightly bigger than 12 inches. Using a 2½-inch round cutter, stamp out 16 circles; do not re-roll trimmings. Transfer to the baking sheet. Prick all over with a fork and bake for 20 to 25 minutes until lightly golden and puffed up. Transfer to wire racks to cool. Best eaten on day of baking.

Hot Herbed Mushroom Bites

Preparation time: 20 minutes + chilling ●
Cooking time: 21 minutes ● *Makes: 16*

Serve these cookies straight from the oven for their melt-in-the-mouth texture.

INGREDIENTS

1 stick lightly salted butter or margarine, softened

⅔ cup fine chopped button mushrooms

2 garlic cloves, crushed

1 tsp dried mixed herbs

1 cup all-purpose flour

½ tsp salt

2 Tbsp fresh chopped chives

Melt half of the fat in a skillet and stir fry the mushrooms, garlic, and mixed herbs over a high heat for 1 minute until softened. Allow to cool.

● Sift the flour and salt into a bowl. Blend the remaining fat into the flour and stir in the chives and mushroom mixture. Mix together to form a dough. Wrap and chill for 1 hour.

● Preheat oven to 375°F. Line a large baking sheet with waxed paper or nonstick baking parchment.

● Form into 16 balls and place on a large baking sheet lined with waxed paper. Bake in the oven for about 15 to 20 minutes until lightly golden. Cool for 10 minutes and then serve. The uncooked dough will keep covered in the refrigerator for 24 hours and so this recipe can be prepared in advance.

Zucchini Triangles

Preparation time: 15 minutes ●
Cooking time: 32 minutes ● *Makes: 18*

An unusual version of this popular cookie. Here shredded zucchini is added to an oat-based mixture and baked.

INGREDIENTS

1 stick lightly salted butter or margarine

2 cups zucchini, trimmed and shredded

1½ cups rolled oats

2 Tbsp + 1 tsp sesame seeds

½ cup plus 2 Tbsp whole-wheat flour

1 tsp salt

Preheat oven to 375°F. Grease and base-line a 7-inch square baking pan.

● Place the butter or margarine in a saucepan to melt. Add the zucchini and gently cook it in the fat, stirring, for 4 to 5 minutes until softened. Remove from the heat and carefully stir in the rolled oats, 2 tablespoons sesame seeds, flour, and salt. Mix well.

● Transfer the mixture to the pan, and press down evenly. Sprinkle the surface with the remaining sesame seeds. Bake for 35 minutes until the flapjack is golden and firm to the touch. Cut into 9 squares and then cut these in half diagonally to make 18 small triangles. Leave the flapjack to cool in the pan. Best eaten on day of baking.

Soft Bake Artichoke and Olive Fingers

Preparation time: 15 minutes ●
Cooking time: 45 minutes ● *Makes: 12*

These luxuriously moist fingers will impress guests at a party or as pre-dinner drinks are served. If preferred, replace the blue cheese with grated block cheese such as Cheddar.

INGREDIENTS

1 cup all-purpose flour

Pinch of salt

¾ stick unsalted butter

¾ cup crumbled blue cheese

⅓ cup canned artichoke hearts, drained and chopped fine

¼ cup fine chopped pitted black olives

1 egg, beaten

½ tsp paprika

Preheat oven to 325°F. Grease and base-line a 7-inch square baking pan.

● Sift the flour and salt into a bowl, then blend in the butter until you have fine crumbs. Stir in the cheese, artichoke, and olives. Add sufficient egg to bring together to form a dough; reserve the rest of the egg for glazing. Turn on to a lightly floured surface and knead until smooth.

● Press the mixture into the prepared pan. Prick all over with a fork and brush lightly with the remaining egg and dust with paprika. Bake in the oven on the middle shelf for 40 to 45 minutes. Slice in half and then into 12 fingers. Allow to cool in the pan. Store in an airtight container for 3 to 4 days.

Carrot, Cumin, and Orange Phyllo Crisps

Preparation time: 25 minutes ●
Cooking time: 25 minutes ● *Makes: 16*

Crisp, buttery phyllo pastry is best eaten warm.

INGREDIENTS

1¼ sticks butter or margarine

½ cup carrot, shredded

1 Tbsp fresh squeezed orange juice

1 tsp cumin seeds, crushed

½ tsp finely grated orange rind

½ tsp salt

Fresh ground black pepper

9 large sheets phyllo pastry, (18 x 12 inches)

Preheat oven to 400°F. Line two baking sheets with waxed or nonstick baking parchment.

● Melt ¼ stick of butter or margarine in a skillet and gently cook the carrot with the orange juice and cumin seeds for 5 minutes until softened. Season and allow to cool.

● In a saucepan, melt the remaining butter or margarine.

● To assemble the phyllo crisps, brush a sheet of pastry with melted butter. Lay 2 more sheets on top, brushing with fat as you go. Spread over one third of the carrot mixture. Prepare 3 more sheets of phyllo as before and place on top of the carrot. Spread with another third of carrot mixture. Prepare the remaining sheets of pastry, place on top and spread with carrot.

● From the shortest side, carefully roll up the pastry like a jelly roll, pressing gently to seal the edge. Slice into 16 pieces and arrange on the baking sheets. Brush with the remaining fat and bake in the oven for 20 minutes until richly golden. Cool for 10 minutes and serve.

Soft Bake Buckwheat Beet Snacks

Preparation time: 20 minutes ● Cooking time: 20 minutes ● Makes: 15

For this recipe, use cooked beet that has not been soaked in vinegar. Buckwheat is a gluten-free grain with a deliciously nutty flavor.

INGREDIENTS

Scant 1 cup buckwheat flour

Pinch of salt

⅔ cup shredded cooked, peeled beet

½ cup fresh grated Parmesan cheese

1 tsp caraway seeds

1 stick lightly salted butter or margarine, softened

Preheat oven to 350°F. Grease or line two baking sheets with nonstick baking parchment.

● Sift the flour and salt together into a bowl, adding any husks which remain in the strainer. Stir in the beet, cheese, and caraway seeds. Using a round bladed knife, stir in the butter or margarine, to form the mixture into a dough.

● Divide into 15 and form into walnut-sized balls. Place on baking sheets, spaced about 2 inches apart. Flatten slightly with a fork and bake for 15 to 20 minutes until lightly golden and firm to the touch. Cool for 10 minutes and then transfer to a wire rack to cool. Best served slightly warm. Store in an airtight container for up to 4 days.

Mexican Potato and Chili Bean Corn Cakes

Preparation time: 10 minutes • Cooking time: 15 minutes • Makes: 14

Little mounds of golden yellow corn with diced potato and kidney beans make these cookies into a substantial snack and ideal lunch box filler or tea-time treat.

INGREDIENTS

⅔ cup cornmeal

½ cup all-purpose flour

2 tsp baking powder

3 Tbsp lightly salted butter or margarine

¾ cup cubed cooked potato

⅓ cup canned kidney beans, drained

1 garlic clove, crushed

½ tsp chili powder

2 Tbsp fresh chopped cilantro

1 egg, beaten

6 Tbsp milk

Preheat oven to 375°F. Grease or line two baking sheets with nonstick baking parchment.

● Sift the cornmeal, flour, baking powder, and salt into a bowl. Blend the butter or margarine into the dry ingredients until well mixed. Stir in the potato, beans, garlic, and cilantro. Make a well in the center and add the egg. Gradually pour in the milk, stirring until the mixture forms a thick batter.

● Using a teaspoon, drop 14 mounds, spaced about 2 inches apart on baking sheets. Bake in the oven for about 15 minutes until lightly golden and firm to the touch. Cool for 10 minutes, then transfer to a wire rack to cool completely. Store in an airtight container for up to 5 days. Not suitable for freezing.

Index

A

almond cookies
Almond Butter Cookies 338
Almond & Chocolate Clusters 187
Almond & Ginger Florentines 375
Almond & Ginger Hearts 339
Almond Macaroons 84
Almond & Orange Sandwich
Cookies 360
Almond & Peach Chews 344
Almond Shortbread 404
Almond Tiles 144
Amoretti 81
Amoretti Drops 159
Apricot & Almond Cookies 246
Chocolate Macaroons 122
Chocolate & Raspberry Macaroon
Bars 387
Eponges 93
Espresso Biscotti 82
Exotic Fruit & Almond Slices 396
Finnish Fingers 98
Fior de Mandorle 81
Fours Poches 90
Lepeshki 98
Middle Eastern Almond Rolls 448
Panforte di Siena 83
Polish Macaroons 97
Scandinavian Slices 99
Vanilla Crescents 85
Wedding Bells 130
Alphabet Cookies 200
altitude adjustments in baking 17
Amaretti 81
Amaretti Drops 159
Anchovy Olive & Basil Spirals 437
Anzacs 102
Apple & Brandy Cookies, Fresh 330
Apple Cheese Cookies 238
Apple & Cinnamon Cookies 49
Apple Cookies 211
Apple & Raisin Cookies 255
Apple Sticky Toffee Treats 278
Apricot & Almond Cookies 246
Apricot & Cheese Cookies 49
Apricot & Chocolate Cookies 160
Apricot Cookies, Honeyed 313
Apricot & Pecan Rye Cookies 446
Apricot & Pistachio Cookies 357
Apricot Slices 28
Apricot Squares, Easy 393
Apricot Wheels 320
Apricot & White Chocolate Cookies,

Big 204
Artichoke & Olive Fingers, Soft Bake 457

B

Bacon, Crispy, & Blue Cheese Melts 434
Baklava 104
Balloon Cookies 203
Banana Chocolate Squares 319
Banana & Cointreau Temptations 309
Banana Cookies 27
Banana Cookies, Double 35
Banana Cookies, The Ultimate 302
Banana & Date Cookies 245
Banana & Walnut Cookies 351
Banoffee Squares 350
bar cookies, method 12
Cranberry 397
Double Ginger 416
Hazelnut 400
Beet Buckwheat Snacks, Soft Bake 458
Birthday Cake Cookies 109
Bitter Chocolate Discs 151
Blue Cheese Shortbread 423
Blueberry Cookies, Truly 322
Blueberry Streusel Bakes 56
Boston Brownies 426
Brandy & Fresh Apple Cookies 330
Brazil Coffee Cookies 354
Brazil Nut Bakes 450
Brazil Nut Blondies 386
Brazil Nut & Drizzled Chocolate Cookies
356
Brazil Nuts, Fruit Salad & 315
Brazil & Orange Chocolate Treats 374
Brownies
Boston 384
Double Chocolate & Mango 394
Microwave 409
Buckwheat Beet Snacks, Soft Bake 458
Butter Currant & Coconut Cookies 43
butter, use of 13-14
Butter Cookies, Dutch 96
Butter Sables, Classic 124
Butter Viennese Fingers 135
Butterflies 211

C

Candied Peel & Dark Chocolate Squares
327
Candy Eggs 221
Cardamom Cookies 61

Cardamom Crisps 147
Caribbean Lime Cookies 245
Carrot Cumin & Orange Phyllo Crisps
457
Carrot & Date Drops 310
Carrot & Walnut Cookies 40
Cashew, Toasted, & Raisin Cookies 348
Cashew Crumbles, Hot 449
Cashew Thins, White Chocolate 167
Cassis Pink Cookies 111
Catherine Wheels 269
Cattern Cakes 294
Celebration Cookies 280
Checkerboards 155
cheese cookies
Apple Cheese Cookies 238
Apricot & Cheese Cookies 49
Blue Cheese Shortbread 423
Cheddar & Peanut Cookies 375
Cheese & Relish Puffs 423
Cream Cheese & Chive Cornbread
Cakes 426
Feta Olive & Sun-dried Tomato Bites
422
Halloumi Cookies 431
Hot Cheese Melts 425
Hot Pizza Snacks 428
Oaty Clusters with Cheese Crumble
Top 428
Parmesan Paprika Crisps 420
Peanut Shortbread Bars 46
Quattro Formaggio 420
Red Cheese & Fruity Relish Palmiers
423
Smoked Cheese Twists 425
Smoked Ham Rings 431
Cherry Chocolate Cookies 315
Cherry Chocolate Dreams 161
Cherry & Cinnamon Candy Bars 389
Cherry Florentines, Candied 325
Cherry Garlands 264
Cherry & Nuts Cookies 365
Cherry Rings 301
Cherry Slices, Candied 112
Cherry & Vanilla Squares 309
Chicks 224
Children's Names Cookies 227
chocolate, use of 14-15
chocolate cookies
Almond & Chocolate Clusters 187
Amaretti Drops 159
Apricot & Chocolate Cookies 160
Banana Chocolate Squares 319

Big White Chocolate & Apricot Cookies 204
Bitter Chocolate Discs 151
Brazil & Orange Chocolate Treats 374
Butterflies 211
Candied Peel & Dark Chocolate Squares 327
Checkerboards 155
Cherry Chocolate Dreams 161
Chocolate & Chili Cookies 190
Chocolate Chip Cookies 217
Chocolate Chip & Pecan Shortbread 390
Chocolate Chip & Raisin cookies 165
Chocolate Crackle-Tops 156
Chocolate & Cream Cheese Marble Fridge Balls 50
Chocolate Cream-filled Hearts 172
Chocolate Crescents 197
Chocolate-dipped Cinnamon Meringues 185
Chocolate-dipped Macaroons 185
Chocolate-dipped Orange Shortbread 178
Chocolate-dipped Palmiers 136
Chocolate-frosted Heart Cookies 182
Chocolate Fudge Cookies 195
Chocolate Ginger Cookies 174
Chocolate & Hazelnut Treats 365
Chocolate Initials 127
Chocolate Macaroons 122
Chocolate Mint Cookies 195
Chocolate Oat Cookies 117
Chocolate Octopus 228
Chocolate Orange Dream Bars 417
Chocolate & Orange Sandwiches 177
Chocolate & Orange Slices 391
Chocolate Pinwheels 162
Chocolate Pistachio Cookies 180
Chocolate Pockets 181
Chocolate Prezels 62
Chocolate & Raspberry Macaroon Bars 387
Chocolate Refrigerator Cookies 175
Chocolate Rugelach 196
Chocolate Snakes 230
Chocolate Speckled Cookies 215
Chocolate Swirls 45
Chocolate Viennese Whirls 190
Chocolate Wafers 181
Coconut & Chocolate Crunch 167
Coconut & Chocolate Swirls 347
Cranberry & White Chocolate Cookies 320
Crunchy Chocolate Chip Cookies 192
Double Chocolate & Mango Brownies 394
Double Chocolate Mint Sandwiches 148
Drizzled Chocolate & Brazil Nut Cookies 356
Flaky Chocolate & Peanut Cookies 359
Granola & Choc-chip Cookies 171
Hazelnut Chocolate Crescents 188
Jeweled Cookie Bars 218
Low Fat Chocolate Brownies 252
Lunchbox Crunchies 154
Macadamia Chocolate Bars 371
Marble Cookies 179
Mocha Chunk Chocs 164
Monkey Puzzles 184
No-cook Peanut Squares 154
Oat Jacks 159
Orange Chocolate Cookies 164
Prune & Two Chocolate Pieces 410
Raspberry & White Chocolate Chunkies 193
Red White & Blue Cookies 174
Sesame Spiced Rum Chocolate Cookies 161
Strawberry Cocoa Sandwich Stars 189
Ultimate Chocolate Chip Cookies 173
White Chocolate Cashew Thins 167
White Chocolate Chunk & Pecan Cookies 168
White Chocolate & Macadamia Nuts Treat 342
White Chocolate Slice 263
Chrabeli Bread 94
Christmas Cookies, Spiced 259
Christmas Puddings, Tipsy 261
Chunky Mixed Fruit Squares 321
Churros, Spanish 88
Cigarettes Russes 90
Cinnamon Balls 283
Cinnamon Candy trees 258
Cinnamon Palmiers 57
Clock Cookies 238
coconut cookies
    Butter, Currant & Coconut Cookies 43
    Coconut & Chocolate Crunch 167
    Coconut & Chocolate Swirls 347
    Coconut Cookies 57
    Coconut Crisps 242
    Coconut Curls 122
    Coconut Fortune Cookies 105
    Coconut & Lime Crunchies 363
    Coconut Macaroons 372
    Coconut Meringues 110
    Coconut & Prune Triangles 420
    Coconut & Rum Cookies 373
    Coconut & Sesame Crunch 384
    Coconut & Walnut Cookies 354
    Exotic Fruit & Coconut Treats 316
    Lime & Coconut Hearts 137
    Stars & Moons 207
Coffee Brazil Cookies 354
Coffee & Ginger Creams 47
Coffee Meringue Snails 143
Coffee Meringues 283
Coffee & Walnut Cookies 359
Coffee and Walnut Numbers 113
Confetti Cookies 134
Cookie Candy Canes 275
cookie dough, keeping 20
cookies, keeping 20
cookies, mailing 21
cooking times 16-17
Corn Cakes, Mexican Potato & Chili Bean 459
Cornflake and Golden Raisin Drop Cookies 35
Cornbread Cakes, Cream Cheese & Chive 426
Cornish Fairings 78
Cranberry Cookies 132
Cranberry Crunch 54
Cranberry Bars 397
Cranberry & Golden Raisin Bars 393
Cranberry & Orange Clusters 277
Cranberry & White Chocolate Cookies 321
Cream Cheese Puff Swirls 36
Crunchy Cereal Bites 41
Crunchy Chocolate Chip Cookies 192
Crunchy Nut Cookies 363
Currant and Almond Cookies 34
Curried Shrimp Diamond Oatcakes 437

D

Danish Piped Cookies 99
Date & Oat Crumb Squares 391
Dates & Cinnamon Cookies 298
Date & Honey Comforts 65
Double Almond Cookies 355
Double Banana Cookies 35
dried Fruit, use of 15
drop cookies, method 10
Dutch Butter Cookies 96

E

eggs, use of 14
Eponges 93
equipment 8-9
Exotic Fruit & Almond Slices 396
Exotic Fruit & Coconut Treats 316

F

Feta Olive & Sun-dried Tomato Bites 422
Fig & Oat Slices 394
Finnish Fingers 98
Fior di Mandorle 81
Fish 231
Florentines
    Almond & Ginger 375
    Candied Cherry 325
    Mini 58
flour, use of 13
Flower Cookies 223
Fours Poches 90
Frosted Easter Ovals 291
Frosting 21
Fruit & Brandy Sticks 399
Fruit & Nut Bars 445
Fruit Salad & Brazil Nuts 315
Fruit Segments 239

G

ginger cookies
    Almond & Ginger Florentines 375
    Almond & Ginger Hearts 339
    Cardamom Crisps 147
    Chocolate Ginger Cookies 175
    Cornish Fairings 78
    Double Ginger Bars 458
    Double Ginger Pecan Cookies 364
    Ginger Bites 42
    Ginger & Coffee Creams 47
    Ginger Cookies, Golden 131
    Ginger Thins 249
    Gingerbread Selection 233
    Golden Ginger Cookies 131
    Grantham Gingerbreads 76
    Grasmere Gingerbread 378
    Mango & Ginger Delights 312
    Pineapple & Ginger Cookies 332
    Triple Ginger Cookies 274
    Whiskey & Ginger Shortbreads 295
Golden Circles 223
Golden Ginger Cookies 131
Granola Bars 24
Granola & Choc-Chip Cookies 171
Grantham Gingerbreads 76

Grapefruit Marmalade & Prune Drops 313
Grasmere Gingerbread 378

H

Halloumi Cookies 431
Ham, Honeyed, & Onion Cookies 439
Ham & Pineapple Corn Cakes 432
Ham Rings, Smoked 431
Hanukkah Sugar Cookies 284
hazelnut cookies
    Buttery Hazelnut Hoops 447
    Hazelnut Chocolate Crescents 188
    Hazelnut & Chocolate Treats 365
    Hazelnut & Cinnamon Rounds with
        Vanilla Glaze 355
    Hazelnut Cookies 71
    Hazelnut Bars 400
    Hazelnut & Molasses Cookies 371
    Hazelnut & Nutmeg Cookies 145
    Hazelnut & Orange Cookies 344
    Lemon & Hazelnut Fingers 404
Herb Crackers 452
Holly Leaves 144
Honey & Date Comforts 65
Honey & Oat Bites 294
Honey & Oat Cookies 32
Honeyed Hearts 287

I

Ice Cream Cone Cookie 214
Ischl Cookies 87

J

Jalebi 105
Jam Heart Cookies 234
Jam Thumbprints 40
Jeweled Cookie Bars 218

K

Knots 215
Kourambiedes 274

L

Lemon Cheesecake Fingers 401
Lemon & Hazelnut Fingers 404
Lemon & Lime Thins 305
Lemon & Pine Nut Cookies 353
Lemon & Poppy Cookies 250
Lemon Rings 133
Lemon-scented Peanut Butter Cookies

206
Lepeshki 98
Lime & Coconut Crunchies 363
Lime & Coconut Hearts 137
Lime Cookies 30
Lime Cookies, Caribbean 245
Lime & Lemon Thins 305
Lime & Rosemary Cookies 139
Linzer Bake 148
Love Hearts 221
Lovers Knots 288
Lovers Scrolls 128
Lunchbox Crunchies 154

M

Macadamia Chocolate Bars 371
Macadamia Cookies, Chunky 102
Macadamia Nut Cookies Syrupy 368
Macadamia & Orange Half Moons 348
macaroons
    Almond 84
    Chocolate 122
    Chocolate Dipped 171
    Chocolate & Raspberry Bars 387
    Coconut 372
    Polish 97
    Simple 255
    Walnut 264
Magical Mushrooms 219
Mandarin Flying saucers 229
Mango & Double Chocolate Brownies 394
Mango & Ginger Delights 312
Mango & Pistachio Slices 149
Maple Moons 268
Maple Pecan Wafers 60
Maple Syrup Cookies 24
Maple Syrup Tartlets 38
Maple Syrup Tuiles 118
Maple Walnut Drops 55
Marble Cookies 179
Marmalade Moons 117
Marmalade & Walnut Cookies 367
Marshmallow & Pecan Cookies 367
Maypole Twists 293
meringues
    Coffee Snails 143
    Spanish Date Meringue Slices 413
    Chocolate-dipped Cinnamon 185
    Coconut 110
    Coffee 283
    Minute 60
    Pink & White 114
Mexican Potato & Chili Bean Corn
    Cakes 459

Microwave Brownies 151
Middle Eastern Almond Rolls 448
Milk Cookies 53
Mixed Seed Crunchies 445
Mocha Chunk Cookies 164
Mocha Mixed Nut Drops 374
Molasses Cookies 249
Monkey Puzzles 184
Mouse Cookies 224
Muesli Cookies 252
Mulberry & Orange Cookies 304
Munch 413
Mushroom Bites, Hot Herbed 454

N

New Orleans Oat Cookies 69
No-bake Chocolate Delight 59
No-cook Peanut Squares 154
Number Cookies 237
Nut Clusters, Mixed, with Cajun Spices 442
Nut Chewies 37
Nut Rocks 62
nuts, use of 15
Nuts & Cherry Cookies 365

O

oat cookies
 Anzacs 102
 Chocolate Oat Cookies 117
 Curried Shrimp Diamond Oatcakes 437
 Date & Oat Crumb Squares 391
 Fig & Oat Slices 394
 Honey & Oat Bites 294
 Honey & Oat Cookies 32
 New Orleans Oat Cookies 69
 Oat Bars 400
 Oat Clusters with Cheese Crumble Top 428
 Oat Jacks 158
 Sesame Oat Crisps 247
 Sour Cherry & Orange Oatmeal Cookies 251
 Wheat-free Fruity Oat Bars 254
oats, use of 15
Onion, Fried, & Thyme Crackers 453
orange
 Almond & Orange Sandwich Cookies 360
 Brazil & Orange Chocolate Treats 374
 Chocolate-dipped Orange Shortbread 178

Chocolate Orange Dream Bars 417
Chocolate Orange Sandwich 177
Chocolate & Orange Slices 391
Carrot Orange & Cumin Phyllo Crisps 457
Cranberry & Orange Clusters 277
Hazelnut & Orange Cookies 344
Orange & Cardamom Filled Thins 298
Orange Carrot Shortbread 235
Orange Chocolate Cookies 164
Orange Flower Cookies 121
Orange & Macadamia Half Moons 348
Orange & Pistachio Thins 352
Orange & Raisin Shortbread 452
Orange Shortbread 34
Orange Spritz Cookies 39
Sour Cherry & Orange Oatmeal Cookies 251

P

Palmiers
 Cinnamon 57
 Parisian 89
 Red Cheese & Fruity Relish 427
pan & baking sheet preparation 16
Panforte di Siena 83
Parisian Palmiers 89
Parmesan Paprika Crisps 420
Papaya Drops, Tropical 307
Passion Fruit Shortbread 311
Passion Fruit Swirls, Valentine 126
Peach & Almond Chews 344
Peach & Cherry Thins, Chewy 332
Peach Shortcake, Grated 101
Peanut Butter Cookies 341
Peanut Butter Cookies, Lemon-scented 206
Peanut Butter & Jelly Cookies 71
Peanut & Lemon Crunch Bars 53
peanuts
 Flaky Chocolate & Peanut Cookies 359
 No-cook Peanut Squares 154
 Peanut & Lemon Crunch Bars 53
 Peanut & Raisin Cookies 244
 Peanut Sesame Carrot & Raisin Pinwheels 440
 Peanut Shortbread Bars 46
Pear Cookies 44
Pear Walnut Cookies 334
Pear Bars 324
Pear Treats, Double 381
pecan

Apricot & Pecan Rye Cookies 446
Chocolate Chip & Pecan Shortbread 390
Double Pecan Ginger Cookies 364
Maple Pecan Wafers 60
Pecan & Cinnamon Cookies 341
Pecan & Marshmallow Cookies 367
Pecan Pinwheel Cookies 140
Pecan & Semi-sweet Chocolate Pebbles 345
Pecan Tassies 75
Roasted Pecan Snacks 444
White Chocolate Chunk Pecan Cookies 168
Pennsylvania Shoofly Slices 68
Peppermint Rings 222
Pepperoni & Peppercorn Shortbreads 435
Pine Nut Biscotti 133
Pine Nut Oat Cookies 27
Pine Nut Horseshoes 129
Pine Nut & Lemon Cookies, Chunky 353
Pine Tree Shillings 360
Pineapple Cookies, Crumbly 331
Pineapple Drops, Chewy 312
Pineapple Shortcake, Grated 101
Pink & White Meringues 115
Pistachio & Apricot Cookies 357
Pistachio Cookies, Chocolate 180
Pistachio Drops, Chunky 338
Pistachio & Mango Slices 149
Pistachio & Mint Creams 364
Pistachio & Orange Thins 352
Pizza, Rocky Road 385
Pizza Snacks, Hot 428
Polish Macaroons 97
Popcorn Balls 43
Poppy Seed Cookies 119
Poppy Seed Pinwheels 237
Poppy Seed Spirals 443
Potato & Chili Bean Corn Cakes, Mexican 459
Praline Sparkler 271
Present Cookies 108
pressed cookies, method 11-12
Prezels, Chocolate 62
problem solving 18-19
Prune & Grapefruit Marmalade Drops 313
Prune & Two Chocolate Pieces 152
Pumpkin Fingers 277
Pumpkin Shorties, Whole-wheat 445
Pumpkin Seed & Bran Cookies 29

Q

Quattro Formaggio 420

R

Raisin Rockies 73
Rascals 92
Raspberry & White Chocolate Chunkies 193
Red White & Blue Cookies 174
Refrigerator Cookies 74
refrigerator cookies, advice on method 10-11
Roast Pepper Cookies 450
Rocky Road 72
Rocky Road Pizza 427
rolled cookies, method 11
Rose Petal Cookies 287
Rosemary & Lime Cookies 139
Rounds, Whole-wheat 77
Rugelach, Chocolate 196
Rum-glazed Wreaths 266
Rum & Raisin Cookies 330

S

Sablés Nantais 91
Scandinavian Slices 99
Scottish Shortbread 78
Sedgemoor Easter Cookies 290
Sesame Chocolate Chewies 180
Sesame & Coconut Crunch 384
Sesame Cracker Cookies 142
Seame Oat Crisps 247
Sesame Seed Sensations 33
Shamrocks 289
Shooting Stars 279
shortbreads & shortcakes
    Almond Shortbread 404
    Blue Cheese Shortbread 423
    Brandied Shortbread 275
    Chocolate Dip & Pecan Shortbread 391
    Chocolate-dipped Orange Shortbread 178
    Fantail Shortbread 142
    Grated Peach (or Pineapple) Shortcake 101
    Orange Carrot Shortbread 235
    Orange & Raisin Shortbread 410
    Orange Shortbread 34
    Passionfruit Shortbread 311
    Pepperoni & Peppercorn Shortbreads 435
    Scottish Shortbread 78

Shortcake with a Hint of Rose 119
    Whole-wheat Pumpkin Shortbread 445
    Whole-wheat Shortbread 242
    Whiskey & Ginger Shortbreads 295
    Wiggly Sheep 213
Shrimp Crackers, Thai 432
Shrimp Diamond Oatcakes, Curried 437
Simnel Bars 382
Smiling Faces 139
Smoked Cheese Twists 425
Smoked Salmon & Lemon Kisses 438
Smoked Salmon & Sour Cream Snacks 453
Snowballs 262
Soft Centers 288
Sour Cherry & Orange Oatmeal Cookies 251
Spanish Churros 88
Spanish Date Meringue Slices 455
Spiced Molasses Drops 52
Spiced Rum Chocolate Cookies 161
Spicy Mixed Fruit Bars 303
Stained Glass Windows 261
Star Cookies 114
Star Fruit Cookies 332
Stars & Moons 207
Sticky Toffee Apple Treats 278
Stollen Bars 414
Strawberry Cocoa Sandwich Stars 189
Strawberry Pinwheels 306
Strawberry Cookies 206
Strawberry Jam Sandwiches 149
sugar, use of 14
Sugar & Spice Stars 267
Sunflower Cookies 205
Sweethearts 285
Syrupy Macadamia Nut Cookies 368

T

Tangerine Fingers 317
Teddy Bears Picnic 200
Thai Shrimp Crackers 432
Tic-Tac Toe 216
Toffee Bars 416
Treasure Coins 229
Tropical Fruit Cookies 64
Tropical Papaya Drops 307
Tutti Frutti Faces 208
Two-toned Cookies 136

V

Valentine Passion Fruit Swirls 126
Valentine's Cookies 125

Vanilla Cookies, Real 150
Vanilla Cream Cheese Cut-outs 112
Vanilla Crescents 85
Vanilla Fudge Crumbles 272

W

walnut Cookies
    Coconut & Walnut Cookies 354
    Coffee & Walnut Cookies 359
    Pear & Walnut Cookies 334
    Maple Walnut Drops 55
    Walnut & Banana Cookies 351
    Walnut & Carrot Cookies 368
    Walnut Crescents 343
    Walnut Macaroons 264
    Walnut & Marmalade Cookies 367
Wedding Bells 130
Wheat-free Fruity Oat Bars 254
Whiskey & Ginger Shortbreads 295
White Chocolate Cashew Thins 167
White Chocolate Chunk & Pecan Cookies 168
White Chocolate & Macadamia Nuts Treat 342
White Chocolate Slice 263
Wholesome Hearts 210
Whole-wheat Rounds 77
Wiggly Sheep 213
Winter Fruit Cookies 334
Winter Logs 267

Z

Zitron 95
Zucchini Triangles 372

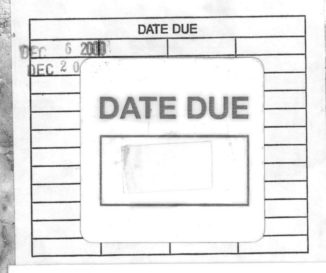

641.8
COL
The Colossal Cookie Cookbook